Primetime 1966–1967

Primetime 1966–1967

The Full Spectrum of Television's First All-Color Season

THOM "BEEFSTEW" SHUBILLA

Foreword by Frank Santopadre

McFarland & Company, Inc., Publishers
Jefferson, North Carolina

LIBRARY OF CONGRESS CATALOGUING-IN-PUBLICATION DATA

Names: Shubilla, Thom, 1984– author. | Santopadre, Frank, writer of foreword.
Title: Primetime 1966–1967 : the full spectrum of television's first all-color season / Thom "Beefstew" Shubilla ; foreword by Frank Santopadre.
Description: Jefferson, North Carolina : McFarland & Company, Inc., Publishers, 2022 | Includes bibliographical references and index.
Identifiers: LCCN 2022011614 | ISBN 9781476683447 (paperback : acid free paper) ∞
ISBN 9781476645025 (ebook)
Subjects: LCSH: Television programs—United States—History—20th century. | Television broadcasting—Technological innovations—United States. | Color television—History. | BISAC: PERFORMING ARTS / Television / History & Criticism | LCGFT: Television criticism and reviews.
Classification: LCC PN1992.3.U5 S5458 2022 | DDC 791.45/75—dc23/eng/20220314
LC record available at https://lccn.loc.gov/2022011614

BRITISH LIBRARY CATALOGUING DATA ARE AVAILABLE

ISBN (print) 978-1-4766-8344-7
ISBN (ebook) 978-1-4766-4502-5

© 2022 Thom "Beefstew" Shubilla. All rights reserved

No part of this book may be reproduced or transmitted in any form or by any means, electronic or mechanical, including photocopying or recording, or by any information storage and retrieval system, without permission in writing from the publisher.

Front cover: Barbara Eden in *I Dream of Jeannie* (NBC/Photofest)

Printed in the United States of America

McFarland & Company, Inc., Publishers
Box 611, Jefferson, North Carolina 28640
www.mcfarlandpub.com

To my parents
who always supported
all my endeavors and pursuits
no matter how outlandish
or unconventional

Table of Contents

Foreword: "Get away from the TV!" by Frank Santopadre   1
Introduction: How the World Turned to Color   3

CHAPTER ONE. Superheroes   11
CHAPTER TWO. Dramas   39
CHAPTER THREE. Action-Adventure   46
CHAPTER FOUR. Law Enforcement   59
CHAPTER FIVE. Science Fiction   70
CHAPTER SIX. World War II   97
CHAPTER SEVEN. Westerns   106
CHAPTER EIGHT. Spies   134
CHAPTER NINE. Southerners   153
CHAPTER TEN. Situation Comedies   165

Works Cited   209
Index   225

Foreword: "Get away from the TV!"

BY FRANK SANTOPADRE

Even 50-something years later, my dad's dire warning that I would somehow be irradiated (or worse) by sinister death beams emanating from the cathode ray tube in our beloved Zenith color TV still rattle around my head.

The old man's hard-and-fast rule for "TV time" was that you had to sit *at least* five feet away from the screen at all times (a life-and-death instruction that would be revised and updated a decade later as "Don't stand so close to the microwave!"). But even at the age of five, my television-induced mesmerization was so complete, that unless such commands were barked in the voices of Lieutenant Commander McHale or *F Troop*'s Sergeant O'Rourke, I would pay little attention.

The year 1966 was the year that TV viewers all over America discovered the wonders of "in living color" (as the famous NBC promos boasted). Sure, my older sister Cathryn and I dutifully followed the black-and-white escapades of Gilligan and Herman Munster and Jeannie and Samantha and Andy and Opie but this was a brave new, uncharted world: When Dad unboxed that brand new Magnavox Manhattan Color Stereo Theater and slid it against the wall, plugged it in and turned it on, he may as well have been President Grover Cleveland throwing the switch that introduced electricity to the 1893 World's Fair. There would be no turning back. TV life now looked exactly like *real* life and from this day forward, the two would be indistinguishable.

My sister and I practically plastered our corneas to that 27-square-inch screen, soaking in those rich reds and brilliant blues, and thrilling to the weekly adventures of Batman, the Green Hornet and even the less compelling superhero knockoffs, Captain Nice and Mr. Terrific. I was too young to appreciate the campiness of Adam West's deadpan Caped Crusader or the Bond-inspired send-ups *Get Smart* and *The Wild Wild West*, but it scarcely mattered. The eye-popping sets and production designs, the tricked-out vehicles and gadgetry, and the singable theme songs that would lodge in our auditory cortexes were more than enough to sustain us. And those colors—those vibrant, dazzling, *glorious* colors! From Jeannie's taffy pink genie bottle to the fire engine red of the Monkeemobile to Special Agent James West's skintight sapphire blue suit, every program seemed to explode across the screen in a fireworks display of brightly saturated images.

Of course, every generation is nostalgic for the pop culture of *their* era, but was there ever a year in American TV history that offered up the variety, creativity and sheer flamboyance that 1966 did? *Lost in Space*! *Get Smart*! *The Monkees*! *Voyage to the Bottom of the Sea*! *Batman*! *Daktari*! *Green Acres*! *Star Trek*! *Bewitched*! *Bonanza*! *Tarzan*! *Flipper*! *The Man from U.N.C.L.E*! A smorgasbord of the wild, the weird, the whacked-out and everything in between.

In this book, a handy viewing guide to the wonderful world of 1966 television, my fellow obsessive Thom Shubilla has painstakingly recreated that initial thrill of discovery and has taken us on a journey back through the decades (without the aid of the Time Tunnel or the *Enterprise*'s transporter room) to those joyful, unforgettable nights spent stretched out on the living room carpet, gazing lovingly, longingly into the magical box that enthralled us for hours on end and entertained us within an inch of our young lives.

(And best of all, you don't have to sit five feet away from the page.)

Frank Santopadre is an Emmy Award–winning comedy writer and producer for television, radio, award shows and celebrity roasts. A staff writer on ABC's The View, *he is co-producer and co-host of* Gilbert Gottfried's Amazing Colossal Podcast, *named by* The Village Voice *"Best Podcast of 2015."*

Introduction:
How the World Turned to Color

Invention

Television is not a natural resource. It is not something given to the world by divine providence. It is a relatively modern invention—introduced after the airplane, electric washing machine, radar and the hair dryer.

Like many modern inventions, television has a timeline that is far from linear. Its earliest form was mechanical television. Developed by Scottish inventor John Logie Baird in 1925, mechanical television was simply scanned images using a rotating disk with holes arranged in a spiral pattern. These images were transmitted to a receiver that did not give viewers much detail; it was only capable of transmitting eerie shadowy images.

Television was greatly improved with the invention of electronic television. which is generally attributed to inventor Philo T. Farnsworth. Electronic television scanned images with beams of electrons and transmitted them to a receiver. This gave the new medium the picture detail viewers would desire. It was such a leap forward in quality, it could best be summed up by what Farnsworth wrote in a telegram to one of his investors: "THE DAMNED THING WORKS!" Soon after the electronic television's first public demonstration, there was a rush to perfect the television by inventors and to monetize it by companies (Poletika).

Commercialization

In November 1928, *Popular Mechanics* asked, "When will radio television and radio movies be available to the average radio fan for home reception?" At the time, "radio movies" referred to what would soon become television. The magazine interviewed several inventors and media executives; their responses varied but all agreed that television "is something that should not be offered to the public until it is as complete, as simple, as perfect and as foolproof as radio broadcasting is today."

Although electronic television was a marked improvement from mechanical television, the quality of the picture was still low. *Popular Mechanics* stated, "One human figure, or at most two, may be produced with fair results, but attempt to crowd a baseball diamond, a prize fight, or a political convention into that space would mean complete loss of detail." Nevertheless, the magazine predicted that with experimentation, television would improve ("What Television Offers You," 820–25).

From 1926 to 1946, several television stations throughout the country were established and aired experimental programming. They only broadcast for several hours a day and the programming was far from consistent. The March 1940 edition of *Electronics Magazine* found only approximately 405 hours of television was broadcast between May 1939 and January 1940 ("The Extent of the Service").

Experimental broadcasts included a weather map broadcast by Jenkins Labs (1926), a comedy set by "Mr. Television" Milton Berle (1927), a *Felix the Cat* cartoon (1927), a *Punch and Judy* puppet show (1931), the musical variety show *Half-Hour on Broadway* (1931), a political show sponsored by the Democratic National Committee (1932), a dramatic monologue from *Tobacco Road* (1936), *Dr. Jekyll and Mr. Hyde* (1940) and *Ringling Brothers Circus* (1946) (Terrace).

A 1940 *Electronics Magazine* article, "The Extent of the Service," indicated that approximately 2000 televisions were sold in the United States and sales only came from five northeastern states where stations were broadcasting; 63.8 percent in New York (31 percent of which came from New York City), 28.9 percent from New Jersey, 5.6 percent from Connecticut, 1.4 percent from Pennsylvania and 0.3 percent from Massachusetts.

Early examples in pop culture of experimental television being demonstrated can be seen in the low-budget Bela Lugosi drama *Murder by Television* (1935) and the Three Stooges short *A Plumbing We Will Go* (1940). Both examples clearly showcase that television was a modern marvel that could only be afforded by wealthy members of society.

Television finally began to commercialize in 1946 and stations began to regularly broadcast programs. That year there were a total of six non-experimental commercial TV stations on the air in the U.S. The first commercial station was in Schenectady, New York (it had also aired experimental programming beginning in 1928), followed by stations in Chicago, Philadelphia, Los Angeles and two channels in New York City. Shows that aired in prime time in 1946 included *Gillette Cavalcade of Sports*, *I Love to Eat, You Are an Artist* and *Let's Rhumba*. The number of stations throughout the U.S. jumped to 98 stations in 1950 and grew to 422 stations by 1955.

Four major networks soon emerged: NBC, CBS, ABC, and DuMont (which folded in 1956). The major networks' programming aired on the growing number of local affiliate stations throughout the country and the number of hours of programming scheduled daily also increased along with the number of TVs purchased (Brooks and Marsh).

Although television had 20 years of experimentation, there was yet to be a standard format. Ed McMahon, who went on to become Johnny Carson's *Tonight Show* sidekick, started his career in the early days of commercial TV in Philadelphia. He once stated, "Every aspect of television was new. You couldn't do anything wrong because there was no right. There was no established structure. Everyone was just making up the rules as they broadcast" (McMahon 25).

Accessibility

Capitalism worked out well for early televisions. More and more companies began to manufacture TVs, which created competition, lowered the price, increased the number of TVs available and sparked a demand for programming. Economists argue that without those steps taking place, television may have stayed a lab experiment (Henderson "Supply").

In 1949, a 16" RCA television cost upwards of $490, during a time when the average American's annual income was $3100 before taxes ("Television Prices," "Income of Families"). The same-size TV just three years later, 1952, cost only $200 ("Christmas RCA Victor"). TVs became a standard piece of furniture in the American living room. In 1948, it was reported that approximately 500,000 TVs were in use in the U.S., and RCA planned on producing 850,000 sets that year ("800,000 Video Sets"). Meanwhile, General Electric sales manager Arthur A. Brandt predicted 12 million would be in use by 1952 ("Big Television Field"). Brandt was off with his prediction: By 1952, there were more than 16.9 million sets in use ("TV Sets").

Furniture manufacturers started marketing their products targeting the TV viewing audience: "Enjoy TV. Relax in a leather upholstered club chair" stated an ad for Nathan's Furniture store in New York City (Grossman 8). Gadgets to improve your TV viewing experience were rolled out; magnifiers to give the illusion of a larger screen and reduce eye strain, attachments to give a 3D effect, glasses to reduce glare, and cheap filters that gave the appearance of color. "Sensational Color-V Filter screen instantly changes dull, dreary black & white pictures to brilliant, eye-filling colors. Attach it yourself in a few seconds. You, your family, your friends will really enjoy the color effects which, while not to be confused with genuine color TV will afford a wonderful treat to the eyes!" claimed one ad by Superior Products (Grossman 18–21).

All of these gadgets were met with less than stellar reviews and typically produced less than optimal results.

The famed TV Dinner was introduced by C.A. Swanson & Sons in 1953 after the company purchased too many frozen turkeys for the Thanksgiving holiday. Gerry Thomas, a Swanson salesman, ordered sectional aluminum trays and loaded them with the leftover turkey, gravy, cornbread stuffing, peas and sweet potatoes. Swanson marketed the product to capitalize on the growing fad of television so busy families could make a quick dinner and eat together in the living room in the glow of the television set (Edwards "How 260").

At the time, most major networks broadcast on Very High Frequency (VHF) channels, a frequency that travels far and is clear as long as the signal does not encounter many physical barriers. In 1962, President John F. Kennedy signed the "All Channel Television Receiver Law," which required all TVs sold in the U.S. to have the ability to pick up VHF and Ultra High Frequency (UHF) channels. UHF has a shorter range than VHF but is better able to pass through the physical barriers that VHF could not. Most markets were able to receive the broadcasts of the major networks on VHF without much trouble; media markets in mountains and valleys had difficulty picking up a clear VHF signal. With the new law, networks could also be broadcast in UHF without fear of some televisions not being able to receive a clear signal ("All Channel Television Receiver Law"). Older televisions could be modified to pick up UHF antenna channels by purchasing an inexpensive antenna ("Converting TV Set").

Cable television was introduced to some media markets in the late 1950s and early 1960s, but it did not start as a medium to receive pay channels, such as HBO and CNN. Cable TV started commercially in 1948 to bring broadcast television to media markets located in the deep valleys of mountain ranges—places even UHF channels had difficulty reaching. In 1947, Mahanoy City, Pennsylvania, located deep in a valley in the Appalachian Mountain Range, was the first town to acquire cable TV thanks to TV appliance owner John Walson. Using his past experience as a lineman-repairman for

Pennsylvania Power and Light, he set an antenna high on a mountain and hooked it to a cable that brought broadcast signals down into town, even from faraway markets, direct to his store for demonstration purposes. Service was soon extended to households in Mahanoy City (Walson).

Walson's idea was quickly adopted by markets with a similar problem (no clear over-the-air TV signal) in Arkansas and Oregon and it expanded media markets throughout the country ("Cable's Story"). In addition to cable, there was even talk that telecasts would soon be beamed from outer space via satellite.

Color TV

Color television was created soon after the development of electronic television by John Logie Baird in 1928. But took nearly three decades to standardize: Not until the 1960s did a color TV become affordable to the average household.

Before a color TV standard was approved, the vast majority of the programming was produced in black and white. There were exceptions. Some television producers, looking to the future, shot in color, correctly predicting that future TV viewers would most likely be watching on a color TV. This made any color program more desirable for syndication once color TVs become commercially available. Examples of this include *The Cisco Kid* (1950–1956), *Sergeant Preston of the Yukon* (1955–1958) and the last four seasons of *Adventures of Superman* (1952–1958).

As early as 1947, the Federal Communications Commission was debating what standard system to use to broadcast color TV. In a 1947 *RCA Radio Age* article, Dr. C.B. Jolliffe of RCA warned, "Much work remains to be done before a determination can be made as to the proper standards for a system of color television which ultimately should be adopted. To adopt standards and authorize commercialization of any system of color television now will probably result in no television rather than improved television" ("Status of Color Television").

The FCC's Fifteenth Annual Report stated, "On September 20, 1948, a hearing was begun to determine the utility of the band 475–890 megacycles for television broadcasting. The purpose of this hearing was to obtain information on the state of development of transmitting and receiving equipment capable of operating in this band in color as well as monochrome," meaning that existing black-and-white TVs still functioned as normal even when a show was broadcast in color ("Federal Communications Commission Fifteenth Annual Report").

The FCC finally settled on the NTSC system, named after the National Television System Committee, on December 17, 1953. This achieved the goal of black-and-white TV sets being compatible with a color signal made. NTSC is also used by most countries in North, Central and South America, Japan, Taiwan and Korea ("Federal Communications Commission Eighteenth Annual Report").

The United Kingdom, most of Europe, China and African Nations chose to adopt the PAL (Phase Alternating Line) format. Many experts felt the PAL format produced a superior picture, but black-and-white sets required a converter to still get a signal. France, the Soviet Union and Middle Eastern countries settled on SECAM (*séquentiel couleur à mémoire*; sequential color with memory), introduced in 1967. SECAM was also compatible with black-and-white televisions.

Just 15 days after the FCC approved NTSC, NBC broadcast the annual Tournament of Roses Parade from Pasadena, California, in color from coast to coast. *The New York Times'* Jack Gould wrote,

> The Tournament of Roses parade had the largest audience thus far, probably several thousand persons to see color TV at one time. The American Telephone and Telegraph Company, in an amazingly speedy engineering accomplishment, put together a color network of 22 cities to which the Radio Corporation of America had rushed equipment. A number of set manufacturers also held demonstrations of color receivers in different cities.

CBS ran *The News Review* in color the same weekend. Gould felt both color broadcasts had their pros and cons. "As the two NBC color cameras scanned a succession of elaborate floats, assorted military units, and other parade features, the scene was a veritable bevy of hues and depth; at other times, the close-up was better. Occasionally there were overcasts of one tint or another but these disappeared with movement of the camera." As for CBS, "[C]onsidering the greater economies of its camera equipment, CBS evidently really has something. The most pressing need at the moment is to improve the lighting in the CBS studio and to get away from pictures that are overly crowded with color. In trade jargon, the CBS color is much too 'busy.'"

Interestingly, Gould mused,

> Soon, incidentally, it is going to be time for both NBC and CBS to present color shows simultaneously so that a viewer can see what happens when he switches between the two. At the moment the two networks are using different hues for test patterns—which can be pretty confusing—and apparently there are other substantial variations. Maybe the engineers have all the answers, but the layman would be well advised to insist on making this basic test of tuning adjustments before plunking down $700 to $1500 for a color receiver [Gould "Television Review: N.B.C. Color"].

Dr. W.G. Baker, vice-president of General Electric and chairman of the National Television System Committee, told reporters in September 1953 it would take three or four years to build up mass production of required color tubes. But TV industry commentators were clearly impatient with the process (Larsen "Color Television Hangs" 14).

In 1956, *Time* magazine asserted, "[C]olor TV has turned out to be the most resounding industrial flop of 1956" ("Industry: Faded Rainbow"). Two years later, it declared,

> In the five years since its ballyhooed debut in 1953, only 325,000 sets have been sold, vs. 10 million black-and-white sets in the comparable first five years of TV broadcasting. Color telecasting still averages only 1½ hours a day, nearly all of it done by NBC alone. And the quality leaves much to be desired, even in the hands of dedicated knob twiddlers ["Television: Chasing the Rainbow"].

Color television was a dream for many viewers. But to most, the dream was unobtainable due to the cost. And in 1955 and '56, although networks did broadcast a number of specials programs in color, only three shows were regularly broadcast in color: *The Red Skelton Hour* on CBS, and *The Milton Berle Show* and *Texaco Star Theater* on NBC. ABC did not regularly air color prime time shows until the 1962–1963 season.

Only four new prime time shows were produced in black and white for the 1965–1966 season: *Lost in Space* on CBS, *F Troop* on ABC, and *I Dream of Jeannie* and *Convoy* on NBC. In 1966, ABC put *The Avengers* on hiatus until the winter so the network could import an entire season of color episodes. That same year, *The Wild Wild West*, *Combat!*, *Lost in Space*, *I Dream of Jeannie*, *The Fugitive*, *F Troop* and *Peyton Place* made the jump to color.

Advertisement for RCA Victor color television console as seen in a 1966 *Reader's Digest* (courtesy Barbara Koulik).

In September 1966, for the first time, all prime time shows on the three major networks were in color. The biggest leap came from CBS: The previous season, approximately 50 percent of the network's prime time programming was in color whereas all of NBC and the vast majority of ABC shows were in color.

Although color came with added expense, networks were requiring sponsors to foot the bill. CBS asked the sponsor of each program to share in the expense of shooting in color, which cost $7000 to $10,000 extra for a half-hour show. NBC was already charging the difference in price to switch to color. But, even if every show were broadcast in color, it would not make a difference if people were still watching that show on a black-and-white set (Humphrey "The Year They Went to Color").

Only nine percent of American households owned a color TV in 1966 but thanks in part to the new all-color prime time lineup, the number jumped to 24.2 percent by 1968 and averaged a nine percent increase each year for the next seven years (Steinberg 144). Consumers now could be part of the new color TV revolution and see all their favorite shows in color.

The Cincinnati Enquirer wrote in September 1966, "No consumer product in the history of American business ever received the potent support that color TV will get this Fall by the three networks in the greatly expanded color broadcasts. ... All in all, it looks like a 'colorful' year for TV" ("1966—Television Is Drenched").

A June 1966 *Business Week* article reported that demand for RCA color TVs outpaced supply and that the average price for a 25" RCA set dropped below $500; just a year earlier, it cost upwards of $700 ("Color TV Demand" 44). A September 1966 *TV Guide* published a "1967 TV Set Buyers Guide" which explained color TV's technical aspects, new color controls, and what was important to look for when buying a set. Advertisements throughout the issue hailed the color quality of each company's new sets.

Even advertisers got into the color game. By the Fall 1966 season, 90 percent of all TV commercials were produced in color—the only holdouts being due to cost restrictions or the "belief that black and white could create surprise or convey mood." Advertising executives considered black and white "dull and drab" ("The Boom" 40).

The number of color TVs sold did not overtake the number of black and white televisions sold until 1972; black-and-white TVs began to be phased out of production. Black and white televisions were not totally phased out until decades later, but the selection of new black and white sets became increasingly sparse with each passing year. A *Los Angeles Times* article in 1992 stated, "Stores that do sell black-and-white TVs usually won't sell anything bigger than the small models, with screen sizes typically ranging from a few inches to 7 inches" (Steinberg 144; Yenkin).

After a Congressional mandate in 2009, television made the switch from an analog to a digital signal, and all televisions were manufactured with a color picture, no matter the size.

Black and white television's fate may have been sealed in the fall of 1966 when for the first time in history, all three major TV networks were broadcasting programs to practically the entire nation in the full color spectrum.

Chapter One

Superheroes

The year 1966 was not the first time superheroes got their own television series. Arguably the first small-screen superhero series was ABC's *The Lone Ranger* (1949–1956). The Ranger did not have superpowers but he did have a secret identity, a secret hideout (a silver mine where he mines and forges silver bullets), gave his foes the perception that he was invincible, rode alongside a sidekick, and always fought for justice.

The Lone Ranger was followed by *Captain Video and His Video Rangers* (1949–1955) and *Flash Gordon* (1954–1955) on the DuMont Network, *Buck Rogers* (1950–1951) and *Zorro* (1957–1959) on ABC, and CBS's *Captain Midnight* (1954–1956). The syndicated series *Adventures of Superman* (1952–1958) and TV's first female superhero *Sheena, Queen of the Jungle* (1955–1956) also joined the television ranks.

From the late 1950s through the early 1960s, superheroes were missing from television lineups. Then in 1966, superheroes came back with a ZZZZZWAP!

Batman

For many people, the premiere of ABC's *Batman* on January 12, 1966, was their introduction to color television. Watching *Batman* in color became an event. It is common to hear stories of kids gathering in one house or traveling to a relative's home with a color television to see the Caped Crusaders, Batman and Robin, in all their color glory. Starting in late 1965, almost every advertisement for this new superhero show mentioned that it would be broadcast in color. Even the introduction illuminated this fact.

In 1966, *Batman* producer and narrator William Dozier was interviewed on an episode of the Canadian Broadcasting Corporation's documentary show *Telescope with Fletcher Markle*, and he described how the show came into fruition.

> About a year ago [1964] I was in New York on a routine business trip and the vice-president in charge of programing and development at ABC, a bright young man named Doug Kramer, asked me to have lunch with him, and he told me that ABC had recently bought the rights to Batman. Not knowing exactly what to do with it or how to do it, just having the kind of seat-of-the-pants hunch that it might be a good television series. And he asked me if I would be interested in producing it in my company at 20th Century–Fox ["The Man Behind Batman"].

Dozier explained that he never actually read a *Batman* comic before producing *Batman*, so he had to catch up with the character. After reading some *Batman* comics, he came up with the idea of how the show should be done:

Batman helped usher in interest in superheroes including movie serials from the 1940, as seen in the one off *Super Heroes Magazine* by Warren Publishing, publisher of *Famous Monsters of Filmland* (courtesy Drew Friedman).

> After a day or so, the fairly obvious idea, it seems obvious now at least, to make it so square, and so serious, and so cliché-ridden, and so overdone, and yet do it with a certain eloquence and style that it would be funny. That it would be so corny and so bad that it would be funny ["The Man Behind TV's *Batman*"].

Chapter One. Superheroes

Adam West was cast as Batman and his millionaire playboy alter ego Bruce Wayne, and an unknown, Burt Ward, was cast as Batman's sidekick Robin the Boy Wonder and his alter ego Dick Grayson.

The supporting cast was comprised of journeymen actors who each made hundreds of appearances in film and television prior to *Batman*. Alan Napier was chosen to play Batman's trusted butler Alfred, Neil Hamilton played Police Commissioner Gordon, Stafford Repp took on the role of Police Chief O'Hara, and Madge Blake portrayed Dick Grayson's Aunt Harriet.

The villains also came with impressive resumés. Cesar Romero, a handsome actor best known for playing "Latin lover" roles in films, portrayed The Joker, and stage, screen and TV actor Burgess Meredith, star of the film classic *Of Mice and Men* (1939), played The Penguin. The Riddler was originally depicted by impressionist Frank Gorshin, but the role was later taken by John Astin, *The Addams Family*'s Gomez. Ice cold villain Mr. Freeze was played by *three* actors throughout the series' run: George Sanders, Otto Preminger and Eli Wallach. Catwoman was first played in the series by Julie Newmar and Eartha Kitt, while Lee Meriwether donned the catsuit for the 1966 *Batman* movie.

Batman first appeared in an issue of *Detective Comics* in 1939; moviegoers first saw Batman and Robin in the serials *Batman* (1943) and *Batman and Robin* (1949). The serials and the TV series differed greatly. The TV series was played for laughs and Batman had the ultimate goal of capturing, understanding and rehabilitating criminal masterminds. The serial Batman was much more violent and had no problem killing the villains he faced.

Before *Batman*'s January 12, 1966, premiere, a nine-minute promotional ABC Network Color Presentation introduced audiences to Batman and Robin. It highlighted scenes from the first episode and, for viewers with color sets, the show's brilliant color sequences.

Each *Batman* adventure was broken up into two episodes. The Wednesday night episode ended in a cliffhanger and viewers were encouraged to tune in to Thursday night's resolution to the story which aired at the "Same Bat-Time. Same Bat-Channel." (Both episodes aired at 7:30 p.m.) The Wednesday night episode took the place of the long-running *The Adventures of Ozzie and Harriet* (1952–1965), which had moved to Saturday night, and the Thursday night episode replaced the newly cancelled musical variety show *Shindig!* (1964–1966).

When *Batman* took to the airwaves, it was the action-packed adventure viewers were looking for. Critics were impressed:

> "Television will never be the same after Wednesday night ... the great appeal of the show is visual. The dialogue is tongue-in-cheek and cleverly written."—Paul Jones, *The Atlanta Constitution* ("New Batman" 10)

> "Television has reached new 'heights' of high camp."—Vernon Scott, United Press International ("ABC's Batman" 60)

> "'The secret ingredient which will make this zany collection a hit is really not secret at all ... it's the way it's played—straight down the middle. The tongue, to be sure, is in the cheek of all the players, but don't go looking for any bumps to show."—Vince Leonard, *Pittsburgh Press* ("Gleeps!" 50)

> "The big brains in televisionland have stumbled onto a new treasure house of material—the comic book."—Charles Witbeck, King Features Syndicate ("Comic Book Heroes" 14)

But not every critic was as excited about *Batman*. Others saw the show as a passing fad:

> "Non-event of the year. ... [*Batman* has] nothing for everyone."—Jack Gould, *New York Times*

> "Not as hip as advertised" and "*Batman* doesn't live up to his publicity."—Rick DuBrow, United Press International (DuBrow "Batman Is Not" 29; DuBrow "Batman Doesn't Live" 5)

Each episode's title card was proudly emblazoned with the fact the show was in color and each week Batman and Robin (aka the Dynamic Duo) took on a variety of colorful villains in Batman's hometown of Gotham City. Within the first few adventures, viewers with color televisions got to see the vivid colors of all of Gotham City's three most iconic villains introduced in *Batman* comic books. Viewers with color televisions were able to see the brilliant green of the Riddler's jumpsuit, the bright red lips and cartoonish green hair of The Joker, and the unique purple hat and bowtie of the Penguin. Many more villains were created specifically for the show, such as Egghead, portrayed by horror legend Vincent Price; King Tut, a role assumed by Victor Buono, and Black Widow, played by Tallulah Bankhead.

Viewers also got to visit the Batcave, located deep below Bruce Wayne's residence of Wayne Manor. The Batcave housed the iconic Batmobile, Bat-computer, the Atomic Pile (which powers the Batcave and Batmobile) and other crime detection and prevention devices. With every punch or kick, the audience saw one of 82 vibrant pop art onomatopoeia graphics such as **Biff! Zap! Crunk! Pow! Bonk!** and **VRONK!**

The first episode of *Batman* ("Hi Diddle Diddle," January 12, 1966) was a bigger success than anyone would have imagined and the series quickly became a cultural phenomenon. The Wednesday night debut episode received a Nielsen rating of 27.3, making it the tenth highest-rated show of the week. There was so much buzz that the second night scored an even higher 29.6 rating, making it the week's fifth highest-rated show (ABC's "Second Season" 9).

Three days later, *New York Times* TV critic George Gent reported that the two episodes were watched by one out of every three viewers in New York City, giving the show more viewers in the city than the Beatles when the group played on *The Ed Sullivan Show* on September 12, 1965 (Gent "Campy Batman").

One of the earliest articles covering "Bat-Mania" appeared in the San Francisco Bay Area newspaper *The Argus* in February 1966. The paper reported that hundreds of the city's residents saw the "Bat Signal" (the light with the Batman logo, used by Commissioner Gordon to summon Batman) flashed on several prominent buildings. Police did not find the persons responsible. San Francisco's Pierce Street Annex bar became the place *Batman* fans gathered to watch the show twice a week. The local ABC affiliate KGO was "deluged by one the largest mail responses in its history. The viewer requests are for fan club cards, Batman T-shirts and for 'Batman for Governor' bumper strips the station offers." *The Argus* also reported that two Bay Area nightclubs went all in with *Batman*: "Big Al in North Beach has converted his night club into a Batcave with topless Batgirls to inhabit it." And a Sunnyvale nightclub, located approximately 40 miles south of San Francisco, "changed its name and décor to 'Wayne Manor' and has installed Batgirl waitresses and drinks like the Batini" ("Bay Area Going 'Ape' Over Batman").

On March 11, 1966, Batman appeared on the cover of *Life* which covered the madness of Bat-mania:

> Batman conquers TV. Kids swing Batman capes in the backyard, and Bat products are everywhere. In the theater, craziness is a new craze. The whole country is going deliberately, and profitably, nuts. ... The hottest place in the San Francisco suburb of Sunnyvale is Wayne Manor, named after Batman's straight self, Bruce Wayne. At the Manor, the Dynamic Duo of Batman and Robin are painted in throbbing colors on the walls, and villains cackle in fluorescence. Behind a plate-glass screen, girls dressed like Robin lead the crowd in the Batusi [a dance Batman performed in the first episode].

Batman and Robin battle infamous foe, the Riddler, in 1966 *Batman* trading cards released by Topps and National Periodical Publications (Shubilla family archives).

Life also gave the account of a Detroit hairdresser who invented the Bat Cut, a women's haircut "in which the girl's eyebrows are shaved off and the hairline imitates Batman's cowl" (Prideaux 19–23).

Soon everything that could be sold with Batman's name, logo and likeness was hitting store shelves: shirts, shoes, belts, card games, board games, rings, model kits, action figures and mugs. *New York Times* financial reporter Vartanig G. Vartain gave Bat-mania credit for a March 1966 stock market gain:

> The onrushing popularity of the Batman ... helped to push shares of National Publications last week to a new high of 45¼. ... [B]rokers were telling the story about a 12-year-old boy who arrived at a magazine store in Manhattan in a chauffeur-driven limousine and paid $25 for three or four vintage books of Batman [Vartain "Batman Fad Aids"]

Adam West as Batman made a public service announcement to encourage children to invest in U.S. Saving stamps and bonds through the Treasury School Savings Program on the behest of President Lyndon Johnson in 1966. "[Children are] learning the lessons of practical citizenship and of wise money management and they're giving important support to the cause of freedom and the men who fight for us in Vietnam," said Batman.

Batman made the cover of *TV Guide* in March 1966, the magazine reporting on the show's status with high society and celebrities: "The afternoon of the premiere ABC set up a campily posh cocktail party at Harlow's, the 'in' New York discotheque, followed by a screening in the hope of completely capturing the in-crowd." Dance instructor Arthur Murray led the attendees in the Batusi. The guests included Andy Warhol, Roy Lichtenstein, Tammy Grimes, Roddy McDowall and about 500 others.

Batman and Robin made the cover of several teen magazines, including *Teen Life*, and was satirized on the cover of *Mad* magazine with the magazine's mascot Alfred E. Neuman dressed as Robin. On June 25, 1966, Batman even headlined his own concert at Shea Stadium in Queens, New York, then home to Major League Baseball's New York Mets. The concert was produced by Harry Bloomfield, a theater producer and restaurateur, and groups that performed included the Young Rascals, the Temptations, Junior Walker and the All-Stars, Shades of Blue, the Chiffons and the Checkmates. Frank Gorshin appeared as the Riddler alongside 26 Batusi Girls introduced by WABC Radio deejay Cousin Brucie Morrow.

The event was almost cancelled by the New York City Parks Department, but was saved when its sponsors "put up $5000 security against possible damage to the park." *The New York Times* reported, "A representative of the sponsors delivered the cash to Mr. Hoving [the Parks Commissioner] in his office at 9 p.m., the deadline the Commissioner had set. 'I was sweating it out,' Mr. Hoving said later. 'I had visions of real screams and teenagers marching on City Hall'" ("Holy Shea Stadium").

The concert had a great turn-out, but with Shea Stadium's 45,000 capacity, the venue appeared empty. Robert Sherman of *The New York Times* wrote,

> The kids impatiently awaited their hero, chomped on hot dogs and, showing remarkably good taste, ignored the gyrating singers on stage. For two and a half hours, one group after another came, screamed and departed, proving conclusively that if there's anything worse than having rock'n'roll groups drowned out by adoring fans—it's having them *not* drowned out. … But when Batman took the field, shouts and cheers rolled down from the stands—the 3000 sounded like 30,000 now—as Batman circled the field in a Cadillac. (The Batmobile was in for repairs, no doubt) [Sherman].

The Shea Stadium event later made more news when *The New York Times* reported that the concert's creditors had not been paid by Harry Bloomfield. The article also stated that the concert producer was previously in hot water with the law and was refused a show license after serving jail time for "failing to turn over to the Federal Government income tax and Social Security money from a [Broadway] production of his that failed" ("Batman Concert").

Not everyone felt *Batman* should be watched by children. A watchdog group, the National Association for Better Broadcasting, charged that *Batman* was "full of torture and brutal death" and called it unsuitable for children (Leonard "What's Out" 78). But *Batman*'s popularity continued to rise.

Throughout the show's run, music artists attempted to capitalize on its success. Neal Hefti, composter of the *Batman* theme, released it as a 45 RPM single which reached #35 on the Billboard Hot 100 charts. On its B-side: "Batman Chase." Hefti later released the LP "*Batman* Theme and 11 Other Bat Songs." Bandleader Nelson Riddle, who recorded the *Batman* theme for the television show, released the "Exclusive Original Television Soundtrack Album." Surf rockers The Ventures and Jan & Dean and University of Central Florida's jazz studies big band *The* Flying Horse Big Band released their own *Batman* theme albums. The Sensational Guitars of Dan & Dale, featuring the instrumental work of avant-experimental jazz musician Sun Ra and members of his Sun Ra Arkestra, and the little-known but very inspired Bat Boys recorded their own *Batman*-inspired LPs.

Rock'n'roll guitarist Link Wray, the English rockers The Who, the German Orchester Friedel Berlipp, the Mexican reggae band Los Batmen, the instrumental surf band The Marketts, the world-famous Boston Pops and scores of other bands all recorded the *Batman* theme as 45 RPM singles. The Marketts' version of the theme reached #17 on the Billboard Hot 100 Charts.

Lavern Baker changed the lyrics to her 1956 hit song "Jim Dandy [to the Rescue]" to "Batman to the Rescue." Peggy Lee belted out the number "That Man"

Adam West as Batman next to the Bat-copter which was introduced in *Batman: The Movie* (1966) (courtesy Ted A. Bohus).

where she exclaimed "I gotta get Batman for me!" Drummer Sandy Nelson released his version of the *Batman* theme song on the record "'In' Beat," alongside his own versions of the songs "Secret Agent Man," "Day Tripper" and "Uptight (Everything is Alright)." Scotty McKay's "Here Comes Batman" was featured in the ultra–low-budget monster movie *Creature of Destruction* (1967). An obscure frat rock band, the Combo Kings, released "Batman a Go Go." Cameo Records released the single "'The Ballad of Batman" with the B-side "Batmobile" by the Camps, who in actuality was Sonny Curtis. (Curtis also wrote "I Fought the Law" and wrote and performed "Love Is All Around," the *Mary Tyler Moore Show* theme.) Garage rockers, the Creation, released the underground favorite "Biff Bang Pow!" In 1967, as an homage to *Batman,* the group opened their live sets with the *Batman* theme ("The Creation"). Two bands from Quebec, André Jean and the Pharaohs and Les Hou-Lops, each put out French-language *Batman*-themed tracks. And the Hullabaloo Dancers danced the Batusi to the *Batman* theme in the second and final season of NBC's prime time dance show *Hullabaloo* (1965–1966).

Golden Records released a spoken word album with Batman's origin story and the adventure "The Joker's Utility Belt." The record came with a Batman comic book, Official Batman Club Card, lapel pin and decoder ring. Wonderland Records released a 45 with the *Batman* theme and "*Superman* Song."

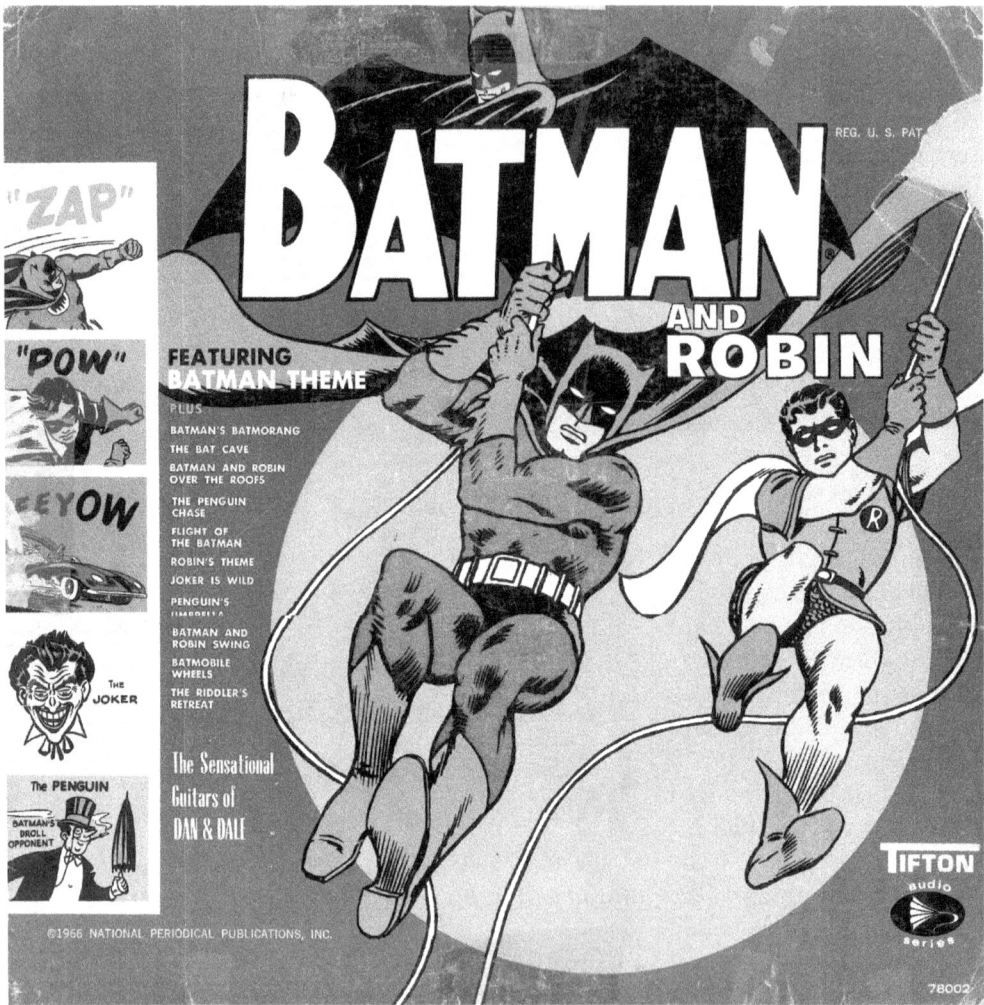

Above and opposite page: Two of the many examples of *Batman*-themed albums released: One released by the aptly named *Batboys*, the other by studio band *The Sensational Dan & Dale* which featured members of *Sun Ra and His Arkestra* (Shubilla family archives).

The show's stars even got in on the act. Adam West recorded the bizarre and unauthorized novelty song "Miranda." In the song, which also featured Burt Ward, he sings that he would do anything for a girl named Miranda, except remove his mask. The names Batman, Bruce Wayne, Caped Crusader, Robin, Dick Grayson, the Boy Wonder are never used in the song. Frank Zappa wrote and arranged a song featuring Burt Ward called "Boy Wonder, I Love You" about a fan who wants Robin to spend the summer with her and writes him a letter. On the B-side, Ward belted out the Nat King Cole song "Orange Colored Sky," presumably because of the onomatopoeia lyrics in the song, including "Wham" and "Bam." Frank Gorshin released a record which included the A-side novelty song "The Riddler" and the B-side "Never Let Her Go," a song originally recorded by David Gates of Bread. Burgess Meredith recorded a spoken word record as the Penguin, telling the story of his capture by Batman and subsequent escape from jail.

Batman was getting attention abroad as well. In the Philippines, three unauthorized

low-budget exploitation movies were quickly released to capitalize on Bat-mania. *Alyas Batman en Robin* (1965), which actually predates the television show; *James Batman* (1966), an attempted cash-in on the Batman and James Bond crazes, and the lost film *Batman Fights Dracula* (1967). They were made by different producers, with different stars, and are not in continuity with the *Batman* television show.

Pravda, the Soviet Communist Party newsletter, reportedly stated that *Batman* brainwashed Americans into becoming "willing murderers in the Vietnam Jungle" (Gent "Pravda"). This was perhaps in response to Batman's PSA encouraging children to invest in U.S. Saving stamps and bonds to help fund the Vietnam War. Additionally, the Soviet satire magazine *Krokodil Today*, famous for lampooning capitalist countries, claimed that Batman and Robin were "like idealized representatives of the F.B.I." *Krokodil Today* also accused the show of "deepening the spiritual vacuum of the United States" and said that Batman's adventures had "hardened American schoolchildren to violence so that they no longer flinched at cruelty and took the death of relatives in their stride" ("Russians Call Batman").

In Great Britain, West appeared as Batman in two PSAs. The first encouraged kids to look both ways before crossing the street. The second, West, alongside Burt Ward as Robin, articulated to youngsters that Batman and Robin "have no wings, and no superhuman powers, and we cannot fly." The PSA was made in response to a report of a British child dying "while imitating his masked and cloaked hero Batman," despite no scenes in the program giving the impression that Batman or Robin had the ability to fly. William Dozier later explained, "In England, kids started jumping out of windows; they thought Batman could fly. They thought the cape was wings" ("Young Britons"; Eisner 31). Both PSAs were produced in black and white because color broadcasts were not available in the United Kingdom until 1967, when the PAL system of color broadcasting was implemented.

Dozier and Greenway Productions toyed with the idea of pairing up with Japanese film studio Toho to produce a crossover movie featuring both Batman and legendary giant monster Godzilla, as seen in an outline for an unrealized feature film, *Batman Meets Godzilla* ("Batman Meets Godzilla").

Bat-mania was riding high in July 1966 when the *Batman* movie was released. Characters from the TV show were originally intended to be introduced to the public by way of the movie, but ABC moved the scheduled debut from September to January 1966. This explains why characters that had been on *Batman* for 34 episodes were introduced in the movie as if they were new.

The movie had a much higher budget than the television show and featured Batman and Robin's four most iconic foes: Riddler, Joker, Penguin and Catwoman. In the movie, the four villains form the United Underworld which purchased a pre-atomic submarine from the U.S. Navy and planned on taking over the world by using their Total Dehydrator to turn delegates from the fictitious United World into dust. Batman and Robin used a variety of gadgets and vehicles in the film, including the Bat-boat, Bat-copter and the ever-popular shark-repellent Bat-spray.

The movie's premiere was held on July 30, 1966, at the Paramount Theater in downtown Austin, Texas. The event was intended as a benefit for and ran parallel to the city's annual Aqua Festival, at the behest of the Austin-based boat company Glastron. Glastron agreed to make the Bat-boat for the movie with the stipulation that the premiere be held in Austin to benefit the Aqua Festival (Rittereiser).

Excitement in Austin grew in intensity in the days leading up to the premiere, as seen in daily updates published in the *Austin American-Statesman* newspaper. The paper promised that the premiere would be "exciting and glamorous," and that the movie was "attracting international press coverage" ("At *Batman* Premiere"; "Preview for Reviewers").

The premiere included two sold-out showings, a five p.m. kiddie premiere and an 8:30 p.m. adult premiere with tickets available for $3 each. Fans lined the streets the day of the premiere, holding signs (including **Batman for President**) during a parade that kicked off at 4:30 and featured William Dozier and stars Adam West, Burt Ward, Cesar Romero, Burgess Meredith and Lee Meriwether ("Austin Aqua"; Johnson "*Batman* World Premiere"; "At *Batman* Premiere").

After the parade, the stars were escorted to an invitational dinner at the luxurious Crest Hotel where they were made Honorary Texans by Texas Secretary of State John L. Hill, under the authority of Governor John Connally. Connally, most famous for being wounded by a stray bullet during President John F. Kennedy's assassination, was in Venezuela promoting the World's Fair, HemisFair '68, which would be taking place in San

Antonio, Texas ("Batman and Robin to Become Texans"). After dinner, the stars were whisked to the Paramount Theater for the 8:30 p.m. showing. An estimated 30,000 people attended the event on Congress Avenue, which was renamed Batman Boulevard for the event (Rittereiser "Holy Superlatives").

Except for Meredith and Romero, *Batman*'s stars stuck around for the Aqua Festival and its National Water-Ski Kite Flying competition at 2 p.m. the next day. At the competition, Miss Aqua Festival Vickie Hudson appeared in her Bat-kini and Adam West posed for pictures with a specially made Bat-kite ("Batman: Hoopla").

After the excitement of the premiere, the cast went back to work. In the summer of 1966, Batman and Robin hosted the ABC Fall Preview, *7 Nights to Remember*, which previewed the 1966–1967 ABC prime time lineup. They pushed the fact that every show that season was airing in color: "Holy Rainbow! Every single program in color. That's really something!" exclaimed Robin.

Also to help promote the show, West hosted the variety show *The Hollywood Palace* on October 8, 1966. He opened the show in full Batman regalia, singing and dancing to his own version of Nat King Cole's "Orange Colored Sky." Also appearing that evening were Western stars Roy Rogers and Dale Evans, singer Ray Charles and comedian George Carlin.

In the 1966–1967 season, *Batman* added new colorful gadgets such as Bat-Jets, radioactive Bat-pellets, Bat X-Ray Deflector, Bat-zooka, Super-Powered Bat-magnet and the Bat-tering ram.

One of the show's highlights was the "Bat-Climb": The Dynamic Duo would scale a building with the aid of the Bat-arang and Bat-rope stored in Batman's utility belt, and while en route to the top would run into a celebrity in a window. The first celebrity featured was comedian Jerry Lewis; other Bat-Climb cameos included Dick Clark, Van Williams and Bruce Lee as the Green Hornet and Kato, Sammy Davis, Jr., Milton Berle, Don Ho, Ted Cassidy as *The Addams Family*'s Lurch, and Werner Klemperer as *Hogan's Heroes*' Colonel Klink. New villains appeared: Art Carney as the Archer, Vincent Price as Egghead, Leslie Gore as Catwoman's sidekick Pussycat, and "Mr. Showmanship" Liberace pulling double duty as evil, piano-playing Chandell and his gangster twin brother Harry.

By late 1966, *Batman* started to see a dip in ratings. Originally the show blamed the media research firms who reported ratings for inaccurate rating reports and even lampooned the firms in the November 1966 two-parter "Hizzoner the Penguin" and "Dizzoner the Penguin." In the episode, Batman defeated the Penguin in an election for mayor of Gotham City despite inaccurate data by pollsters named after polling firms: Gallup, Roper and Trendex. It was remarked that these pollsters could get jobs reporting TV ratings after doing such a poor job predicting the outcome of the Gotham mayoral election.

Soon William Dozier realized the low ratings were not due to polling error: *Batman* **was** losing viewers. Changes needed to be made to keep *Batman* fresh and regain viewership. Dozier announced he felt the show had become formulaic and would start doing three-part episodes. Terry Moore, known for her role in the movie *Peyton Place* (1957), was cast as villain Venus Flytrap and love interest of Bruce Wayne. Dozier revealed, "[This season] Batman has his first big love scene with Terry Moore and Robin doesn't mind at all. ... We've gotten better in the humor area; we're much more titillating" (Leonard 82).

By the end of the second season, the Thursday night edition of *Batman* dropped to the 37th highest-rated show, regularly trounced in the ratings by NBC's *Daniel Boone*, and Wednesday night's *Batman* finished a dreadful 58th, crushed by CBS's *Lost in Space* and NBC's *The Virginian* (Brooks and Marsh; Spencer "TVs Vast" 54).

Rumors began swirling about *Batman*'s demise. Although ABC was disappointed by the ratings, the network announced at their annual affiliates meeting that *Batman* would indeed return the next season. But the network relegated the show to one night a week ("ABC Cancels" 16).

Feeling the series needed spicing up, producers introduced a new character, Batgirl. The plan to introduce Batgirl was considered as early as 1966, seeing as the character was included in the script for *Batman Meets Godzilla* ("Batman Meets Godzilla").

In the summer of 1967, Yvonne Craig was cast as Batgirl and her alter-ego Barbara Gordon, daughter of Police Commissioner Gordon and an employee at the Gotham City Library.

William Dozier and Greenway Productions shot an unaired seven-minute color clip in 1967 to convince the ABC network that new characters were needed to help with the serious ratings decline. The short presentation included Batman, Robin and Commissioner Gordon and introduced the villain Killer Moth (Tim Herbert). Dozier produced similar short subjects for *Dick Tracy* (1966) and *Wonder Woman* (1967), but they were made with the intention of selling a possible show to a network. Neither were picked up.

Craig first publicly appeared in her Batgirl attire on *The Merv Griffin Show* on

Despite riding in on her Bat-Cycle for the 1967–1968 season of *Batman*, according to the show's budget, Yvonne Craig made $1050 more per episode than Burt Ward (courtesy Ted A. Bohus).

September 15, 1967, to help promote *Batman,* and debuted on *Batman* in the first episode of season three, "Enter Batgirl."

Although Batgirl was a youthful, strong and smart female character that young girls could look up to (and had plenty of sex appeal), the other additions to the cast looked to the past. Instead of attempting to recapture the younger audience, the show added guest villains who primarily were known for their work in the 1930s, '40s and '50s: Rudy Vallee as larcenous Londoner Marmaduke Ffogg, Joan Collins as the Cleopatra-esque baddie Siren, Ethel Merman as Penguin co-conspirator Lola Lasagna and Zsa Zsa Gabor as diamond thief Minerva. Milton Berle played zoot suit–wearing mobster Louie the Lilac and Henny Youngman ("Take my wife—please!") played Manny the Mesopotamian, despite Dozier's previous feelings that comedians should not be cast as villains ("The Man Behind TV's *Batman*").

The downward spiral continued even after adding Bat-gadgets such as the Bat-Bomb Shield, Bat-Alert Buzzer and a portable Bat-Phone. *Batman* dropped to the 48th place in the Nielsen ratings ("Curses!!!").

At the end of season three, *The New York Times* reported that *Batman*—once touted as the biggest thing since The Beatles—was about to end. Dozier conceded, "There will be no *Batman* next season." Leonard Goldberg, ABC's vice-president of programming, announced, "Mr. Dozier had not been told the program would not be renewed," but he admitted, "[Dozier] probably came to that conclusion after looking at the ratings" ("Curses!!!").

In February 1968, *The New York Times* reported that ABC confirmed *Batman* had been cancelled ("Batman's TV Spot"). ABC replaced *Batman* with a short-lived and poorly reviewed sitcom, *Ugliest Girl in Town.*

Along with the ratings decline, *Batman*'s production cost was also often cited as a reason for cancellation. The show's post-production coordinator Robert Mintz stated, "The expenses for the optics from the series were enormous." But William Dozier maintained, "It was the network's decision to cancel the series because it wasn't delivering a big enough audience of the right kind, it wasn't delivering enough adults who buy things" (Eisner 10–11).

It has long been believed that *Batman*'s producers were looking to move the show to another network for a fourth season. The rumor was most notably repeated by Batgirl herself, Yvonne Craig: She claimed that NBC was looking to pick up the series, then didn't, because the sets were destroyed and it would be too expensive to duplicate them (Eisner 163).

Craig reprised her Batgirl role four years later in a very progressive 1972 PSA for the U.S. Department of Labor promoting the Equal Pay for Equal Work Act of 1963. Along with Craig, the PSA featured two other *Batman* alumni—William Dozier, who narrated, and Burt Ward, playing Robin. Missing was Adam West, who declined to reprise his role as the Caped Crusader. Dick Gautier, best known for playing Hymie the Robot on *Get Smart* (1965–1970), donned the Bat-costume in West's absence. When he wore the Batman cowl, the resemblance was uncanny.

Asked about taking on the role of Batman, Gautier stated, "They called me in, hoping I'd fit into the Batman costume. I could and did and then I imitated Adam's peculiar cadence of delivery and they bought it. Let me rephrase that ... there was no money." Craig maintained that her Batgirl costume and wig were provided by Burt Ward, who pilfered them when the series ended (Kimbal).

The PSA was not the last time Ward put on his Robin tights. And Adam West, who rejected reprising his Batman role to avoid typecasting, soon began appearing as Batman again at circuses, grand openings, parades, car shows and comic book conventions. ("Without Cape" 24; "Drat! Adam West" 35). In 1976, he even appeared in the Batman cowl and a black Lacoste brand tracksuit at a Memphis area pro wrestling event to trade barbs with infamous wrestling villain Jerry "The King" Lawler. West began the odd encounter by admitting that he snuck into the arena but warned kids not to do the same. West claimed to be in Memphis to investigate a rumor that Mr. Freeze, Penguin and "the evil King of Memphis" (Lawler) were causing a radical change in the weather and that he was not wearing his full Batman outfit because he was attempting to go incognito. Lawler walked on camera wearing a Superman style "Super King" outfit. "I've heard he had his problems with the Joker, and the Penguin and Mr. Freeze, but he hasn't handled the King yet," declared Lawler. The encounter takes an even stranger turn when West exclaimed, "That costume that you are wearing ... has been stolen from a friend of mine, 'Supe.' Superman, I call him 'Supe.' And I think that Spider-Man, Spidey baby, would probably object too." West went on to state that it may not be too late for Jerry Lawler to transform: "I think possibly if you change some of your habits, some of your methods of wrestling, if you used your left and right turn indicator in your car, did other things that people normally do when they are polite and courteous and you weren't such a naughty mean person." In true wrestling heel fashion, Lawler quickly changes the subject and calls the Memphis wrestling crowd "a bunch of rednecks." But Batman came to the crowd's defense: "They look like splendid people to me, and Bat-fans ... It's insulting to call them rednecks," and added that he felt that Lawler could be rehabilitated, "possibly in Gotham State Prison." West never got in the ring to wrestle Lawler.

In 1976, West officially portrayed Batman again in the two-part Hanna-Barbera–produced *Legends of the Superheroes,* reuniting with Burt Ward as Robin. Campy even for *Batman* standards, *Legends of the Superheroes* featured a number of other DC Comics superheroes such as the Flash, Captain Marvel, Hawkman and the Green Lantern, and supervillains Weather Wizard, Solomon Grundy, Sinestro and the Riddler (Frank Gorshin player the latter character). The second part of the special featured a celebrity-style roast at the Hall of Heroes hosted by Ed McMahon.

In even stranger circumstances, West continued to appear as Batman in an unofficial capacity throughout the 1970s and even claimed to have been shot out of a cannon while in full Batman garb at a circus in Indiana in 1976. In mid-flight after the cannon shot, he made the decision to never appear as Batman again (Adam West: *Batman Unmasked*). There is no concrete evidence of the event taking place. However, advertisements for a Evansville, Indiana, Thanksgiving week Hadi Shrine Circus in 1977 promised that Batman, portrayed by Adam West, would "roar into the stadium on his Batcycle in person" and that he would be "bringing chilling accounts of the Joker, Steam Head, King Tut and the daring exploits of Robin and Batwoman." No one's quite sure who "Steam Head" is, as it's not the name of a recorded Batman villain. It might be a typo, or an erroneous reference to the Batman villain Egghead. Either way, West's performance was later panned by the *Evansville Press Metro* in an article titled "Shrine Circus is a Smash: Batman Is a Flop": "[West is] strictly a tongue-in-cheek actor, or rather, talker—there is no act as such. ... His appearance is followed by one final act that most people left the stadium without seeing. It's sort of a takeoff on the popular *Star Wars* movie theme, with a man and woman performing an aerial act from a rocket" ("Batman Roars" 36; Heiman "Shrine Circus").

West continued to make appearances and sign autographs as Batman throughout the country. Meanwhile, rumors began to surface that he was being considered to reprise his role as Batman when producers Jon Peters and Peter Guber purchased the rights to make a *Batman* movie in 1979. In 1981 when the *Los Angeles Times* asked Peters and Guber about West's possible casting, Peters responded, "Who's Adam West?" (Broeske).

In the meantime, West and Ward continued to appear as the Dynamic Duo. In 1986, they were in full costume at Toronto's Metro Convention Center to meet fans and sign autographs to help commemorate the 20th anniversary of *Batman*. In 1988, they were honored by the Georgia State House of Representatives.

Artist's rendition of Adam West's supposed 1976 human cannonball act (illustration by Bennett Lipski).

West continued to lobby for the part of Batman throughout the 1980s until Michael Keaton was cast in the title role in *Batman* (1989); produced by Peters and Gruber, it was the first live-action Batman movie since 1966. That year, West stated that he was upset he was not given the role but understood the producers wanted to go in a new direction (Watkiss; "Drat! Adam West" 35).

West and Ward appeared together on screen one last time in CBS-TV's *Return to the Batcave: The Misadventures of Adam and Burt* (2003). Not a Batman adventure per se, the movie portrays West as himself, living in a home with a Bat-Pole and an Alfred-type butler. He reteams with Ward after the Batmobile used in the 1966–1968 series had been stolen. The movie featured flashbacks to *Batman*'s production, and behind-the-scenes stories with actors reenacting the memories. *Return to the Batcave* also featured *Batman* alumni Frank Gorshin and Julie Newmar and was narrated by Lyle Waggoner, famous for his roles on *Wonder Woman* and *The Carol Burnett Show*. (Waggoner auditioned for the role of Batman in 1965.)

West told *The Guardian* in 2014,

> I decided early on to embrace the character, I mean, how many actors are lucky enough to play a character that becomes iconic? … Some actors get reputations that just won't go away.

… Maybe they're famous for being divas on the set. Maybe they're famous for only playing certain roles—or even worse, only playing one role. Nobody will let them forget it. They can struggle mightily to earn a new reputation … or they can resign themselves to their fate and make a career out of it [Tan "Beyond Batman"].

Batman made its way into TV syndication in 1969. Starting in the 1980s, Bat-fans who did not want to wait for TV to air their favorite *Batman* adventure purchased bootleg versions of the complete series on VHS because the show never had an official home video release. The unauthorized versions varied in quality and were commonly found at comic book and film conventions. A *Batman* DVD–Blu-Ray collection received an official release in 2014 after years of legal wrangling and confusion of rights between 20th Century–Fox, who owned the distribution rights, and Greenway Productions, who owned the footage.

Until his death in 2017, West provided the voice of Batman in several direct-to-video animated *Batman* movies, including *Batman: Return of the Caped Crusaders* (2016) with Burt Ward as Robin and Julie Newmar as Catwoman. Astute viewers of *Batman: Return of the Caped Crusaders* (2016) will observe parodies of West's October 1966 appearance on *Hollywood Palace*, Batman's 1966 British road safety PSA, and Bat-Climbs from the original series.

In 2019, Burt Ward appeared as Robin in the CW Network's DC Comics superhero special event *Crisis on Infinite Earths,* where Ward exclaimed, "Holy crimson skies of death!" The event linked many DC movies and television shows to the classic *Batman* series. The story of *Batman Meets Godzilla* was finally brought to life via an unauthorized web comic book in 2020.

Clearly, critics like Rick DuBrow and Jack Gould were wrong in January 1966 when they wrote that *Batman* was nothing but a passing fad (DuBrow "Batman Is Not" 29; Gould "*Batman* Nothing" 93).

The Green Hornet

Because of the early success of *Batman,* ABC sought another live-action superhero series as a companion piece.

Prior to the premiere of *Batman*, its production company Greenway and its president William Dozier were looking to bring the vintage radio drama *The Green Hornet* to TV sets in the late 1960s. But *Batman*'s success in early 1966 kicked *The Green Hornet*'s production into high gear, along with expectations.

The Green Hornet made his official debut in 1936 on his own radio show. Its popularity brought the character to the big screen in a black-and-white serial released in 1940. A year later, there was a sequel, *The Green Hornet Strikes Again.*

Before Greenway's Green Hornet was cast, 24-year-old martial artist Bruce Lee, then a relative unknown, was cast as the Hornet's sidekick and valet Kato. In Lee's screen test, he talked about the different types of martial arts, most notably his personal style known as Gung Fu. While wearing a slim-fitting suit, he demonstrated punches and kicks for the camera. At the time of the screen test, Lee's wife had just given birth to their son Brandon Lee.

On February 17, 1965, William Dozier wrote a letter to Lee, who was in Hong Kong due to the death of his father: "The film you shot when here looks very good, and when you return to San Francisco, please let me know" (Dozier "Dozier to Lee").

Lee modestly responded on the 21st, "I'm glad to hear that the screen test was all right. That day having waited for seven hours I was in no shape for that test. Anyway, I'm glad I've done something that pleased you" (Lee).

In hopes of finding the lead, two separate five-minute test episodes were shot. Both featured Lee as Kato with different actors playing the Green Hornet: one was comedian and character actor Jay Murray and the other, TV actor Michael Lipton. Ultimately, neither was chosen: Greenway cast Van Williams in the title role. Williams previously played on the ABC shows *Bourbon Street Beat* (1959–1960) and *Surfside 6* (1960–1962), and starred in the ABC pilot *Locate, Pursue and Destroy* (1965), about a World War II submarine crew.

Production on *The Green Hornet* started on June 7, 1966 ("Green Hornet Series Budget").

Like Batman, the Green Hornet's alter ego, newspaper publisher Britt Reid, created the perception that he was a wealthy and eccentric playboy. As a crime fighter, he had a distinct car and a masked sidekick, and he used unusual gadgets. Unlike Batman, the Hornet was officially a wanted man, and he kept up the ruse of being a villain to provide cover for his crime-fighting.

Although *Batman* and *Green Hornet* are forever linked, the two shows did have big differences. Dozier, executive producer and narrator of both *Batman* and *The Green Hornet*, stated that he tried to avoid making the shows too similar. "How are you going to be serious about a guy who runs a newspaper in the daytime and goes out at night and hunts criminals? How can you be funny with it? It just fell in the middle. It was neither serious nor funny" (Eisner 114).

In a November 1966 interview with the Rochester, New York, newspaper *Democrat and Chronicle,* Williams said, "This is not a 'way-out' show like *Batman*. It's not 'camp.' We're playing this straight, with a lot of action. As a matter of fact, I wouldn't have done the show if it were going to be like *Batman*" (Heisner).

Before *The Green Hornet*'s debut, the show got a push from another ABC talent, "Mr. Television" Milton Berle, on *The Milton Berle Show*. In one episode, Berle predicted, "ABCs *Green Hornet* show with Van Williams and Bruce Lee will become as popular as the *Batman* show starring Adam West." Williams, Lee and Adam West appeared in a slapstick comedy skit where Berle played an actor who was cast as a villain simultaneously on both *Batman* and *The Green Hornet*. This would not be the last time the Green Hornet and Batman met.

Prior to the premiere, *The New York Times* ran an article about the Hornet's car, "The Black Beauty." The article revealed that, stripped down to its essentials, the car was a 1966 Chrysler Imperial. "But $50,000 was spent to rebuild it with flair, style and class that might make even James Bond envious. The job was done by Dean Jefferies who operates an automotive styling company in Hollywood and also designs and builds racing cars." The article went on to describe the car's devices, such as a secret compartment for guns, a TV camera on a closed circuit to make recordings, and brooms under the car to sweep away tire marks. *The New York Times* even teased a crossover episode: "Whether the Batmobile and Black Beauty will ever meet grill to grill on some lonely road is not known. But ABC ought to consider putting them in a drag race" ("Moving Up to a Black Beauty").

Viewers first look at *The Green Hornet* was on the 1966 ABC Fall Preview, *7 Nights to Remember*, hosted by Batman and Robin. The preview's narrator exclaimed, "7:30 will start Friday's buzzing with *The Green Hornet*, that legendary nemesis of crime with his wild companion Kato, who thrilled most of us as kids in one of radio's longest runs!"

The first *Green Hornet* episode was not complete at the time of the Fall Preview so viewers did not see much action, just the Green Hornet and Kato moving a wooden sawhorse from the road and driving around in the Black Beauty. ABC later released another promo with action and explosions.

TV Guide's "Fall Preview 1966–1967 Shows" issue gave *The Green Hornet* a spread and attempted to differentiate it from *Batman*: "The show is produced by William Dozier, the man behind Batman. Unlike *Batman*, however, *The Green Hornet* will have no cliffhangers and no recurring villains and it's not *intentionally* funny" ("Fall Preview").

Neil LeVang and Buddy Merrill shredded the *Green Hornet* theme song on guitar on ABC's *The Lawrence Welk Show*, to help promote the series. Welk, with his pronounced accent, stated, "I'm sure many of you folks remember the fine radio show *The Green Hornet*. You'll be glad to know that this show had been adapted for television and is one of the Friday night features on ABC this season. We're going to call on Buddy Merrill and Neil LeVang for their recording version of *Green Hornet*'s theme." A long-time guitarist for Welk, LeVang had an impressive resumé and had a connection with other shows in the 1966–1967 Fall lineup: He played on a number of TV and film projects including *Batman*, *Green Acres* (1965–1971), *The Ed Sullivan Show* (1948–1971), *The Monkees* (1966–1968) and *Petticoat Junction* (1963–70) (Meeker).

Even Dozier helped promote *The Green Hornet* to ABC executives at affiliate stations at a network convention where he said,

> I think it's easier to tell you what *The Green Hornet* will not be. It will not be an imitation of *Batman*. I would question anyone who would want to imitate *Batman*. *Green Hornet* will stand very much on its own, as an action-adventure with plenty of exciting gadgets and gimmicks for the youngsters at 7:30. It will be done with elegance and style, all its own. I believe a style that will match *Batman*'s style and a result that will match *Batman*'s result, but entirely unique unto itself. So those of you who have BAT-ed 1000 with us at 7:30 on Wednesday and Thursday nights, get buzzing with us on *Green Hornet* at 7:30 next year on Friday ["Green Hornet William Dozier"].

ABC held a press conference hosted by Dozier and Adam West, to help introduce audiences to Van Williams and Bruce Lee. West thanked the press for the amount of coverage *Batman* had received, stating, "[*Batman* has] been written about a great deal in the past six months; quantitatively it's been marvelous! Qualitatively? You're beginning to understand the show a bit." West and Williams also gave a peculiar interview at the while in their respective characters. The pair were even asked about several accusations by Pravda, the Soviet Party newsletter, that Batman and Green Hornet were "representatives of U.S. millionaires." West, as Batman, stated, "I represent U.S. millions, however I do not represent U.S. millionaires. … I presume anyone that carries the cape of freedom would be accused … of this nature." Williams, as the Green Hornet, went on to defend U.S. capitalism: "I protect the money interests in this country, and one thing I can say is, we should be very proud of this country that you can make more money than the other guy if you want to. … Anybody who has the ability—they can do it." The reporter also asked both stars about the Pravda accusation that both shows were training Americans to kill in Vietnam; both wholeheartedly stated that their characters don't kill, but are only interested in the rehabilitation of criminals ("Adam West, Bruce Lee").

Two days before the *Green Hornet* debut, Dozier—nervous about how the show would be viewed—wrote to Van Williams, "On Friday, our collective necks will start sticking out. I simply want you to know, regardless of the reception, that I think you have worked magnificently and well, and I am very grateful for your high degree of dedication, professionalism and cooperation" (Dozier "Dozier to Van Williams").

Despite Dozier's nerves, hopes were high for the new show and retailers predicted that the Green Hornet would become the next fad. *The Greenville News* in Greenville, South Carolina, wrote, "It is rumored the Batman is quickly dying, and a more exciting character will flash across the television screens and claim new fortunes in the T-shirt business." The paper interviewed Frank Plummer, manager of Grant's Department Store in Greenville, who said, "The Green Hornet's the thing," while displaying his store's Green Hornet T-shirts. "I expect we'll be getting more and more of these things, but Batman is gone … all washed up" (Boley).

The *Green Hornet* debut episode, "The Silent Gun," aired on Friday, September 9, 1966, at 7:30 p.m. For viewers not familiar with *The Green Hornet*, the show's introduction stated the premise: "Another challenge for the Green Hornet, his aide Kato, and their rolling arsenal, the Black Beauty! On police records a wanted criminal, the Green Hornet is really Britt Reid, owner-publisher of *The Daily Sentinel*, His dual identity known only to his secretary, and to the district attorney. And now, to protect the rights and lives of decent citizens, rides the Green Hornet!"

Reviews from around the country were less than complimentary:

> "Just sluggishly old hat rather than divertingly awful."—Jack Gould, *The New York Times*
>
> "It isn't funny and it isn't much fun."—Ann Hodges, *Houston Chronicle*
>
> "What that handsome young publisher needs is psychiatric help."—Laurence Laurent, *Washington Post*
>
> "Humorless, unimaginative, unimportant and unnecessary."—Dwight Newton, *San Francisco Examiner*
>
> "Generates nothing but boredom."—Walt Dutton, *Los Angeles Times*
>
> "So bad it almost defies description."—C.J. Skreen, *Seattle Times*
>
> "Let's face it, Mr. Dozier, your hornet has no sting."—Bob Tweedell, *Denver Post* ("Critic's Views" 58–62)

According to *TV Channels,* a northern Maryland–Washington, D.C., metro area magazine:

> It was easier to be serious in the '30s. … America isn't as square today, despite what a majority of TV producers like to believe. We'll tolerate a lot of junk, more out of apathy than curiosity, but occasionally we rebel and draw the line. Unfortunately, the TV producer finds all kind of "analytical" reasons for the show's failure, yet refused to face the fact that it was a lousy show, and that this time the public blew the whistle on [Dozier] ["Justice Will Out"].

The National Association for Better Broadcasting, a watchdog organization, criticized the show for its content: "Stories of concentrated viciousness make this show wrong on every count for teens and children" (Leonard "What's Out" 78).

The first episode received a Trendex rating of 21.5 with a 54.8 share of the audience, beating out NBC's American Football League Football game of the Jets vs. Dolphins and a *Wild Wild West* rerun on CBS ("Numbers Game" 58; Brooks and Marsh).

But *The Green Hornet* would not rise to become one of the season's top-rated shows as *Batman* did nine months earlier. The next week, it slid to a 14.8 rating with a 36.0 share ("Latest from the Sheet" 66–69). This time *The Green Hornet* went against the series premiere of *The Wild Wild West* and *Tarzan*. The show slid even further each subsequent week. By October, the program was the 73rd most watched show between the hours of six p.m. and one a.m. ("The Ratings").

The Green Hornet's ratings never took off and *Batman*'s ratings were on a downward trajectory so both programs needed a jump start. Batman and the Green Hornet officially met in late 1966. Since both shows had the same producer and network, a crossover episode was inevitable.

On the *Batman* episode "The Spell of Tut," the Green Hornet and Kato made an appearance during one of Batman and Robin's infamous Bat-Climbs. While Batman lectured Robin about the importance of exercise, the Hornet and Kato stuck their heads out of a window and let Batman know that they are in Gotham City on a "special assignment for *The Daily Sentinel*" and "pursuing the enemies of law and order wherever they happen to be."

Later that season, in the two-part adventure "A Piece of the Action" and "Batman's Satisfaction," Reid and Kato made yet another trip to Gotham City. Unfortunately, the superhero duos do not tangle with a well-known villain. Both superhero teams broke up a rare postal stamp forging ring led by new *Batman* villain Colonel Gumm, and even fought *each other*. Colonel Gumm counterfeits rare stamps in a factory unbeknownst to its owner Pinky Pinkston (the heart interest of both Britt Reid and Bruce Wayne). Batman and Robin save the Hornet and Kato from being crushed in a stamp-making machine. After the superheroes take out Gumm's henchmen in a fight, they go after each other (Robin vs. Kato, the Hornet vs. Batman). The fight wound up being a draw, or a "Mexican Standoff," as narrator Dozier put it. When the police arrived, they broke up the rumble and arrested Gumm as the Hornet and Kato escaped.

In the episode, *Batman* took advantage of color in the storyline, something that *The Green Hornet* continually failed to do. Those watching on a black-and-white TV would not have had the same experience as those with a color set. Pinky Pinkston sported bright pink hair, owned a pink dog and operated a pink-colored stamp factory, and narrator Dozier made it a point to mention Wayne Manor's red brick color and the red Bat-phone. In addition, the Green Hornet and Kato are made into life-size, full-color stamps after being thrown into a stamp-making machine by Gumm's henchmen.

Batman and Robin never got a chance to take a trip to *The Daily Sentinel* to take on Green Hornet and Kato for a rematch. However, in the *Batman* episode "The Impractical Joker," Bruce and Dick sit down to watch an episode of *The Green Hornet* on TV, before being interrupted by the Joker. And in *The Green Hornet* episode "Ace in the Hole," Batman and Robin can be seen on TV in the midst of a Bat-Climb.

Although both show's ratings were on the decline, *Batman* continued to overshadow *The Green Hornet* in the media. A close-up of a masked Van Williams as the Hornet appeared on the cover of the horror movie magazine *Castle of Frankenstein* in February 1967. yet Batman still found a way to outshine his fellow hero. Inside there was a page dedicated to the *Batman* movie, released the previous year. Inside the magazine

Jazz trumpeter Al Hirt's album *The Horn Meets the Hornet* featured a number of iconic theme songs from the 1966–1967 season (Shubilla family archives).

was only a small blurb on *The Green Hornet,* concerning how the original design for the Green Hornet's mask was rejected because it muffled Van Williams' voice. To make matters worse for *Green Hornet,* the previous *Castle of Frankenstein* featured a full-page close up of Cesar Romero as the Joker on the cover, alongside photos of Batman, Robin, Catwoman and Penguin with a multi-page article about *Batman.* That issue failed to mention *Green Hornet* (Mitchel 42).

The Green Hornet radio program, movie serials and TV series all featured the iconic theme "Flight of the Bumblebee" by Russian composer Nikolai Rimsky-Korsakov from his opera *The Tale of Tsar Saltan*, composed at the turn of the 20th century. Many records were produced in 1966–1967 featuring the *Green Hornet* theme. Versions of "Flight of the Bumblebee" were done by surf rockers The Ventures, instrumental group B. Bumble and the Stingers, funk band Lee Merril and the Golden Horns, Latin Jazz combo The Mexicali-Brass, and composer Billy May, who arranged the song for the TV show. Al Hirt, who performed "Flight of the Bumblebee" for the show, released the LP "The Horn Meets 'The Hornet'" on RCA Records which featured an image of Hirt holding his trumpet alongside Van Williams as the Hornet holding his program's logo. The album also featured themes from several other new prime time shows: *Get Smart,*

Tarzan, The Monkees, Run, Buddy, Run, T.H.E. Cat and *Batman.* Hirt's album reached #126 on the Billboard charts.

Even with the push by Milton Berle, *The New York Times*, the NBC Fall Preview *7 Nights to Remember, TV Guide*, Welk, ABC, Dozier, and the many musical collaborations; *The Green Hornet* never took off in the ratings because the show missed many opportunities to appeal to youth and younger adult audiences. According to *7 Nights to Remember, The Green Hornet* "had thrilled most of us as kids" and had "one of radio's longest runs." That statement made it clear from the start the show was not going to seek to appeal to a new generation of fans. Instead it would focus on fans who listened to the radio show which premiered 30 years earlier (and had not been on the radio airwaves in 14 years). In all likelihood, this decision was due to one of the Hornet's creators and the owner of the Green Hornet franchise, George Trendle. Trendle repeatedly urged Dozier and the show's writers to harken back to the radio program and base the stories in reality rather than take the show in a new direction (Trendle "Trendle to Dozier" 13 May 1966; 2 June 1966; 21 July 1966; 22 September 1966; 26 November 1966).

Example of one of the few promotional items for *The Green Hornet* in comparison to Batman (courtesy Kevin Daugherty Collection).

Even though Trendle and Dozier agreed they did not want to simply recreate *Batman*, they had very different ideas about what should be the foundation of the series. Trendle did not believe the show should concentrate on gadgets and gimmicks, such as the Green Hornet's gas gun and his Black Beauty. Instead, Trendle envisioned *The Green Hornet* as more of a police procedural, as opposed to Dozier's vision of an action-adventure program. Trendle believed *The Green Hornet's* "appeal rested in its ability to teach viewers about civic duty and police work" (Trendle "Trendle to Dozier," 13 May 1966).

Trendle also believed nostalgia for the old radio show would be a driving force for

The Green Hornet, as seen in many of his letters to Dozier. However, Dozier imagined that gadgets and over-the-top storylines were the key to merchandising and achieving success.

Without the over-the-top camp storylines, the show did not appeal to a younger demographic, like *Batman* did, and the older generation who once listened to the radio show had presumably outgrown it. *The Green Hornet*'s storylines may have appealed to a teenage and college-age audience. But the 7:30 p.m. Friday time slot was terrible for a series that would rely on a teenage and college-age audience. Staying home to watch *Batman* at 7:30 p.m. on Wednesday and Thursday night was not unheard of, but any number of social activities could keep teens and young adults out of the house on a Friday at 7:30 p.m. *The Green Hornet* may have done better at a later time slot or during the week.

A combination of several other factors caused *The Green Hornet* to fail. The first could possibly be that Batmania was waning and the audience's desire for masked superheroes was already in decline by the fall of 1966. There was not enough wind for the Hornet to ride Batman's cape to the top. The series also did not offer much in terms of color and there was nothing innovative that made it a must-see in color, especially in comparison to *Batman*; just the Black Beauty's green lights, the Hornet's gas gun's green smoke and the Hornet graphic between scenes. The sets were dark, Kato and the Hornet wore black (with the exception of the Green Hornet's mask), and the sets and villains were not colorful.

The series also failed to get the most out of merchandising, especially in comparison to *Batman*. A study conducted by Avi Santo and published in the Winter 2010 *Cinema Journal* argued that the series failed to capitalize on merchandising rights because of Trendle and the influence he had on scripts (Santo 63–85).

Batman was owned by Licensing Corporation of America (LCA), a subsidiary of National Periodical Publications which owned DC Comics, publisher of *Batman* comics. LCA encouraged *Batman* to introduce new gadgets for more merchandising opportunities. *The Green Hornet* was owned by Trendle, who also controlled merchandising and licensing for *The Lone Ranger* and *Sergeant Preston of the Yukon*. Although Trendle was very successful with both *The Lone Ranger* and *Sergeant Preston* properties from the 1930s through the 1950s, he failed to change with the times and offer the more outlandish merchandise that fans clamored for in the '60s (Santo 63–85).

Even before *Batman* was on the air, Dozier was looking ahead to *The Green Hornet*. In a November 16, 1965, letter, he asked Trendle to watch *Batman*'s premiere episode: "I am sure you will agree that we can't do straight *Green Hornet* stories today as they were done on radio. We must give the characters an added style and dimension which they didn't have on radio in order to make the grade in the present-day sophisticated television market" (Dozier "Dozier to Trendle").

However, a straight Green Hornet was exactly what Trendle wanted to see. Throughout the program's production, he wrote Dozier on many occasions to complain about *The Green Hornet*'s scripts being over the top and urged the writers to go back and listen to the *Green Hornet* radio program for inspiration. For example, Trendle wrote on May 13, 1966, "I'm a nut for trying to keep these things logical, so that when they're viewed, the audience won't say … 'that's crazy!' … or 'that's fantastic' … or 'this couldn't be done!' I like to stay within the realm of reality as far as we can. Give the audience all the action you want but keep it believable" (Trendle "Trendle to Dozier" 13 May 1966).

Two of the most iconic covers of *Castle of Frankenstein* featuring Cesar Romero as the Joker and Van Williams as the Green Hornet (courtesy Drew Friedman).

Dozier wrote to Trendle on January 3, 1967, about his displeasure with Trendle's interference:

> It has not been easy, George, to work around your particular brand of censorship, and I must tell you if I have my way about it again, I would never go into another deal where a basking owner of a property has any rights of final approval of scripts. I think one thing that has been wrong with *Green Hornet* is that we have tried too hard to make it too much like the radio show, whereas had been left to our own devices we would have probably gone much more in the modern direction—and even in the direction of *Batman*, which is what I think the public was expecting and also what the network was expecting. Everyone was expecting that but you, and I think we have let everyone down and apparently we have let you down [Dozier "Dozier to Trendle" 3 January 1967].

Dozier addressed his frustration and the audience's lack of interest eight days later: "The trouble is we set out not to do another *Batman*. And the crimes committed under a newspaper publisher are limited." He went on to state: "Perhaps if the show were an hour which I'd like it to be next year, we could say something about Britt Reid, how he met Kato, for instance. We'd like to open up in the human area" (Leonard 82).

But Dozier would never get the chance to expand the show's time slot or storylines. ABC announced on January 21, 1967, that it would not be picking the show up for another season.

Dozier's wrote in a March 7, 1967, letter to Van Williams, "Well, it looks like our friend the Green Hornet is just going to buzz off into oblivion. I'm sorry, as I am sure you are. Everyone tried, very hard, and you above all. None of us need be ashamed of the show, and we all gave it a hell of a shot. That's all anyone can be expected to do" (Dozier "Dozier to Van Williams").

In the last *Green Hornet* episode, "Invasion from Outer Space," the Hornet and Kato do battle with what appears to be alien invaders who wear colorful costumes and brandish exotic, futuristic weapons. The show seemingly was planning to take a more creative approach to storylines and break away from Trendle's vision.

The 27 episodes of *The Green Hornet* went into syndication that spring, and reruns aired on ABC throughout the summer of 1967 ("Syndicators" 100).

Unlike Adam West, Williams never put the mask back on to play his most iconic character. In a 2007 interview, he said he was a fan of the *Green Hornet* radio show and serial as a kid but was unsure if he wanted to play the character on a TV series. He thought it would be the "kiss of death" to his career, much like it was for George Reeves after playing Superman. However, he was talked into taking the role by his agent at the William Morris Agency. Williams left show business soon after *The Green Hornet* to become a real-life crime fighter by joining the Los Angeles Police Department. He said that he felt pride when fans told him they went into law enforcement after learning he had done the same. "That is probably the best thing that ever came out of my working in show business," the actor said. "It was wonderful for me to learn that I'd had some kind of a positive effect on them" (Barnum).

Then relative unknown Bruce Lee went on to become a movie legend with a legacy that extends far beyond his death. After *The Green Hornet*, he moved to Hong Kong where *The Green Hornet* was known as *The Kato Show* and was still popular on television. Lee got the opportunity to star in a string of kung fu movies that became very popular in America and throughout the world before his untimely death in 1973. To exploit Lee's death, several *Green Hornet* episodes were edited together and released as a feature-length film in 1974. The movie's poster and trailer prominently featured Lee.

Lee's life was chronicled in the 1993 biopic *Dragon: The Bruce Lee Story*. In it, Van Williams played the role of a *Green Hornet* episode director.

The Green Hornet did not make another official live-action appearance on TV or movies until 2011 when he came to the big screen in a film featuring Seth Rogen in the title role.

When pitching the show's reruns to station managers and program directors in the 1980s, 20th Century Television sent out a promo tape promising that *The Green Hornet* will put a "charge in your station's lineup, ignite your station's ratings, help you kick your competition, and make your station money" and that the 27 episodes will provide "flexibility as a summer strip or ideal for weekends … or in its own marathon! If you're looking for a program to solve problem time periods, *The Green Hornet* is your answer." The pitch also prominently featured Bruce Lee as Kato, stating that in 1986, Lee was "ranked 12th amongst kids, and would you believe that his Q score [a measurement of audience familiarity] placed him above Paul McCartney, Leonard Nimoy and Larry Hagman?—just to name a few!"

Better late than never to appeal to a younger generation.

Mr. Terrific and *Captain Nice*

In January 1967, both CBS and NBC tried to recreate ABC's success with *Batman* by airing two very similar color superhero comedies on Monday nights: *Mr. Terrific* at 8:00 on CBS and *Captain Nice* in the 8:30 slot on NBC. Both shows were announced in the

Superheroes were not relegated only to primetime television in 1966. A vast array of Saturday Morning cartoons featured superheroes on ABC that season (Shubilla family archives).

article "Hyped Heroes Fly High" in *The New York Times* on November 13, 1966. The article stated, "Don't kick in your TV screen. Beginning Monday, Jan. 9, television will be 'nice' and 'terrific.' *Captain Nice* will be introduced by the National Broadcasting Company and *Mr. Terrific* by the Columbia Broadcasting System" (Adams "Hyped Heroes").

In *Mr. Terrific*, the United States government's Bureau of Secret Projects gives a nebbish gas station attendant, Stanley Beamish, the opportunity to become crime-fighting superhero Mr. Terrific by way of a power pill. Beamish was selected because he happened to be the only person in the country the pill will work for. The power pill gave him superhuman strength and the ability to fly, with the assistance of a special flying suit. The pill worked for one hour, and taking more than one pill a day would have caused him to explode, as explained in the pilot episode. Mr. Terrific could get more time with his superpowers with the aid of booster pills.

The role of Mr. Terrific in the unaired pilot was played by Alan Young, coming off the lead role as Wilbur Post on *Mr. Ed* (1961–1966). But by January 1967, when the series began running as a mid-season replacement for *Run, Buddy, Run*, Mr. Terrific was played by Stephen Strimpell.

Mr. Terrific's co-worker at the gas station, Hal Walters, was played by Dick Gautier, who also played Hymie the Robot on *Get Smart* and later replaced Adam West in the role of Batman in a 1972 PSA for the Department of Labor and Industry.

Executive producer Jack Arnold was most famous for directing some of the biggest and most famous monster movies of the previous decade at Universal: *It Came from Outer Space* (1953), *Creature from the Black Lagoon* (1954), *Tarantula* (1955) and *Monster* on the Campus (1958). He also directed episodes of *Gilligan's Island, Rawhide, It's About Time, Peter Gunn*, etc.

The *Mr. Terrific* premiere on January 9, 1967, received an Arbitron rating of 22.7 with a 38 share, beating out time slot rivals *The Iron Horse* on ABC and *I Dream of Jeannie* on NBC. It was the third most-watched show of the entire evening ("How Critics" 50).

Mr. Terrific started off on a ratings hot streak. The February 13, 1967, issue of the industry magazine *Broadcasting* reported that *Mr. Terrific* and ABC's science fiction show *The Invaders* were two of the highest-rated new shows of the season. *Mr. Terrific* was the 14th most watched show in prime time, receiving a 24.5 rating ("CBS Leads Latest" 66). On February 20, *Broadcasting* reported that CBS was "mulling over the slotting of *Mr. Terrific* or *Gilligan's Island* to open Monday at 7:30, followed by *Hogan's Heroes* which moved to Friday at 8:30–9:00 p.m." ("Annual Chess Game" 58).

But the good news did not last for *Mr. Terrific*. Three days later, George Gent of *The New York Times* reported that CBS was not picking it up for another season because it was being watched by the wrong demographic: "[*Mr. Terrific*] was considered one of the more successful mid-season programs and was in the top 30 shows in the last Nielsen report. CBS apparently felt that the series had reached its peak audience with the children and was not likely to pick up steam" (Gent "Marshal Dillon"). The February 27 *Broadcasting* confirmed the report of its cancellation ("Ten Shows" 25).

NBC's answer to *Batman* and *The Green Hornet, Captain Nice,* was the mid-season replacement for the variety series *The Roger Miller Show*. Captain Nice was played by character actor William Daniels, who went on to play roles on *St. Elsewhere* (1982–1988) and *Boy Meets World* (1993–2000) and provided the voice of the car K.I.T.T. on *Knight Rider* (1982–1986). Daniels asserted that the role was written with him in mind by Buck Henry after Henry saw him on a poster ("William Daniels").

On the show, chemist Carter Nash (Daniels) discovers a formula that will turn him into a superhero, but only for a short amount of time. The first time he makes his superhero transformation, most of his clothes are blown off, only leaving his monogrammed belt buckle. Keeping the same initials, Carter Nash went by Captain Nice. He donned a pajama-ish superhero costume, created by his mother who browbeat him to use his powers for good.

Executive producer Buck Henry had an impressive resumé: He was co-creator of *Get Smart* (1965–1970) and co-wrote (with Calder Willingham) *The Graduate* (1967), which was being produced at the time.

Captain Nice's January 9, 1967, debut scored a 17.9 rating with a 29 share of the viewing audience, beating its competitors on CBS (*The Lucy Show* and ABC (*The Rat Patrol*). The high rating put the show in the top five shows in prime time that week ("How Critics" 50–51).

But ratings quickly dropped; later that month, *Captain Nice* was the time slot loser. Arbitron reported that *Captain Nice* received a 15.1 rating/24 share, losing to *Lucy* and *Rat Patrol*. *Lucy* received a 22.9 rating with a 37 share and *Rat Patrol* an 18.5/30 share ("CBS Edges" 60). *The New York Times* reported on February 28, 1967, less than two months into *Captain Nice*'s run, that NBC had announced that it would not be picked up for a second season. Other cancelled shows: *Hey Landlord!, The Andy Williams Show, The Road West, The Girl from U.N.C.L.E., Occasional Wife, Bob Hope Presents the Chrysler Theatre, T.H.E. Cat, Laredo, Please Don't Eat the Daisies* and *Flipper* (Gent "NBC to Cancel").

Both were seemingly doomed from the start, as seen by the many mediocre reviews from around the country:

> "*Terrific* is terrible. *Nice* was Nicer than *Terrific* but not by much."—Percy Shain, *Boston Globe*

> "Both embarrassing likenesses in theme, costume and gags."—Bob Hull, *Los Angeles Herald-Examiner*

> "So unbelievably bad [*Mr. Terrific* and *Captain Nice*] further emphasize how disastrous the current season is."—Paul Molley, *Chicago Sun-Times*

> "If you've seen one cape you've seen them all."—Dean Gysel, *Chicago Daily News*

The negative reviews overwhelmingly outnumbered the positive ones:

> "[*Mr. Terrific*] got off to a faster start and packed more action."—Wade Mosby, *Milwaukee Journal*

> "[*Captain Nice* is] smartly written ... moves briskly and ingeniously."—Bernie Harrison, *Washington Evening Star* ("How Critics" 50–51)

Both shows lasted half a season, 17 episodes for *Mr. Terrific,* 15 for *Captain Nice*. Both aired on Monday nights, debuted on the same day and aired their last episodes on the same day, August 28, 1967.

Mr. Terrific was replaced by the second half-hour of *Gunsmoke,* which moved to Monday from 10:00 p.m. Saturday. *Captain Nice* was replaced by the second half hour of *The Man from U.N.C.L.E.,* which moved from its 8:00 p.m. Friday time slot (Brooks and Marsh).

The shows are remembered due in part to *Batman* and the superhero craze of the mid–1960s, because of their story similarities, and adjoining time slots. And, for being just a knob-turn away from each other, they will be forever linked. Even the titles are often misremembered as *Captain Terrific* and/or *Mr. Nice*.

Chapter Two

Dramas

Dramatic shows were few and far between in the 1966–1967 season. Associated Press TV critic Cynthia Lowry proclaimed that the shortage of drama was "the disappointment of the year" (Lowry "The Television Year" 8).

When networks announced their pilot shows for the season, ABC vice-president Edgar Scherick believed that "far-out" comedy was getting stronger and realistic drama was on the wane. Other networks felt the same way ("Bumper Crop" 28). Clearly television executives did not see much future in dramas; they did not make a resurgence on TV until the early 1970s.

Peyton Place

The only prime time soap opera in the 1966–1967 season, *Peyton Place* was based on the popular 1956 novel by Grace Metalious and the racy (for 1957) film starring Lana Turner and Lee Philips. The TV series was the serialized story of residents of a small Massachusetts town. In January 1964, it was first announced that the ABC show would be the "first half-hour TV series to be shown twice-weekly on a network in prime evening time" (Gardella "Dems to Join" 442).

Producer Richard Goldstone stated, "It's an exciting concept, but one that presents all kinds of logistical problems. ... The writing is difficult, because we have to keep several different plots going to involve a number of people in the town. ... We require a large cast ... and we have two directors leap-frogging their units, each working every other week" (Thomas "TV's *Peyton Place*" 6).

When it came to time period and themes, the series was different from the novel and the movie. *Peyton Place* the novel and movie both take place during World War II, whereas the TV show was set in contemporary times. The show's production company 20th Century–Fox promised the show would have "fresh storylines" but with "the basic characters of the movie" and gave the show a "top-flight" budget (Gardella "Dems to Join" 442; Thomas "TV's Peyton Place" 6).

The movie was considered lurid because of its adult themes. Associated Press writer Cynthia Lowry wrote that the show would be "a watered-down child of the book" that would air "after the kiddies have gone to bed" (Lowry "Loss of Lucille" 12).

Producer Richard Goldstone stated that the show could not deal with the issues dealt with in the book or the movie: "We'll deal with contemporary problems, without getting into the sexy material Grace Metalious had in her book. I expect we'll be scrutinized because of the sensitivity of the title. But we are out to entertain, not shock"

(Thomas "TV's *Peyton Place*" 6). United Press International wrote that the show could be viewed by the entire family—even children: "[*Peyton Place*] has been dry cleaned, scoured and scrubbed until it bears almost no resemblance to the Grace Metalious original. The sins and crimes of passion are omitted" ("*Peyton Place*—A Show" 14).

With high hopes for *Peyton Place,* ABC brought in top soap opera consultant Irna Phillips and aired the show two nights a week. The network even hoped to air it on *more* than two nights a week if it caught on with audiences (Du Brow "Television Review" 29).

Peyton Place hit the airwaves in September 1964, playing on Tuesdays and Thursdays at 9:30 p.m. It starred Dorothy Malone, Warner Anderson, Ed Nelson, Ryan O'Neal, Barbara Parkins and Mia Farrow. It had a revolving cast of characters and, like any other soap opera, it focused on a variety of dramatic storylines and characters—including love and betrayal.

In that first season, *Peyton Place* met the network's expectations of high ratings, scoring on average 25.5 in the Nielsens. The 9:30 p.m. Tuesday episode was the 20th highest-rated show and Thursday did even better. The Thursday episode was the ninth highest-rated show that season ("Critics Views" 60; "The Latest" 69; Brooks and Marsh).

ABC's high hopes and investment paid off and they extended the show from two shows a week to three midway through the first season, adding a 9:30 Friday night episode. The unprecedented move to air new episodes three nights a week was satirized on the prime time cartoon *The Flintstones* (1960–1966) in the January 1966 episode "The Long, Long, Long Weekend": The Stone Age characters take a trip to the 21st century, where *Pey-Rock Place* is the only show on television.

In the second season, *Peyton Place* continued to air three nights a week (Mondays, Tuesdays and Thursdays) at 9:30. But it never again got the high ratings it had in the first season. In the second season, *Peyton Place* did earn a respectable average 19.5 Nielsen rating (Morris "Primetime").

Originally in black in white, *Peyton Place* made the jump to color in the fall of 1966 for the third season. Most daytime soap operas, including *Dark Shadows, General Hospital* and *The Guiding Light,* did not switch to color until the fall of 1967.

When *Peyton Place* gained color, it lost one of its stars. The 1965–1966 season was the last season for Mia Farrow after she married crooner Frank Sinatra and accepted more prominent roles in feature films. Farrow was replaced by Leigh Taylor-Young who *TV Guide* described as "doe-eyed" and her acting as "intense" (Lew "New Girl" 25–26).

In 1966–1967, ABC dropped the show back to two episodes a week, Mondays and Wednesdays in the fall of 1966 and Mondays and Tuesdays in the winter of 1967, all at 9:30. The season's ratings dropped once again: a 17.7 average Nielsen rating for both shows, the Monday night episode ranking 38 and Tuesday a dismal 61 (Morris "Primetime"; Spencer "TV's Vast" 54).

Theories on why viewership fell ranged from Mia Farrow's absence, scheduling changes, and increased competition from CBS's *Family Affair* on Monday and *Petticoat Junction* on Tuesday.

ABC continued to move the show around on the schedule each year and ratings continued to plummet (Morris "Primetime"). In 1969, after five years on the air, ABC did not renew the contract with 20th Century–Fox to produce more episodes. Not long after the cancellation, it was announced that *Peyton Place* reruns were being sold into syndication and that the show had the biggest syndicated TV sale ever. 20th Century–Fox vice-president in charge of syndication Alan Silverbach stated the show was sold for "top dollar" and would start airing in the fall of 1970 (Morris "Primetime"; "Strong Start" 3).

After the cancellation, TV critic Richard K. Shull was asked in his "Shull's Mailbag" syndicated newspaper column, "Why was *Peyton Place* taken off the air when it had such a large following?" Shull answered, "Its following had diminished considerably. The show's content—racy stuff a half-dozen years ago—had become pretty tepid for modern audiences" (Shull "The Following" 19).

Thanks to success in syndication, NBC brought the series back and continued the original storylines in 1972–1974 with *Return to Peyton Place*, a daytime soap opera that lasted 425 episodes along with one prime time special.

Peyton Place is considered to be one of the most successful prime time soap operas.

Lassie

Originally conceived as a short story and later a novel in 1940 by Eric Knight; *Lassie* was the tale of an intelligent, loyal and heroic female Rough Collie. The rights to *Lassie* were purchased by MGM just three years later and turned into seven successful feature films, starting with *Lassie Come Home* (1943). Because of the films' critical and financial success, Lassie got her own weekly ABC radio series in 1948, and her own CBS-TV show in 1954.

Lassie began her time on television owned by the Miller family, consisting of young Jeff (Tommy Rettig), his widowed mother Ellen (Jan Clayton) and Timmy's paternal grandfather (George Cleveland). Once Rettig's Jeff started getting too old for the part, he was replaced by seven-year-old orphan Timmy (Jon Provost).

In the fourth season, due in part to the real-life death of George Cleveland, Jeff and his mother Ellen moved to the city and left Lassie with Timmy and his newly introduced foster parents. The seasons Lassie spent with Jeff became known in syndication as *Jeff's Collie*. Timmy's foster father Paul was first played by Jon Shepodd (1957–1958) and then by Hugh Reilly (1958–1964), his foster mother Ruth by Cloris Leachman (1957–1958) and then June Lockhart (1958–1964). They took care of Lassie for seven seasons.

In a three-part episode at the start of the 11th season in 1964, the Martin family learn that they have the opportunity to move to Australia: Paul has been offered a "square mile of good farmland, with the option to buy a lot more land." He believes that Australia "could be one of the largest food sources in the world but it takes people with a lot of technical know-how," and Paul believes he is one of these people. But Lassie would have to be quarantined in Great Britain for up to six months before being allowed to take the trip to Australia with the rest of the family. Despite Lassie having saved Timmy and the rest of the Martin family on numerous occasions from a number of predicaments each and every week, they decided to leave her in the States with neighbor Cully Wilson (Andy Clyde). After the Martins left for Australia, Cully suffered a heart attack and was, of course, saved by Lassie. Cully could now no longer take care of Lassie, so he gave the heroic dog to Forest Ranger Cory Stuart (Robert Bray). Previous to this, Ranger Cory helped Lassie and the Martin family on many occasions. Now Lassie began working alongside Ranger Cory in the Forestry Service.

Television critic Hal Humphrey reported that there was some dispute on why the change in characters was made. June Lockhart stated that Jon Provost's mother wanted too much money for the child star, who was reportedly making $60,000 compared to Lassie's $100,000. But *Lassie* associate producer Bonita Granville stated that the show needed to appeal more to adult viewers, which was one-half of its audience, so that it became "the type of show that can go indefinitely" (Humphrey "Out of the Air" 15). In the 1964–1965 season, *Lassie* fetched the 17th highest-rated spot in prime time (Brooks and Marsh).

The seven years Lassie spent with Timmy and the Martin family were the most successful in terms of both ratings and syndication. As early as 1965, the 1957–1964 years of *Lassie* were sold into syndication with the title *Timmy and Lassie*, to differentiate it from new episodes in prime time. The company in charge of syndication, Telesynd, ran advertisements in TV broadcasting trade magazines boasting that *Timmy and Lassie* was popular with both kids and adults and claimed that according to a January 1966 Nielsen survey, "56% of Lassie audience are adults," adults being the ones who have buying power for the household ("Family Pet" 16).

Lassie became a color series in its 12th season (1965–1966). Switching to color oftentimes gave shows a ratings boost, but it did the opposite for *Lassie*. *Lassie* was consistently one of the top-rated shows of the year almost every year since 1961, but ratings dropped in the 1965–1966 season. In the 1966–1967 season, the downward slide continued. Although early in the season *Lassie* did see some ratings victories, winning the Sunday 7:00 p.m. time slot against ABC's *Voyage to the Bottom of the Sea* and the *NBC News/Bell Telephone Hour*, the show dropped to the 33rd highest-rated show of the season ("The Latest Form Sheet" 68; "ARB Top 20" 59; Spencer "TV's Vast 54"). That season, Lassie was up to her usual heroics: saving a missing calf, a female bear in a pit trap, a trapped raccoon, a steer from an abusive owner, and even Ranger Cory and a negligent ski slope owner from a faulty ski lift.

Lassie's work in the Forestry Service led to the opportunity to become the face of the "Keep America Beautiful" anti-littering ad campaign led by First Lady Lady Bird Johnson. On May 3, 1967, a ceremony was held to promote the unveiling of the Keep America Beautiful poster featuring Lassie. Lassie was on hand to celebrate the occasion on the White House lawn by picking a piece of crumpled paper off the ground and carrying it to a wicker trash basket. Lassie also presented the First Lady with a bouquet of flowers ("Keep America Beautiful"). At the ceremony, the world officially learned that Lassie was a male dog that playing a female role (Buchwald 6).

In the 1968 season, Ranger Cory was injured in a forest fire so Lassie went to work with several other Rangers, and by the 1970–1971 season she knew Forest Service so well that she spent much of her time alone in the forest saving other animals.

The show's 1971 cancellation was due to declining ratings, an FCC ruling that stations needed to make more room for local and syndicated programing, and CBS executives' Rural Purge (the elimination of rural and Southern-based shows). Pat Buttram, who played Mr. Haney on *Green Acres* which was cancelled around the same time, reportedly quipped about the Rural Purge, "It was the year CBS cancelled everything with a tree—including *Lassie*" (Harkins 203).

New episodes of *Lassie* were produced and the show went on for another two seasons in syndication, due in part to a continued sponsorship by Campbell Soup. In those two seasons, *Lassie* was picked up by many NBC affiliate channels ("Some Network O&O's"). In her two seasons in syndication, Lassie left the Forest Service, settled down with another collie that she met in the last episode of the 17th season, and eventually had

First Lady of the United States Lady Bird Johnson with Lassie to help with the Keep America Beautiful Campaign (LBJ Library, photo by Robert Knudsen).

a litter of puppies while living at their new home, Garth Holden's [Ron Hayes] ranch. Despite being tied down with a family, Lassie still found time to save the day on numerous occasions.

Throughout the 19-season run, six different collies played Lassie. All six dogs came from the same bloodline of collies owned by animal trainer Rudd Weatherwax. The most notable was Pal, the original Lassie: Pal starred in the MGM *Lassie* films and even the *Lassie* TV pilot in 1953. The Lassie bloodline is still going strong and is maintained by the Weatherwax family ("Bob Weatherwax").

In 2013, the American Kennel Club recognized the Weatherwax Lassie collies as a verified pedigree of dog. Dogs in the Lassie bloodline have "white blaze, full white ruff, and four white paws; superior intelligence and trainability; and inherent charisma" ("Weatherwax Collies Gains AKC").

Daktari

Daktari, debuting in color in January 1966, was based on the movie *Clarence, the Cross-Eyed Lion* (1965). It chronicled a young woman, Paula Tracy (Cheryl Miller), and her father Dr. Marsh Tracy (Marshall Thompson), who move to Africa to save animals from poachers and hunters. The show also featured Clarence, the Cross-Eyed Lion, and Judy the Chimp. *Daktari* was a mid-season replacement for the cancelled black-and-white *Rawhide* on Tuesdays at 7:30 p.m. giving CBS another full hour of color programming. *Daktari* quickly became one of the season's highest-rated shows, averaging a 23.9 rating which made it the 14th highest-rated show of the season (Brooks and Marsh).

Daktari did not kick off as a roaring success. In the second season's first three weeks, it was not even one of the top 40 shows ("Numbers Game" 60; "The Latest Form Sheet" 69; "Few Cheers" 58). But *Daktari* could not be caged. In the fourth week, the show picked up the pace, jumping to the 27th highest-rated show, according to Arbitron Ratings ("ARB's Top-20" 68). Eventually it rose to the seventh highest-rated show of the season with an average rating of 23.9—a 10.6 rating point increase from the season premiere, now beating out time slot rivals *Combat!* and *The Girl from U.N.C.L.E.* ("Numbers Game" 60; Brooks and Marsh).

The parental TV watchdog group National Association for Better Broadcasting not only announced that the show could be watched by the entire family but felt that it made a marked improvement in story, writing: "New season episodes show improvement in this series, which in the past had captivating animal sequences but poor plots. Good show for children" (Leonard "What's Out" 78).

At the start of the new season, once again *Daktari* did not get off on the right paw, losing out to ABC's World War II adventure series *Garrison's Gorillas* and CBS's sitcom *I Dream of Jeannie* and the first half-hour of the comedic *Jerry Lewis Show* ("CBS, ABC Race" 45; "Specials Confuse" 77).

In the 1968–1969 season, ratings did not bounce back. In an effort to boost viewership, *Daktari* was moved to Wednesdays at 7:30 p.m., but ratings continued to plummet. *Daktari* was cancelled in January 1969 and replaced by the variety show *The Glen Campbell Goodtime Hour* which rose to the 15th highest rating show in its first season and ran until 1972 (Brooks and Marsh).

MGM Television sold *Flipper, The Man from U.N.C.L.E., Please Don't Eat the Daisies, Dr. Kildare* and *Daktari* as a package deal to air in syndication. *Daktari*'s main selling point in syndication was that all 89 hours were in color ("Advertisement for MGM Television" 3).

After the show's cancellation, the Soviet Union began running the show on Soviet State-sponsored television. *The New York Times* reported, "The Russians acquired 26 episodes for cash and started showing them in 1970 but they did not clearly identify the source of the film each time it was shown." It was also believed that *Daktari* was the first and only American TV series shown in the Soviet Union at the time (Shaba 16). Although the Soviets had adopted the color TV system SECAM in 1967, color TV sets were not widely available there until the mid–1980s, when strict Communist policies were relaxed (Boutenko and Razlogov 237).

Chapter Three

Action-Adventure

TV audiences had an appetite for action-adventure programs in the 1966–1967 season. Not only did they tune in for superhero adventures, World War II battles, law enforcement procedurals, science fiction cliffhangers and espionage mysteries, they also favored a number of dramatic action-adventure thrillers which kept them on the edge of their couch every week.

The Saint

Just making the cut to be considered part of the 1966–1967 prime time lineup was hour-long English import, *The Saint*, starring a future James Bond, Roger Moore. Even before *The Saint*, it was rumored that Moore was being eyed as a potential replacement for Sean Connery as Bond, so *The Saint* is often considered Moore's warm-up for the role of Bond.

Moore took on the role of James Bond in 1973, starting with *Live and Let Die,* but in 1967 Moore stated that he considered Bond "an immoral, amoral character. He's a man who is glamorized because he can kill, and this is rather sick." The Saint, aka Simon Templar, never killed anyone in his six seasons on the air (Van Gelder 5).

On *The Saint*, Moore played dapper, wealthy international playboy Simon Templar. Templar, who is often described as a modern-day Robin Hood, takes on swindlers and confidence men around the globe and uses his skills for the greater good by protecting the helpless. He is known the world over by his calling card which features a drawing of a stick figure with a halo, giving him his nickname, the Saint.

Moore was previously cast in the English series *Ivanhoe* (1958–1959) and two American Westerns, *The Alaskans* (1959–1960) and *Maverick* (1960–1961). After *Maverick* left the airwaves, Moore headed back to the British Isles to take on the role of Simon Templar. *The Saint* debuted on ITV in the United Kingdom on October 4, 1962, in black and white.

Not only were both British and American audiences familiar with Moore, audiences were familiar with the Saint. The character first appeared in the Leslie Charteris novel *Meet the Tiger* in 1928. Charteris wrote and published 36 *Saint* books. There was also a radio series (1947–1951) with Vincent Price and ten films, starting with *The Saint in New York* (1938).

Although Moore's *The Saint* did not begin airing in prime time on NBC Stateside until May 21, 1967, it was seen in syndication throughout the U.S. starting in 1963. It was often played by TV stations in less than desirable time slots (against the local news, older films and TV reruns late at night or in the early morning). For example, in New York City, *The Saint* aired on Sundays at 11:15 p.m. on Channel 4, New York's NBC affiliate. Roger Moore acknowledged that up until that point, *The Saint* did not have much in terms of competition in the U.S.:

> We've been doing remarkably well against nothing ... we're seen on Sunday night opposite an assortment of old, old movies all playing for the 50th time. ... NBC checked the ratings and found we had a higher share than many of their other programs. But next season we go in against regularly scheduled programs and we may fall flat on our faces [Jordan 52; Pack 22].

The Saint switched to color starting in the fifth season in September 1966, despite color TV not being available in the U.K. until July 1967, when the country adopted the PAL system. The switch to color was made in anticipation of future color broadcasts in the U.K. and to appease the new American network standard of all prime time shows being in color (Pack 22).

When picked up by NBC to air in prime time, *The Saint* ran on Sundays at ten, replacing the variety series *The Andy Williams Show* for the summer months. NBC did not air new episodes until February through September 1968, Saturdays at 7:30 p.m., replacing the Jay North series *Maya*. The last season of *The Saint* wrapped up in the U.K. in February 1969 after 118 episodes in six seasons, 47 of them in color. But the last season of *The Saint* would not air in the United States until April 1969, again airing on a new timeslot, Fridays at 10:00 p.m., replacing drama *Bracken's World*.

Although *The Saint* never ascended to the top of the ratings in the U.S., it proved to be a good replacement throughout the summer months and quickly gained a cult following. It was also a favorite in the Eastern European Communist Bloc nations Czechoslovakia, Romania, Hungary, Bulgaria and Poland. *The Saint* was so popular in Poland it was reported that Communist Party branches never scheduled meetings when *The Saint* was on the TV schedule ("Red Viewers" 10). But *The Saint* was not shown in the Soviet Union; the first American show broadcast in the USSR was *Daktari* in 1973 (Shaba 16).

The show's cult following brought Simon Templar back to television in 1978 in *Return of the Saint*, this time starring Ian Ogilvy. *Return of the Saint*, which lasted one season, aired on ITV in the U.K. and CBS in the U.S. *The Saint* was brought back to the big screen in 1997 starring Val Kilmer. In the film, Roger Moore made a voice-only appearance as a radio news broadcaster. The film was financially successful but unlike the earlier films, it did not spawn any sequels.

Audiences had to wait another 20 years before getting another version of *The Saint*, this time in the form of a 2017 TV movie starring English actor Adam Rayner. It was originally intended to be a new TV series and started shooting in 2013, but production got off to a rocky start and the episodes were instead turned into a TV movie. The TV movie also featured the final acting role by Roger Moore before his death that same year.

Flipper

Accompanied by an infectious theme song written by Henry Vars and William "By" Dunham, *Flipper* swam into America's living rooms in September 1964. The show was created by Jack Cowden and his brother-in-law Ricou Browning. Cowden did not have much prior experience in film or television, while Browning was known for his underwater stunt work as the Gill Man in three of the most iconic Universal horror films, *Creature from the Black Lagoon* (1954), *Revenge of the Creature* (1955) and *The Creature Walks Among Us* (1956).

The two came up with the concept for *Flipper* and wrote a rough draft of the story while on vacation. After several failed attempts to sell the story to publishers, movie–TV producer Ivan Tors read the pitch and wrote to the *Flipper* creators "This is really good. We're going to make a movie" (Goodman).

Flipper was seen on the big screen in 1963 starring Chuck Connors and child actor Luke Halpin; the sequel was *Flipper's New Adventure* (1964). Cowden and Browning brought *Flipper* in color to TV in the fall of 1964. The show aired on NBC on Fridays at 7:30, which was perfect for the school age audience that *Flipper* attracted.

Throughout three seasons, Flipper helped numerous marine and land wildlife off the coast of Florida. The human characters were Porter Ricks (Brian Kelly), a park warden at Coral Key Park and Marine Preserve, and his two young sons Sandy (Halpin) and Bud (Tommy Norden). They seem to encounter an unusually high number of criminal elements for a Marine Preserve.

Flipper also featured colorful and advanced underwater camerawork. Co-creator and producer Ricou Browning was also in charge of underwater operations. He wrote in a July 1966 article about how he directed the dolphin: "To me, Flipper is a person. … Anybody who can train a child can train a dolphin … it takes as long for me to teach Flipper a trick as it takes me to get the idea across to him as to what I want him to do. And he never forgets." He went on to state that Flipper is rewarded with food and eats on average 12 pounds of fish a day plus vitamins (Browning 11).

Browning also got help from a team of trainers headed by Ric O'Barry. O'Barry stated that Flipper was kept in "pools, lakes or penned areas" because, despite him being one of the smartest animals underwater, the trainers could not trust him to swim back to the set in time for every shot—or at *all* (Witbeck "Flipper Learns" 20). O'Barry would later disavow aquatic animals being held in captivity, especially those being made to do tricks and stunts.

Although Flipper was made to do tricks and stunts, Browning assured the TV viewing audience that he was well taken care of:

> All dolphins are moody and Flipper's no exception. When she wants to play, she's fantastic. Flipper will rest in my arms and nuzzle me. We can persuade her to perform for an hour at a clip, twice a day. … But when Flipper decides to call it a halt, that's it. There's nothing we can do. Flipper will just ignore everyone completely [Lardine 8].

Although the show was named after its title character, most of the heavy lifting was done by the human actors. Kelly stated, "The dolphin is in the periphery. If fans don't like myself and the two boys, they won't care about the dolphin." He added that he knows that the fans mostly are interested in seeing the dolphin (Witbeck "Flipper" 20).

To keep things fresh in the 1966–1967 season, producers gave Flipper a playmate named Lorelei. The same year *Batman* introduced the Bat-copter, *Flipper* introduced its own unique mode of air transportation. In addition to the Kellys' speedboat, his regular mode of aquatic transportation, the show also introduced a Cessna 185 seaplane, flown by Kelly and equipped with a water-filled pouch so Flipper could fly with the family as well ("Flipper Will Take to Air"). Flipper's adventures that season included saving Lorelei via a "commando-style rescue" with the new Cessna 185 seaplane, catching a thief who turns out to be a seal, and rescuing his friends from the middle of a Navy firing range. Guest stars included Huntz Hall (most famous for the Dead End Kids–East Side Kids–Bowery Boys movies), David Soul, Karen Steele, Stuart Getz and Heather MacRae ("Flipper Flips" 11A).

The added gadgets, dolphins and guest stars did not equal a ratings boost for *Flipper*. Although the show averaged a 22.5 rating in its first two seasons, ratings took a dive in the third season: It consistently lost to CBS's *The Jackie Gleason Show*, the season's fifth highest-rated show (Brooks and Marsh; "The Numbers Game" 58; "Few Cheers" 58; "CBS Edges" 60). In the 1966–1967 season, *Flipper* was the 56th highest-rated show, putting it in the bottom third (Spencer "TV's Vast" 54).

In February 1967, NBC announced that *Flipper* would not be back next season. *Flipper*'s last episode aired on Friday, April 15, 1967.

Tarzan

In the fall of 1966, the American public was very familiar with Tarzan. At that point, 31 films had been produced and 26 official books were published featuring the character Tarzan, "King of the Apes," created by Edgar Rice Burroughs. Audiences were also used to seeing Tarzan swinging from vine to vine in color. Seven color *Tarzan* films had been released before *Tarzan*'s color TV debut.

But bringing Tarzan to TV was a difficult task. In 1958, Banner Productions, headed by producer Sy Weintraub, purchased the rights to Tarzan for $3,500,000 and worked for seven years to bring *Tarzan* to television (Lewis "It Shouldn't Happen" 24). It was finally announced in November 1965 that the role of Tarzan was going to former professional football player Mike Henry ("Bumper Crop" 32).

Just two days before the start of filming, Henry left the set in Brazil and pulled out of the role after a chimpanzee bit him on the chin, leaving a wound requiring 18 stitches. Henry sued Banner Productions for $875,000 for hazardous working conditions and mental anguish. Henry would never play Tarzan on TV, but due to contract obligations he did play the Ape Man in three movie adventures: *Tarzan and the Valley of Gold* (1966), *Tarzan and the Great River* (1967) and *Tarzan and the Jungle Boy* (1968) (Lewis "It Shouldn't Happen" 24).

The TV role of Tarzan was then given to Ron Ely. Ely previously played in CBS's action-adventure show *The Aquanauts* (1960–1961) and went on to play Doc Savage in a 1975 movie. Ely played a much different type of Tarzan: one who was well-spoken and always sported a fresh haircut. This version of Tarzan was earlier seen in *Tarzan's Greatest Adventure* (1959), the first in a long string of movies to feature the jungle hero speaking proper English rather than his usual primitive English ("Me Tarzan, you Jane"). Also missing from the TV show is Tarzan's mate, Jane. Jane was excluded from the show so that it could focus more on action and avoid the repetitive storyline of Tarzan having to save Jane from jungle perils. However, Tarzan's chimpanzee Cheetah, from the books and movies, joined Tarzan on TV.

NBC's hour-long *Tarzan* debuted on Thursday night, September 8, 1966, at 7:30. Its first half-hour aired opposite the first episode of the second season of *Batman* and its second half-hour opposite *F Troop* on ABC and the hour-long CBS presentation *World of Wheels*. That evening, *Tarzan* held its own, receiving a 14.6 rating with 33.3 percent share of the audience, losing by only 1.4 ratings points to *Batman* and beating out the first half-hour of *World of Wheels*. In the second half-hour, *Tarzan's* ratings rose to 15.3, taking a 36.4 percent share of the audience and beating out the second half-hour of *World of Wheels* and *F Troop* ("Critics Views" 59).

The first episode provided viewers with exposition:

> The dark land of the jungle is the country of the unknown Of savagery, terror and peril beyond the imagination of men. Here in the forbidden tangle of the jungle, a child was found and raised by the great apes. The boy took the name Tarzan and later was educated in civilization. But then Tarzan returned to the deadly land he knew so well, and everywhere deep in the jungle Tarzan continues to enforce his law, the law of right! Tarzan's awesome warning cry is known to every living creature in the jungle.

In the second week, *Tarzan* aired in its permanent time slot, Fridays at 7:30, going head to head with *The Wild Wild West* on CBS and *The Green Hornet* and *The Time Tunnel* on ABC.

The early reviews were negative:

> "Crude and corny."—Bob Tweedell, *Denver Post*
>
> "Active scene bogged down in sterile dialogue and badly paced direction."—Hal Humphrey, *Los Angeles Times*
>
> "Incredibly naïve and corny."—Percy Shain, *Boston Globe*
>
> "Looks exactly like those tired, old, infinitely inept Hollywood jungle epics TV keeps re-running."—Harry Harris, *Philadelphia Inquirer* ("Critics Views" 60).

One of the only favorable reviews came from *The New York Times'* Jack Gould: "[The cast] contributed portrayals that were consistent with the producer's hopes of providing a unique bridge between primitive and civilized existence" (Gould "TV: N.B.C. Tarzan").

Tarzan was originally filmed in Brazil and later Mexico, the South American countries standing in for the African jungle where *Tarzan* took on ivory poachers, evil scientists, smugglers and hostile natives (LoBrutto 315). Tarzan rescued villagers and animals alike from natural disasters. No matter the foe, Tarzan managed to save the day in every episode in the lush jungle backdrop featuring waterfalls, plains, mountains and volcanos.

Ely appeared in full Tarzan garb on the cover of *TV Guide* on November 26, 1966, to help promote the show and was featured in a "TV Close-Up" article which revealed that filming was far from smooth: A number of delays cost Banner Productions $450,000. Ely had several injuries from the animals, including a welt from an alligator, scars from both a leopard and a puma, and stitches from a lion. He also suffered non–animal-related injuries, including a slipped disc, severe muscle strain, numerous foot injuries and burns from swinging on vines. Most notably, he required surgery for a separated shoulder after a 28-foot fall from a vine. The fall also broke Ely's orbital bone. The actor missed only three days of shooting for the surgery. The fall was incorporated into a later show's plot. Insuring Ely reportedly cost producers $65,000 annually (Lewis "It Shouldn't Happen" 23–25).

The series' theme "Tarzan's March," composed by Sydney Lee, also had a connection with two other shows on the 1966–1967 schedule, *The Green Hornet* and *The*

Lawrence Welk Show. Lawrence Welk and His Orchestra recorded the song and released it on a 7" 45 RPM single, and Al Hirt recorded it for his TV theme album "The Horn Meets the Hornet."

Tarzan never made a splash in the ratings. By the second season, it was one of the 20 least watched shows on television ("New Shows Get" 60). Producers did very little to change the format or formula to gain viewership.

In February 1968, it was announced that *Tarzan* might not be back for the new season. And it wasn't. Very few newspapers or trade publications made mention of its cancellation ("TV Networks Hurry" 50).

The show was replaced on the NBC schedule by the Western *The High Chaparral*. CBS showed reruns from June 1968 to September 1969. Several *Tarzan* episodes were pieced together to create two feature-length films for theaters, *Tarzan's Jungle Rebellion* (1966) and *Tarzan's Deadly Silence* (1970) (Brooks and Marsh).

Tarzan as a live-action television series was never a successful adventure. Tarzan did not get back into the TV series swing until 1991: A syndicated series portrayed Tarzan as an environmentalist fighting to save the rainforest. The show ran until 1994. TV executives keep trying with *Tarzan*, presenting viewers with a 1996–1997 syndicated series, a 2003 WB network series, and a 2017 Netflix original series—all with a more traditional Tarzan character and with very limited success.

Coronet Blue

The last show to debut in the 1966–1967 season was Larry Cohen's *Coronet Blue*, which first aired Monday, May 29, 1967, at 10:00 on CBS. It was shot much earlier than its airdate: Production of *Coronet Blue* was first announced in December 1964 by *The New York Times*. According to the *Times,* it was one of several shows that could possibly be picked up by CBS for the 1965–1966 schedule; others included *The Wild Wild West, Lost in Space, The Haunted* and *The Quest*—the last two of which never made it to air. Two months later, *Coronet Blue* was "tentatively scheduled" to air Fridays at 10:00 (Adams "C.B.S. Fall Slate"). And in March 1965, it was revealed that Shakespearean actor Frank Converse would take on the starring role (Gardner "A.C.L.U. Lifts Bars").

In April 1965, CBS revealed they no longer planned to air the show that season and that no new premiere date was set (Adams "A.B.C. Prepares"). Despite the start date being in limbo, *Coronet Blue* reportedly had a 22-episode commitment from CBS, and received more than two million dollars from investors. So *Coronet Blue* producer Herbert Brodkin of Plautus Productions began shooting the series in New York City, in the hopes of being picked up mid-season or for the Fall 1966 lineup ("A slot on the network" 29; "*Coronet Blue* Series"). Three short-lived shows aired in the Friday 10–11 p.m. time slot instead during the 1965–1966 season: *Slattery's People* in the fall, *The Trials of O'Brien* in the spring, and *Wayne and Shuster Take an Affectionate Look At...* in the summer.

CBS program vice-president Michael Dann said, "We have enormous enthusiasm for *Coronet Blue* and expect that it will be on our schedule in 1966," but when the 1966–1967 season lineup was announced, *Coronet Blue* remained in limbo. Then after two years, in the summer of 1967, the hour-long *Coronet Blue* finally made it to TV, as a summer replacement for the game shows *To Tell the Truth* and *I've Got a Secret* after the shows "failed to attract enough viewers" (Laurent "*Coronet Blue* a Good Show" 10). The sudden decision to air the show came as a surprise to star Frank Converse. "I've never talked to anyone since the end of work on the show in September 1965," said Converse. "I learned *Coronet Blue* was going on the air this summer from reading newspapers" (Shull "Converse Applauded" 8).

Coronet Blue was the story of a man who regains consciousness and pulls himself out of the river after waking up from an attack. It is clear that he suffers from amnesia, and the only thing he remembers about his attack are the words "coronet blue." To make matters worse, the man, who later adopts the name Michael Alden, quickly learns that his attackers, nicknamed Greybeards, are continuing to attempt to kill him.

Larry Cohen also explored paranoia, particularly justified paranoia, in TV's *The Fugitive* (1963–1967) and *The Invaders* (1967–1968) and in the film *The Stuff* (1985). But producer Herbert Brodkin played down the paranoia storyline and described the show as a "search for identity," and that the amnesia suffered by the main character was "only symbolic" and that that search for identity was explored throughout the series ("Plautus May Have" 74).

Before the show aired, the 6'2", handsome 29-year-old blonde Frank Converse started getting a lot of attention. "It's a weird experience," he said. "I'm getting large with the teeny boppers and the crayon set. I'm getting a lot of mail, mostly from the same types who like Richard Chamberlain or Troy Donahue" (Shull "Converse Applauded" 8).

Coronet Blue viewers overwhelmingly enjoyed the show. In a survey, 70.2 percent of respondents rated *Coronet Blue* as "very good," more so than any other summer replacement that season, beating out *The Saint*, *The Lucy Desi Comedy Hour* and *The Steve Allen Comedy Hour* (Williamson "Top View" 35).

Critics were not as kind. One exception: *Washington Post* columnist Lawrence Laurent called it "a good show" and compared it to Cohen's long-running and critically acclaimed *The Fugitive* (Laurent "*Coronet Blue* a Good Show" 10). *New York Times* TV critic Jack Gould reported the CBS finally aired the show to "recoup their production cost" and described the summer replacement as "dull in any weather" and having "sticky dialogue and cory villains" (Gould "TV: Crisis"). Syndicated TV columnist Rick Du Brow wrote, "No matter how you size up the young man of *Coronet Blue,* he is still just another twist on television's old pitch for the juvenile audience through the glorification of a poor, misunderstood punk" and *Pittsburgh Post-Gazette*'s Win Fanning penned, "I simply can't imagine how such a decision was made by any program manager in his right mind [to air the show]." Fanning applauded Brodkin for filming in color in 1965 because "the 1965 season still harbored a lot of black and white series." If the show's producers did not have the foresight to shoot *Coronet Blue* in color, it is doubtful the show would ever have ever made it to a primetime schedule" (Du Brow "*Coronet Blue* Tagged" 7; Fanning "Auspicious Debut" 29).

After 13 episodes, CBS cancelled the show despite good ratings and the fact that Converse "has become a darling of the teen-agers" (Gent "TV Show to Take Secret").

To make matters worse, viewers were never told the story's outcome or Alden's true identity. Creator Cohen stated,

> I know how it ends but I can't tell you. ... I'm negotiating with *TV Guide* to do an article on how it would have ended, but even that depends on whether or not someone decides to revive

the series. With all this attention, it could happen. I can say this: All the clues to Michael Alden's identity are contained in the first episode [Gent "TV Show to Take Secret"].

But Frank Converse believed that no one knew how it would have ended: "No thought was ever given to a wrap-up show"; and an unidentified CBS executive disclosed to *The New York Times*' George Gent that the network had no plans to bring back the series (Shull "Converse Applauded"; Gent "TV Show to Take Secret").

In 1997, Cohen revealed the ending in the book *Larry Cohen: The Radical Allegories of an Independent Filmmaker*, which chronicled his career:

> When the Brodkin Organization [Plautus Productions] took over the series, they wanted to turn it into an anthology … so they played down the amnesia aspect until there was nothing about it at all in the show. … [The show] was just Frank Converse wandering from one story to the next with no connective format at all [Williams "Larry Cohen: The Radical"].

Brodkin downplaying the amnesia storyline could be seen as early as January 1965 when Brodkin stated that the amnesia was "only symbolic" and was an abstract quest for identity ("Plautus May Have" 74).

Cohen also revealed the ending he originally envisioned:

> The actual secret is that Converse was not really an American at all. He was a Russian who had been trained to appear like an American and was sent to the U.S. as a spy. He belonged to a spy unit called Coronet Blue. He decided to defect, so the Russians tried to kill him before he could give away the identities of the other Soviet agents. And nobody can really identify him because he doesn't exist as an American [Williams "Larry Cohen: The Radical"].

Coronet Blue was replaced by *The Carol Burnett Show* (1967–1978) in the fall of 1967. Converse starred alongside Jack Warden on the ABC police drama *N.Y.P.D.* (1967–1969) the next season.

Decades later, perhaps to avoid similar bad press, the shows *Twin Peaks* (1990–1991) and *Life on Mars* (2008–2009) were cancelled and then given the opportunity to quickly wrap up their story arcs and give viewers some closure.

T.H.E. Cat

Robert Loggia played the title role, a cat burglar and aerialist turned bodyguard named Thomas Hewett Edward Cat, also known as T.H.E. Cat and Tom Cat. Each week he found himself hired by a client facing certain death from various assassins on NBC's *T.H.E. Cat*, which debuted on September 16, 1966.

Loggia described his character as someone who "moves and thinks like a cat. He likes wine and beautiful girls. He doesn't go around flexing his muscles. Tom Cat is vicious and lethal but with it all a pretty suave character. You get the feeling his background is strictly continental, that he grew up in wealth" (Stellwag "This is One" 59).

Loggia also said:

> There is lots of physical action. … In each half-hour show there's a physical payoff which chews up about 15 minutes. For example, in the pilot film, I kept leaping across ledges which are supposed to be 80 feet above the ground. I recently completed a show which had a big fencing scene, a sort of throwback to the Errol Flynn movies [Messina "Action, No Gimmicks" 256].

Loggia claimed that he did his own stunt work:

> [The show is] not a put-on or a spoof. ... I do most of the stunt work myself, anything I won't get killed at. You can't fool the people any more. They're hep. They're sophisticated enough to know when a stuntman is used in place of the star. We don't use a lot of gimmicks like that Bond fellow or Man from U.N.C.L.E. Our trademark is authenticity [Stellwag "This is One" 59].

T.H.E. Cat featured a jazz theme and music throughout the show. The theme was featured on trumpeter Al Hirt's album "The Horn Meets the Hornet." Loggia's character even operated out of a smoky jazz nightclub called Casa del Gato.

The series, which aired Fridays at 9:30, never found its niche. It competed with *The CBS Friday Night Movies* and the second half hour of *The Milton Berle Show* in the fall, and *The Phyllis Diller Show* in the Spring. Although *The CBS Friday Night Movies* did score high ratings, *The Milton Berle Show* and *The Phyllis Diller Show* were not well received by critics or viewers, which should have translated to success for *T.H.E. Cat* ... but didn't. *T.H.E. Cat* received very little attention from critics and scored even lower ratings than *The Milton Berle Show*. In the show's defense, Loggia asserted, "It's the best show we can possibly do, and I think it compares favorably with any of its type" (Kleiner "Series 'Purrfect'" 6). In early March 1967, the show was cancelled by NBC. In total, 26 episodes were produced and aired. In the fall of 1967, it was replaced by the Jerry Van Dyke sitcom *Accidental Family*—which was subsequently cancelled after only 16 episodes on the air.

The Fugitive

In 1963, David Janssen accepted the role of Richard Kimble in the Quinn Martin production *The Fugitive*. At that point, Janssen was most famous for his role on TV's *Richard Diamond: Private Detective* (1957–1960), a show he left to focus on his film career. Janssen returned to TV after ABC bought the pilot to *The Fugitive*, created by Roy Huggins (Parsons "Tiff Between" 10).

The Fugitive, which was loosely based on a true story, debuted in black and white on September 17, 1963. It aired on Tuesdays at 10:00 opposite the CBS variety series *The Garry Moore Show* and NBC's orchestral musical presentation *The Bell Telephone Hour*.

The opening segment laid out *The Fugitive*'s premise:

> The name: Dr. Richard Kimble. The destination: Death Row, State Prison. The irony: Richard Kimble is innocent. Proved guilty, what Richard Kimble could not prove was that moments before discovering his murdered wife's body, he encountered a one-armed man running from the vicinity of his home. Richard Kimble ponders his fate as he looks at the world for the last time and sees only darkness. But in that darkness, fate moves its huge hand.

A train derailment gives Kimble an opportunity to escape and begin his quest to prove his innocence by finding the one-armed man (Bill Raisch). Throughout the series, Kimble is pursued by by-the-book Police Lt. Philip Gerard (Barry Morse).

"Our series isn't necessarily a chase or a cops'n'robber show," said Janssen. "Here is a man who was once a respected doctor—how does he operate in the shadows of society? What we have here is a story of survival" (Freeman "Fugitive Gains" 21). To survive,

Janssen took on odd jobs, including a lab tech, peanut farmer, beet picker, kennel attendant, barrel loader, cut man for a boxer, sailmaker, bartender, roller rink attendant, and construction company first aid man.

TV critic Donald Freeman wrote on October 30, 1963, "*The Fugitive* is the sleeper of the year and already—believe the ratings or not—it has won itself a sizable following" (Freeman "Fugitive Gains" 21). Janssen was not surprised by its success:

> If you have faith in the integrity of the people involved in a production, as I did with Quinn Martin and his staff, then you don't worry so much about whether a premise is going to pay off. Actually, we're not as limited in this show as you might think. Sure, the doctor has to keep on the move, but that can be an advantage. There is no sameness to the show.

When asked how long *The Fugitive* can keep running, the actor countered, "How long can *Wagon Train* keep rolling? My guess is that we could go three years without exhausting the story possibilities" (Thomas "Fugitive Janssen" 9).

In the second season, ratings exploded. *The Fugitive* destroyed its competition and became the fifth highest-rated show of the season (Brooks and Marsh). Hollywood reporter Bob Thomas wrote that the series "has ascended to the upper reaches of the audience ratings. ... Many theories have been offered for the success of *The Fugitive*— realistic production, endless suspense, etc. A strong factor must be Janssen himself and the fact that his presence is not dissipated by a team of co-stars" (Thomas "*Fugitive* Janssen" 2).

In the second season, and in every subsequent season, the show opened with the narrator explaining:

> Dr. Richard Kimble, an innocent victim of blind justice. Falsely convicted for the murder of his wife, reprieved by fate when a train wreck freed him en route to the death house. Freed him to hide in lonely desperation ... to change his identity ... to toil at many jobs. Freed him to search for a one-armed man he saw leave the scene of the crime. Freed him to run before the relentless pursuit of the police lieutenant obsessed with his capture.

After the second season, ratings settled, but it still did well in its Tuesday time slot in 1965–1966, now opposite *CBS News Hour* and *NBC Tuesday Night at the Movies* (Brooks and Marsh).

ABC was reportedly comfortable with ratings, despite *The Fugitive* not reaching the same heights it did in 1964–1965. The network planned "several exciting new features" in the 1966–1967 season, including "exotic and international settings" by shooting in Mexico and Hawaii. Additionally, *The Fugitive* would now be shot in color (Coffee "Exciting New" 22). It was also reported that the show might introduce a young son for Richard Kimble, but that never came to fruition (Coffee "Exciting New" 22).

Two months into the 1966–67 season, *The Fugitive* found itself at the lower third of the Nielsen ratings with competition coming from the popular *NBC Tuesday Night at the Movies* and *CBS News Hour* (Scott "Jack Benny" 14; Spencer "TV's Vast" 54). ABC announced that *The Fugitive* would not be renewed for the 1967–1968 season.

On April 19, *1967, The Chicago Tribune* asked ABC about the possibility of a resolution for the series. ABC responded, "There *will* be an ending. The whole thing probably will be settled sometime between now and September when the show goes off the air. One or two more episodes will be shot to resolve the unanswered: Was Kimble the criminal or the one-armed man?" (Wolfe "Alas" C8). On July 10, the *Los Angeles*

Times announced that two final episodes, airing on August 22 and 29, would wrap up the series (Humphrey "*Fugitive* Pauses" 18).

Leonard Goldberg, then ABC's vice-president of programming, told *Vanity Fair* in 2007, "I realized we were going to leave viewers empty-handed, and that was wrong. I went to the [network higher-ups] and said, 'We have to give people a conclusion.'" Goldberg stated that some of the ABC executives felt that a conclusion would hurt *The Fugitive* in syndication and that the show did not need a proper ending. Goldberg responded, "But they are deeply invested. This is our business; we are selling advertisers on the power of television, and yet we ourselves don't believe it? That seems odd" (Liebenson "How *The Fugitive*'s").

Audiences desperately wanted a conclusion. Both David Janssen and Quinn Martin were tight-lipped about it, as to not spoil the ending for audiences. "A great many people worked hard to do these two final episodes, so I'd be a real louse to ad-lib it for you now in five minutes," said Janssen. Martin echoed Janssen's sentiment: "To discuss the conclusion now would only spoil it for the audience. Suffice it to say the concluding two episodes are the culmination of the entire series—and I feel sure no one will be disappointed" (Humphrey "*Fugitive* Pauses" 18; "*The Fugitive* Finally" 14).

The second part of the two-parter "The Judgment" gave viewers closure to the story, when Kimble and the one-armed man met and justice was served. Both "Judgment"s reaped big ratings, especially the second part which aired on August 29: It had a massive 45.9 Nielsen rating with an unbelievable 72 share, making it the most watched television episode of all time, remarkable for a series that was not one of *the* top-rated shows. The episode held that record until November 21, 1980, when audiences learned who shot the character J.R. (Larry Hagman) on *Dallas*' fourth episode of the fourth season, "Who Done It." (Liebenson "How *The Fugitive*'s"; Brooks and Marsh).

After *The Fugitive* went off the air, ABC paid a licensing fee of $10,000 per day, five days a week for one year, for the right to rebroadcast *Fugitive* episodes on daytime TV ("Expensive Rerun" 5).

In the days before home video recording devices and on-demand viewing, people who missed the nail-biting conclusion would have had to wait until 1971 to finally see it air on television. Ron Simon, curator of Television and Radio at the Paley Center for Media in New York, claimed that U.S. service members who were in Vietnam when "The Judgment" aired flocked to the Paley Center for Media to watch the conclusion. It was one of the museum's most requested shows ("Fugitive Captured" 107; Liebenson "How *The Fugitive*'s").

After "The Judgment—Part II" aired, David Janssen appeared on the ABC late night talk show *The Joey Bishop Show* (1967–1969) to discuss it. That *Joey Bishop* episode was one of its highest-rated (and one of the rare occasions when *Joey Bishop* beat out a new episode of *The Tonight Show Starring Johnny Carson* ("Fugitive Captured" 107).

The Fugitive was nominated for five Emmy Awards and won the Emmy for Outstanding Dramatic Series for the 1965–1966 season. It was also nominated for three Golden Globes; David Janssen won for Best Male TV Star.

Fugitive reruns played on TV for decades. There was also a big-budget 1993 film adaptation with Harrison Ford and Tommy Lee Jones and its indirect sequel, *U.S. Marshals* (1998) with Jones. The show's concept had two other short-lived versions on television: the first in 2000 on CBS and 20 years later in 2020 on the short-form mobile video platform Quibi.

Run for Your Life

The NBC drama *Run for Your Life* chronicles young lawyer Paul Bryan (Ben Gazzara), who has been diagnosed with an unnamed disease and given two years to live. Bryan dedicates the rest of his short life to getting as much as he can out of life and helping as many people as he can along the way.

Creator Roy Huggins, who also created *The Fugitive* (1963–1967), called Paul Bryan a traditional American hero: "People love Paul Bryan because of his ability to live to the fullest. Their sympathy for him is a bonus. ... "We all assume we are immortal, and we remind the audience that we aren't. Paul Bryan lives on hope like everyone else, and he does it like all of us—to keep to himself from thinking about his mortal predicament" ("How Gutsy" 64).

Run for Your Life's lounge music theme song (created by jazz composer Pete Rugolo) not only kicked off the show each week but was also featured on the Al Hirt album "The Horn Meets the Horn." Rugolo composed music for several other 1966–1967 shows (*The Fugitive*, *The Felony Squad*, *Lost in Space*).

Paul Bryan was first introduced to TV audiences on April 15, 1965, in an episode of the anthology series *Kraft Suspense Theater* which had acted as *Run for Your Life*'s pilot episode. The color, hour-long series began its run on Monday, September 13, 1965. With a 10:00 time slot, it had some big running shoes to fill, taking over the *Alfred Hitchcock Hour* (1962–1965) slot.

Critics had a clear difference in opinion when it came to *Run for Your Life*:

> "After 15 minutes we were ready to put on our track shoes and make an escape."—Eleanor Roberts, *Boston Traveler*

> "A real bomb."—Henry Mitchell, *Memphis Commercial Appeal*

> "Trite and currently imitative."—Frank Judge, *Detroit News*

> "The hero has an unnamed disease that will finish him off by March 1967—if the ratings don't beat the mortician."—Terrence O'Flaherty, *San Francisco Chronicle*

> "Seems the most promising of the new Monday-night entries."—Bob Williams, *New York Post*

> "One of the coolest heroes in a long time."—Rick Du Brow, United Press International

> "NBC may have a winner ... [This series] may just have a good run."—Bill Irwin, *Chicago American* ("How Critics" 34)

NBC renewed the show for a second season but *New York Times* critic Val Adams questioned how much longer the show actually had on the air. "*Run for Your Life* may be boxed in," Adams wrote. "If the young lawyer has only 18–24 months to look forward to, NBC would have to cancel *Run for Your Life* in the middle of next season" (Adams "People Just" 46). In the 1966–1967 season, *Run for Your Life* again aired in the Monday 10:00 slot, opposite *The Big Valley* on ABC and *The Jean Arthur Show* and *I've Got a Secret* on CBS. Syndicated TV columnist Charles Witbeck stated that its ratings were not as high as the network had hoped and that it was saved by praise from the press. The show's creator Roy Huggins was actively seeking that praise: "The press used to shower attention on *Slattery's People* for tackling touchy subjects. Well, I believe we've attempted themes just as delicate, only to be ignored by TV critics" (Witbeck "TV-Radio Chatter" 61).

Huggins suspected that it was a conspiracy from certain Nielsen households with rating Audiometers:

> They do this to punish a producer who has made a social statement with which they disagree. We did an episode last season called "The Assassin," which condemned our lax gun laws. Thousands of organized-type letters, probably inspired by the National Rifle Association, protested our show. That was to be expected, but what wasn't expected was a five-point drop in the Nielsen rating one week later.

Huggins also believed the same thing happened when the show dropped two Nielsen points after the episode "A Rage for Justice" which focused on social justice and race relations; and also after an episode which shined a light on the "unsavoriness of the gambling element in Las Vegas" (Humphrey "A New Race" 16).

None of the controversial episodes aired in the summer of 1967 and Huggins stopped pushing the network for permission to tackle more controversial episodes (Humphrey "A New Race" 16).

Despite the show being one of the lowest rated of the season, Paul Bryan outlived his two-year diagnosis and was given another season. The show was finally cancelled after the 1967–1968 season. Bryan's story, unlike Fugitive Richard Kimble's, did not get a proper resolution.

In the three years on the air, Bryan took on many foes and problems with varying degrees of controversy behind them including Communism, the Mob, Nazi war criminals and smugglers. "The ratings were soft," Gazzara admitted. "We were beaten by *The Big Valley* much of the time. We ranked about 47th among all the network shows, which is only fair. But we had a very loyal audience and quality audience too. … Okay, so we had 30 million viewers. What I want to know is: What's wrong with 30 million viewers?"

Run for Your Life aired for a total of 85 color episodes. It was subsequently sold into syndication, excluding the *Kraft Suspense Theater* pilot episode ("'Life' Begins" 56). NBC replaced the show with the detective drama *The Outsider* (1968–1969), which also boasted Pete Rugolo music.

CHAPTER FOUR

Law Enforcement

Four shows in the 1966–1967 season featured stories of law enforcement: *The F.B.I., Hawk, The Felony Squad* and *Dragnet*. These shows featured realistic, often gritty stories and hard-nosed police work, a stark contrast from that season's many quixotic action-adventure programs and James Bond–inspired spy stories that featured outlandish stories, gadgets, sensational locations and jet-setting international playboys.

The F.B.I.

In March 1965, it was announced that Efrem Zimbalist, Jr., previously the star of ABC's detective drama *77 Sunset Strip* (1958–1964), would take the lead role of Inspector Lewis Erskine on a new ABC show revolving around the cases of the Federal Bureau of Investigation and appropriately titled *The F.B.I.* (Hopper 31).

The F.B.I. was one of the rare TV shows made without a pilot episode and green-lit simply based on the reputation of executive producer Quinn Martin, who was already in the midst of producing *Twelve O'Clock High* and *The Fugitive* for ABC (Rich 16).

Prior to 1965, Martin had produced another crime-busting show, ABC's *The Untouchables* (1959–1963). *The Untouchables* starred Robert Stack as Prohibition-era agent Eliot Ness. Martin noted that *The F.B.I.* "is almost opposite in direction to *The Untouchables*. ... *The F.B.I.* is more a cerebral show compared with the ordinary police series. In 1965, laboratory investigation is the kingpin, not guns. *The Untouchables* was based on a wild and highly theatrical era of Prohibition when crime was wide open hostility to the police. In the F.B.I. today, you don't pull a gun unless you have to kill a man" (Witbeck "*FBI* After Sullivan" 16).

Martin worked in conjunction with the real F.B.I. and its long-time director J. Edgar Hoover. In 1958, Hoover called television "an affront to the national conscience" because of what he called a "dangerous trend to glorification of crime on television programs and motion pictures" (United States Congress Senate Committee on the Judiciary, page 1898).

But in subsequent years, Hoover worked with Hollywood executives like Martin to strengthen the image of the Bureau. *The F.B.I.* was one of the first TV shows to work with Hoover (Rich 16). The end titles even personally thanked the FBI director: "The Producers extend appreciation to J. Edgar Hoover, Director, Federal Bureau of Investigation and his associates for the assistance in the production of this series."

Martin made sure that the F.B.I. was portrayed in a positive light and even sent all the scripts to F.B.I. officials in Washington, D.C., for their review. In return Quinn Martin was given real life cases by the FBI.

> I was also given 1,000 cases to read and I happily accepted them. It's silly to have such material available and not use it. Why, we've found things in those files our writers could never have dreamed up. ... Outside of making money, the only reason I'm doing the show is to try and build a respect for law and order. We need it and I hope our series can do it without resorting to a soapbox [Witbeck "*FBI* After Sullivan" 16].

The show was not done to advance a political agenda for Martin. He described himself as a "liberal Democrat" which is in contrast to common conceptions of the F.B.I. Martin wanted to learn for himself if the Bureau was as right-wing as he had heard. After a tour of FBI headquarters, he stated, "I explored and I found them apolitical ... and a great outfit" (Humphrey "Twin Faces" 59).

Although Martin was able to use actual FBI case files, both he and Hoover agreed there would have to be some dramatic license with their stories to create more tension and bloodshed; considering there had only been 13 FBI agents shot in 32 years (Lowry "Job Jeopardy" 21).

Despite the close coordination of Hoover, the show was not approved by the National Association for Better Broadcasting, which stated,

> The F.B.I. producer Quinn Martin has used all of the gory and horror-inducing tricks that are the trademarks of his many similar shows. If a man is assassinated, the audience gets a close-up view of the automatic rifle and of the victim's squirming body. [The show has] a tasteless view of psychopathic criminals, program shows brutality and sadism in sordid detail [Horn 10; Leonard "What's Out" 78].

Unlike many shows which aired in color that season, *The F.B.I.* did not advertise that fact in any promos or in the show's introduction or title sequences. The approximately 90 percent of American households with black-and-white TVs would have no idea that the new show was in color.

The F.B.I. was given a patriotic score by Bronislau Kaper, an Oscar winner for MGM's *Lili* (1952). It played along with the main title sequence which featured pictures of the Federal Bureau of Investigation's official seal, the White House, the Capitol Building, the Washington Monument, the Lincoln Memorial and the FBI building ("Bronislau Kaper Scores").

The FBI debuted on Sunday, September 19, 1965, at 8:00. The first half-hour went up against the last half-hour of NBC's *Walt Disney's Wonderful World of Color* and the second half-hour against NBC's black-and-white Western *Branded*. It went against *The Ed Sullivan Show* on CBS.

After its first week on the air, nationally syndicated Hollywood TV reporter Charles Witbeck wrote about *The F.B.I.*'s ratings battle. "Cocky underweight ABC, the third network which is elbowing in on its competitors, has thrown a big haymaker this fall on Sunday nights with *The F.B.I.*" Quinn Martin was quoted as stating, "We're not going to hurt Walt Disney one bit," and then adding, "Ed Sullivan hasn't had adult competition for years" (Witbeck "*F.B.I.* After Sullivan." 16).

Critics in that first week throughout the country largely ridiculed *The F.B.I.*:

> "Week's most depressing event."—Jack Gould, *The New York Times*
>
> "A fraud."—Percy Shain, *Boston Globe*

"Easily the week's biggest disappointment."—Bernie Harrison, *Washington Evening Star*

"One suspected that by F.B.I. they meant the Federal Bureau of Idiocy."—Dwight Newton, *San Francisco Examiner*

"They don't need tommy guns anymore. They need Ann Landers."—Jack Anderson, *Miami Herald*

"Stilted dialogue and weak attempts at humor."—Hal Humphrey, *Los Angeles Times* ("The Critics' View, part 2" 69)

The F.B.I. had a strong start, but regularly finished third in the ratings. *The Ed Sullivan Show* was the 18th highest-rated show of the season and *Walt Disney's Wonderful World of Color* the 17th (Brooks and Marsh). But ABC saw promise and in the ABC Fall Preview *7 Nights to Remember*, the network stated, "*The F.B.I.* returns at 8:00. This show has been gaining steadily in popularity and ratings." *The F.B.I.*'s new main title sequence was similar, but one exception: It now proudly exclaimed "*The F.B.I.:* In Color."

In *The F.B.I.*'s first six years on the air, its main competitors *Ed Sullivan* and *Wonderful World of Color* were regularly listed as being among the highest-rated shows (Brooks and Marsh). But *The F.B.I.* held its own: It was the 32nd highest-rated show in the 1966–1967 season and one of the top 25 shows in the 1967–1968, 1968–1969, 1970–1971 and 1971–1972 seasons (Spencer "TV's Vast" 54; Brooks and Marsh). ABC cancelled *The FBI* in September 1974 when the network saw a downward slope in the ratings. At the time, it was the third longest running show that was broadcast entirely in color (Stanley "The Day Hoover" 255).

Quinn Martin was not finished with F.B.I.-oriented drama. In 1974, he produced the TV movie *The FBI Story: The FBI Versus Alvin Karpis, Public Enemy Number One* and the next year *Attack on Terror: The FBI vs. the Ku Klux Klan*, both for CBS. In addition, Martin produced several other shows and made-for-TV movies focused on law enforcement: *Travis Logan, D.A.* (1971), *The Streets of San Francisco* (1972–1977) and *Most Wanted* (1976–1977).

The F.B.I. found a modern-day renaissance of interest in 2019 when the Quintin Tarantino film *Once Upon a Time in Hollywood* (2019) used footage from the 1969 episode "All the Streets Are Silent," which guest starred Burt Reynolds. In *Once Upon a Time in Hollywood*, Reynolds was digitally replaced by Leonardo DiCaprio's character, former Western star turned character actor, Rick Dalton.

Hawk

After Burt Reynolds' *Gunsmoke* stint as Native American blacksmith Quint Asper (1962–1965), but before he became the mustached, hairy-chested sex symbol of the 1970s, the actor was cast as another Native American character—this time in a contemporary setting. Reynolds portrayed Police Lt. John Hawk in ABC's *Hawk*. From the show's advertisements: "A full-blooded Indian, he prowls New York at night, stalking those who prey on the innocent."

Reynolds claimed to be part–Cherokee, and that same year he took on another Native American role in the Italian Spaghetti Western *Navajo Joe* (1966) Even at the time, folks were skeptical of the claim that Reynolds was part–Native American. When a letter was sent to the *Pittsburgh Press*' TV-Radio Editor Vince Leonard asking "Is [Reynolds] really an Indian?" Leonard responded, "You must be hiding your TV in a teepee … he's part Irish, part French, part Italian and all American" (Leonard "*Time Tunnel* Goes to the Well" 52).

Reynolds did not want to play a stereotypical Native American character, stating. "Every time they write in a scene in which I spout like an Indian, I cut it out. Okay, he's an Indian. But why make a big deal out of it?" (Byers "Burt Reynolds" 17). Reynolds was later quoted as saying, "I'm not running around in moccasins or anything like that," and "I wanted to play this Indian my way—after all those years of watching TV Indians getting undignified treatment" (Dutton "*Hawk*" 556; Lowry "Hero of Dying" 176).

Reynolds wanted to play Hawk differently than other TV detectives:

> I think Hawk is a valid cop—outwardly cold and calculating as you'd have to be to survive in this type of job, but he gets upset inside. I wanted to play him the way Kirk Douglas played *Detective Story* [1951] or like John Garfield always played cops—tough and hard. I hope that with all his hostility and obvious appearance—how many cops do you see in a Brooks Brothers suit?—the audience will appreciate the character's qualities [Lowry "Hero of Dying" 176].

The color series was shot on the streets of New York, a city where filming is expensive and difficult. To make matters worse, the show was actually filmed at night. Reynolds stated, "They're shooting it like in Europe, where they put a camera on your back and you run down the street and they shoot a lot with available light, which causes a lot of shadows, but adds something to the overall effect." He added that sometimes there were "a strange breed of people on the streets at two or three a.m." but noted that the production team had the full cooperation of Mayor Lindsay and his special police force, tasked to aid film crews working in the city (Dutton "*Hawk*" 556).

According to *Hawk*'s production manager Hal Schaeffle, who also worked on the similar shows *Naked City* (1958–1963) and *The Defenders* (1961–1965), "The one thing we have succeeded in doing with this series is breaking through red tape," in reference to the legal difficulties of shooting in New York. "We met all one afternoon with Mayor Lindsay's office and griped and out of these gripes came the most constructive changes [the industry] has ever had. … We now have one permit for the entire show, whereas they used to have one permit for each shot on each street, right through the whole shooting schedule" (Mead "Burt Hark Reynolds" 45).

Critics were mostly impressed and believed the show had a lot of upside:

> "Taut, suspenseful."—Harry Harris, *Philadelphia Inquirer*

> "Enough virtues to suggest the series may find a niche for itself."—Jack Gould, *The New York Times*

> "The best mix and action flow of any show unveiled to date."—Percy Shain, *Boston Globe*

> "For viewers who like tales of criminal action in New York after sundown, *Hawk* had to be a hit."—Peggy Constantine, *Chicago Sun Times*

> "One of the best crafted of the new television programs."—Terrence O'Flaherty, *San Francisco Chronicle*

> "Tension built nicely."—Aleene MacMin, *Los Angeles Times*

> "May be pretty exciting."—Joseph T. Sullivan, *Boston Herald*

"Unique flavor of harsh and brittle realism."—Bill Barret, *Cleveland Press* ("Critics' Views" 59–60)

Viewers did not feel the same way. After the September 8, 1966, premiere, *Hawk* quickly fell to the bottom of the ratings, even doing worse than the disastrous sitcom *The Tammy Grimes Show* which was cancelled by ABC after four episodes ("The Ratings" 68).

ABC announced that *Hawk*, along with their Western *Shane*, would be cancelled and conclude at the end of the calendar year despite slowly rising in the ratings ("Second Season" 56; Stephen 37). The show only lasted 17 episodes. It aired until December 27, 1966, and was replaced in January 1967 with a show moved from the Monday 10:00 time slot, *ABC Stage 67*, a multi-genre show which featured various dramas, documentaries and musicals, and was seen as "experimental television programming" (Jones "*Hawk* Is Above" 76).

Hawk aired opposite *The CBS Thursday Night Movie,* which that year aired popular films such as *The Music Man* (1962) and *Breakfast at Tiffany's* (1961); Reynolds saw this as the probable cause of the show's cancellation. That season, even *The Dean Martin Show*, which aired in the same time slot on NBC and was the 14th highest-rated show of the season, fell in the ratings when a popular movie aired. Reynolds was quoted as saying, "It's not fair to put our $80,000 show against a $2,000,000 movie. If [the network] would stay with us for a whole season, give us a chance to build an audience, I think *Hawk* would be around for years." But his pleas fell on deaf ears (Stoyer "It Was All" 105; Brooks and Marsh). Reynolds had a message for TV network decision-makers who believed that airing feature-length movies was better than investing in a new series: "Movies don't build an audience. Viewers don't get involved with a series like *Bonanza*. People will watch a series like that no matter what the story is because they feel they know the people in it. But before they sit down to spend two hours watching a movie, they want to know what it is" (Stoyer "It Was All" 105).

After *Hawk* wrapped, Reynolds was in high demand and was offered a number of other shows including a war series "very similar to *Rat Patrol*" and a show based on the Clark Gable–Burt Lancaster movie *Run Silent Run Deep* (1958). Instead he signed to do a television show entitled *Lassiter*, a drama to be shot in Europe, about a "magazine writer who becomes involved with people as he moves about" ("*Hawk* to *Lassiter*" 7). Reynolds claimed that he earned $2000 each episode of *Hawk* but would be paid $12,500 for doing the pilot to *Lassiter* ("*Hawk* Reynolds Still Flying").

Lassiter was never picked up by a network. The pilot episode made it to the airwaves in 1968 via CBS's anthology series *Premiere*.

Reynolds went on to bigger and better things: the TV series *Dan August* (1970–1971) and the films *Sam Whiskey* (1969), *Impasse* (1969) and *Skullduggery* (1970), and he became a popular late-night talk show guest. He finally got his breakout role in the film *Deliverance* (1972).

Dragnet

Jack Webb served as producer, director and star of the police procedural *Dragnet*, based on actual police case files.

Dragnet was originally a radio drama that aired from 1949 to 1957 for 240 original episodes. It featured Los Angeles Police Department Sergeant Joe Friday (Webb) and his partner, Officer Ben Romero (Barton Yarborough) in the first season. After Season One, Romero's replacement was Officer Frank Smith (Ben Alexander). *Dragnet* hit the NBC-TV airwaves in 1952 on Thursdays at 9:00. Once again Webb directed, produced and starred as Joe Friday, with Alexander as Frank Smith.

The first TV season of the noirish, black-and-white *Dragnet* was immensely popular. It averaged a 46.8 Nielsen rating, making it the fourth most popular show of the year. That season, *I Love Lucy* was the #1 show with a colossal 67.3 rating. The second season, *Dragnet's* ratings jumped even higher, to 53.2, but again it lost to *I Love Lucy*. Although ratings cooled, the show aired until 1959 (Brooks and Marsh).

Dragnet even became a part of popular culture: The theme, written by Walter Schumann and performed by the Ray Anthony Orchestra, went to #3 on the Billboard charts in 1953, and the show was parodied in films, cartoons, comedy albums and even by the Three Stooges (Brooks and Marsh). In 1954, *Dragnet* made its way to the big screen via a feature film released by Warner Brothers (and for the first time in color), once again starring Webb and Alexander.

The original *Dragnet* TV series boasted 276 episodes in its eight seasons, which made it easy to syndicate. A TV station that needed to fill a half-hour weekday time slot could easily air *Dragnet,* entitled *Badge 714* in syndication, without repeating a single episode within the course of a year. *Dragnet's* popularity in syndication and the initial success of the L.A.–based TV crime drama *The Felony Squad,* which debuted in September 1966, led to *Dragnet's* revival in 1967. Once again Webb produced and directed and took on the role of Sergeant Friday. Ben Alexander was unavailable to reprise his role as Frank Smith due to his *Felony Squad* gig, so character actor and future *M*A*S*H* star Harry Morgan enlisted as Friday's new partner Officer Bill Gannon ("*Felony Squad* Rates High" 31).

Alexander did return to his role as Frank Smith with a brief cameo in an October 1966 *Batman* in where he recited a line attributed to Joe Friday (but which in actuality was never uttered): "Just the facts, ma'am."

In the years since 1959, President John F. Kennedy and Malcolm X were assassinated, the U.S. involvement in Vietnam escalated, censorship in film and television was loosening, President Johnson signed the 1965 Voting Rights Act, the Beatles transformed music, culture and fashion, and the hippy counterculture movement gained momentum. The world may have changed, but Jack Webb assured his audience that some things would remain the same. From the *Los Angeles Times' Dragnet* preview:

> The new *Dragnet* will be dressed up in color, and Webb reports the Los Angeles Police Department's terminology has changed considerably since he left the beat, all which will be included in place of the old glossary of terms. He is not, however, leaving his old "dum-de-dum-dum" music for any rock'n'roll [Humphrey "Dragnet Returns"].

Although some things remained the same, *Dragnet's* storylines did change with the times. Two minutes into *Dragnet's* Thursday, January 12, 1967, premiere at 9:30, the show dove headfirst into 1960s psychedelic drug counterculture: In the episode "The LSD Story," Captain Richey (Art Balinger) sent Friday and Gannon out on a call regarding a juvenile "painted up like an Indian" and chewing the bark off a tree. When Friday and Gannon arrived, the juvenile (Michael Burns) had his head buried in dirt while hallucinating on LSD. They pulled him off the ground, revealing that he had his face painted blue and yellow and wore a leather vest with "Live and let live. Down with the fuzz" on the back. Friday and Gannon found LSD on him. Asked for his name, the juvenile exclaimed. "Don't you know my name? I'm Blueboy!" He was later released at the urging of his doting parents and because, at the time the story took place, LSD was not yet illegal in California. Friday stated in a long exposition:

> LSD users were increasing at an alarming rate, particularly among juveniles. By now, users have already established their own language. The drug itself was now called "the ticket," "the ghost," "the beast," "the chief," "the hawk" or simply "25" [referring to the drug's clinical name Lysergic acid diethylamide 25]. Users usually refer to themselves as acid heads or acid freaks. A trip still referred to having taken the drug but now more often the words a "bum trip" and "freak-out" were being used and heard, meaning a bad LSD experience. The pusher or supplier became known as "the travel agent." ... [A]fter consuming LSD, it requires 45 minutes to an hour for the drug to take effect. Most users were now spending this waiting period inhaling marijuana.

After learning that California passed a law which made LSD illegal, Friday and Gannon got tipped off about Blueboy's location: an acid party in the Hollywood Hills. When the pair went to break up the party, they entered a house with far-out red lighting, a woman snapping her fingers offbeat to a groovy tune on reel-to-reel tape, a girl trying to climb the walls, and even a beatnik eating green paint from his paint brush. The room's psychedelic colors were in sharp contrast to Friday and Gannon's gray suits, crisp white shirts and solid blue ties. But Friday and Gannon were too late to the party: Blueboy overdosed on "acid, reds, yellows, rainbows." His roommate acknowledged, "[Blueboy] kept wanting to get further out, further out, further out."

The next day, the *Indianapolis News* called the episode a "teenage LSD shocker": "Webb's new *Dragnet* ... has considerably more cool than the old series. It's in color. It's contemporary, and as in the case of last night's show, it's willing to tackle a current police problem and preach as little-sermon along the way" (Shull *"Dragnet* is Back").

Dragnet's second episode, "The Big Explosion," tackled yet another hot button 1960s issue: the racial integration of schools. Neo-Nazi Donald Chapman (Don Dubbins) hijacked "a large quantity of high velocity gelatin dynamite," and police felt that he intended to use it based on a prior racially motivated assault charge. When Friday and Gannon raided his house, they found some of the missing dynamite, rifles, machine-guns, hand grenades, World War II–era Nazi helmets, flags, weapons and, according to Gannon, "hate literature by the ton." When Chapman was interrogated, he spouted hateful Nazi propaganda until Friday lectured, "Now you listen to me, you wide-mouth punk, we've heard about all we want from you. ... Try to put that walnut-sized brain of yours to work on this. You keep harping about minorities. Well, mister, you're a psycho and they're a minority too."

Eventually, Chapman revealed he was planning on blowing up a school because it was going to be integrated that day. The bomb squad proceeded to dismantle the bomb. At the end of the episode, the camera panned to the deep red Nazi flag hanging from Chapman's wall, which helped make a powerful statement about the ugliness of hate and bigotry.

Other episodes highlighted more traditional topics: burglary, con men, gambling, juvenile delinquency, missing persons, murder investigations and, in December 1968, "The Christmas Story," an account of a baby Jesus statue stolen from the Nativity Scene right before Christmas from a mostly Hispanic Catholic Church. "The Christmas Story" was also featured on the radio show and in the first incarnation of the TV show in 1953.

Clearly one of Jack Webb's favorite *Dragnet* casefiles, "The Christmas Story" was released on 7" vinyl in 1954 (Internet Archive).

Other unconventional episodes chronicled a police shooting review board, the organization of a school youth group against drugs, debunking of a pyramid scheme, preparing for a possible riot following Martin Luther King, Jr.'s, assassination, and Friday and Gannon appearing on an avant-garde community access show to debate police issues with hippies.

Dragnet had a reputation for being a right-wing police show, mostly for its stance on drugs and its admiration of authority. But throughout the revamped series, it took on right-wing militias. It was pro-community policing, and Friday lectured about the political correctness needed in language. It even spotlighted police brutality.

The accusation that Webb and *Dragnet* were too right-wing went as far back as 1954 and the *Dragnet* movie. The *New York Times* reviewer stated,

> Mr. Friday does little more to solve it than browbeat the three most likely thugs and throw a few sharp insinuations at a couple of balky witnesses. This is the character of the fellow. He is a pretty brutal and ruthless sort. And if that's what the TV audience worships, it's a

frightening and unfortunate thing. ... It is also significant that Friday makes a pitch in this film for tapping wires and shows an obvious distaste for the Fifth Amendment to the Constitution, behind which he feels his criminals hide. That's Joe Friday as we see him. And since he and Mr. Webb are virtually one—Mr. Webb being player and director—that is substantially Mr. Webb [Crowther "*Dragnet* Has Debut"].

Dragnet worked closely with the LAPD for accuracy of stories. Webb reportedly paid anywhere from $50 to $100 to any police officer who submitted one of their own cases that was selected for the show, $150 to off-duty police officers to act as technical advisors on set, and $25 to a public relations officer to check scripts for inaccuracies (Hayde 48). An early 1990s Nick at Nite *Dragnet* promo ("Preserving Our Television Heritage") claimed that on-set technical advisors "assured that the gun, the badge, even the telephone on Joe Friday's desk were authentic." The promo also reported that the show was so realistic, citizens came to LAPD headquarters and asked to meet Sergeant Friday. The standard reply from the front desk was, "Sorry, it's Joe's day off."

Despite close ties to the LAPD, *Dragnet* still depicted the department's flaws. In one episode, Friday acknowledged that police officers are not perfect: "We have one big problem in selecting police officers ... we have to recruit from the human race."

A *Los Angeles Times* preview of *Dragnet* stated, "Jack Webb has decided there is a definite social need for a show like *Dragnet* and offers this as his primary reason for reviving the famous TV series." Webb was quoted in the article as saying, "There's been a breakdown in our mores, a total disregard for constituted authority, and I hope a series like *Dragnet* can do something to help restore respect for the law." He went on to state that the show would not focus on "weightier" civil rights issues because "many of these things ... a detective sergeant and officer wouldn't be called in" (Humphrey "*Dragnet* Returns").

The revived *Dragnet* averaged a 21.0 rating in its first season, in spite of competition from the popular *CBS Thursday Night Movie* (Brooks and Marsh). The first episode, "The LSD Story," lost in the ratings to the *CBS Thursday Night Movie*'s airing of *A Summer Place* (1959) but then the two shows traded ratings wins throughout the season ("Second Season Loses" 60; "CBS Edges Ahead" 60, Brooks and Marsh).

Before the television revival of *Dragnet,* Webb produced a two-hour made-for-TV *Dragnet* movie that was supposed to serve as a pilot and introduce Bill Gannon as Joe Friday's partner. According to the *Indianapolis News,* "The two-hour version has been shelved for a while. Among other things, Webb pointed out if his new TV series plays well with the public, the two-hour film may be released in the theaters for a larger profit" (Shull "*Dragnet* Is Back"). The movie did finally play on TV in 1969.

Dragnet's ratings held steady until the 1969–1970 season, when they took a downward tumble. NBC announced the cancellation of *Dragnet* in May 1970. Webb was not upset: "Never cry or bellyache about being cancelled," he said. "Go and find something else to do" (Laurent "You Needn't Weep" 46).

Webb took his own advice and his production company, Mark VII Limited, produced many other shows portraying public servants: the LAPD police procedural *Adam-12* (1968–1975), the legal drama *The D.A.* (1971–1972), a crime drama focusing on federal crime, *O'Hara, United States Treasury* (1971–1972), the medical drama *Emergency!* (1972–1977), the LAPD special case drama *Chase* (1973–1974), the National Park Service rescue drama *Sierra* (1974) and the police dog procedural *Sam* (1978).

In 1987, *Dragnet* became a buddy cop film comedy starring Dan Aykroyd and Tom

Hanks. It was also rebooted on TV as *LA Dragnet* (2003–2004): Ed O'Neill, most famous for his role as Al Bundy on *Married with Children* (1987–1997), played Joe Friday.

The Felony Squad

In November 1965, ABC announced the production of a pilot for a police drama titled *Men Against Evil*. It starred Howard Duff as Police Sergeant Sam Stone and Jeanne Crain as his alcoholic wife. The episode featured a *Peyton Place*–like dramatic serialized format to "present police melodrama-style" (Gysel "Ben Alexander Sounds" 67).

ABC picked up *Men Against Evil* and slated the show to air in the 1966 fall season and originally planned for two half-hour episodes each week. But by March 1966, that plan was scrapped and the show was slated to air once a week on Mondays at 9:00 (Adams "A.B.C. Picks 16").

In addition to being knocked down to one night a week, the show's format underwent changes. It was originally pitched as a show about "policemen and their tensed-up wives"; in April 1966, Crain was removed because, according to TV columnist Alex Freeman, producers felt she "didn't have some things they wanted and too much of some that they didn't want" ("The New Shows" 37; Freeman "Animals' Returning" 8). All the main female characters were removed, and the show focused strictly on police work instead of the officers' personal lives.

The show was also given a title change. *Men Against Evil,* an odd and vague title for a police drama, was changed, reportedly due to objections from an unnamed sponsor. Producers considered changing the name to *The Force* or *The Heavy Squad* but settled on *The Felony Squad* (Adams "Friday's Friend"; Lowry "Ben Playing Cop" 8-C).

The Felony Squad hit the ABC airwaves on September 12, 1966, with opening credits that featured a groovy theme song with colorful four-panel Andy Warhol polyptych pop art–style visuals. Opening text stated "The Place—A City. The Time—Now. The Story of *The Felony Squad*." *Television Magazine* described the new show as being "dolled up in living color" ("The New Shows" 37).

Felony Squad executive producer Walter Grauman described the show as a

> cops-and-robbers show, but with a difference. The police have an emotional relationship to each other and to the case that they're on. … The show is given a style of harsh realism by using real locations as much as possible. I think of it as an action show, even a chase, and I like to keep 50 percent of it in movement. I hammer at the writers: Let us learn about the characters in action.

Grauman also stated that he "wanted a contrast" between characters. Sergeant Stone (Duff) who is a more mature detective "who operates by instinct" contrasts with the by the book young police officer Jim Briggs (Dennis Cole) who has been taught by his father battle-scarred officer Sergeant Dan Briggs (Ben Alexander) (Thomas "Plots in *Felony Squad*" 62).

TV reporter Charles Witbeck described the show as

> an honest to goodness, old-fashioned police show minus the fancy frills of karate, James Bond, gods or eye-wrenching sirens. … Each episode opens on the crime of the night—the preparation, the actual act, or the results of the deed—then the camera shifts as Howard Duff and his sidekick Dennis Cole swing into action, checking out cases on police brutality, dope,

vice, kidnapping and murder, along with the usual petty theft and arson jobs [Witbeck "*Felony Squad* Not Armed" 126].

Witbeck's positive reaction was not typical. After the first week, TV critics were less than kind to the new police drama:

"A vicious and stupid show."—Dwight Newton, *San Francisco Examiner*

"Nothing slightly distinctive."—Bob Williams, *New York Post*

"Seems concerned with supporting police viewpoints, which may [upset] the social-protest class in some circles."—Bob Hull, *Los Angeles Herald*

"A tough, almost brutal show with unbelievably bad writing."—Lawrence Laurent, *Washington Post*

"Another tired extension of the detective theme."—Dean Gysel, *Chicago Daily News* ("Critics' Views" 64)

The National Association for Better Broadcasting did not like the show: The watchdog organization felt that it presented "a violent and unconvincing portrayal of police war against criminals" and that it was unsuitable for children (Leonard "What's Out" 78).

Two first-season *Felony Squad* episodes *seemed* to have been ripped from the headlines. In "Between Two Fires," a right-wing militia stocks weapons to go to war with left-wing organizations; this closely mirrored the story of Robert DePugh and his Minuteman militia, arrested in 1966 on federal weapons charges. "The Immaculate Killer" seemed directly inspired by the deadly 1966 sniper shooting at the University of Texas. Actually, both episodes were written and filmed before the events took place (Thomas "Plots in *Felony Squad*" 62).

By December 1966, *The Felony Squad* was one of the season's three top-rated new series, the others being *The Rat Patrol* and *Family Affair* (Thomas "Plots in *Felony Squad*" 62). Howard Duff appeared on *Batman* (1966–1968) as his *Felony Squad* character Sam Stone in a Bat-Climb segment in the episode "The Impractical Joker" (November 16, 1966). *Felony Squad* co-star Ben Alexander had appeared on *Batman* as his *Dragnet* character, Frank Smith, a month earlier.

The Felony Squad held its own in the ratings with CBS's immensely popular *The Andy Griffith Show* which aired at the same time ("ABR Top-20" 69). *The Felony Squad*'s success was reportedly one of the reasons that NBC brought *Dragnet* back in January 1967. Ben Alexander played Joe Friday's partner Frank Smith in the original *Dragnet* but was unable to return to *Dragnet* because of his obligations to *The Felony Squad* ("*Felony Squad* Rates High" 31).

The Felony Squad got off to a hot start but cooled down by January 1967 and was the 47th most watched show of the season (Spencer "TV's Vast" 54). It ran for another two seasons but never picked back up in the ratings. In November 1968, ABC announced that it was scheduled for cancellation after running for 73 episodes. The last episode aired January 31, 1969. It was replaced by the very short-lived prime time game show *The Generation Gap* (Brooks and Marsh; "A.B.C. to Replace").

Chapter Five

Science Fiction

With the exception of the anthology series *The Twilight Zone* (1959–1964) and *The Outer Limits* (1963–1965), the quality of pre-1966 science fiction TV programs was less than stellar. But the 1966–1967 season brought viewers several of the most iconic SF TV programs of all time.

Star Trek

In September 1966, TV viewers with an affinity for space exploration, science, horror or fantasy were no doubt talking about one of the most revolutionary science fiction shows to hit the airwaves: *Star Trek*.

Star Trek was initially pitched in March 1964 by its creator, TV writer Gene Roddenberry, who called it "a *Wagon Train* concept—built around characters who travel to worlds 'similar' to our own, and meet the action-adventure-dramas which became our stories." (*Wagon Train* [1957–1965] was a Western series wherein the main characters encountered different people and situations as they moved from place to place.) Roddenberry added that *Star Trek* should be set "'somewhere in the future,' it could be 1995 or maybe even 2995. In other words, close enough to our own time for our continuing characters to be fully identifiable as people like us, but far enough into the future for galaxy travel to be thoroughly established [happily eliminating the need to encumber our stories with tiresome scientific explanation]" (Roddenberry "*Star Trek* Pitch").

Lucille Ball's Desilu Productions went into production with the color pilot episode, "The Cage," in late 1964. The episode cost $600,000 and had the USS *Enterprise* commanded by Captain Pike (Jeffrey Hunter). *Star Trek* was rejected by CBS and was labeled "too cerebral" when shown to NBC network brass. But then NBC gave it another chance ("Entertainment Weekly: The Ultimate Guide").

NBC commissioned a second color pilot episode, "Where No Man Has Gone Before," with Captain Pike replaced by Captain Kirk (William Shatner). While on their mission, the *Enterprise* crew came across green-skinned slave girls. The green body paint was applied by Fred Phillips, who also did the makeup for the TV shows *Bat Masterson* (1958–1961) and *The Outer Limits,* and John Chambers, who went on do the prosthetics in the *Planet of the Apes* films. When the processed film was viewed, their skin was not green; it looked normal. It was assumed that a mistake was made in filming and the scenes were reshot, but with the same result. After a call to the film lab, a color correction technician explained that he thought that the lab had accidently turned the slave girls green while processing the film. On both occasions, the lab then worked overtime to do color correction to make the slave girls' skin appear normal (Whitfield and Roddenberry 78).

NBC picked up *Star Trek* for the 1966–1967 lineup. "Where No Man Has Gone Before" was broadcast later in the first season and "The Cage" was recut and the footage used in the two-parter "The Menagerie." In 1986, the original version of "The Cage" was released on VHS, and in November 1988 it aired on TV.

On June 25, 1966, a little more than two months before the premiere, Roddenberry was tasked with selling the show to the viewing public via an article in *TV Week*. He wrote, "[*Star Trek*] may be the most difficult television series ever attempted. Certainly, the most challenging and exciting." The article also highlighted that every detail on the set, even the beds, hairstyles and wardrobe, was the producers' attempt to create a look of how the world would look, hundreds of years in the future (Roddenberry "TV's Newest").

NBC began running 60-second promos before the premiere stating, "Here among a billion stars—a lonely ship streaks along an endless path. It's the men of Starship *Enterprise*! Follow her trackless journey each week on *Star Trek*." The promo presented several of the villains the crew encounters on their journey, introduced Captain Kirk (William Shatner) and Mr. Spock (Leonard Nimoy) and stressed that that show was in color. A week before the premiere, Roddenberry screened both "The Cage" and "Where No Man Has Gone Before" for attendees of the Tricon World Science Fiction Convention in Cleveland, Ohio.

The Dallas Morning News previewed *Star Trek*, calling it "definitely a superior effort. It is a highly imaginative project and was engrossing and intriguing" (Bowman "NBC 'Sneaks'").

The Newspaper Enterprise Association reported,

> William Shatner, the handsome green-eyed Canadian actor, had just given one of the most impressive performances of his life. He had convinced a crowd of skeptical television editors that his new NBC-TV series *Star Trek* is more than a gimmick-bound, monster-ridden, machine-made science fiction series. He had convinced them that the series will have stories "in the realm of possibility based on scientific knowledge" and that human emotions will be important to the plot. ... There were times when this one showed signs of becoming a little too gimmicky for its own good but it was nevertheless a high-quality production with top-notch acting and was a fascinating hour ["*Star Trek* Real Science Fiction"].

Star Trek took place in the year 2265; the *Enterprise* was on a mission "to seek out new life and new civilizations. To boldly go where no man has gone before," as stated in Captain Kirk's intro in the Thursday, September 8, 1966, premiere episode "The Man Trap."

The premiere scored high ratings (a 40.6 share of viewers) and averaged a 19.8 rating as seen in a Trendex ratings study. But the high ratings were partially due to *Star Trek* being one of the only new shows in the hour-long 8:30 p.m. time slot that evening, with the only exception being the infamously short-lived and unpopular sitcom *The Tammy Grimes Show*. With the second episode "Charlie X," ratings fell to 16.5, according to a Trendex ratings study; this time, *Star Trek* was defeated by the season premieres of *My Three Sons*, *Bewitched* and *The CBS Thursday Night Movie*, which that night featured *The Music Man* (1962) ("The Numbers Game" 59–60).

After the first two episodes, mixed opinions about *Star Trek* started to pour in from around the country:

> "Too clumsily conceived and poorly developed to rate as an A-1 effort."—Percy Shain, *Boston Globe*
>
> "You may need something of a pointed head to get involved."—Bob Williams, *New York Times*
>
> "Suspenseful, puzzling and ultra imaginative yarn."—Harry Harris, *Philadelphia Inquirer*
>
> "The plots may be space opera, but the show has been produced with care and lots of money."—Lawrence Laurent, *Washington Post*
>
> "Opening yarn was a breath-catcher."—Terrence O'Flaherty, *San Francisco Chronicle*
>
> "Disappointingly bizarre hour … things better improve, or this won't be a lengthy mission."—Ann Hodges, *Houston Chronicle* ("Critics Views" 58–59)

The third episode, "Where No Man Has Gone Before," drew an even lower rating—15.6—and that's where ratings approximately stayed for the rest of the season ("The Latest Form Sheet" 69).

Although *Star Trek* was getting subpar ratings, the impact was being seen: The series began breaking new ground for television, pioneering new uses for color television, and amassed a following like no other television show had before. According to the *TV Guide* 1966–1967 Fall Preview,

> Star Trek takes us on a journey into the unexplored regions of space, aboard the USS *Enterprise*, a huge "star ship." … Its officers and crew include representatives of every known race and gender, plus one startling character called Mr. Spock (Leonard Nimoy), who has pointy ears, slanty eyebrows and Beatle bangs, and turns out to be half–Earthling, half–Vulcanian and all business (creatures from the planet Vulcanis, as we all know, never display any emotion). What these galaxy-trotters run into out there is even stranger to behold than spooky–Spocky ["Fall Preview"].

The cast included "representatives of every known race and gender" which was an important aspect of *Star Trek*. On the *Enterprise*, men and women and people of all races worked as equals. In many science fiction films in the 1950s and early 1960s, women were taken on missions and portrayed scientists and doctors but were never treated as equal partners; and people of color were often relegated in film and TV to the roles of servants, comedic relief, or both. This was not the case in *Star Trek*. Characters included Captain Kirk and Mr. Spock in the Command Department, the ship's medical doctor Leonard "Bones" McCoy (DeForest Kelley), Communications Officer Lieutenant Uhura (Nichelle Nichols), engineer Montgomery "Scotty" Scott (James Doohan), nurse Christine Chapel (Majel Barrett) and helmsman Sulu (George Takei). To many viewers, *Star Trek* proved that women and people of color could be strong main characters and positive role models.

Nichelle Nichols appeared on the cover of the African-American magazine *Ebony* in January 1967. *Ebony* praised the show for including women and people of color in roles of importance and power "in anticipation of a multi-racial society." Inside the magazine an article about Nichols entitled "Role Plugs Women, Negros" stated, "The communications officer she portrays was in the pilot film, played by a man. Anticipating the future, however, planners decided to give the role to a woman and a Negro at that" ("Role Plugs").

Color was an integral part of the show. *Star Trek* helped usher in the age of color and made viewing in color and owning a color TV more desirable. In 1966, RCA Victor made Captain Kirk and Mr. Spock the face of their color television advertising campaign (RCA Victor advertisement).

When the crew of the *Enterprise* were beamed to other planets or other spaceships, the effect was generated by a series of glowing orange lights. The phaser, the crew's preferred weapon, blasted blue or red electronic beams. Many of the episodes featured very colorful planets, villains, monsters and alien beings such as the green-skinned Gorn, purple Giant Space Amoeba and the psychedelic Melkotian.

Even the color of the crew's clothing was significant. The color of each crew member's shirt represented their role on the ship. Olive shirts were worn by the command division, red shirts by engineering and communications, and blue shirts in the science and medical staff.

Much has been written about the innovative and colorful technology featured on *Star Trek*. Creator Roddenberry stated, "Everything we do is based on fact. We've consulted with aeronautical engineers and the Rand Corp." The horror-sci-fi magazine *Castle of Frankenstein* featured an article in early 1967 about *Star Trek*'s special effects. The article stressed the importance of the behind-the-scenes crew, most notably special effects artist Jimmy Rugg:

> Rugg is most proud of the intricate bridge, the nerve-center of the craft. Rugg had this set built in eight sections; when these sections are rolled together on their special hydraulic jacks, they form a complete circle. ... [H]undreds of hours were required to complete the wiring job. When asked how many feet of wiring went into construction of the bridge, Rugg laughingly replied, "You'd have to measure it in miles, I think" [Page "*Star Trek* Is Costly"; Asherman 8–10].

Apart from the premiere episode "The Man Trap," *Star Trek* was never a ratings winner. It ended the season the 52nd highest-rated show of the season and was one of the lowest rated shows renewed by a network that season (Spencer "TV's Vast" 54).

In the fall 1966–1967 season, audiences preferred the two popular and established shows *Star Trek* went up against: CBS's *My Three Sons* and ABC's *Bewitched*. According to the Nielsen ratings, *Bewitched* was the eighth most popular show of the season, pulling in a 23.4 rating, and *My Three Sons* was the 27th highest-rated show and received a 20.2 rating (Brooks and Marsh).

In its second season, *Star Trek* moved to Fridays at 8:30 p.m., which pitted the show against CBS's *Gomer Pyle, U.S.M.C.*, which averaged a 25.6 rating and was the third highest-rated show of the season (Brooks and Marsh).

Despite the ratings lag, *Star Trek* came with merchandising opportunities. In 1966, Aluminum Model Toys (AMT) released a model kit of the *Enterprise* and in 1968 a Klingon Battle Cruiser. In 1967, Remco released several toys with the *Star Trek* name. They had nothing to do with stories or characters: *Star Trek* Astro, Astro Tank, Astrocopter and Astrotrain (Toys That Made Us).

But much of the *Star Trek* merchandising was done in-house by Star Trek Enterprises (later renamed Lincoln Enterprises). Star Trek Enterprises was set up by Roddenberry, Roddenberry's future wife and *Star Trek* actress Majel Barrett, and *Star Trek* superfans Betty Jo "Bjo" and John Trimble in 1967 to handle fan mail, serve as an official fan club, and conduct business for a mail order catalogue after Desilu-Paramount began putting budgetary restrictions on promotional material ("Bjo Trimble: The Woman Who").

The idea for Star Trek Enterprises came about after a personal letter from science fiction writer Isaac Asimov was misclassified as fan mail by Desilu Studios and Asimov received a signed photo from the cast (Sawyer "A Collector's Trek"). There are also conflicting stories about how "official" the fan club was, considering Desilu, who owned the *Star Trek* property, did not have their hand in the direction or profits of Star Trek Enterprises.

Roddenberry sent out a press release that was published in a number of science fiction magazines and fanzines and newsletters to publicize Star Trek Enterprises:

> PUBLICITY RELEASE FROM GENE RODDENBERRY. Because so many *Star Trek* fans have written requesting souvenirs from our show, we have made up a list of items most asked for. They include actual film clips from *Star Trek*, the official *Star Trek* Writer's Guide, large color photographs of our stars, genuine scripts from this and past seasons, and dozens of other exciting and authentic items, all at as minimal a price as we can arrange. If you wish to receive this list, send your name and address and request to: STAR TREK, 6725 Sunset Blvd., Suite 205A, Hollywood, California 90028 [Roddenberry "Publicity Release"].

Above and opposite page: **Fans of horror, science fiction, and fantasy were some of *Star Trek*'s earliest supporters as seen in *Castle of Frankenstein* magazine (courtesy Drew Friedman).**

Star Trek's earliest group of core fans and supporters were, of course, aficionados of science fiction, horror and fantasy. An issue of *Castle of Frankenstein* magazine from early 1967 included a full-throated endorsement of the show that would be the envy of any presidential candidate:

> *Star Trek* is the best dramatic TV series ever made! ... Whether it's the ideal combination of Gene Roddenberry's ingenuity and outstanding scripts plus handsome décor and winning special effects; whether [it is] heroic William Shatner who as a futuristic Odysseus has a fine cast for his galactic Argonauts—one thing emerges with brilliant clarity: LEONARD NIMOY! He of pointed ears, piercing eyes—and inscrutable face! He who carried himself with Olympian dignity and touch of elfin magic with each movement!! ... Exit the past. Enter the future. Let us

all gird our loins for a new era ushered in by the starship *Enterprise*. And now ... being it is time to end compromise, let the veil be torn asunder; let the curtains be parted and the windows opened all the way for badly wanted fresh air. This is the *Star Trek* age—the era to begin sweeping always clouds of creative enslavement—the age of blowing minds! [Beck "*Star Trek* Forever"].

The *Castle of Frankenstein* article also reported on the rumors that NBC was planning on cancelling the show after the less than stellar first season's ratings. The article warned,

If there should ever be danger of a show like *Star Trek* getting cancelled, vitally needed (though vulgarly overlooked) good-will for the TV industry not only will be in jeopardy but irreparably damaged. In the eyes of our nation's mushrooming educated population, TV's image is now badly tarnished. Only rare brilliant morsels like *Star Trek* help ward off impending doom [Beck "*Star Trek* Forever"].

As early as the end of the first season, a letter- writing campaign to save the show was organized by a number of science fiction writers. Star Trek Enterprise's Bjo Tremble stated, "Their main push was to save the only TV show that actually bought scripts from writers who knew the subject, so not many fans were involved. Details are hazy on just what happened, but NBC at least did not cancel the show, so it must have worked."

The show was brought back the next season but moved to the less desirable 8:30 Friday night time slot. In the 1967–1968 season, the *Enterprise* crew's missions included being sent to a parallel universe, destroying a deadly alien probe, landing on a planet with a haunted castle (complete with black cats, witches and goblins), time-traveling back to 1920s Prohibition Era America, visiting a planet that was patterned after Nazi Germany, and dealing with cute, fluffy, and quickly multiplying creatures called Tribbles.

In the second season, the series also added a new character. When George Takei took a leave of absence at the start of the second season to play a role in the 1968 John Wayne film *The Green Berets*, a Russian character, Ensign Chekov (Walter Koenig), became the *Enterprise*'s helmsman. Legend has it that, prior to

Chekov's debut, the Soviet Communist Party newsletter *Pravda* wrote that *Star Trek* was being "typically capitalistic" by not including a Russian character. Roddenberry was famously quoted about the situation:

> The Chekov thing was a major error on our part, and I'm still embarrassed by the fact that we didn't include a Russian right from the beginning. However, now it is Russia's turn to be embarrassed. After we wrote Chekov into the show, we sent a long, polite letter to the minister of cultural affairs in Moscow, apologizing for the error and telling him about Chekov. That was over a year ago, and they still haven't answered us. So we're square [Whitfield and Roddenberry 249–251].

It is unlikely that citizens of the USSR were able to see the Chekov character. In 1966, Moscow had three TV stations and residents were getting a combined average of 16.4 hours of programming per day. It is believed that the first American TV show to air in the Soviet Union was *Daktari* in 1970 (Paulu; Shaba 16).

After the second season's ratings fell even lower, the rumors of cancellation began getting louder. Bjo Trimble stated, "We'd mapped out a basic plan of action. So, we called Gene Roddenberry to see if he was okay with this idea. Gene had just told his staff that it would be wonderful if there was just some way to reach fans and get their support. So, things began to happen." Members of the *Star Trek* fan club were instructed to write to NBC to help save the show. The plea also was also published in many *Star Trek* fan newsletters and fanzines ("Bjo Tremble: The Woman Who"). This ran in the inaugural issue (December 13, 1967) of the *Star Trek* fan newsletter *Plak-Tow*:

> STAR TREK NEEDS HELP!!! The *Enterprise* faces a deadly menace and could be destroyed. Is it the Romulans? The Klingons? The Orions? No, worse still—the Nielsens. ... As Bjo Trimble says, "If thousands of fans just sit around moaning about the death of *Star Trek*, they get exactly what they deserve, *Gomer Pyle*!" We must show that there are more people who want *Star Trek* than who don't really care one way or another. So, pass the word and write some letters, people; it's up to us fans to keep *Star Trek* on TV. Our own inaction will assure that it never sees a third season! Write NBC ... set phasers for heavy stun" [Meech "From the Editor"].

CBS's *Gomer Pyle, U.S.M.C.*, that season's third highest-rated show, aired opposite *Star Trek* (Brooks and Marsh).

The January 29, 1968, issue of *Plak-Tow* updated fans: "[T]he effects of the 'Save *Star Trek*' campaign was beginning to be felt. Letters have been pouring in to NBC, to *TV Guide*, and other magazines and newspapers" (Meech "Encouragement").

In an unprecedented move, NBC announced the renewal of *Star Trek* on March 1, 1968: "And now, an announcement of interest to all viewers of *Star Trek*. We are pleased to tell you that Star Trek will continue to be seen on NBC television. We know you will be looking forward to seeing the weekly adventures in space on *Star Trek*." It was rumored that NBC put out the announcement to stop letters from inundating the company's mail room.

On March 4, 1968, NBC stated, "Somehow word was circulated that *Star Trek* might be off the schedule next season, though that never was our intention." The report also claimed that the network "has had 115,000 letters from viewers including two governors, several mayors and corporate executives, pleading for [*Star Trek*'s] return." The TV industry magazine *Broadcasting* reported that the show was moving to 8:00 on Monday; at the time, the NBC 8:00 Monday time slot was held by the wildly popular *Rowan*

Chapter Five. Science Fiction

& Martin's Laugh-In, the highest-rated show of the 1968–1969 season, receiving a Nielsen rating of 29.1 rating ("NBC-TV Aims" 28; Brooks and Marsh).

Ultimately, NBC did not move *Star Trek* to Monday at 8:00 p.m. Instead, the third season of *Star Trek* was relegated to the timeslot doldrums at 10:00 p.m. Friday night and the show took an even deeper plunge in the ratings—losing weekly to *The CBS Friday Night Movie* ("NBC takes 6 of 7" 58). In her biography *Beyond Uhura:* Star Trek *and Other Memories,* Nichelle Nichols wrote that NBC had no intention of giving the show a chance after the third season: "While NBC paid lip service to expanding *Star Trek*'s audience ... [NBC] slashed our production budget until it was actually ten percent lower than it had been in our first season. ... This is why in the third season you saw fewer outdoor location shots. ... *Star Trek*'s demise became a self-fulfilling prophecy. And I can assure you, that is exactly as it was meant to be" (Nichols 188).

Star Trek's opening narration by Captain Kirk stated that the *Enterprise* had a "five-year mission: to explore strange new worlds, to seek out new life and new civilizations, to boldly go where no man has gone before." That mission was cut two years short by NBC. After much speculation and two seasons of being on the brink of cancellation; NBC took *Star Trek* off the air.

Once again Bjo and John Trimble and Star Trek Enterprises sprang into action. Fans received a Star Trek Enterprises flyer urging them to help save *Star Trek* yet again in early 1969. The flyer informed fans that although the show was not "officially cancelled," Roddenberry and Paramount were informed that it had indeed been cancelled but could possibly be saved by another letter writing campaign. Fans were told, "YOU SAVED *STAR TREK* LAST YEAR—CAN YOU DO IT AGAIN?" (Bjo Trimble "Save *Star Trek*").

But this time NBC did not change its mind: *Star Trek*'s last episode, "Turnabout Intruder," aired June 3, 1969.

But *Star Trek* did not just go away: Its stars were not done with their characters, interest in the series remained high, reruns went into syndication, and some of *Star Trek*'s most iconic toys were released in the mid–1970s, Star Trek/Lincoln Enterprises remained dedicated to the *Star Trek* Fan Club and the mail order business, and maybe most importantly, fans of *Star Trek* began building their own social network.

Shortly after the show was cancelled, Roddenberry made a July 4, 1968, guest appearance at Future Unbounded Science Fiction Show and Convention [FunCon] at the Statler Hotel in Los Angeles. Although not entirely *Star Trek*–themed, the convention featured *Star Trek* stars George Takei and Walter Koenig, a surprise appearance by William Shatner, screenings of a *Star Trek* blooper reel and "Menagerie," and a display of *Star Trek* props and costumes (Meech "FunCon Planning"; Meech "Con Report").

In September 1967, while *Star Trek* was still on the air, *Spockanalia*, considered the first *Star Trek* fanzine, was first published. It lasted until 1970. The first edition of the 'zine featured *Star Trek*–related art, poetry, fan fiction, news, lyrics to fan-created songs about the show, a review of the LP *Leonard Nimoy Presents Mr. Spock's Music from Outer Space* and a preview of the album *The Two Sides of Leonard Nimoy*. *Spockanalia*'s publishers organized "The *Star Trek* Con," held March 1, 1969, at the Newark Public Library in Newark, New Jersey. Although there were no special guests, the convention is considered the first *Star Trek* convention due to it being a coordinated event that only focused on *Star Trek* (Comerford "*Spockanalia*").

The term "Trekkies" began to be used around 1968 to describe fans of *Star Trek*.

An early example is an essay titled "A Mid-Spring's Night's Dream, or, Journey to Backstage," written by Ruth Burman and Dorothy Jones, found in the June 30, 1968, edition of *Star Trek* fan newsletter essay in *Plak-Tow* #8. The essay discussed meeting actor Mark Lenard, who played Sarek, the father of Spock. Burman wrote,

> I don't know about other people, but I'm afraid I was acting out of snobbery in cataloguing the roles I'd seen Mr. Lenard play when I sent him a fan letter—I'd wanted to make it clear I wasn't just a trekkie in love with Spock and therefore with all things Vulcan, especially Spock's father, but rather a sophisticated, mature admirer of good acting wherever it appears. Which I hope is true—but I'm in love with Sarek anyway.

Dorothy Jones missed out by several lines on being considered the first person to have the word "Trekkie" in print: In the same piece, she recalled,

> His appearance won't hurt any [in his roles], either. He is one of the most beautiful men I've ever seen in my life. He doesn't look much like Sarek, except for the bone structure. Colonel Kessler had the closest thing to his own face. His hair is black, flecked with grey (and curly—putting bangs on Sarek must have driven the hairdresser nuts). His great, warm brown eyes are guaranteed to melt any trekkie into a helpless pool of protoplasm [Berman].

The first dedicated *Star Trek* convention with guests, *Star Trek* Lives!," was held from January 21 to 23, 1972, at the Statler Hilton in New York City. It was organized by super-fan Joan Winston and Star Trek Enterprises' Bjo Trimble. Programs were hand-stamped "Late Flash: Gene Roddenberry will speak early Saturday afternoon," and famed science fiction writer-*Star Trek* fan Isaac Asimov was in attendance ("Celebrating 40 Years"; "*Star Trek* Lives").

Gene Roddenberry showed the original pilot episode "The Cage" and a *Star Trek* blooper reel. According to multiple news reports, between 3000 and 3500 people were in attendance (Roberts; "Celebrating 40 Years"; Shult; "The '72 Star Trek Con").

The Portsmouth Herald in Portsmouth, New Hampshire, featured an article about two high school seniors who attended that convention. According to the article, merchandise was on sale at the con, including amateur fan magazines about *Star Trek*, Trek 'Zines,' photos, scripts and even Tribbles. Phasers, tricorders, *Star Trek* artwork and uniforms were on display (Roberts "*Star Trek* Fans Attend").

According to the *Los Angeles Times Service* article "Cult Fans, Reruns Give *Star Trek* an Out of This World Popularity" (July 3, 1972), the *Star Trek* Lives! organizers expected 800 people but had over 3000. The article went on to discuss the series' continued popularity, quoting the programming director at L.A.'s Channel 13 as saying, "The interest in the show is greater now than it was last year, or for that matter, when the show was on the air in prime time. ... We get more mail and phone calls on this show than any other show." The article also mentioned college-age fans' passion for the shows. Students at some L.A. area colleges started their own fan clubs, one boasting more than 4000 members (Shult "Cult Fans").

In 1973, a horror–sci-fi publication, *The Monster Times,* printed a "Sci-fi Super TV Special Issue" which reviewed the 1972 convention and promoted the upcoming 1973 convention. The article stated that 3500 people showed up and claimed the attendance was "more than any other science fiction convention in the history of this planet." The review gushed over guests Roddenberry, Asimov, science fiction author Hal Clement and Oscar Katz, Desilu's executive vice-president of production between 1964 and 1966. According to the article,

A gala *Star Trek* costume ball was one of the final festivities and one of the most frequently attended ones. Dozens of *Star Trek* fans paraded about the Grand Ballroom, dressed as the U.S.S. *Enterprise* crew, as well as some of the numerous and picturesque villains and lifeforms. ... One lady portrayed a Tribble (a fuzz-ball critter), various persons paraded about as Klingon and Romulan officers. Mr. Spock was impersonated by at least a dozen fans. ... [T]he First Annual *Star Trek* Convention was such an overwhelming success, that there will definitely be another one Next Year! ["The '72 *Star Trek* Con"].

The 1973 convention was the first to bring in major stars from the show: announced guests were James Doohan and George Takei. Leonard Nimoy made a brief, unannounced appearance to thank *Star Trek*'s fans. The 1974 program book stated,

Leonard Nimoy. That was a surprise. ... After his speech, we spirited Leonard out of the Ballroom, down the back stairs and out of the lobby to get a cab. A host of fans coming out of the Howard Johnson's across the street spotted him and the shriek of "Spooocck" split the 42nd Street air. The cab took off as two trucks and a crosstown bus slewed across the icy street trying not to hit the hysterical fans. The fans in the hotel would not believe that Leonard had left; they even cased the Ladies room [Winston "*Star Trek* Lives!"].

The New York Times reported that at least 7000 people paid the $5 admission (Montgomery "Star Trekkie Show").

The 1974 *Star Trek* Lives! convention took place at the larger Americana Hotel in New York and also had a larger guest list including DeForest Kelley, Walter Koenig, Nichelle Nichols and George Takei. It was reported the convention had an attendance of 15,000, much larger than any science fiction convention at the time (Verba "Boldly Writing").

In 1975, a schism in the *Star Trek* convention community occurred. Albert Schuster, who was involved in the original *Star Trek* Lives! conventions started his own rival convention in New York, Schuster *Star Trek* Conventions. *The New York Times* reported on February 22, 1976, that "The *Star Trek* convention that opens at the Commodore Hotel today is the third here in a month, and perhaps the 20th in the country in the last year." The article went on to say that *Star Trek* Lives! promoter Joan Winston said "Albert Schuster is a man who is interested only in making money. Mr. Schuster, promoter of a rival convention here last month that lost money, considers Miss Winston and her collaborators 'childishly naive.'"

Both Winston and Schuster had a distinct disagreement with the conventions regarding money and what a *Star Trek* convention means. "Miss Winston ... proclaims herself a 'Trekkie.' To her, the conventions are a means of propagating the Star Trek 'message'—one of a future when life on earth will be peaceful, and multinational crews travel through space in search of other forms of life" wrote *The New York Times* ("*Star Trek* Promoters").

Schuster stated, "there is no such thing as altruism. It is fine ... if the conventions inspire their patrons," and went on to admit he's running the convention for the money and wants to "to exploit the series commercially." He added that although some of the *Star Trek* episodes were good, others were "pure tripe, utter bunk, complete garbage" ("*Star Trek* Promoters").

But another promoter caught the ire of both Winston and Schuster, Lisa Boynton. *The New York Times* reported that "If [Winston and Schuster] agree on anything, it is that Lisa Boynton of Chicago, promoter of yet another convention, which drew more than 20,000 people to the New York Hilton Hotel, was an out-and-out interloper." Winston told *The New York Times*, "She just came in, raped and pillaged, then left." Said

Mr. Schuster, "She's strictly a businesswoman, out for the buck." Mr. Schuster believed that Boynton's advertising confused "thousands of 'Trekkies'—acolytes of the cult—into patronizing her convention rather than his" ("*Star Trek* Promoters").

Schuster also stated in a June 12, 1976, edition of the UK newspaper *The Guardian* that the first of three of his New York *Star Trek* conventions at the Statler Hilton, "drew a relatively modest" 4,000 fans to the convention. But Boynton's rival convention "cut his throat" due to Boynton's event being attended by 20,000 attendees ("Ears Today...").

Although they now had competition, the 1975 *Star Trek* Lives! convention moved back to the Commodore Hotel, but this time brought William Shatner to the convention for his first official advertised convention appearance. The *New York News Service* reported on March 4, 1975, that the "1975 *Star Trek* Lives! convention was attended by 7,200 trekkies" (Maksian).

The *Star Trek* Lives! conventions ran until 1976, when the promoters announced:

> Back in 1971 we had an idea—we thought we'd run a special kind of science fiction convention—one dedicated to one of the few really good SF television programs, *Star Trek*. It seemed like a good idea, even if many people thought we were crazy. After all, the stars were in California and we were in New York. So, they laughed. That is, until we broke all records. Our small convention for several hundred turned into a small convention for several thousand! The very first *Star Trek* Convention, held at the Statler Hilton Hotel in New York City, January 21–23, 1972, had an attendance of 3500—almost double that of the largest SF con held at that time. ... When Captain Kirk was given command of the *Enterprise*, he was assigned a five-year mission. Unfortunately, this mission was aborted after only three years. We've been luckier. With this convention comes the end of the *Star Trek* Convention in New York—the end of our five-year mission. Should we decide to do something in the future, we'll let you know. You'll recognize us by our name and our symbol, accept no substitutes! [Rosenstein].

Star Trek conventions made their way to the West Coast in 1975 beginning on February 22 with the Red Hour Festival at Lincoln High School in San Francisco. The *Star Trek* fanzine *A Piece of the Action*, issue #24, reported that it was "great fun. Dealers with all kinds of *Star Trek* and science fiction items to buy, a great carnival with Federation credits that one could trade for *Star Trek* prizes." The convention included 16mm screenings of *Star Trek* episodes in the high school's theater and boasted appearances by James Doohan, George Takei, Walter Koenig and the actress who played Spock's bride-to-be in "Amok Time," Arlene Martel (Walker and Young). The *Piece of the Action* article continued, "If memory serves, almost 4000 fans were there. Another fan disputes that number, saying 2000 tickets were sold" (Walker "One Small Step"; Walker and Young).

The next year, a much larger convention was brought to the West Coast: The *Star Trek* and Space Science Convention, held at the Oakland Municipal Auditorium on August 7 and 8, 1976. This convention featured the all-star lineup of Shatner, Nimoy, Kelley, Doohan and Takei ("Star Trek and Space"). *Star Trek* conventions began popping up throughout the country and eventually throughout the world, ranging from small gatherings in hotel ballrooms with vendors and a movie screening room to large gala events featuring guests and exclusive *Star Trek* content.

Soon after the 1969 cancellation of *Star Trek*, rumors circulated about the possibility of a series revival, and NBC continued receiving letters urging them to bring the series back. In May 1972, the *St. Petersburg* (Florida) *Times* spotlighted *Star Trek* fan Dale Surran, who started the *Star Trek* Association for Revival, dedicated to getting the show back on TV: "[Surran] simply doesn't understand why *Star Trek* went off the air.

And now she knows there are many others who can't understand it either, she's not going to take it anymore." Although Surran did not have a lot of money to spend on the project, she put took out two ads encouraging fans to write and made phone calls to NBC and to Paramount, and she began receiving letters herself from people supportive of the cause. Surran stated, "I don't know what prompts these men to make the decisions they do. Maybe there's somebody's wife up there that didn't like the show. Certainly, logic, intelligence and viewer response aren't prompting them" (Sedgeman "Fan of *Star Trek*").

Fandom surrounding the series was so strong that some considered *Star Trek* to be better than the real-life space exploration happening at the time. On July 22, 1969, *The Calgary Herald* in Calgary Alberta, Canada, reported that the Ottawa TV station CJOH-TV received 15 complaints because a *Star Trek* rerun was preempted by the telecast of the Apollo 11 moon flight ("They Wanted *Star Trek*").

The Associated Press reported in March 1972, "*Star Trek* has engendered a cult unlike any other series, and for thousands of people the StarShip *Enterprise* is still out there exploring new worlds." The article covered the convention phenomenon and the fans who were unwilling to let their favorite show die. Examples were Emerson College using episodes in graduate seminars, community playhouses putting on original plays, and the 100-plus "privately published fan magazines" where fans "write episodes, poetry, and music" (Buck "*Star Trek* Engenders").

On September 8, 1973, seven years to the day after *Star Trek* debuted, these fans got their wish—in a way. *Star Trek* returned as a Gene Roddenberry–produced NBC Saturday morning cartoon show, *Star Trek: The Animated Series*. It was very well received by *Star Trek* fans and, because it was produced by Roddenberry, episodes are considered official *Star Trek* story canon. Much of the original cast members were slated to return to voice their characters. Shatner returned as Captain Kirk, Nimoy as Spock, Kelley as McCoy, Doohan as "Scotty" and Gene Roddenberry's now wife, Majel Barrett, as the voice of the *Enterprise* computer. Absent were George Takei and Nichelle Nichols. They were added to the cast after pressure from Nimoy, who held out voicing Spock unless Takei and Nichelle Nichols were added ("The Howard Stern Show").

On October 12, 1974, *Star Trek* fans once again received bad news: *The Animated Series* was cancelled. The show lasted two seasons with a total of 22 episodes.

But with the cancellation came good news. *Knight Newspapers* wrote, "*Star Trek* fans, a plump morsel of good news and a sad blot of bad news are available for you." The article mentioned the cancellation of *The Animated Series* because "it did not do well in the Nielsen ratings," running third against *The Hudson Brothers* on CBS and *Super Friends* on ABC. It also announced the good news that the rumors were true that *Star Trek* would be made into a major motion picture with plans to include the original cast: "Paramount said it was too early to say when shooting would start or when the movie might be finished. But you can get your money ready, Trekkies, for they are going to do it" (Winfrey).

According to *The Miami Herald*, the *Star Trek* movie was scheduled for 1976 release, and that Roddenberry had announced at the *Star Trek* convention at New York's Commodore Hotel that he had received financial backing for the project. The article went on to say that NBC has been flooded with letters since the show went off the air and quoted George Takei as saying that the reason the show was not brought back was a matter of economics. "Why should they release a new series when Paramount can make so much money on the reruns? ... They're past their tenth rerun in schedule now so they don't have to pay the cost of any residuals. The reruns are all gravy for them, and they are still being played all over the country. The cost of producing a new series, manufacturing new sets and costumes, is astronomical." Takei also stated that the set was donated to the UCLA Theater Arts department and "subsequently destroyed because of lack of space," and that the original *Enterprise* model was on display in the Smithsonian Institution in Washington, D.C. Therefore, a new film would have to "start from scratch" (Maksian).

The Monster Times reported in its July 1975 edition that Paramount and Roddenberry signed a contract to produce a *Star Trek* movie and promised new aero-space designs, digital instruments and controls, and stretch-knit material uniforms for the cast ("*Star Trek* Lives!"). The magazine also published a phone interview with Roddenberry, conducted on April 8, 1975, in which Roddenberry admitted that no one had signed on to the film yet; that most of the script was still in his head; and that he was still "playing around" with ideas such as making the film about the crew's origin. Roddenberry said that the actors all wanted to do a film and hoped that they would sign on once the script was completed ("*Star Trek* Lives!" 4–6).

Roddenberry spoke too soon: A *Star Trek* movie did not get produced in 1976. But other big *Star Trek* news was coming though the galaxy.

In 1976, once again due to a letter-writing campaign from *Star Trek* fans, NASA named the first orbiter of the Space Shuttle system after the *Enterprise*. In March 1976, a flyer began circulating asking *Trek* fans to write to President Gerald Ford to encourage him to attend the unveiling of the new shuttle and christen it with the name *Enterprise*. The flyer called readers to action by stating, "This is the beginning of making the *Star Trek* Dream a reality. ... Do you want to be a participant ... or do you merely want to observe others pass you by, while they reach for the future?" ("The *Enterprise* Needs Your Help").

A Piece of the Action #39 implied that someone within NASA came to Roddenberry about the naming possibility stating,

> If there has been enough support, and the new shuttle is named after the "Big E," then there will be all kinds of *Star Trek* tie-ins. So, the christening will tie in both the past and the future. When Dick Hoagland [NASA] approached Gene Roddenberry with the possibilities, GR was amazed, thought fast, and finally came up with "Well, I can give the president a Flight Deck Certificate!" [Walker].

Despite the fanzine's claim, Dick Hoagland did not work for NASA in any capacity. He was a CBS News science advisor during the Apollo program (1968–1971). Interestingly, Hoagland was also the originator and publisher of many conspiracy theories involving NASA and alien civilizations. A 2008 NASA report credited him as the originator of the letter-writing campaign to name the shuttle *Enterprise* ("NASA-Wide Survey"). According to a September 9, 1976, Associated Press article,

> [NASA] had suggested the name of "The *Constitution*" and had even planned to unveil the shuttle orbiter on Sept. 17, 1976, Constitution Day. But *Star Trek* fans initiated a letter-writing campaign to President Ford to name the shuttle for the starship *Enterprise* in the televised science fiction drama. The show has been out of production for years, but reruns are popular. Mr. Ford did not refer to the letters, but White House sources said that he overruled NASA officials after the letter-writing campaign ["A New Space Craft Is Named *Enterprise*"].

The U.S. Navy has had a number of ships named the *Enterprise* throughout its history, and *Enterprise* was the name of one of the first reconnaissance balloons used by the Union Army during the Civil War. This caused a lot of speculation on whether the letter-writing campaign was the real driving force behind the naming of the shuttle. Two declassified Ford White House documents revealed that the letters did play a role in the decision. William F. Gorog, deputy director of economic policy, wrote a memo to President Ford on September 3, 1967:

> NASA has not announced a name as of yet for the shuttle, and they are holding this announcement until your meeting with Fletcher. Dr. Fletcher is not averse to the name *Enterprise* for the space shuttle, and I suggest that you ask that it be so named for the following reasons:
> - NASA has received hundreds of thousands of letters from the space-oriented *Star Trek* group asking that the name *Enterprise* be given to the craft. This group comprises millions of individuals who are deeply interested in our space program.
> - The name *Enterprise* is tied in with the system on which the Nation's economic structure is built.
> - Use of the name would provide a substantial human interest appeal to the rollout ceremonies scheduled for this month in California, where the aeronautical industry is of vital importance [Gorog].

On September 7, 1976, Jim Conner, White House staff secretary and Cabinet secretary, compiled a memo with comments and recommendations for the space shuttle's name from White House staff members. Jim Cannon, assistant to the president of the United States for foreign affairs, seemed enthusiastic about naming the shuttle the *Enterprise*: "It seems to me *Enterprise* is an excellent name. ... It would be personally gratifying to several million followers of the television show *Star Trek*, one of the most dedicated constituencies in the country. Moreover, the name *Enterprise* is a hallowed Navy tradition."

White House counsel Phil Buchen and National Security advisor Brent Scowcroft concurred with the recommendation. Jack Marsh, assistant secretary of defense, stated, "I have no objection to this selection of a name; however, I am not enthusiastic about the rationale for the selection. *Enterprise* is a famous name for vessels since the early days of the Republic. I think that is a far better reason than appealing to a TV fad" (Conner).

President Ford officially named the shuttle "The *Enterprise*" and, although he was not in attendance to christen the new shuttle as it was originally hoped, Roddenberry, Nimoy, Kelley, Takei, Doohan, Nichols and Koenig were present when the ship rolled off the assembly line at Rockwell's Air Force Plant 42, Site 1, Palmdale, California, on September 17, 1976. In photos, Roddenberry and the cast members look properly excited.

Star Trek's popularity in syndication, the growing fan base, and the *Star Wars*–inspired popularity of space movies led to Paramount finally producing and releasing *Star Trek: The Motion Picture* (1979). It was the first of six *Star Trek* movies starring the original series cast, between 1979 and 1991; the others were *Star Trek II: The Wrath of Khan* (1982), *Star Trek III: The Search for Spock* (1984), *Star Trek IV: The Voyage Home* (1986), *Star Trek V: The Final Frontier* (1989) and *Star Trek VI: The Undiscovered Country* (1991).

The original series remained popular in syndication. In 1986, *The New York Times* wrote:

> [N]obody expected much success when *Star Trek* was syndicated. ... Certainly, no one expected that, in 1986, 17 years after it was placed in syndication, it would be listed by the A.C. Nielsen Co. as No. 1, the most watched show in syndication. But, freed from the tyranny of

being broadcast everywhere at 8:30 p.m. on Thursday, *Star Trek* found a welcome in the late afternoon in one city, in the early evening or late night in another [Harmetz].

Nichelle Nichols made her final appearance as Uhura in *Star Trek: The Animated Series*, but others stayed aboard the *Enterprise* for many years to come. Majel Barrett voiced her character, Christine Chapel, in *The Animated Series* and appeared in *Star Trek: The Motion Picture* and *Star Trek IV*. DeForest Kelley made his final appearance as Dr. Leonard "Bones" McCoy in *Star Trek VI*. George Takei played in all six original *Star Trek* movies and his character Sulu was even promoted to captain in *Star Trek VI*.

In 1994, a new cast enlisted for *Star Trek: The Next Generation* [*TNG*]. *TNG*, like the original series, was featured both on TV and in the movies. Shatner as Captain Kirk, Doohan as "Scotty" and Koenig as Chekov made their final appearances as their respective characters in the first *TNG* film, *Star Trek Generations* (1994).

In total, eight variations of the *Star Trek* franchise made it to TV after the original series. In film, the *Star Trek* franchise was rebooted in 2009 into an alternative timeline of the original series. Leonard Nimoy, who reprised his role as Mr. Spock in the franchise, was the only original series cast member to appear in *Star Trek* (2009) and *Star Trek: Into Darkness* (2013), where he was known as Spock Prime.

It's About Time

The best way to describe *It's About Time* is "Prehistoric *Gilligan's Island*."

Like other Sherwood Schwartz–produced shows such as *Gilligan's Island* and *The Brady Bunch*, *It's About Time* described its premise in the opening theme. Astronauts Hector (Jack Mullaney) and Mac (Frank Aletter) land on what is seemingly an exotic planet but similar to Earth in atmosphere and gravity. But after observing cavemen and dinosaurs, the astronauts realize they *are* on Earth: They had broken the time barrier and went back approximately a million years. The cave people the astronauts run into speak a primitive form of English, and soon Hector and Mac become involved with their lives. Notable events included rescuing a young caveman from a dinosaur attack, teaching cave people how to use a slingshot, showing cavemen the proper courtship of women, and introducing them to the concept of the birthday.

At the time, Mullaney was best known for his role as Professor in *South Pacific* (1958) and Igor in *Dr. Goldfoot and the Bikini Machine* (1965). Character actor Frank Aletter was married to Lee Meriwether and appeared on episodes of *12 O'Clock High*, *The Twilight Zone* and *The Lucy Show*.

One of the cave people, Shag, was played by Imogene Coca, best known for playing on Sid Caesar's *Your Show of Shows* (1950–1954) and for the movie *National Lampoon's Vacation* (1983). The other main cave-person, Gronk, was played by night club comedian Joe E. Ross, memorable as Sgt. Rupert Ritzik on *The Phil Silvers Show* aka *Sergeant Bilko* aka *You'll Never Get Rich* (1955–1959) and as Officer Toody on *Car 54 Where Are You?* (1961–1963).

Production of *It's About Time* was first announced in November 1965 and it was quickly picked up by CBS ("Bumper Crop" 29). Viewers got their first look at the series on CBS's 1966–1967 Fall Preview show, *You'll See Stars*. It was then covered in *TV Guide*'s 1966–67 Fall Preview issue: "It's about dinosaur hunts, mastodon steaks, evil spirits and cavemen dragging cavewomen around by the hair. It's about eternal verities.

(Caveman: 'Man say, woman do.' Astronaut: 'I wonder how we let that custom get away.') It's about 30 minutes long" ("Fall Preview").

It's About Time's backdrops and sets could be easily recognized by fans of *Gilligan's Island* and the stop-motion dinosaurs were leftovers from the science fiction films *The Beast of Hollow Mountain* (1956) and *Dinosaurus!* (1960).

On September 19, 1966, the syndication service Newspaper Enterprise Association presented an interview with Mullaney, who stated,

> In the pilot, everyone was trying too hard to be funny. I play a goofy astronaut. ... There has to be a basis in reality because I am playing an astronaut. But if you see a dinosaur, even if you're an astronaut, you scream, don't you? ... I'm a sweater, and someone has to get inside my helmet and wipe the visor because it keeps fogging up. And now we have those damn caveman furs to wear. I like clothes. I feel funny if I'm not wearing them, because I'm kind of skinny ["*Star Trek* Real Science Fiction"].

The first episode, "And Then I Wrote 'Happy Birthday to You'" (September 11, 1966) was the highest-rated show on network TV in the 7:30 p.m. time slot with an Arbitron rating of 20.9 with a 47 share of the audience ("Numbers Game" 59). The show was up against reruns of NBC's *The Wonderful World of Disney* and ABC's *Voyage to the Bottom of the Sea*. Despite the high ratings, critics published many scathing reviews:

> "One of the silliest shows of the season."—Bob Hull, *Los Angeles Herald-Examiner*
>
> "*Gilligan's Island* looks good now."—Jack Gould, *New York Times*
>
> "I kept waiting for [it] to start but the show never came."—Bernie Harrison, *Washington Evening Star*
>
> "An arrogant insult to everyone over the age of 5."—Hal Humphrey, *Los Angeles Times*
>
> "Momentarily funny."—Bob Williams, *New York Post*
>
> "A wild comedy ... [T]he jokes are terrible."—Harriet Van Horne, *New York World Journal Tribune*
>
> "I suspect that [it] heads the first annual casualty list."—Ann Hodges, *Houston Chronicle*
>
> "Corny ... but if *Gilligan's Island* can make it big, this one should also."—Fairfax Nisbet, *Dallas Morning News* ("Critics Views" 62)

Although *It's About Time* was blasted by critics, it managed to maintain respectable ratings for the first several weeks, even beating out favorites such as *The Andy Griffith Show*, *The Lawrence Welk Show* and *Gomer Pyle, U.S.M.C.* ("The Latest Form Sheet" 68). But a downward spiral soon began. Just a few weeks later, on October 17, *It's About Time* fell to the 39th most-watched show, according to Arbitron Ratings ("The Ratings: A Photo" 68). The next week, the industry magazine *Broadcasting* reported that "the future of *It's About Time* is suspect and some changes may be forthcoming" ("Second Season to Exceed" 56).

CBS was looking to cancel the show, but producer Schwartz proposed several changes and the network agreed. The changes came three months later, after a continuing ratings slide. Schwartz felt the caveman motif was starting to get stale and limited story potential, so he planned on bringing the cave people to the 20th century.

In a December 28, 1966, Associated Press article, movie-television writer Bob Thomas reported Schwartz stated that, although it was difficult to analyze his own show to make the appropriate changes, he came to three conclusions about what should be changed: the storylines, dialogue and color. Schwartz believed that "giving cavemen the opportunity to react to modern conveniences and situations, rather than astronauts reacting to prehistoric storylines," would give the writers opportunity for new storylines. Having all the characters with the exception of the cave people speak normally was easier for the viewer, and it expanded opportunities for dialogue. Maybe most importantly, bringing the show to the 20th century "expanded the color pallet" because when the show was set in prehistoric times, "the look of the show, especially in color, is monotonous—caves, trees, dirt streets, mangy-looking furs" (Thomas 24).

On January 22, 1967, during the 19th episode of *It's About Time*, astronauts got into their spaceship to once again break the time barrier, but this time with their Stone Age pals. The cave people were now thrown into modern situations, such as signing up for gym memberships, joining the Army, going to school, starting a rock'n'roll band, and getting evicted from an apartment. The show's theme song was even updated to reflect the switch.

Despite the changes, CBS cancelled the show, only producing six new episodes after making the leap to contemporary 1967. In the February 23, 1967, *New York Times*, George Gent announced *It's About Time*'s cancellation (Gent "Marshal Dillon"). The last new episode, "The Stowaway," aired on April 2, but was produced before the jump to the 20th century and took place in the Stone Age rather than in 1967.

Schwartz later admitted that one problem the show had was being up against the popular *Walt Disney's Wonderful World of Color*, the 19th highest-rated show of the season. Another problem was the show's concept. Schwartz stated,

> I did *It's About Time* two years too soon. Comedy by its very nature is satire. Drama doesn't have to be. [Satire] has to have a precursor. It has to have something that you're satirizing. Two years after *It's About Time* was the first time that we walked on the moon. … We were doing a satire on man walking on the moon. [Man walking on the moon] hadn't happened yet ["Sherwood Schwartz"; Brooks and Marsh].

Voyage to the Bottom of the Sea

Producer Irwin Allen had three science fiction shows on the air during the 1966–1967 season: *Voyage to the Bottom of the Sea, Lost in Space* and *The Time Tunnel*. Prior to coming to TV, Allen worked for RKO and Warner Brothers as a producer. In 1960, he moved to 20th Century–Fox where he directed *The Lost World* (1960), *Voyage to the Bottom of the Sea* (1961) and *Five Weeks in a Balloon* (1962). Allen quickly became known as the King of Special Effects. Allen's actors sometimes felt that he was too focused on the effects and not focused on *them*. *Lost in Space* actor Mark Goddard later joked, "[Allen] loved special effects … hated actors."

By 1964, 20th Century–Fox was focusing more attention on television so Allen changed gears and began work on a TV show based on his film *Voyage to the Bottom of the Sea* (Royal "Time Bothered Him" 13; Marta Kristen and Mark Goddard).

Allen first fell in love with the sea when, as a child, he first witnessed an epidemic of whooping cough sweep through New York City. At the time it was believed that the change in pressure from going up or down in the water would relieve the cough. Allen recalled that he, and hundreds of other kids, were taken to the Brooklyn Navy Yard and put in a submarine to help with the cough. Allen did not remember if the submarine ride had any effect on him or any other kid, but it was his first memory of the ocean (Witbeck "*Voyage* Has High Adventure").

Voyage to the Bottom of the Sea used "most of the picture props, sets, miniatures and underwater gimmicks—valued at $2 million by creator Irwin Allen." Without the existing sets and props, Allen's new weekly TV show would not have been affordable (Witbeck "*Voyage* Has High Adventure").

Production was nothing less than impressive. Critic Charles Witbeck wrote that Allen

> has four separate units shooting at once on location in spots like Catalina Island for underwater sequences, and he has two stunt units going full-time as well. A 20th Century–Fox stage holding the innards of the atomic sub is almost like a fancy toy store. There are banks of dials for the sub men to concentrate upon, and all the dials light up at one time or another. The computer companies would be proud of the lighting effects even if the dials don't mean anything [Witbeck "Dials Light Up" 4].

The hour-long, black-and-white *Voyage to the Bottom of the Sea* debuted on September 14, 1964. The show sailed into the color world after one season, making it the first color prime time live-action science fiction show. (The cartoon series *The Jetsons* has the distinction of being the first science fiction show in color to air on prime time; it debuted in the fall of 1962.)

Voyage's introduction laid out the series basic premise: "This is the *Seaview*, the most extraordinary submarine in all the seven seas. Its public image is that of an instrument of marine research. In actuality, it is the mightiest weapon afloat and is secretly assigned the most dangerous missions against the enemies of mankind."

The *Seaview*'s main crew included Admiral Harriman Nelson (Richard Basehart), Captain Lee Crane (David Hedison), Lieutenant Commander Chip Morton (Robert Dowdell), Seaman Kowalski (Del Monroe) and Chief Petty Officer Curly Jones (Henry Kulky). In its first season, it aired on Mondays at 7:30 (Witbeck "*Voyage* Has High Adventure"). According to Charles Witbeck,

> Eight-year-old minds will certainly buy this heady stuff and homework may be junked. ... It's clear to all that *Voyage* is a kids' show, filled with stern men concentrating on dials, conversing in thin-lipped tones, using dialogue sprinkled with pseudo-scientific jargon. ... The high adventure comic book material has come to the TV screen, produced with care and effort [Witbeck "*Voyage* Has High Adventure"].

Starting in the second season, bumpers and promos proudly declared that the show was now "In Color." Star Basehart, approved of the switch: "The move to color was right. So what if it takes a little longer to light and is a little hotter working. Ours *is* a color show if there was one. Our special effects really warrant it" (Thompson "Basehart Pleased").

That season, the show moved to Sundays at 7:00 and added a yellow flying submarine to expand storylines and keep the show fresh. "Now we can get ashore more," said Basehart. "It's no longer a matter of the cast going into a state of shock at the sight of a woman." And the cast clearly wanted more women featured. So producers slowly added more women guest stars. Basehart recalled his scenes in the second episode of the

To promote the television series, Milton Bradley released the *Voyage to the Bottom of the Sea* board game in 1964 (courtesy Peter Biscontini Law Firm Media Library).

second season, "Time Bomb," with actress Ina Balin: "[She was] very good in the kissing department" (Thompson "Basehart Pleased").

David Hedison wanted even more women on the show: "You might think that in a series based on Navy life, there would be a few trim young things in uniform. But the only Waves we've had in our series so far are the watery kind" ("*Voyage* Lacking" 20).

Although the show had action, adventure, good-looking women and special effects, it was in rough waters ratings-wise. In the 1966–1967 season, it went up against *Lassie* on CBS and the *NBC News/Bell Telephone Hour* on alternating weeks in the first half-hour and then the very popular *Walt Disney's Wonderful World of Color*, the 19th highest-rated show that year (Brooks and Marsh).

In its first two seasons, *Voyage* did feature some sci-fi and supernatural elements, but most of the episodes had more straightforward action-adventure storylines. Then in the 1966–1967 season, the show took on more "creature feature" elements. Episodes featured monsters from the ocean floor, werewolves, a mummy, mermaids, haunted submarines, alien-controlled toys, a seaweed creature and a deadly cloud. Not everyone was amused. The National Association for Better Broadcasting remarked that the show had "terrifying characters, such as monsters and werewolves," which made it inappropriate pre-bedtime viewing for young children ("Shock Appeal" 44).

TV critics felt that *Voyage* was starting to lose its potential and grew tired of the show's storylines. "[*Voyage*] has an intriguing setting and the plus factor of the excellent acting talents of Richard Basehart," wrote critic Marian Dern. But she added that the show, "once a unique sci-fi, futuristic series that had class and quality. [But] now that they've married the monster format-wise, it's a B picture version of the horde of monster pix turned out en masse years ago" (Dern "Will *Time Tunnel*" 15).

Bringing horror elements to the show was not enough to boost ratings. In four seasons, *Voyage to the Bottom of the Sea* was often one of the lowest-rated shows of the season (Brooks and Marsh; Spencer "TV's Vast" 54–55).

Voyage lasted one more season. In March 1968, ABC announced eight new shows for the upcoming 1968–1969 season and the end of nine others, including *Voyage*. It was replaced by another Irwin Allen production, *Land of the Giants* (1968–1970). The hour-long *Land of the Giants* ran for 51 episodes in two seasons (Lowry "TV Winter").

Allen went on to produce the big-budget disaster flicks *The Poseidon Adventure* (1972) and *The Towering Inferno* (1974), which earned him his most famous nickname, "The Master of Disaster."

Lost in Space

Lost in Space was described as an "Out-of-This-World Interplanetary Cliff-Hanger" by critic Don Royal. Royal also compared the show to movie serials of the 1930s and 1940s:

> Grandfather no longer has a monopoly on stories on the great old "continued next week" gaspers of an earlier era. True, the heroine won't be tied to the railroad track, but what happens in late 20th-century guise will offer just as many possibilities for excited speculation as to what comes next. *Lost in Space* is literally a "cliffhanger," one of the first prime-time television shows to use such a technique [Royal 9].

The show was also described as "*Swiss Family Robinson* in space," because of similarities to that German novel about a family shipwrecked in the East Indies.

The connection to *Swiss Family Robinson* was not coincidental. The premise of the show was lifted from a 1962 Gold Key comic, *Space Family Robinson*. The show was described as such in pre-production as early as December 1964. It's reported that Irwin Allen and CBS did not get the rights from Western Publishing, Gold Key's parent company, but later reached a settlement over the rights ("Television Pilot Program").

In the far-off year of 1997, with the Earth dangerously overcrowded, the Robinson family is selected by a worldwide computer system as the best family to embark on a mission to new planets that may support life. But Dr. Zachary Smith (Jonathan Harris), who works for an unnamed foreign government, attempts to sabotage their spacecraft, the *Jupiter 2*—and then finds himself trapped aboard. Soon he, too, is lost in space.

Each week the cast were at odds with a new monster, creature or disaster. And there were internal struggles amongst the group—most notably between Dr. Smith and the rest of the group.

June Lockhart was cast as biochemist, wife and mother Maureen Robinson. Prior to *Lost in Space*, Lockhart was best known for her role on *Lassie* where she played somber farm woman Ruth Martin. Lockhart stated that after she left *Lassie* "I looked around for another series. They called me up and said, 'We have a *Space Family Robinson* you might like.' It was so imaginative and such a commercial property that I was delighted. They sort of cast the rest of it around me." Although again playing a mother role, as on *Lassie*, Lockhart traded in her matronly drab farm dress for a form-fitting space uniform. "The suits are very uncomfortable," she said, "They're standard racing drivers' suits, canvas-covered in aluminum and fine plastic sprayed on top for fireproofing. They're horribly hot, and my suit is so tight and fits so well I can't sit down." She added, "Of course, the men's suits are loose, but they wanted mine to be more, well—attractive."

After the 1966–1967 season, Lockhart had a change of heart: "In *Lassie* I was allowed to wear only gingham gowns and aprons, and no one knew I had a body under those aprons. But in *Lost in Space* I wear form-fitting silver lamé jumpsuits while I float around the wild blue yonder. Those women of the future do know how to dress" (Mead 10B; Humphrey "Out of the Air" 15; "June Lockhart Is Still").

Lockhart was cast opposite handsome Guy Williams as astrophysicist Dr. John Robinson. Williams was best known for starring in Disney's *Zorro* (1957–1959), a role that he feared he would be stuck with his entire life—but he broke free thanks to *Lost in Space*. When *Zorro* was on the air, Disney was sued by ABC over the handling of the series. Williams recalled, "The suit was in court for two years and meanwhile I wasn't allowed to do anything. I felt like a kept man; all I did was collect my ever-increasing salary. During that time, I had no chance to prove I could do anything else besides Zorro." Williams later made *The Prince and the Pauper* (1962) for Disney and three films in Europe, then landed the *Lost in Space* role (Thomas "Batman, Zorro" 10).

The Robinson children were Judy (Marta Kristen), Penny (Angela Cartwright) and Will (Billy Mumy). The Robinsons were joined by Dr. Smith, Major Don West (Mark Goddard) and a Class M3 Model B9 General Utility Non-Theorizing Environmental Control Robot simply known as the Robot (piloted by Bob May and voiced by the show's narrator Dick Tufeld). The Robot was created by Bob Kinoshita, who also created *Forbidden Planet*'s (1956) Robby the Robot and *Tobor the Great* (1954). The Robot took special care of young Will Robinson. Whenever Will was in trouble, the Robot would famously call out, "Danger! Danger, Will Robinson!"

Despite being a dastardly character, Dr. Smith quickly became a fan favorite, despite one Los Angeles TV critic calling Jonathan Harris "the worst actor of the year." Harris laughed off the criticism: "I'm playing this role with my tongue so far in my cheek it hurts to talk. It's all spoof. I just can't understand a critic trying to take part seriously. I'm having a ball playing Smith, he's such a nut. And I'm not really overplaying him, he's just over-extended. He's such a pompous ass but he's really a simple soul who is a dreadful coward" (Johnson "Jonathan Harris" 28).

Billy Mumy recalled that Harris helped create the character of Dr. Smith. Originally Smith was strictly a villain, but he had to learn to live with the Robinsons in order to survive, and he made his character a comedic one. Mumy said that Harris "single-handedly created the character of Dr. Smith. He knew from the very beginning that this snarling, nefarious, spy-saboteur would be old quick—that the audience would want to see him killed off ... so he very quickly started turning the character into a comedic Dr. Smith that we love to hate." Mumy and Harris worked well together and had a lot of scenes together, because they practiced lines together after Harris had rewritten his part. They usually did scenes in one take ("Bill Mumy").

Irwin Allen produced an hour-long black and white pilot episode, "No Place to Hide," which helped sell the show to CBS. *Lost in Space* debuted in black and white on September 15, 1965, and was rumored to have been picked up that season by CBS over *Star Trek*. Brand-new CBS-TV president Jack Schneider indicated that the show could "hit in a big way or miss in a big way." He later added, "In my position, one has to take chances" ("Schneider Comes On" 61).

Lost in Space was one of the last four shows to debut in black in white on prime time TV, along with *I Dream of Jeannie*, *F Troop* and *Convoy*. Scenes from the show's unaired pilot episode were reused in several episodes in the first season.

Most critics did not appreciate *Lost in Space*.

"Has to be seen to be disbelieved."—Clay Gowran, *Chicago Tribune*

"Looked like the poor man's *Outer Limits*."—Louis R. Cedrone, Jr., *Baltimore Evening Sun*

"Pure grade B hokum."—John Horn, *New York Herald-Tribune*

"*Lost in Space* … should be."—Jack O'Brian, *New York Journal American* ("How Critics See" 34)

On top of poor critical reviews, *Lost in Space* had out-of-this-world competition in the first half-hour of its hour-long time slot: *Batman*. In the winter of 1966, *Batman* was red hot. But Paul Zastupnevich, assistant to the *Lost in Space* producer, had confidence in the series and predicted the end of Bat-Mania: "We have no doubt about *Lost in Space* surviving against *Batman*. … Strange as it may seem, our space villains are quite realistic compared to these comic book characters. We may be far-out, but we do relate to current space ideas" (Witbeck "Small Fry Love" 8).

When the show switched to color for the 1966–1967 season, some changes had to be made. Mark Goddard stated, "[A]ll the colors came out … they brought all these plants in and they changed our outfits—they made us look like Easter Bunny outfits. [Everyone else] had beautiful uniforms, but they kept me in gray." Marta Kristen added that she felt that color of the uniforms was due to a trendy art movement. "What was happening at the time was, everything became sort of 'pop art'" (Marta Kristen and Mark Goddard).

The producers wanted more "imaginative monsters" so, as Zastupnevich stated, "then we can fight [*Batman*] on even terms." The episodes' storylines began to focus more on fantasy elements rather than the family struggles (Witbeck "Small Fry Love" 8).

The show's stars felt confident about going up against *Batman*. Marta Kristen stated in a summer 1966 interview, "We have a much more stable show than *Batman*. Our show is more honest" (Heisner "Most Honest Than *Batman*" 3).

The investment in color and creatures worked for CBS. Although *Lost in Space* was never one of the highest-rated shows in its four years on the air, it was very popular with kids and held its own against *The Virginian* on NBC and *Batman* in the first half-hour and *The Monroes* in the second half-hour on ABC. The show even received an Emmy nomination for Cinematography—Special Photographic Effects (Brooks and Marsh; "Critics' Views" 60; "The Latest" 69).

By January 1967, *Lost in Space* actually started to beat out *Batman* in the ratings. In January 1967, TV critic John Heisner wrote that his two children watched *Batman* every Wednesday "with only passing concern about the many Robinson family and Dr. Smith." But soon the children were changing the channel to *Lost in Space* during commercials, and then after *Batman* ended; which eventually led to the children sticking with *Lost in Space* over *Batman*. Heisner also stated that *Lost in Space* had "recaptured most of its lost viewers" and that *Batman* has "dropped from the ranks of the sensational just a year ago, into the non-distinct middle of the pack somewhere. … No, *Lost in Space* isn't setting any ratings' worlds on fire. But it is quite well set in the safe area and is very far from being wiped out by *Batman*, as so many had predicted a year ago" ("2d Season" 51; Heisner "More Honest Than *Batman*" 3). Meanwhile, the National Association for Better Broadcasting wrote: "Frightening scenes and cliffhanger endings leave the space family in continuous peril from week to week. The program is too scary for very young children" ("Shock Appeal" 8).

Lost in Space was the 44th highest-rated show in the 1966–1967 season (Spencer

"TV's Vast" 54). It aired for one more season but was ultimately stranded after three seasons by CBS. Although no official reason was given, odds are the show was cancelled due to the same reasons *Batman* would be cancelled a year later: ratings not high enough for a show that was expensive to produce. In addition, the cliffhanger format, which *Batman* dropped after 1967, became passé. The audience was younger and lacked buying power, so sponsor and advertiser money was not as high.

According to Bill Mumy, his agent said it was a money issue that finally ended the show before the fourth season even started: "What I was told was, CBS wanted to cut the budget because the numbers weren't that great and Irwin [Allen] said, 'I'm not going to cut the budget—I can't cut the budget' and [Allen] had these other shows ... and he said, 'If you're not going to give me the money, I want then to let it go.'" So the show ended with the cast still lost in space. CBS moved *Daktari* into *Lost in Space*'s Wednesday night time slot.

Allen went on to make a more traditional *Swiss Family Robinson* TV series in 1975. *Lost in Space* was made into a feature film in 1998 with William Hurt, Matt LeBlanc, Gary Oldman and, as the voice of the Robot, Dick Tufeld. There were also cameo appearances by June Lockhart, Mark Goddard, Marta Kristen and Angela Cartwright. Although the film did well at the box office, it was almost universally panned by critics. *Lost in Space* was given a reimagining in a critically acclaimed and popular 2018 Netflix series, which gave guest roles to Bill Mumy and Angela Cartwright.

The Time Tunnel

Irwin Allen's *The Time Tunnel,* opened with a color spinning psychedelic sequence with exposition from the narrator:

> Two American scientists are lost in the swirling maze of past and future ages during the first experiments of America's greatest and most secret project: The Time Tunnel. Tony Newman and Doug Phillips now tumble helplessly towards a new and fantastic adventure somewhere along the infinite corridors of time.

Allen created the show in part due to his aversion to the concept of time, declaring, "I have always disliked the limitations of time. Clocks annoy me and I have never worn a wristwatch" (Royal "Time Bothered Him" 13).

Allen reportedly spent a million dollars on the pilot episode (Dern "Will *Time Tunnel*" 15). *The Time Tunnel* was seen as the one Allen show that was geared more toward an adult audience. TV critic Marian Dern wrote, "Only time ... will tell if *Time Tunnel* keeps its own potential promise or descends ... into a show about which even a representative of that often referred to '12-year-old mind' was heard to say recently: 'It's just too stupid to watch anymore'" (Dern "Will *Time Tunnel*" 15).

The Time Tunnel was set in the not far-off year of 1968.

Tony (James Darren) and Doug (Robert Colbert) have been working on a government-funded Time Tunnel experiment, Project Tic-Toc, which used an hourglass as a symbol of both time travel and time running out. They volunteered to be sent into the Time Tunnel to keep the government from pulling the plug on the expensive operation. The two men found themselves lost in time in an hour-long ABC adventure series seen each Friday at 8:00.

The Time Tunnel also featured three Project Tic-Toc scientists: Lt. General

Heywood Kirk (Whit Bissell), electronics expert Dr. Raymond Swain (John Zaremba) and Dr. Ann MacGregor (Lee Meriwether). Bissell is best known for his roles in the 1957 horror movies *I Was a Teenage Werewolf* and *I Was a Teenage Frankenstein*. For 14 years, Zaremba portrayed the Hills Brothers Coffee Broker in a series of commercials. Meriwether played the villainous Catwoman in the 1966 *Batman* movie.

Each week, Tony and Doug found themselves in a life-or-death predicament somewhere in time, like being placed on the deck of the *Titanic*, at the Battle of Gettysburg, in the French penal colony of Devil's Island in 1852. They also needed to be careful not to alter the course of history—like when they were transported to Hawaii in 1941 and Tony could not warn his own father of the coming Pearl Harbor invasion in which his father would die. Of course, the scientists back in the Project Tic-Toc lab in 1968 would find a way to rescue the main characters at the end of every episode, sending them back through the Time Tunnel to another point in history.

Footage of pirates on ships, armies fighting in the desert, hordes of men on horseback, volcanic eruptions, jets in the sky, etc., gave the show an expensive look and feel. However much of the footage was taken directly from 20th Century–Fox's stock footage library, and other footage came from MGM, Disney, Columbia and Republic at the request of Allen (Grams "*The Time Tunnel*").

The multi-colored opening and closing sequences were greatly inspired by the op-art movement, art that gave the perception of movement, which was very popular in the 1960s (Seitz).

The series was scored by composer John Williams, credited as Johnny Williams, who went on to score films such as *Jaws* (1975), *Star Wars* (1977), *Close Encounters of the Third Kind* (1977) and *Raiders of the Lost Ark* (1981).

The night before the show hit the airwaves, *The Time Tunnel* was screened at the 24th annual World Science Fiction Convention in Cleveland, where it received a very favorable reaction from science fiction fans (Royal "Time Bothered Him" 13).

That season, ABC aired several of their new shows a week earlier than other shows' season premieres. *The Time Tunnel*'s premiere episode was preceded by the first episode of the highly anticipated *The Green Hornet*. *The New York Times* gave it a negative review: "*Time Tunnel* may have better luck when it looks into the future and can take narrative refuge in the plausible climax of justifiable uncertainty" (Gould "Milton Berle"). Other critics felt differently:

> "Fine acting and a highly professional gave it all a gloss of wonder."—Harriet Van Horne, *New York World Journal Tribune*
>
> "An ingenious scene-changer for a dramatic-history series."—Terrence O'Flaherty, *San Francisco Chronicle*
>
> "Rates as a superior effort in the science fiction realm."—C.J. Skreen, *Seattle Times*
>
> "Provocative possibilities."—Dwight Newton, *San Francisco Examiner*
>
> "A good deal more promising than many."—John Voorhees, *Seattle Post-Intelligencer* ("Critics' Views" 62)

In addition to good ratings, *The Time Tunnel* was one of the most recognizable new shows with the TV viewing audience, second only to *Star Trek*, especially with viewers aged 6–16 ("Movies are Favorites" 74).

For a show that was popular with younger audiences, made at a time when TV programs were willing to put their show's name on anything everything and, there was a surprising lack of merchandise released. There was a board game where the objective was to be the first player to time travel through prehistoric, medieval, present and future time periods; a *Time Tunnel* novel from Pyramid Books (actually a time travel novel originally published two years earlier, and rewritten to become a *Time Tunnel* novel); two Gold Key comic books, and a View-Master reel highlighting exciting scenes from the show. A blue-colored vinyl LP of the *Time Tunnel* story "Adventure in the Lost World" was released in Japan.

The Time Tunnel got off to a great start, but Friday night was not the best night for a show with more grownup storylines. Although the show may have been popular with youngsters, older teens and young adults were not typically home to watch TV. Also, *The Time Tunnel* was not a show that would be watched by the whole family: The older the audience, the less they were inclined to watch it ("Movies are Favorites" 74).

After several episodes, the show became too formulaic and predictable: Tony and Doug would find themselves in a historical period and get into a dangerous situation, only to be saved by the scientists back in 1968, and sent into another point in time.

The Time Tunnel was cancelled after only 30 episodes. Perhaps if it had appealed more to its younger audience base, like Irwin Allen's *Lost in Space* and *Voyage to the Bottom of the Sea*, the show may have lost favor with critics but lasted on television.

Much like the show itself, there was not a happy ending for the on-screen characters. At the end of the 30th and final episode, Newman and Phillips found themselves back on the deck of the *Titanic*, where they were in the first episode, signaling to the audience that the duo were in a never-ending loop in the Time Tunnel.

Even though it lasted only one season, *The Time Tunnel* must have made an impression on some. After it was cancelled, *The Time Tunnel*'s special effects photographer, L.B. Abbott, won an Emmy in 1967 for Individual Achievements in Cinematography for his *Time Tunnel* work. The later TV shows *Quantum Leap* (1989–1993) and *Sliders* (1995–2000) were similar to *The Time Tunnel*. There was an attempt to remake *The Time Tunnel* in 2002. Although a pilot episode was made, it never aired, and the show was not picked up by a network.

The Invaders

Nearly two years before its debut, *The Invaders* was first announced by ABC in November 1965. At the time, ABC was "reluctant to discuss its theme" and only announced a title ("Bumper Crop" 28). *The Invaders* was given the green light by ABC in mid–September 1966 and began filming on October 10 ("ABC OK's" 76).

The show was the brainchild of producer Larry Cohen, who was 30 when it debuted but already a TV veteran. Cohen got his start in TV at age 22 by submitting scripts to NBC's anthology series *Kraft Television Theater* in 1958 and by 1966 he had an impressive resumé, writing episodes for *The Rat Patrol*, *The Fugitive* and *The Defenders*. In addition, he created and produced the Western *Branded* (1965–1966) and the World War II spy series *Blue Light* (1966). Those shows were not long for the TV world: They were cancelled before the fall of 1966.

Cohen was disappointed over their cancellation but looked forward to his new show. Known for being a fiercely independent producer, he was thankful that ABC had his back—especially financially. He confessed, "I'd rather have a network own a piece of my package than not. After all, I'm not financially big enough to produce a costly TV series today without a larger company to absorb the shock" (Gardella 11). Production was overseen by famed producer Quinn Martin, who that year also produced *The Fugitive, 12 O'Clock High* and *The F.B.I.*

The Invaders plot felt like a fever dream. Cohen described the show thusly: "One man, the show's hero, is the only person on Earth who's aware our planet is being infiltrated by people from another planet ... they're the vanguard of a big invasion being planned. And naturally, when he tries to warn people, they think he's flaky" (Gardella 11).

The opening narration:

> *The Invaders!* A Quinn Martin Production. Starring Roy Thinnes as architect David Vincent. *The Invaders*, alien beings from a dying planet. Their destination: the Earth. Their purpose: to make it their world. David Vincent has seen them. For him, it began one lost night on a lonely country road, looking for a shortcut that he never found. It began with a closed deserted diner, and a man too long without sleep to continue his journey. It began with the landing of a craft from another galaxy. Now David Vincent knows that the Invaders are here, that they have taken human form. Somehow he must convince a disbelieving world that the nightmare has already begun.

Roy Thinnes had starred on the daytime soap opera *General Hospital* for two seasons starting in 1963, and the prime time drama *The Long Hot Summer* (1965–1966). "I've been told that fan mail gave me this third chance [*The Invaders*] and I'm grateful, believe me" (Johnson "Roy Thinnes"). Before the show debuted on January 10, 1967, Thinnes looked forward to playing the role of a man who knows the truth about aliens invading Earth: "It's challenging to say the least. There will be no time for comedy" (Johnson "Roy Thinnes").

David Vincent learns of certain characteristics the aliens have that could give away their identity, such as lack of pulse and lack of dexterity in certain fingers. Vincent also learns that the alien invaders were attempting to deplete oxygen levels on Earth to make the planet more inhabitable for the alien race. Each week a new guest star also learned the truth about the invaders; a group called the Believers formed, and ultimately met with David Vincent. Guest stars included Roddy McDowall, Kevin McCarthy, Dawn Wells, Gene Hackman, Peter Graves, Andrew Prine, Ed Begley, Michael Constantine and Norman Fell.

Although ABC reportedly held "particularly high hopes" for the show, critics were not convinced:

> "ABC-TV has another weekly hour of filler."—Rick Du Brow, United Press International

> "Silly ... and plodding."—George Gent, *The New York Times*

> "The show fascinated at first, then dissolved in its own credibility gap."—Dwight Newton, *San Francisco Examiner*

> "Carbon Copy TV."—Clay Gowran, *Chicago Tribune*

But the reviews for *The Invaders* were not all negative:

"Weird and, in a way, wonderful."—Donald Kirkley, *Baltimore Sun*

"May have a winner here."—Kay Gardella, *New York Daily News*

"Tautly and crisply put together."—Julia Inman, *Indianapolis Star*

"A fascinating new ... chiller that is certain to catch on as quickly as *The Fugitive*."—Terrence O'Flaherty, *San Francisco Chronicle*

"Spooky, kooky, and, for my taste, absolutely divine."—Harriet Van Horne, *New York World Journal Tribune* ("2d Season" 50; "How the Critics" 51)

After two weeks on the air, *The Invaders* failed to win in the ratings vs. CBS's *Red Skelton Hour* and NBC's *Tuesday Night at the Movies* but it was reported that "several agency programmers felt *The Invaders* held 'the most promise for sustained popularity'" ("CBS Edges" 60). And after three weeks it was reported that *The Invaders* "continued to score several points higher than its lead-in show, *Combat!*" ("Second Season Loses" 60).

Although it was reported that networks were disappointed in the viewership with most mid-season replacement shows, three shows did "increase audience shares over previous audience levels in the same time period": *Dragnet* on NBC, *Mr. Terrific* on CBS and *The Invaders* on ABC ("CBS Edges" 60).

The show was renewed for the 1967–1968 season, after it scored decent ratings (the 39th highest-rated show of the season), and it went against *The Red Skelton Hour* and the last half-hour of the new variety show *Jerry Lewis Show* and the first half hour of *Tuesday Night at the Movies* on NBC (Spencer "TV's Vast" 54; "ABC-TV Sets" 114).

Although *The Invaders* increased the audience share by 14 percent in new prime time periods by January 1968, the network was still undecided if they would renew the show for another season ("ABC-TV Moves Up" 9; "QM to Make ABC" 43).

By late February, ABC executives cancelled *The Invaders*, along with *Cowboy in Africa*, *The Rat Patrol*, *N.Y.P.D.*, *The Second Hundred Years*, *Off to See the Wizard* and *Voyage to the Bottom of the Sea*. *The Invaders* was replaced by *It Takes a Thief* ("Networks Start Race" 28).

The show did not have an official conclusion. In the last episode, "Inquisition," David Vincent destroyed an alien transmitter, thwarting an incoming alien invasion.

The Invaders may be the perfect example of a show that did not succeed but for all intents and purposes should have. Like *The Green Hornet*, storylines were marketed and geared towards younger adults but, unlike *The Green Hornet*, *The Invaders* had a perfect time slot for that age demographic: Tuesday at 8:30. Also, the storylines stayed geared to younger adults and did not get silly or over-the-top, like *Voyage to the Bottom of the Sea* and episodes of *Star Trek*.

The Invaders was regularly routed in the ratings by *The Red Skelton Hour*, but the two shows were not in direct competition in terms of audience demographics. Red Skelton was a veteran of vaudeville, radio, film and television and had viewers who were typically older than those of *The Invaders*. *The Invaders* also aired at a time when interest in space, UFOs and aliens was at an all-time high.

After *The Invaders*' cancellation, Larry Cohen produced and directed the exploitation horror films *It's Alive* (1974), *God Told Me To* (1976), *Q: The Winged Serpent* (1982) and *The Stuff* (1985) and continued to write for both film and TV. *The Invaders* returned in 1995 as a two-part Sci-Fi Channel mini-series starring Scott Bakula as believer Nolan Wood and Thinnes as David Vincent. The mini-series finally gave the saga a proper conclusion.

Chapter Six

World War II

By September 1966, it had been 21 years since the official end of World War II, but based on the fall TV lineup, it was clear that Americans could not get enough of World War II adventures. Five shows revolving around World War II were beaming into American living rooms: *Combat!, Jericho, 12 O'Clock High, Hogan's Heroes* and *The Rat Patrol*.

In addition to the shows that made the network airwaves, a number of pilots were produced, but ultimately never picked up: *Locate, Pursue and Destroy, Assault* and *Off We Go* ("Bumper Crops" 27–32).

Combat!

Television programs in the 1950s all but ignored the subject of World War II, but 1962 brought three World War II–themed series: *Combat!, The Gallant Men* and *McHale's Navy*. The year also brought three other military-themed shows, *Don't Call Me Charlie, McKeever and the Colonel* and *Ensign O'Toole*. By the 1966–1967 season, only *Combat!* Remained.

The hour-long ABC drama depicted a U.S. Army platoon's trek across Europe to defeat the Nazis following the D-Day invasion. It starred Rick Jason as 2nd Lieutenant Gil Hanley and Vic Morrow as Sergeant Chip Saunders. The show debuted in black and white on October 2, 1962, and aired on Tuesdays at 7:30; it kept that time slot its entire run. In the 1962–1963 season, *Combat!* battled *Gunsmoke* (the tenth most popular show that season), *Laramie* and Aaron Spelling's short-lived anthology show *The Lloyd Bridges Show*.

In its first three seasons, *Combat!* was not scoring high ratings, but advertisers felt that it was one of the best shows for reaching men 18-to-34 and this helped keep it from being cancelled. In the 1964–1965 season, the investment in *Combat!* paid off. That season, *Combat!* was the tenth highest-rated show, even beating out time slot rival *Gunsmoke* ("ABC-TV Affiliates" 104; "ABC Reveals" 59; "What kind of 'Top 10'" 15; "Millions at ABC" 9; Brooks and Marsh). When ABC and the show's sponsors brought *Combat!* back for the 1966–1967 season, it was now in color ("On the Networks" 119; "Affiliates Hear ABC-TV's" 86).

Combat! was one of the many shows that switched to color in time for the Fall 1966 season, but it did not change much in terms of storylines. The introduction did get a makeover, now exclaiming that the show was "In Color!"

That season, *Combat!* averaged an 18.8 rating. But most of the show's viewing audience was not the World War II generation. Instead, *Combat!* was mostly being watched by the World War II generation's children in the 49-and-under viewing audience, twice the size of the audience over 50 ("CBS Reshuffle: Emphasis" 26).

Combat! was even popular with the real military. It was one of the first programs to air on Armed Forces Television for troops in Vietnam, along with *Bonanza* and *The Beverly Hillbillies*. Captain Willis Haas, who was in charge of the station, believed that Armed Forces Television would have 5000 to 10,000 viewers and eventually there would be 56 hours a week of programming that would reach all 24,000 troops. An Armed Forces Television station technician, interviewed by *The New York Times*, stated, "We might even have our own version of *Combat!* one of these nights. We have an alert about once a week because of the Vietcong." It was also reported that 12 men were assigned to the station, which was located in an 11-ton TV van atop an 1800-foot mountain. It transmitted from a 132-foot tower ("G.I.'s in Vietnam" 6).

Combat! was cancelled after finishing the 1966–1967 season with lower-than-expected ratings. Its five seasons on the air made it TV's longest running World War II drama ever. After leaving the airwaves, *Combat!* was replaced with another hour-long World War II action-adventure drama, *Garrison's Gorillas* ("Fall Schedule Announced" 26).

Combat!'s 152 episodes (25 of them in color) went into syndication in 1967. ABC Films called the show "[p]erhaps the most important hour series ever released in syndication" ("Syndicators Have Pitches" 102; Advertisement for ABC Films 41).

Jericho

Garry Moore, who hosted the game show *To Tell the Truth* and his own variety show *The Garry Moore Show,* also hosted *You'll See Stars*, the CBS 1966–1967 Fall Preview show. Regarding CBS's new series *Jericho*, the *You'll See Stars* narrator exclaimed, "Code name: Jericho. Assignment: counterintelligence. It's nerve-tingling World War II adventure behind enemy lines as Don Franks, John Leyton and Marino Masé star in *Jericho* ... in color."

The one-hour show's counterintelligence agents worked behind enemy lines in World War II Germany to sabotage the Nazi war effort. The Jericho team was comprised of Franklin Shepard (Don Franks), an American explosives and demolition expert; Lieutenant Jean-Gaston Andre (Italian-born actor Marino Masé), weapons expert from the Free French Air Force; and Nicholas Gage (John Leyton), a British Royal Navy lieutenant who in peacetime was an acrobat and aerialist; Gage often got the team out of high-risk situations. Leyton was best known for his song "Johnny Remember Me" and his roles in *The Great Escape* (1963) and *Von Ryan's Express* (1965).

The Jericho team took on Nazi soldiers and Gestapo agents on their own turf. The show was not unlike *Mission: Impossible*: The team was given seemingly impossible objectives, such as moving an entire symphony orchestra out of occupied France, as seen in the first episode.

Reviews were mixed after *Jericho*'s premiere on Thursday, September 15, 1966, at 8:00 p.m. Jack Gould of *The New York Times* was mostly negative, stating that the show was an attempt to

> capitalize on the enduring appeal of underground commandos who worked behind Nazi lines, preferably with a touch of comedy as a bonus. ... The suspense that almost

automatically attends the art of outwitting the Nazis somehow became subordinate to a prolonged gag of one of the characters about his incipient cowardice [Gould "TV: Spies"].

Bob Hull (*Los Angeles Herald-Examiner*) wrote that the series "is neither worse nor better than others of its kind." Walt Dutton of the *Los Angeles Times* believed that it "has potential through the development of its characters" ("How Critics Assess" 76).

But *Jericho* never got to develop. In the winter of 1967, after only 16 episodes, it was replaced by the very short-lived variety show *Coliseum*, which did not fare much better. (*Coliseum* was cancelled after half a season despite all-star hosts and musical guests such as Paul Revere and the Raiders.)

Jericho's ratings failure is often attributed to going head to head with the ABC shows *Batman* and *F Troop*. Even *Jericho* star Don Franks believed *Batman* was the reason behind the show's demise: Clearly frustrated with the situation, he later stated, "All we had was a kid show playing against us" (Cole "Franks"). But the popularity of *Batman* and *F Troop* was waning, so odds are that *Jericho*'s ratings failure had more to do with its NBC competition, the frontiersman action-adventure series *Daniel Boone*, which was a ratings winner that season with an average Nielsen rating of 20.8 (Brooks and Marsh).

12 O'Clock High

Air Force Magazine called the Gregory Peck movie *12 O'Clock High* (1949) "the best movie ever made about the Air Force":

> [It] had an authenticity seldom seen in war movies. It pushed all the right buttons for airmen, who held it in such regard that the movie became something of a cult film for several generations of Air Force members. In those days, almost everybody in the Air Force had seen it at least once, and the film was used for many years in USAF leadership courses [Correll].

Thanks in part to its "cult following," *12 O'Clock High* was brought to the small screen in the fall of 1964: Producer Quinn Martin's hour-long World War II drama aired in black and white Fridays at 9:30 and followed the missions of a U.S. Air Force Heavy Bombardment Group stationed in England. Characters from the film appeared in the show, including Brigadier General Frank Savage (Robert Lansing), Major Harvey Stovall (Frank Overton), Major Cobb (Lew Gallo), Major "Doc" Kaiser (Barney Phillips) and General Pritchard (Paul Newlan).

12 O'Clock High aired in a difficult time slot that season, running opposite the popular military-themed Southern comedy *Gomer Pyle, U.S.M.C.* and the drama *The Reporter* on CBS and *The Jack Benny Show* and the prime time talk show *The Jack Paar Program* on NBC. All of them continuously beat out *12 O'Clock High*, which was soon at the bottom of the ratings barrel ("Thursday Night Still" 10). But *12 O'Clock High* still had its "cult following" of current and former Air Force members so it picked up major sponsors, such as Frigidaire. In January 1965, ABC moved the show to a less competitive 10:00 time slot so that it aired opposite the low-rated *Slattery's People* on CBS and *The Jack Paar Program* on NBC. Ratings improved and ABC renewed the show ("Business Briefly" 52; Spencer "TV's Vast 55"; "ABC-TV Renews" 62).

After the first season, *TV Guide* announced that *12 O'Clock High* would be moving to Monday at 7:30 p.m., but star Robert Lansing would not be returning because of the time slot move. Quinn Martin stated,

ABC is very high on Lansing and asked me to find another series for him. They said they want him for a 10 p.m. show. Had we remained at 10 p.m. Bob would have continued. ... Ever since the story broke in print, Hollywood has been trying to figure it out. One observer speculated that to appeal to the 7:30 audience, which contains more juveniles, the show will have to feature more physical action, which calls for a younger star.

TV Guide also reported, "Instead of diving back into TV, Lansing hopefully intends to concentrate on working in feature films, where not only the stature is higher and the money is better, but careers last longer." Lansing was quoted as saying, "Once an actor stays with a series too long, movie producers' lose interest in him. TV is great for a certain amount of public recognition. Then, if he can leave TV when he's riding high, he's in a position to make his move—the way Steve McQueen, James Garner and Rod Taylor did" (Lewis 24). Lansing was replaced in the second season with Paul Burke who, although four years older than Lansing, had a more youthful look.

The appeal to a younger audience did not work, ratings did not improve, and *12 O'Clock High* was moved back to Friday's at 10:00 p.m. in the 1966–1967 season. Lansing went on to star in the ABC series *The Man Who Never Was* in the fall of 1966.

Although the first two seasons were shot in black and white, the show flew into the world of color for the 1966–1967 season. One of the main problems the show had when transitioning to color was that it relied heavily on World War II–era black and white stock footage of Allied bombing raids, takeoffs, landings and dogfights. The show's solution was to simply give the existing footage a blue tint that gave the appearance of color.

Color did not improve *12 O'Clock High*'s ratings. The show continued to struggle in 1966 opposite the Western *Laredo* on NBC and the popular *CBS Friday Night Movie*. By October 17, 1966, it was the lowest rated scripted show in prime time ("ARB's Top-20 Oct 2–8"). Cancellation came in January 1967, only 17 episodes into its color run, and it was replaced by the first color season of the British import *The Avengers*.

Hogan's Heroes

In January 1965, CBS announced that Bob Crane, who had previously appeared on *The Donna Reed Show* (1958–1966), would take the title role on one of their new show *Hogan's Heroes*. Very little information was provided about the show (Graham "TV People" 6). But soon it was revealed that it was a comedy about a Nazi prisoner of war camp, Stalag 13, during World War II. The camp consisted of captured Allied airmen led by Colonel Robert E. Hogan (Crane). His crew: Sergeant James "Kinch" Kinchloe (Ivan Dixon), Sergeant Andrew Carter (Larry Hovis), Corporal Peter Newkirk (Richard Dawson) and Corporal Louis LeBeau (Robert Clary). The captured airmen could easily escape the camp at any time but were on a secret mission, spying on the Germans and sabotaging the German war effort.

The POWs were being watched by the incompetent and easily manipulated camp commandant, Wilhelm Klink (Werner Klemperer), and the equally incompetent Sergeant Schultz (John Banner). Klink and Schultz were under constant threat of being sent to the Russian front if the camp fell into disarray, so they did everything in their power to convince Nazi leaders it was well-run.

Several of the actors playing Nazi soldiers were of Jewish descent, starting with Klemperer and Banner. Perhaps it exacted some revenge on the Nazis—even if it was the comedic kind. Syndicated gossip columnist Walter Winchell reported in April 1965, "In CBS's new comedy series for next season many make-believe Nazis are acted by Jewish lads"—but he asked, "What's so comical about a concentration camp?" (Winchell "Hubert's Big Role" 5).

The show's stars never saw it as anything but funny. In 1965, Klemperer defended the show:

> We are working with a time in Germany never treated with any kind of humor. We have proper respect for the time. We by no means excuse the events that happened. We are not ridiculing Germans. We are wringing humor from situations that existed—as *McHale's Navy* does with the war in the Pacific. ... [A] prisoner of war camp was not the same as a concentration camp for political enemies and Jews [Newton "Comedy in a War" 38].

In a 2013 *Los Angeles Times* interview, Clary, who was a Nazi concentration camp survivor, stated, "True, they were in a camp, but they were not treated the same as a concentration camp. It was a stalag." Despite his background, Clary claimed he did not think twice about taking the role. (King "Robert Clary").

In May 1965, CBS announced that the show would debut in color, and that six other CBS shows would make the jump to color: *My Favorite Martian, Lassie, The Lucy Show, The Beverly Hillbillies and Gilligan's Island* (Wister "It's a Colorful Race" 38; "*Hogan's Heroes* Readies").

The show started to get traction with the critics before debuting and it was considered CBS's "hottest prospect for hit comedy" (DuBrow "Negroes Getting Regular TV Roles" 43). It was praised for the casting of African-American actor Ivan Dixon as communications specialist James "Kinch" Kinchloe. At the time, Dixon was active in a movement to get more TV roles for African-Americans (DuBrow "Negroes Getting Regular TV Roles" 43).

Hogan's Heroes debuted in color on Friday, September 17, 1965, at 8:30. Despite some early trepidation about a comedy set in a Nazi POW camp, it was almost universally praised by critics:

> "Life in a German POW camp can be beautiful."—Don Page, *Los Angeles Times*
>
> "First program was hilarious."—Agnes Ash, *Miami News*
>
> "Wild, completely unbelievable and fun."—Frank Wilson, *Indianapolis News*
>
> "Wildest and zaniest."—Bill Irwin, *Chicago's American*
>
> "According to this show, all was riotous fun in those days."—Dwight Newton, *San Francisco Examiner* ("The Critics' View, Part 2" 68–69)

In the first season, *Hogan's Heroes* was one of the most-watched new shows. It ended up the ninth highest-rated show that season with a 24.9 Nielsen rating (Adams "*Bonanza* Leads Nielsen"; Brooks and Marsh).

On the 1966–1967 prime time schedule, Friday nights became one of the most competitive time slots. *Hogan's Heroes* went up against two popular newcomers, *The Time Tunnel* on ABC and *The Man from U.N.C.L.E.* on NBC. But *Hogan's Heroes* found its niche audience: families. Families would be watching television together and in 1966 the generation who served in World War II were now in their 40s and 50s and had children in record numbers between 1946 and 1964. *Hogan's Heroes* was seen by those who served in World War II as a comedic escape; many of them had fought against the Nazi soldiers who were now comedic foils week after week. The show also had humor that the younger set could enjoy. The show perhaps opened dialogue between generations about the war.

The first two weeks of the 1966–1967 season, *The Time Tunnel* won in the time slot war. But by the third week, the novelty of *The Time Tunnel* wore off, and *Hogan's Heroes* consistently won out the time slot the remainder of the season. It was the 18th most-watched show of the season with an average 21.8 Nielsen rating, tied with *The CBS Friday Night Movie* ("The Latest" 66; "Few Cheers" 58; Brooks and Marsh).

In 1966, *Hogan's Heroes* was enjoying success in both ratings and in promotion. Bob Crane and Robert Clary appeared on the cover of the November 19, 1966, *TV Guide*, the series was parodied in *Mad* magazine and it was made into a Dell comic book.

After the 1966–1967 season, *Hogan's Heroes* moved to Saturdays at 9:00. In its final season in 1970, the show moved to Sundays at 7:30. No matter when it aired, *Hogan's Heroes* never saw the same ratings success it did in its first two seasons and it was cancelled in 1971 during CBS's famed Rural Purge which eliminated many shows with Southern or rural themes or, in the case of *Hogan's Heroes*, shows that appealed to an older audience (Gould "C.B.S. Line-Up for Fall Omits"; "TV Shows Biting" 1).

The show had success in reruns and syndication due in part to its timeless humor. The fact that all the episodes were in color gave it a uniform look.

The Rat Patrol

ABC announced the production of several new shows in February 1966, among them two World War II dramas. The first was the submarine adventure program *Locate, Pursue and Destroy*, a show that most likely would have been picked up *except* that its star Van Williams instead took on the role of the Green Hornet. The other was the desert warfare action-adventure *The Rat Patrol* (Adams "ABC's Fall Schedule to Omit" 53).

The show was the brainchild of Tom Gries, who also served as a writer, producer and director. Gries came up with the idea after doing research on a World War II British armored-car outfit, the Long Rang Desert Group, which fought against the Nazi Afrika Korps (Hobson "The War" 18).

After *The Rat Patrol* was sold to ABC, the network hired Mirisch-Rich Television Productions as producers. *TV Guide* reported that Mirisch-Rich brought on producer Stan Shpetner, who wanted to "put his own stamp on the show": "[H]e wanted a hipper show than the pilot; farther out, more razzamatazz. He wanted pungent dialog, yet no soggy beating of breasts or 'identity crises.' He wanted action, excitement, guts; he wanted the screen to jump." Shpetner described his idea for the show as "Audacious, Gassy and Cool" (Hobson 15–16).

The pilot episode was shot in three locations: Arizona, Hollywood and Camp Pendleton, California. TV reporter Dwight Newton reported that the cost, $650,000, was "enough to finance five *Bonanzas*" (Newton 37). Production was moved to Almeria, Spain, "to make use of Allied and German tanks, half-tracks, troop carries, mortars and artillery pieces" which were assembled for the films *The Great Escape* (1963) and *The Battle of the Bulge* (1965) (Witbeck "*Rat Patrol* Premieres" 41).

The ABC Fall Preview *7 Nights to Remember*, hosted by Batman and Robin, featured *Rat Patrol* footage, including an exciting desert armored vehicle shootout with

Nazi Afrika Korps troops. *Rat Patrol* featured square-jawed Sergeant Sam Troy (Christopher George), Private Tully Pettigrew (Justin Tarr), Private Mark Hitchcock (Lawrence Casey) and English Sergeant Jack Moffitt (Gary Raymond). The group's mission: "to attack, harass and wreak havoc on Field Marshal Rommel's vaunted Afrika Korps." *New York Times* TV critic Jack Gould described the show thusly: "A unit of four commandos of mixed Allied nationality taking on Rommel's Afrika Korps during World War II." He went to state that the show was not for viewers interested in plot or exposition:

> The program's chief appeal for those who want their action not to be materially interrupted by any characterization or dialogue is the unit's frenzied jockeying of Jeeps over the sand dunes. With swiveling machine guns mounted on the rear of the vehicles, the commandos ride their Jeeps as if they were staging an automated version of an Indian raid on a stalled wagon train [Gould "TV: *Rat Patrol*" 93].

ABC's expectations were reported to be low, despite their financial investment ("*Rat Patrol* Rates High"). Critics did not see much potential for *Rat Patrol*:

> "The same old clichés abound."—Percy Shain, *Boston Globe*

> "Opening plot came out of someone's mimeograph file."—Lawrence Laurent, *Washington Post* ("Critics Views" 64)

ABC and the critics may not have been sold on *The Rat Patrol,* but the public was. Despite getting little network support and having a cast of relative unknowns, the first episode (Monday, September 12, 8:30) was the 12th highest-rated show that week, scoring a 19.8 Arbitron rating. It beat out NBC's musical variety series *The Roger Miller Show* by six ratings points and barely lost out to perennial favorite *The Lucy Show,* which earned a 21.4 rating ("The Numbers Game" 59; "ARB Top-20 Programs Sept. 11–17" 68).

In the second week, *The Rat Patrol* was the fifth highest-rated show with a 22.7 Arbitron rating, this time beating out *The Lucy Show* ("*Rat Patrol* Rates High" 48; "ARB Top-20 Programs Sept. 18–24" 68).

But some industry insiders believed that its success would be short lived. Critics worried that it would follow in the footsteps of *A Man Called Shenandoah* which the previous season "zoomed away to a spectacularly high start then plummeted sharply" and was cancelled ("*Rat Patrol* Rates High").

The Rat Patrol continued to beat *The Lucy Show* for the next six weeks, averaging a 20.9 Arbitron rating. But by October 31, things had changed ("ARB's Top-20 Programs Sept. 25–Oct. 1" 59; "ARB Top-20 Programs Oct. 2–8" 68; "Top-20 Arbitrons Oct. 9–15" 56 ; "Top-20 Arbitron's Oct. 16–22" 64; "Top-20 Arbitrons Oct. 23–29" 56).

Although *The Rat Patrol* concluded the season as the 23rd highest-rated show, with an average Nielsen rating of 20.9, it dropped well below *The Lucy Show,* which ended the season as the fourth highest-rated show with an average 26.2 Nielsen rating (Brooks and Marsh; "Top-20 Arbitrons Oct. 30–Nov 5" 72; "The Arbitrons Nov 13–19" 84).

Filming in Spain was an expensive venture and it did not bring down costs as producers had originally hoped. At the same time, trade unions in Hollywood, including the AFL Hollywood Film Council, were putting pressure on the show's sponsors to force producers to bring *The Rat Patrol*'s production to the U.S. and hire union workers. The series' producers bowed to the pressure and moved the show back to the U.S. after 17 weeks of filming overseas in October 1966 (Hobson "The War" 18).

Two months into the season, *The Rat Patrol* was the only new show to make the top 20 most-watched shows list, but it was steadily dropping in the ratings ("Two More Shows" 72). At the end of the 1966–1967 season, only two shows that debuted in the Fall 1966 were among the highest-rated: *Family Affair* and *The Rat Patrol*. Two mid-season replacements made the list as well: *The Smothers Brothers Comedy Hour* and *Dragnet* (Brooks and Marsh).

The show was not popular in England and Australia. After airing six episodes, the BBC dropped *The Rat Patrol* due to viewer complaints, most notably by parents of British soldiers who died in Africa during World War II: They complained that the show depicted a small number of Americans winning the war against Rommel's Afrika Korps, when in fact much of the campaign was fought by British forces. One of the show's stars, Gary Raymond, who was from England, stated, "I didn't think the BBC would buy the series at all. ... Then I was surprised they took it so seriously that it had to be cancelled. ... It's rather flattering to the actors. Of course, I may be shot when I get home." Although the show was never picked up by stations in Australia or New Zealand, Australians were reportedly offended due to Christopher George, an American, wearing an Aussie Brush Hat. It was reported that Australian felt that they should have been represented on the show (Humphrey "Gary May be No. 1").

Despite being cancelled by the BBC, high production costs and declining ratings, *The Rat Patrol* was picked up by ABC in November 1966 for another season. But Gary Raymond wanted to see some changes. "Our pilot film had a sense of the period in which the stories are laid, but now that seems to be gone and it's difficult to tell just where we are now." TV reporter Hal Humphrey reported that executive producer Lee Rich was a "strong believer in not fooling around with successful formulae." Rich added that the show would occasionally "take the boys out of the desert. ... We're buying some more tanks, too. But the people like what they see now" (Humphrey "Gary May be No. 1").

To cash in on the success of *The Rat Patrol*, a number of toys and collectables were released in coordination with the show. Remco released several *Rat Patrol* action figures and play sets, Aurora produced *Rat Patrol*–themed model kits, Topps trading cards produced 66 collectable cards, and five books based on the show's characters were published. *The Rat Patrol* even had a metal lunch box with thermos featuring the Rat Patrol blowing up a Nazi Jeep.

The Rat Patrol once again went head to head with *The Lucy Show* in the 8:30 time slot in 1967–1968. But that season, CBS had a loaded Monday night schedule that featured four of the year's most popular shows: *The Lucy Show, Gunsmoke, The Andy Griffith Show* and *Family Affair* (Brooks and Marsh). It was clear that many TV viewers were not changing the channel from CBS on Monday nights that season, which made it difficult for any other network's shows to improve their share of the viewership. *The Lucy Show* was the second most watched show of the year. *The Rat Patrol* was still an expensive show to produce, even after moving back to the States, especially for a show with slumping ratings. Making matters still worse: In the winter of 1968, NBC's *The Man from U.N.C.L.E.* was replaced by the cultural sensation *Rowan & Martin's Laugh-In*, which rose to become the 21st most watched show that season (Brooks and Marsh).

In February 1968, ABC announced that *The Rat Patrol* would not return for the 1968–1969 season ("Network Race" 23). By 1968, it was clear that TV viewers had had enough of the war: That year, *Hogan's Heroes* (1965–1971) was the only World War II–themed show left.

After *The Rat Patrol*'s cancellation, several episodes were edited together to make the 1968 feature *Massacre Harbor,* with the tagline "The Hit-and-Run Heroes of *Rat Patrol* Hit the Big Screen! Bigger and better—as they take on a town … and wipe it off the map!"

Chapter Seven

Westerns

In 1960, Westerns filled the prime time TV landscape. Twenty-one Westerns aired between 7:30 and 11:00 p.m. on the three major networks, filling approximately 16 hours of TV in an average week, or roughly 22 percent of the week's prime time programming. But just six years later, in the fall of 1966, the number dropped to just 13. Although Westerns were being phased out of the prime time schedule, many older series were still being run heavily in syndication in daytime and late-night slots on local channels. The older Westerns were remarkably more violent than Westerns in production in 1966 and 1967 due to recent pressure on producers from parental groups such as the National Association for Better Broadcasting, the Congress of Women's Clubs, various religious organizations, and a Congressional subcommittee. All aforementioned groups blamed TV violence and lewd comics for a rise in juvenile delinquency (Mosby 6; Torre 45; White 1; "Urge Reduction" 1).

Bonanza

It was widely reported that NBC's *Bonanza* was the first color Western, although in reality it was actually the third. *The Cisco Kid* (1950–1958) and *Sergeant Preston of the Yukon* (1955–1958) were the first two Westerns shot in color. But they were not originally *broadcast* in color ("On Television" 71). *The Cisco Kid* and *Sergeant Preston* were first seen in color when they went into syndication in the 1960s, when color TVs were more abundant and stations were equipped to broadcast in color. Both shows remained popular throughout the 1960s and 1970s in syndication thanks to forward-thinking producers who decided to dole out extra money to shoot in color.

Even though *Bonanza* was not the first color Western, it was the first Western show that was broadcast in color when it debuted on September 12, 1959.

The show's creator David Dortort pitched the idea of the show being shot in color to NBC (then a subsidiary of RCA), as a way to help sales of RCA color TVs. Dortort also felt that the show *needed* to be seen in color and stated that he told NBC, "I understand in the RCA labs in Indiana they have been developing color television and I want to shoot this show in color." NBC believed that it was too expensive to produce in color, but acquiesced after Dortort described how the show's vast landscape (shot in Lake Tahoe) needed to be shot, broadcast and seen in color. Dortort also stated that the show's producer Tom Sarnoff's influence at NBC helped lead to the network agreeing to the added expense of color ("David Dortort").

Shooting in color cost approximately 25 percent more, but it paid off for everyone

Chapter Seven. Westerns

involved. Dortort said that *Bonanza* was shot in color "from the very first foot of film" and recalled, "People were flocking to RCA dealers and they were selling thousands of color television sets. Anybody who had a color set would watch the only color show on the air" ("David Dortort").

In 1959, less than a million households owned a TV set and *Bonanza* was not a ratings success or a success with the critics. According to the TV industry magazine *Broadcasting*, "What must have looked like a sure winner on the planning boards is just embarrassing on the TV screen. ... [C]onceivably the program's planners thought this would be the Westerns to end all westers. It just might" ("The New NBC-TV").

Bonanza is the story of the prosperous Cartwright family. Their Ponderosa ranch (located between Virginia City, Reno and Carson City, Nevada) is run by Ben Cartwright (Lorne Greene) and his three son Adam (Pernell Roberts), Hoss (Dan Blocker) and, the youngest, Little Joe (Michael Landon).

The Cast of *Bonanza*, left to right: Dan Blocker (Hoss), Lorne Greene (Ben Cartwright), Pernell Roberts (Adam Cartwright), Michael Landon (Joseph "Little Joe" Cartwright) (Internet Archive).

In its first season, *Bonanza* was not a ratings hit. It ran opposite the tenth highest-rated show of the season, the courtroom drama *Perry Mason* on CBS and the musical variety series *The Dick Clark Show* on ABC. NBC stuck with *Bonanza* despite the high cost of color (Brooks and Marsh).

The show's rise in popularity is often credited to its move to Sunday nights in the third season, but in the second season the show did make some ratings gains and became the season's 17th highest-rated show (Brooks and Marsh). In 1965, *The New York Times* TV columnist Jack Gould wrote,

> Mr. Dortort's contemporary epic is a lesson for TV's eager beavers; it did not catch on in 13 weeks. Indeed, *Bonanza* needed several seasons of nurturing before it bloomed statistically and dramatically, and it did not really make the grade until it took over the 9 o'clock niche. ... That time period is now recognized as belonging so firmly to Ben Cartwright and sons that a

rival impresario who is asked to compete is usually aware that he is getting the pink slip in the grand manner [Gould "TV: Why a 'Bonanza?'" 75].

Even for those who could not see the "vast landscape" in color, the show's story was more than enough to make audiences tune in. *Bonanza* was not your typical shoot-'em-up. Dortort believed that the show would not be a typical Western and would use historical fact as a basis for stories. He stated:

> The men who shaped the west were men of power and drive—not a bunch of half-brained, gun-happy semi-delinquents. ... There won't be anything aimless about *Bonanza*'s gun-slingers. They'll be the executioners hired by the silver kings, and their violence will be for a good reason. And we certainly won't glamorize them; we'll show them for precisely what they are—murderous mercenaries for hire ["History to Be Used" 16].

Bonanza was much less violent than many Westerns of the 1950s and early 1960s, and yet the National Association for Better Broadcasting considered "some episodes too violent for young children." But they conceded that *Bonanza* "had appealing scenic backgrounds and constructive social attitudes," and added that the show was "fine for older audiences" (Leonard "What's Out" 78).

The show's intro had an infectious instrumental theme (written by Jay Livingston and Ray Evans) that played over a burning map of the Ponderosa Ranch making way for the show's stars riding on horseback. Al Caiola and His Orchestra scored a hit with a recording of the theme in 1961: It reached #19 on the Billboard Hot 100 charts. The theme was given lyrics in 1962 by Johnny Cash and Johnny Western, and that version reached #94 on the Billboard Hot 100 charts. The show's theme with Cash and Western's lyrics was recorded by *Bonanza* star Lorne Greene and later recorded by the entire cast of *Bonanza* when RCA Victor released the album *Ponderosa Party Time!*

In the third season, NBC moved the show to Sunday at 9:00, perfect for family viewing. That season, *Bonanza* jumped in the ratings and became the year's second highest-rated show, averaging a 30.0 rating (second only to fellow NBC Western *Wagon Train*). It averaged a 33.3 rating for the next two years and in the 1964–1965 season it began a three-year run as the highest-rated show (Brooks and Marsh).

In 1963, the larger-than-life Dan Blocker capitalized on the show's success by opening a chain of Bonanza Steakhouses which quickly spread throughout the country. In 1965, businessmen Dan Lasater, Norm Wiese and Charles Kleptz started their own *Bonanza*-themed chain named after the Cartwright ranch, Ponderosa. The chains merged in 1989, and both Bonanza and Ponderosa Steakhouses are in operation throughout the world.

NBC's *Bonanza* color gamble eventually paid off and in 1964 RCA even made the show the face of its color TV sales campaign. In 1964, approximately 1,610,000 Americans (3.1 percent of American households) owned a color TV, and the number steadily increased to 5,220,000 (9.6 percent of households) by 1966 (Steinberg 144).

Bonanza once again took top Nielsen honors when the season kicked off in September 1966, rustling up a 27.3 rating ("The Numbers Game" 59). In the second week, it had added competition with a new *ABC Sunday Night Movie* but still led the pack with a 28.7 rating ("ABR Top 20 Programs Sept. 18–24" 59).

In the third week of the season, ratings took a plunge and it was not even on the list of the top 40 highest-rated shows of the week, despite having a new episode ("A Time to Step Down" with guest star Ed Begley). That week ratings were taken over by the ABC presentation of *The Bridge on the River Kwai* (1957), which dominated the ratings in every category that week and aired the same time as *Bonanza*. Jack Gould of *The New York Times* wrote:

> When the history of the 1966–67 television season is finally written, it is not likely that any great percentage of the new half-hours or hours will be remembered. The bona fide bombshell was last Sunday's full evening presentation of *The Bridge on the River Kwai*, the prize-winning movie of 1957. ... [It] completely ran roughshod over all its competition including *Bonanza* and *The Ed Sullivan Show*. For just slightly over three hours the film swept the rating boards and afforded the viewer one of the most satisfying evenings of entertainment TV has ever offered [Gould "Why *Kwai*" 135].

The next week, the *Sunday Night Movie* (*Move Over Darling* [1963] with Doris Day and James Garner) was again the ratings winner, but *Bonanza* regained its top spot the following week and remained there most of the season. (ARB's Top 20 Programs Sept. 25–Oct. 1; ARB's Top 20 Programs Oct. 2–8; Brooks and Marsh).

Bonanza received time slot competition from CBS on February 5, 1967, with the premiere of the sketch comedy variety show *The Smothers Brothers Comedy Hour*, which defeated *Bonanza* in the ratings in its first two weeks on the air. *The New York Times* wrote that *Smothers Brothers*

> did even better in the Nielsen 30 major market cities, where the comedians outdrew the cowboys 24 to 17.4 and got a 36 share of the available audience to *Bonanza*'s 26. And even wondered if *Bonanza*'s days were numbered. ... It's probably too early to tell for sure but Madison Avenue saloons are beginning to favor two slick newcomers to town named Tom and Dick Smothers [Gent "*Bonanza* Faces" 87].

Before this point, very few would have believed that any TV show could take down *Bonanza*. An unnamed NBC spokesman stated, "There's no panic here. There is no doubt that the Smothers Brothers are doing better than the other CBS shows in that period, but *Bonanza* will remain in the 9 p.m. time slot" (Gent "*Bonanza* Faces" 87).

As predicted, *Bonanza* eventually overtook *The Smothers Brothers Comedy Hour* and went on to become the highest-rated show of the season, averaging a 29.1 rating. *The Smothers Brothers Comedy Hour* finished the season the 16th highest-rated show, averaging a 22.2 rating (Brooks and Marsh).

Even American troops halfway around the globe in Vietnam watched *Bonanza* when it became one of the first two shows, along with *Combat!*, to air on the Armed Forces Television Service in September 1966 ("G.I.'s in Vietnam" 6).

Bonanza remained in the top ten shows each year until 1971. In 1971–1972, *Bonanza* finally fell to #20. Around that time, many other rural-based shows (*Green Acres, The Beverly Hillbillies, The Lawrence Welk Show*) fell out of favor with audiences (Brooks and Marsh).

To make matters worse for *Bonanza*, after the 13th season ended, on May 13, 1972, Dan Blocker died of a pulmonary embolism. Syndicated Hollywood reporter Dick Kleiner reported his death "has been handled with great discretion" and that "there has been no attempt—nor will there be any—to capitalize on it, to sentimentalize it, to turn it to program advantage," much like studios did with the death of Clark Gable, Gary Cooper, Spencer Tracy and Humphrey Bogart. But his death was not ignored altogether: The death of Hoss was "referred to in scripts as a family would refer to a loved one" (Kleiner "*Bonanza* Faces Up" 15B). Hoss' big shoes were filled by a hired hand named Candy (David Canary).

In 1973, NBC played reruns of *Bonanza* (under the title *Ponderosa*) on Tuesday nights, to prepare the show for a move to Tuesday at 8:00. After *Bonanza* moved to Tuesdays in the fall, it found itself trailing in its new time slot against CBS's *All in the Family* spin-off *Maude* and the ABC sitcom *Temperatures Rising*. For the first time since its first season on the air in 1959–1960, *Bonanza* was not one of TV's most popular shows (Brooks and Marsh). NBC considered moving *Bonanza* to Saturday to take on CBS's *All in the Family*—but cancelled the show instead midway through the 1972–1973 season (Shull "Fading *Bonanza* Near End"). *Bonanza*'s last episode aired on January 16, 1973, and it was replaced the next week by *NBC Tuesday Night at the Movies* for the rest of the season.

Associated Press writer Jay Sharbutt wrote,

> *Bonanza* remained a durable attraction on NBC throughout the years, doing battle against both bad men and good series on opposing networks.... It remained that way until last September when it was pitted against a loud-mouthed lady called *Maude*.... [R]atings for *Bonanza* dropped dramatically despite a good start. NBC decided in late November to put the show out to pasture [Sharbutt "Network to Broadcast" 14].

When *Bonanza* was cancelled, not only were there 13½ seasons of shows to air in reruns, it had 13½ seasons of episodes in color—more than any other show at the time. Associated Press TV writer Jerry Buck reported: "Despite its removal from the network there is no chance that *Bonanza* will fade away like a played-out silver mine.... The show, with 431 episodes in living color, had entered the fabric of American folklore" (Buck "There's No Death Knell" 6A).

Three made-for-television *Bonanza* movies followed: *Bonanza: The Next Generation* (1988), *Bonanza: The Return* (1993) and *Bonanza: Under Attack* (1995). Twenty-two years after the show's cancellation, there was also *Ponderosa* (2001), a short-lived prequel on ION Television.

The Wild Wild West

The Wild Wild West could just as easily be put into the category of a spy series as much as it is a Western. The show was pitched to CBS by creator Michael Garrison as "James Bond on horseback." It has been described as "James Bond in a Western outfit," and the show's star Robert Conrad stated, "You might call me Agent 001 because I'm 95 years ahead of Bond, who as everybody knows, is 007" (Kesler *The Wild Wild West*; Dilego 19; Wolters 8).

James T. West, played by former *Hawaiian Eye* (1959–1963) star Conrad, was a secret agent for President Grant, battling radical groups looking to undermine the federal government in the aftermath of the Civil War. West traveled from location to location on a private train with his sidekick, master of disguise Artemus Gordon (Ross Martin). Like James Bond, West always found himself in the company of very beautiful women throughout the course of his adventures. Among the most notable: Suzanne Pleshette, Diane McBain, Lisa Gaye, Dawn Wells and Yvonne Craig. The comparison to Bond continues with West's numerous gadgets, such as his sleeve gun, various explosive and escape devices, and a switchblade knife in the toe of his shoe.

The 1965 *Wild Wild West* pilot commercial called it "Western adventure with the excitement of espionage" and featured Conrad's James West going through his arsenal of weapons and gadgets and fighting a Fu Manchu–style Chinese villain.

The Wild Wild West debuted on September 17, 1965, at 7:30, right before *Hogan's Heroes*. There was a joint promo sponsored by the TWA airline with Conrad as James West arresting John Banner as *Hogan's Heroes*' Sergeant Schultz in an airport terminal.

In its first season, *The Wild Wild West* was the 23rd highest-rated show with a 22.0 average Nielsen rating (Brooks and Marsh). But it had very little time slot competition: It went up against *The Flintstones* and the fish-out-of-water sitcom *Tammy* on ABC, and two short-lived sitcoms, *Camp Runamuck* and *Hank*, on NBC.

In the 1966–1967 season, *Wild Wild West* went to color and got some stiff competition from *The Green Hornet* and *The Time Tunnel* on ABC and *Tarzan* on NBC. All three came into the 1966–1967 season as some of the most hyped and talked-about shows ("The Numbers Game" 59; "The Latest Form" 66).

By mid-season, after the hype of the other shows died down, *The Wild Wild West* began scoring ratings wins but it nothing close to the 22.0 rating it received in its first year. It ended the season as the 53rd highest-rated show ("Second Season Loses" 60; Brooks and Marsh; Spencer "TV's Vast" 54).

The Wild Wild West featured colorful and outlandish villains who would have easily fit in on shows like *Batman*, among them Dr. Loveless (Michael Dunn), Count Manzeppi (Victor Buono), Mr. Singh (Boris Karloff) and Professor Cadwallader (Burgess Meredith).

The Wild Wild West was never able to replicate the ratings success it had in the 1965–1966 season, but when CBS cancelled it in February 1969, ratings was not the reason. After the June 1968 assassination of Robert Kennedy, several activist groups focused their attention on TV violence. Initially the *Wild Wild West*'s producers and stars pushed back. Producer Bruce Lansbury said, "We are a different kind of show—unrealistic, preposterous, escapist—a comic strip," and Conrad asked, "The question is, did or did not John Wilkes Booth's mother let him watch television?" (Crosby "Tube Moves Boobs" 14; Kleiner "Hollywood Making Reappraisal" 30).

But the groups kept up their crusade, often focusing solely on *The Wild Wild West*. It was called one of TV's most violent shows by *The Christian Science Monitor*. The National Association for Better Broadcasting listed it as one of the most detrimental shows on TV for children. Rhode Island Democratic Senator John O. Pastore began holding Congressional hearings which condemned the show's sex and violence, and other members of Congress were organizing a National Commission on Violence. The commission believed that shows like *The Wild Wild West* encouraged violent forms of behavior and fostered moral and social values about violence in daily life "which are unacceptable in a civilized society" ("TV Violence Continues" 8; Pearson "Reappraising TV Violence" 6; Inman "New Violence" 25; Mohibat 38).

Eventually the network caved to pressure and cancelled *The Wild Wild West*. The last new episode aired on April 11, 1969. The cancellation was seen by many as a sacrifice to appease the activist groups. The Associated Press wrote, "*The Wild Wild West* despite high ratings, because of criticism. It was seen by the network as a gesture of good intentions" (Mohibat 38).

After the show was cancelled, activist groups tried to keep reruns off the airwaves. The Foundation to Improve Television filed suit in U.S. District Court seeking an injunction to keep *The Wild Wild West* off TV before 9 p.m., believing that children were "being force-fed a steady diet of murder and mayhem. [TV viewers] have the right to be free from the daily diet of violence and horror served by the broadcast industry." The group said *The Wild Wild West* was chosen because "it is a good example of the kind of program the foundation is trying to stop." They added, "Children have a constitutional right under the Fifth Amendment to be free from mental harm caused by viewing television programs that portray fictional violence and horror." The suit ultimately failed and *The Wild Wild West* continued to air at all hours of the day (Hall "Group Files" 15).

The show was replaced on the CBS Friday night schedule with *Get Smart* and the sitcom *The Good Guys*, with Bob Denver as the driver of a George Barris–designed 1924 taxi cab ("*Get Smart* Switches" 64; Brooks and Marsh).

Robert Conrad and Ross Martin reprised their *Wild Wild West* roles in the made-for-TV movies *The Wild Wild West Revisited* (1979) and *More Wild Wild West* (1980). Like many shows of the era, *The Wild Wild West* was turned into a big-budget movie: Warner Brothers' *The Wild Wild West* (1999) starred Will Smith as James West and Kevin Kline as Artemus Gordon. It was a critical and box office failure, but its theme "Wild Wild West" by Will Smith reached #1 on the Billboard Hot 100.

Pistols'n'Petticoats

CBS had two shows in the 1966–1967 season with the word *Petticoat* in the title, the more popular and well-known being *Petticoat Junction*, the less popular being *Pistols'n'Petticoats*. It aired Saturdays at 8:30.

According to *TV Guide*'s "1966–1967 Fall Preview Guide," "*Pistols'n'Petticoats* brings back the 'Oomph Girl' of the movies, Ann Sheridan, as the deadliest pistol-packin' mama since Ma Barker" ("1966–1967 Fall Preview"). (On March 16, 1939, in connection with a Warner Brothers publicity stunt, she was giving the nickname "Oomph Girl" by "a score" of Hollywood male celebrities [Busch 64].)

TV Guide went on to describe the show's premise and characters:

> The setting is the town of Wretched, Colo., where we find Henrietta Hanks (Sheridan), the lady known as Hank who totes a .38 in her shopping bag but prefers to dispose of desperados and pests by whacking them with her purse. Hank has a kindly old mother (Ruth McDevitt), who perpetually wears a sweet smile and a tiny derringer, both of which she uses with a devastating effect; a father (Douglas Fowley) who's as nearsighted as Mr. Magoo but somehow never misses what he's shooting at; a daughter Lucy (Carole Wells), who has just come back from finishing school but hasn't forgotten how to handle a shootin' arm; and who [has] cuddly pets—a wildcat named Kitty and a timber wolf called Bowser. Then there's Sheriff Harold Sikes (Gary Vinson), who's courting Miss Lucy and wishes her kinfolk would stick to their crocheting and leave at least some of the bad guys to him. Not a chance.

CBS's 1966–1967 Fall Preview show, *You'll See Stars,* showed clips from the new series and stated that the family "can out-shoot and out-talk any bad guy from miles around, and they get a lot more laughs. In color this channel heads 'that-a-way' for comedy as Ann Sheridan, Douglas Fowly and Ruth McDevitt star in *Pistols'n'Petticoats*."

The crispness of the photography and the clarity of the color presentation stood out with *Pistols'n'Petticoats*. The color quality was due in part to color coordinator Robert Brower and cinematographer Benjamin H. Kline. Brower was best known for doing the color coordination for *Dragnet* (1967–1970), *Laredo* (1965–1967), *Tammy* (1965–1966) and *Run for Your Life* (1966–1968). Kline was known for his camerawork on many Three Stooges shorts, and films such as *The Man They Could Not Hang* (1939), *Before I Hang* (1940) and *Detour* (1945).

The nation's TV critics were not very fond of *Pistols'n'Petticoats* writing that the show was "another piece of hillbilly trash that CBS-TV seems to find in abundance" (Du Brow "*Mission: Impossible* Beats" 7). Another wrote that the series "[made] its first appearance with a not very funny story about tactics of a pioneer woman" (Lowry "*Mission Impossible* Long" 19).

The show's early ratings were not good. Although the first episode won a showdown with a rerun of the popular *The Lawrence Welk Show* on ABC, scoring 15.0 to Welk's 14.8, it lost a shootout to NBC's *Get Smart*, which scored a 19.4 rating ("The Latest" 68). By the second week, *Pistols* was shooting blanks: It lost to both *Lawrence Welk* and *Get Smart* on a weekly basis ("The Latest" 68; "Few Cheers" 58; "ARB's Top 20" 68; "Second Season" 60).

In hopes of improving the series' ratings, CBS moved it to 8:00 in the winter of 1967. The switch helped *Mission: Impossible,* the show that now followed it, but it did not help *Pistols.* To make matters worse, *Pistols* star Ann Sheridan died of cancer at the age of 51 on January 21, 1967. A little more than a month after her death, it was announced that CBS was cancelling *Pistols* along with nine other shows ("Ten Show to Get" 25).

The show did shoot and air five more episodes (without Sheridan) until March 11, 1967. It finished the season as the least watched program on the prime time schedule (Spencer "TV's Vast" 54).

Even before Sheridan's untimely death, it was clear that in an era that brought us the miniskirt, TV viewers were not interested in petticoats.

Daniel Boone

In 1954, 6'6" World War II veteran turned actor Fess Parker took on the role of American folk hero Davy Crockett, "King of the Wild Frontier," in a *Walt Disney's Disneyland* mini-series. The role made him famous, made Davy Crockett a household name, and it made the coonskin cap, Crockett's signature hat, a popular fashion choice for many youngsters (Le Zotte "The Invention").

Crockett's popularity was not confined to the under–21 crowd. The famous frontiersman was so popular that he was "elected" to the office of judge of elections by one vote in a ward in Pittsburgh, 119 years after his death, in the 1955 primary election ("Davy Crockett Elected").

Davy Crockett's theme song "The Ballad of Davy Crockett" by Bill Hayes even reached #1 on the Billboard Hot 100 Chart; cover versions of the song by Fess Parker, Walter Schumann and Tennessee Ernie Ford made the Billboard charts as well.

Parker went on to star in several other Disney productions throughout the 1950s, but by 1964 he was freelancing and was hired by 20th Century–Fox to play the role of pioneer Daniel Boone. It was rumored that Fox attempted to purchase the rights to Davy Crockett from Disney, to no avail. So, Fox settled on another American folk hero, Daniel Boone, who in many ways was similar to Crockett. Both future American folk heroes helped the U.S. expand westward and were elected to political office in their later lives.

There *were* differences between the two. Davy is considered a frontiersman due to being born soon after the American Revolution in the mountains of Tennessee, which at the time was considered the Western United States. Boone on the other hand is considered a pioneer because he was born in 1734, before the Revolution in the already settled and populated Eastern Pennsylvania, and he journeyed westward to create a settlement in Kentucky and later Missouri. But in the eyes of 20th Century–Fox they were one and the same. Fox even dressed Parker in the same buckskin clothes (complete with leather tassels and coonskin cap) he wore as Davy Crockett.

The hour-long show premiered in black and white on Thursday, September 24, 1964, at 7:30. In the premiere episode, President George Washington (Stephen Courtleigh) sent Boone to Kentucky to broker peace with Native American tribes and find a location to build a new American fort. In that episode, Boone befriended a Harvard-educated Native American, Mingo (Ed Ames), who joined him for the rest of the series.

Daniel Boone was not wildly successful in its first season, but it had stiff competition from the prehistoric cartoon *The Flintstones* and the long-running sitcom *The Donna Reed Show* on ABC and *The Munsters* and the first half-hour of the courtroom drama *Perry Mason* on CBS.

To help promote the show and show off the axe-throwing skills he picked up playing the role of Mingo, Ed Ames went on *The Tonight Show Starring Johnny Carson* on April 27, 1965. On a piece of wood he drew an outline of a cowboy, and with his first throw he hit the cowboy outline below the belt, in the groin area. Ames, clearly embarrassed, went to pull the axe from the cowboy but was stopped by Carson, who exclaimed "Welcome to *Frontier Bris*!" and "I didn't even know you were Jewish!" Ames asked Carson if he would like to throw the axe, and Carson replied, "I can't hurt him any more than you did!" The clip became one of *The Tonight Show*'s most iconic moments and was replayed many times throughout Carson's run as the host. Carson's sidekick Ed McMahon later claimed that all three lines were ad-libbed by Carson and that they got the three biggest and longest-running laughs on television ("Ed McMahon on Ed Ames").

Despite less than optimal ratings, the network stuck with *Daniel Boone* and transitioned the show to color for the 1965–1966 season. At the start of that season, it aired opposite the musical variety show *Shindig!* and the sitcom *The Donna Reed Show* on ABC and the monster comedy *The Munsters,* and the season's 19th highest-rated show *Gilligan's Island* on CBS.

Daniel Boone's color production had a cinema quality created by Deluxe, which used Eastman Color film. Eastman Color film was higher in quality than most color film and did not require special development, which made it perfect for weekly TV which required a quick turnaround.

Many of the exterior scenes were shot on a stage, which gave the show a unique and surreal look. Exterior shots were filmed in Kane County, Utah, at the Grand Staircase-Escalante National Monument, Bryce Canyon National Park, Zion National Park and Glen Canyon National Recreation Area, which made the show look expensive.

Not everyone was impressed with *Daniel Boone*. Kentucky lawmakers voted 38 to 26 to formally voice their displeasure over the series' historical inaccuracies, stating that it was "an inexcusable farce." The lawmakers noted that Boone never had an Indian companion with a cultured Harvard accent, never encountered Inca Indians, and documented that on the show, Daniel Boone was introduced as being from Boonesborough, Kentucky, a town not founded until two decades after Boone's death. Parker defended his show in a telegram to the same Kentucky lawmakers, stating that they had "turned into a passel of television critics" and that the show was "a mixture of fact and legend that was designed to entertain." Parker claimed that Boone did at one time have a Harvard-educated Indian friend and that the legislature should have checked their facts before voting (Gent "Coonskin Parker").

Viewers were not deterred by the Kentucky resolution and in the 1966–1967 season the show rose to 25th place with a 20.8 rating average (Brooks and Marsh). The increase in ratings that season was thanks in part to *Batman*'s sharp decline.

Daniel Boone started to take more creative liberties with stories, getting away from any historical accuracy the show once had. That season, Boone saved President Washington from assassination in Kentucky, recovered the stolen Liberty Bell and delivered ransom money for a kidnapped President Adams. Perhaps the Kentucky legislature had a point when it called the show "an inexcusable farce."

Although the show never made it back into the top 30 after the 1966–1967 season, it ran for a total of six seasons until the 1969–1970 season in the same 7:30 Thursday night time slot.

Despite Thursday nights traditionally being a strong night for TV, *Daniel Boone* did not have much competition in the 7:30–8:30 time slot; it ran opposite the lackluster shows *The Flying Nun*, *The Ghost and Mrs. Muir*, *Blondie*, *Ugliest Girl in Town* and *Cimarron Strip*.

Until 1969. In the 1969–1970 season, *Daniel Boone* saw its first real competition since 1967: It ran opposite CBS's *Family Affair*, the fifth highest-rated show of the season, and the first half-hour of the 12th highest-rated series, *The Jim Nabors Hour*. They took away what was left of *Daniel Boone*'s share of the TV audience and this led to the show's demise.

The last *Daniel Boone* aired on May 7, 1970. It was replaced by the weekly variety series *The Flip Wilson Show*. The change worked out very well for NBC. While *Daniel Boone* seemingly remained stagnant in the ratings in its six seasons, *Flip Wilson* in its first season rose to the second highest-rated show on TV, scoring a 27.9 rating average (Brooks and Marsh).

Iron Horse

Iron Horse was the story of gambler and womanizer Ben Calhoun (Dale Robertson), who was best described as a "cowboy's cowboy" ("The cowboy's cowboy" 12). Calhoun won big in a poker game and took control of the Buffalo Pass, Scalplock and Defiance railroad lines. Unfortunately for Calhoun, the lines were unfinished and almost bankrupt. So it was up to Calhoun, his construction engineer Dave Tarrant (Gary Collins), crew member Nils Torvald (Roger Torrey) and clerk Barnabas Rogers (Bob Random) to complete the work. They must overcome obstacles such as crooked financiers, mobsters, native tribes and the hardships of the Old West landscape. Of course, Calhoun still had the ability to make time with the ladies in towns along the rail lines.

The show's production came with a high price tag. It was reported that it had "no trick photography" and was shot with real trains and actual stunts. *Iron Horse* also took advantage of being produced in color. Syndicated TV columnist Edgar Penton wrote, "The bright red and green colors of the *Iron Horse* are reminiscent of the gay '90s when red velvet, gold flock wallpaper and a gold watchchain across the vest were high fashion" (Penton "*Iron Horse* Chugs" 18).

The *Iron Horse* characters were introduced to audiences on April 10, 1966, in the two-hour TV movie *Scalplock*. The TV series debuted on Monday, September 12. *Iron Horse* received mostly positive reviews and showed a lot of promise among the crop of new shows that season:

> "Has every prospect of being an enduring lusty Western."—Jack E. Anderson, *Miami Herald*
>
> "Another winning series."—Paul Henniger, *Los Angeles Times*
>
> "Dale Robertson ... comes off as the most engaging rogue since James Garner quick playing *Maverick*."—Lawrence Laurent, *Washington Post*
>
> "Featured more action and more chest hair than other oaters."—Bob Hull, *Los Angeles Herald Examiner*

Even the negative reviews were not particularly damning:

> "Strictly conventional movie stuff."—Kay Gardella, *New York Daily News*
>
> "There's no mistaking this horse opera. It's strictly for the kids."—Dean Gysel, *Chicago Daily News* ("Critics' Views" 63).

The only real criticism came from TV watchdog groups and crusaders against TV violence. According to the National Association for Better Broadcasting, "The hero is unattractive and there's practically no storyline—just one brutal incident after another" (Leonard "What's Out" 78).

Although the show received mostly positive reviews, the show's star Dale Robertson was allegedly pessimistic about the first several episodes but hoped viewers would stick with the show "until the tenth or twelfth episode" because by then he felt the show would be "on the road" (Jones "TV's *Iron Horse*" 14).

Even though critics saw potential, *Iron Horse* was not a ratings success. The show initially held its own in the 7:30 hour-long Monday night slot against *Gilligan's Island* and *Run, Buddy, Run* and its replacement *Mr. Terrific* in the winter of 1967 on CBS and *The Monkees* and *I Dream of Jeannie* on NBC. Soon *Iron Horse* found itself at the bottom of the ratings barrel as the season's 48th most-watched show (Powers "*Gunsmoke* Shift" 89; Spencer "TV's Vast" 54).

Unimpressed with *Iron Horse*'s ratings, ABC took it off the 1967–1968 schedule but changed their minds after CBS moved the long-running Saturday night Western *Gunsmoke* to Mondays. ABC hoped *Iron Horse* would pick up in the ratings from viewers turning on the TV on Saturday night hoping to catch a Western (Powers "*Gunsmoke* Shift" 89).

Iron Horse had stiff competition on Saturdays at 9:30 against *Petticoat Junction* and *Mannix* on CBS and the popular *NBC Saturday Night at the Movies*. Its ratings did not improve and the show did not capture *Gunsmoke*'s former audience. ABC announced in November 1967 that *Iron Horse* was being cancelled, along with *Little Big Horn* and *Good Company*. ABC aired new *Iron Horse* episodes until January 9, 1968, when the show was replaced by the variety show *The Hollywood Palace*, which moved from Tuesday nights (Bender "Goodbye *Iron Horse*" 36; Fisher "*Little Big Horn*" 68; Newton "Requiem" 43; "House Cleaning" 6).

Gunsmoke

Gunsmoke was the story of the quiet, tough and fair Marshal Matt Dillon, who was in charge of the wild and unruly town of Dodge City, Kansas, in post–Civil War. Other characters included Dillon's partner Chester Goode, the town's only physician Galen "Doc" Adams, and saloon owner Kathleen "Kitty" Russell.

Gunsmoke was first introduced to audiences in 1952 on radio but was not the typical radio Western. CBS Radio producer Norman Macdonnell was quoted as saying, "[R]adio Westerns generally are written and played for kids, with lots of fistfights and bang-bang stuff. We decided to do *Gunsmoke* as a straight, adult drama" (Danson 23).

Radio columnist Tom E. Danson wrote, "*Gunsmoke* bears as little relation to the average radio or TV Western as great dramatic films like *The Gunfighter* (1950) or *The Ox-Bow Incident* (1943) to have to the average cowboy movie" (Danson "Show Has Cows" 5). The radio show's main character, Marshal Dillon, was voiced by character actor William Conrad. It aired on CBS Radio until 1961.

In 1955, CBS brought the adult Western to TV. On TV, the Dillon role was taken on by James Arness. Arness, already an established actor, played in a number of Westerns, such as *Wagon Master* (1950), *Sierra* (1950) and *Hondo* (1953), and even played the bloodsucking giant bulb-headed alien in the science fiction thriller *The Thing from Another World* (1951). Arness was joined by Milburn Stone as Doc, Amanda Blake as Kitty and Dennis Weaver as Chester. The show later added more characters: bartender Sam

Gunsmoke's James Arness as Marshal Dillon in full color on the cover of the show's own Dell Comic Book. Dell Comics also released 1966–1967 television titles: *Lassie, Mission: Impossible, Hogan's Heroes, The Monkees, Get Smart, Bewitched, F-Troop, Bewitched, I Dream of Jeannie, Bonanza, Daktari, The Monroes,* and *T.H.E. Cat* (Internet Archive).

Noonan (Glenn Strange), Native American blacksmith Quint Asper (Burt Reynolds), stable keeper Hank Miller (Hank Patterson) and stagecoach driver Jim Buck (Robert Brubaker).

Every week Marshal Dillon took on outlaws, robbers, killers, dishonest gamblers, con artists, cattle rustlers and human traffickers (or "white slavery rings," as they were known on the show). Occasionally the show would even take on subject matters such as racism, religious intolerance and civil rights. It aired on Saturdays at 10:00.

The TV show was not an instant ratings success. But by the second season, *Gunsmoke* jumped to the season's seventh highest-rated show; in the third season, it began a four-year run as TV's highest-rated shown—and it remained one of the top 25 shows of the year for the next seven seasons (Brooks and Marsh).

The half-hour show was so popular that in 1961, CBS announced that it would expand to one hour, stating that the added time would give the show "added scope in terms of greater character and plot development." Reruns of the show became known as *Marshal Dillon* in syndication (Adams "*Gunsmoke* Plans").

In 1964, all three major networks covered practically every aspect of Democratic and Republican conventions in place of regularly scheduled programs. One unnamed network executive was quoted as saying, "The politicians of both parties would scream to high heaven if they thought they had to compete with *Gunsmoke*. They know they would be clobbered and they'd never stand for it" (Gould "Should All 3" 20).

Gunsmoke ratings started to falter in the 1964–1965 season and fell even further in 1965–1966. The black-and-white Western got a color makeover for the 1966–1967 season. For the first time, viewers who owned color TVs could see Marshal Dillon's blue eyes and Kitty's red hair. A syndicated newspaper report wrote,

> The addition of color brings an exciting new dimension to the classic Western drama. The series will have its own distinctive color quality through the use of subdued hues, keyed to the earthiness of the dusty frontier town and the surrounding countryside. ... [T]he action itself will be more colorful this season, involving Marshal Dillon and his friends in more far-reaching adventures in and out of Dodge City [Brooks and Marsh; "12th Season" 9].

According to a *TV Week* Cover Close-Up, shooting in color did not change much in terms of the male wardrobe: "[T]he predominantly male cast will continue to wear the subdued, almost drab colors that typified the era. The splashes of color will come primarily from Kitty's totally redesigned wardrobe" ("There's No Sunshine" 54). One of the show's directors, Philip Leacock, remarked, "When it was announced that we were going to color, some of the people on the show said we could now repaint all the sets brilliant colors, put bright green curtains in the Long Branch Saloon and new dresses on the girls. I said no. Dodge City will look pretty much the same. It would be easy to lose the dusty atmosphere of the town by going wild in color. But we'd also be destroying the essential quality of the show" (Thomas "*Gunsmoke* in Color" 10).

But the switch to color did not translate to a ratings turnaround. That season, Saturday night audiences preferred *NBC Saturday Night at the Movies,* which featured *Stalag 17* (1953) and *Roman Holiday* (1953) that season (Brooks and Marsh).

On February 23, 1967, *The New York Times* announced that CBS "gunned down" *Gunsmoke* and that it would not be on the Fall 1967 lineup. The paper also reported that the network cancelled the show even though it was still doing well in the ratings and was the 26th highest-rated show that season, pulling in a 21.7 rating and getting 35 percent of the audience share (Gent "Marshal Dillon Gunned"). But *Gunsmoke* was soon brought back to life. George Gent of *The New York Times* wrote that *Gunsmoke* "appealed to older people, and advertisers are busily courting children and the young married these days. ... But then last Tuesday, CBS announced a change of heart. It attributed the reversal to a strong pro–*Gunsmoke* reaction from the press, from the public and from its own affiliates." Milburn Stone was quoted as saying, "They told us we were dead. We even had the wake, complete with flowers. Now we've been resurrected. It feels great" (Gent "*Gunsmoke*'s Doc").

Gunsmoke had a very powerful ally on its side, CBS president William Paley. Paley greenlit the *Gunsmoke* radio program for CBS Radio in 1951 so he lobbied the network to keep the show on the air (Potts 9).

Once CBS brought back *Gunsmoke*, they needed to clear an hour's worth of programming to make room for it. They cancelled *Gilligan's Island* and knocked off the schedule of the new comedy *Doc* (no relation to Gunsmoke character Milburn Stone's character Dr. Galen "Doc" Adams), which never made it to the airwaves.

One of the major changes was moving the show from its usual Saturday 10:00 slot to Mondays at 7:30. The move paid off. *Gunsmoke* saw a ratings resurgence and became the fourth highest-rated show that season; it stayed in the top 15 the next seven seasons (Brooks and Marsh).

By 1971, CBS started to favor contemporary comedy shows, such as *All in the Family* and *The Mary Tyler Moore Show*, over rural and Western shows that catered to an older audience as per a decision by CBS chairman William Paley and CBS president Robert Wood. This movement became known as the Rural Purge (Gent "*All in the Family*"; Brooks and Marsh).

But CBS stuck with *Gunsmoke*, which was still doing very well in the ratings. However, in the 1974–1975 season, the show took yet another ratings dip and it was cancelled in 1975 after 20 seasons on the air (Brown "CBS Will Drop").

CBS program chief Fred Silverman said the cancellation came as a "result of ratings attrition over the past several seasons," despite *Gunsmoke* picking up in the ratings in the second half of the season. Clearly CBS execs had made up their minds about the final cancellation of *Gunsmoke* (Keating "Smoke Will Linger" 13; "CBS Doesn't Plan" 26). *Gunsmoke*'s time slot was filled by two *Mary Tyler Moore Show* (1970–1977) spin-offs, *Rhoda* (1974–1978) and *Phyllis* (1975–1977).

James Arness returned to the role of Marshal Dillon in five made-for-TV movies: *Gunsmoke: Return to Dodge* (1987), *Gunsmoke II: The Last Apache* (1990), *Gunsmoke: To the Last Man* (1992), *Gunsmoke IV: The Long Ride* (1993) and *Gunsmoke V: One Man's Justice* (1993).

Gunsmoke left the airwaves after 635 episodes, 202 of them in color.

Shane

Based on the Academy Award–winning 1953 movie of the same name starring Alan Ladd and Jean Arthur, ABC's *Shane* was an hour-long Western which aired in color Saturdays at 7:30. It told the story of a gunfighter looking to get out of the business by taking a job as a ranch hand on land owned by a widowed woman who lives with her young son and father-in-law. But week after week, Shane was forced to once again pick up his gun to defend the ranch's inhabitants.

Producer Herbert Brodkin, who previously produced *The Defenders* (1961–1965) and *The Nurses* (1962–1965), cast then relative unknown David Carradine in the title role. At the time, Carradine was starring on Broadway in the play *Royal Hunt of the Sun* and had several small film and TV roles to his credit but was best known for being the son of actor John Carradine. John was renowned for his roles in hundreds of films since the 1930s; the same year David was cast in *Shane,* John starred in the cult classic *Billy the Kid versus Dracula* (Doan "Between Channels" 3; "Changes in Cast" 24; "Carradine to Star").

In 1953, when the movie *Shane* was released, the plot of a retired gunfighter forced to kill once again may have been original; but by 1966, scores of TV series and movies were made with the similar plot. Reviews reflected this:

> "Any resemblance to the movie was without intent one could hope."—Bob Hull, *Los Angeles Herald Examiner*
>
> "Instead of suspense, they built tedium."—Lawrence Laurent, *Washington Post*
>
> "Awfully long hour."—Paul Henniger, *Los Angeles Times*
>
> "It's a shame. ... I had great expectations."—Dean Gysel, *Chicago Daily News* ("Critics' Views" 61)

On top of unfavorable reviews, the show aired at the same time as the popular *The Jackie Gleason Show* on CBS, which that season reunited Gleason and Art Carney for new *Honeymooners* sketches.

Due to the reviews, stale storyline and time slot competition, *Shane* was one of TV's lowest rated shows. The network cancelled it by October but continued to air *Shane* through December ("ARB's Top-20" 68; "Second Season to Exceed" 56). It was replaced in the ABC lineup by two game shows: *The Dating Game* at 7:30 and *The Newlywed Game* at 8:00.

David Carradine went on to much bigger and better things: He starred in the hit TV series *Kung Fu* (1972–1975) and films such as *Death Race 2000* (1975), *Bound for Glory* (1976), *Q—The Winged Serpent* (1982) and Quentin Tarantino's *Kill Bill: Vol. 1* (2003) & *Kill Bill: Vol. II* (2004).

The Big Valley

When Four Star Productions announced in August 1964 that their newest television property, the Western *The Big Valley,* was being put into production, Patrick Wayne, son of John Wayne, was reportedly in talks to star in the series (Grant "TV News Beat" 129). Ultimately, Wayne was not cast; he went on to star in *The Rounders* that season. In his place, Richard Long, who starred in the show *Bourbon Street Beat* (1959–1960), was cast as the male lead. Soon after Long's casting, seasoned actress Barbara Stanwyck, the star of many film noir productions such as *Double Indemnity* (1944), signed on. Once Stanwyck and Long were cast, Four Star Productions brought on beautiful blonde actress Linda Evans in her first starring role; Peter Breck, who was best known for his role in Western *Black Saddle* (1959–1960), and Lee Majors, who went on to star in *The Six Million Dollar Man* (1973–1978) (Grant "TV News" 6; "Richard Long's Hunch" 20; Thomas "Barbara Stanwyck Stars" 34).

Stanwyck starred as the widowed Victoria Barkley, matriarch of the wealthy Barkley family. Victoria and her offspring Jarron (Long), Heath (Majors), Nick (Breck) and Audra (Linda Evans) run the prosperous Barkley Ranch in Stockton, California, in the 1870s. Stanwyck's character was often described as a "female father Cartwright of *Bonanza*" due to the family's ranch and wealth ("TV Has 'New' Star" 19). Long felt that the comparison to *Bonanza* was "unjust ... but inevitable" but hoped the comparisons would end once *The Big Valley* made its mark ("Richard Long's" 20). Breck took it a step further, stating, "The difference between *Bonanza* and *The Big Valley* is that when the Barkley boys get in trouble, they solve it. When the Cartwrights get in trouble, they run to papa" (Crawford "Breck Says" 184).

Despite starring alongside three young male actors, Stanwyck stated that she missed her former male co-stars and, more specifically, their masculinity:

> Most of my co-stars were real men—Clark Gable, Walter Huston, Robert Ryan, Spencer Tracy—and when you act with them, you knew they were male. Today—well, don't ask me what's happening to the guys. They're petulant. They're worried about their hair more than their performance. The young men today look like they're made of paper. They dance a lot. But don't ask them to push a lawnmower. They'd faint!

It was not reported what Long, Breck or Majors felt about Stanwyck's statement. But there *was* a quote attributed to "one of the young crop of leading men who once played with Miss Stanwyck": "Anyone who played opposite her—even a gorilla—would come out looking like a sissy" ("TV Has 'New' Star" 19).

ABC picked up the series for the 1965–1966 season. Although more comedies and less Westerns were being placed on the schedule, Stanwyck felt confident about Westerns and believed that viewers and networks would come back to the genre. She asserted, "This was to be the big season for comedy. Well, everybody was to fall on the floor laughing. Well, everybody fell on the floor, but they weren't laughing. So, we're falling back on Westerns" (Battelle "Barbara Stanwyck" 4). According to Long, "Westerns were going to make a television comeback as long as the focus was on people, not horses" ("Richard Long's" 20).

Before the September 16, 1965, debut of the new hour-long color show, ABC sent Long, Breck, Evans and Majors all over the country to help promote it. They made a combined 109 personal appearances. But Stanwyck stayed on the set where she reportedly put in 12-hour days ("Barbara Stanwyck Stars" 34).

In the first season, *The Big Valley* had some stiff competition on Wednesday at 9:00: On CBS, there was the popular new rural comedy *Green Acres*, which was the 11th highest-rated show of the season, and the last season of the sitcom *The Dick Van Dyke Show*, the season's 16th highest-rated show. On NBC was *Bob Hope Presents the Chrysler Theatre*. *The Big Valley* was not a sensation, but its ratings did steadily climb throughout the first season. It also did well outside the States, particularly in England where it was the #1 show (Thomas "Acting 'Rookie'" 7).

The Big Valley was also being recognized by critics. In the first season, Stanwyck won the Primetime Emmy Award for Outstanding Continued Performance by an Actress in a Leading Role.

Despite the accolades, Breck felt the show was putting too much emphasis on dramatics. "If the show becomes '*Peyton Place* Goes West,' I'll go East," he stated. "I signed up for a horse opera, not a soap opera." Breck put the blame on the network, not the writers: "They are demanding the soapy stories. As a show we have no argument with them. The rating is climbing. But I do have an argument because I think there is room on television for a true Western" ("The ABC West" 22).

Heading into the 1966–1967 season, *The Big Valley* relocated to Mondays at 10:00 where it had much less competition, airing against the CBS sitcom *The Jean Arthur Show* which suffered from low ratings and NBC's man-on-the-run drama *Run for Your Life*. *The Big Valley* was the 45th most-watched show of the season (Spencer "TV's Vast" 45).

The producers listened to Breck's recommendation and had more Western- and action-adventure–themed episodes: The Barkley brothers took on a Mexican dictator, stopped a train station robbery, and were stranded in the desert by stagecoach robbers.

Not everyone was happy about the change of format. The National Association for Better Broadcasting called it "a rough and rowdy show" (Leonard "What's On" 78). *The Big Valley* aired in the Monday 10:00 time slot for a total of three seasons. In February 1969, it was announced that the series would not be renewed.

In four seasons on the air, *The Big Valley* never got high ratings, but ABC's decision to cancel it was based more on demographics than ratings: ABC executive Leonard H. Goldenson stated that the network was focusing on the 16-to-40-year-old market with its Monday night lineup (Cray "ABC, TV's Question").

At the end of the season, Four Star Entertainment offered *The Big Valley* into syndication boasting "112 big, beautiful hours in color" ("Advertisement for *The Big Valley*" 62–63).

The Rounders

Loosely based on the 1965 Glenn Ford–Henry Fonda Western film of the same name, *The Rounders* was a Western set in the contemporary 1960s which aired opposite CBS's *The Red Skelton Hour* and the NBC sitcom *Occasional Wife* Tuesdays at 8:30. "Rounders" was a term in Texas that, according to TV critic Charles Witbeck, meant "people who go round and round in a circle and never get any place" and more often than not was in reference to "cowboys who keep aiming to get out of the saddle but never do, winding up drunk on Saturday night" (Witbeck "Texas Tall-Talk" 32).

The Rounders was a story of just that. Ron Hayes and Patrick Wayne (son of Western legend John Wayne) starred as ranch hands Ben Jones and Howdy Lewis, who are in debt to JL Ranch owner Jim Ed Love, a con artist played by Western character star Chill Wills. Wills played the same role in the film *The Rounders* and a similar role in hundreds of Westerns since the late 1930s. Each week, Ben and Howdy would try to find a way to pay off Jim Ed but always ended up owing Jim Ed even more money.

Rounding off the cast was a trick horse named Old Fooler, which was sold to Jones by Jim Ed. The problem was, Old Fooler performed tricks for everyone except Jones and Lewis. The horse was one of the reasons why Jones and Lewis were in hock to Jim Ed, considering they owed for the horse's upkeep and well-being. To make matters worse, Old Fooler has a habit of kicking in barn doors and walls, which Jones and Lewis must pay for as well.

An ABC press releases described the show as a "contemporary lusty comedy" but syndicated TV-radio writer Cynthia Lowry was quick to point out, "[I]t is doubtful whether any early-evening television program, including *The Rounders*, could really be described as lusty. Anything broadcast before 9 p.m. must be fit for tender young eyes and ears" (Lowry "New TV Season" 22).

Seemingly the only "lusty" part was when Jones and Lewis went into town to the bar, The Hi Lo, and attempted to flirt with pretty ladies. More often than not, their trip to the Hi Lo would lead to a fight and a night in jail. Of course, Jim Ed would bail out his best ranch hands, which only increased their debt.

Although not necessarily "lusty," *The Rounders* was a dusty Western that would have lent itself to black and white just as well as it did in color, with the exception of the costumes of the ladies that Jones and Lewis would chat up at the Hi Lo Saloon.

The Rounders was the first new show to air in the 1966–1967 on Tuesday, September 6, 1966. Critic Joan Crosby included it on her list of "Best Bets" of the season:

> [I]t's nice to report [*The Rounders*] is good. Ron Hayes is attractive and funny as a happy-go-lucky cowpoke, and Patrick Wayne is handsome and toothy as his partner, Chill Wills plays Jim Ed Love, their wealthy conniving Texas-talking boss. Also, prominent and a scene stealer if there ever was one, is Old Fooler, the horse. ... This is not subtle comedy, but it's fast paced, zany, obvious stuff and fun [Crosby "*Rounders* Kicks" 63].

Other critics were not as impressed:

> "Poorly motivated free-for-all made [it] seem square."—Harry Harris, *Philadelphia Enquirer*
>
> "Faintly amusing in spots."—Bernie Harrison, *Washington Evening Star*
>
> "An unfortunate something of a present-day Western comedy."—Bob Williams, *New York Post*
>
> "Floundered into a dull review."—Dwight Newton, *San Francisco Examiner*
>
> "Comedy is predictable, broad stuff aimed at the kiddie audience or young-in-heart adults who don't mind an obvious laugh track plus and overdose of cornball dialogue."—Pete Rahn, *St. Louis Globe-Democrat*

The majority of the positive reviews focused on Chill Wills and the show's horse:

> "Wills gives some solid professional touches to this otherwise bland entry."—Katy Gardella, *New York Daily News*
>
> "Actors play straight men to one of the funniest animals on the screen."—Bob Hull, *Los Angeles Herald-Examiner*
>
> "Chill Wills ... and a trick horse are the only hope for this one."—Bill Barrett, *Cleveland Press* ("The Critics Review" 36)

The show's debut episode received a 23.1 rating along with a 43.2 share of the audience but had little competition: It aired against a repeat showing of the film *Home from the Hill* (1960) on the *NBC Tuesday Night at the Movies* and the last episode of the CBS summer replacement *Hippodrome*, which was hosted by Eddie Albert and featured Nancy Sinatra, British singers Paul and Barry Ryan, and a troupe of European circus performers ("Peeks at Ratings" 35).

After the initial ratings success, *The Rounders* found itself at the bottom of the ratings bin. Now airing at the same time was the second highest-rated show of the year, *The Red Skelton Hour* on CBS. Less than a month into the series run, ABC had the show marked for "replacement or shuffling." It was cancelled in November but ran on the network until January 3, 1967 ("NBC Claims" 10; Gysel "Ratings KO" 40).

The Rounders was replaced by the Larry Cohen–created, Quinn Martin–produced science fiction series *The Invaders*.

The Monroes

The Monroe family—father, mother and five children—made their way west to the state of Wyoming in the mid-1800s. But along the way, the Monroe parents drowned in the Snake River. Now forced to make it in the wild frontier alone, the Monroe children: 18-year-old Clay (Michael Anderson, Jr.), daughter Kathy (Barbara Hershey), twin boys Jefferson (Keith Schultz) and Kevin (Kevin Schultz) and the youngest, Amy (Tammy Locke). They are aided by a Native American, Dirty Jim (Ron Soble), who came along on the family's journey. Soble was not of Native American ancestry but stated that he abhorred the way Native Americans were typically portrayed in film and television: "I'm nauseated by the stoic picture of the noble redman. I did a lot of homework on the Indian for my part" (Leonard "Soble on Indian" 42).

The hour-long ABC Western debuted on Wednesday, September 7, 1966, at 8:00. At the time, most prime time Westerns were being watched by an older audience; *The Monroes* was directly aimed at teenagers and young adults and had characters their own age with whom they could identify. *The Monroes* showed early promise and received mostly positive reviews:

> "Like a breath of fresh air amid the synthetics and forced humor of most TV programming."—Percy Shaim, *Boston Globe*
>
> "Carefully aimed at that 50% of the population that is under the age of 25 years."—Laurence Laurent, *Washington Post*
>
> "This one should make it with the kids."—Louis R. Cedrone, Jr., *Baltimore Sun*
>
> "A believable, sensitive and often touching story."—Rex Polier, *Philadelphia Evening Bulletin*
>
> "Has all the makings of a winner."—Walt Dutton, *Los Angeles Times* ("The Critics Review" 36)
>
> "Lots of beautiful scenery. Most of the early episodes, in fact, were shot in color near historic Jackson's Hole in the picturesque Grand Teton National Forest in Wyoming."—Martin Hogan, Jr., *Cincinnati Enquirer* (Hogan "What Makes" 6)
>
> "The scenery is the star of *The Monroes*. ... That opening shot of the Grand Tetons rising above the valley—it was awesome and magnificent and truly overpowering."—Donald Freeman, *Copley News Service* (Freeman "'Monroes' Hailed" 15)
>
> "Filmed entirely in the Jackson Hole region of Wyoming in the shadow of the spectacular Grand Teton mountains, so there's a large factor for those who have color sets."—Ernie Kreiling, *Salina Journal* (Kreiling "Actors, Sets" 6)
>
> "If you don't have a color set, you are cheated."—Dean Gysel, *Chicago Daily News* ("The Critics Review" 36)

> "Small-fry Western has big Wyoming scenery for background."—Bob Williams, *New York Post* ("The Critics Review" 36)
>
> "The scenery ... spectacular."—Harry Harris, *Philadelphia Inquirer* ("The Critics Review" 36)
>
> "If this newcomer didn't have any plot at all, it could be still enjoyable for its truly impressive color photography."—Clay Gowran, *Chicago Tribune* ("The Critics Review" 36)

Monroes writer-producer Al C. Ward said, "The public is just too sophisticated to accept the old sound stage shots with mountain backdrop. Viewers today know every rock in the San Fernando Valley by sight. Jackson Hole brings TV a fresh look and a new vista" (Freeman "*Monroes* Hailed" 15).

Although critics were almost universally impressed by both the story and the photography, viewers did not take to *The Monroes* and it constantly lost out to *Lost in Space* and *The Beverly Hillbillies* on CBS and *The Virginian* on NBC. The National Association for Better Broadcasting called it "one of the biggest disappointments of the new season, being too violent for children and full of contrived situations" (Brooks and Marsh; "Shock Appeal" 44). After one episode, *Washington Post* TV writer Lawrence Laurent asked,

> Can the Monroes survive in the low Nielsens? Last night's episode had drownings in the Snake River, a thunderstorm, a renegade Indian who is struck by lightning, a six-year-old girl who survives a fever along with the usual assortment of horsemanship and fistfighting. ... The first episode ended without victory, without defeat. The kids were left in that cold, lonely county and armed with little more than a saying from an almanac: "Pride digs in: vanity runs away." Pride, however, isn't likely to carry this series ... through the chill and even lonelier feeling that goes with a low Nielsen rating [Laurent "Can *Monroes*" 28].

When ratings are on the decline, a typical TV tactic is the addition of new characters. *The Monroes* did just that, only this character was of the four-legged variety. In October 1966, *The Monroes* added a family dog, a white great Pyrenees named Snow—and rearranged the entire series to do so. "Seventeen scripts already were written without a dog, so this meant re-writing roughly half of those scripts," said Ward. He added that he and the network were convinced that Snow would help in the ratings (Humphrey "Monroes Go" 19).

Ratings did not improve.

The Monroes barely survived being cancelled in mid-season. In January 1967, executives were looking to improve the ratings and changed the overall feel of the show in an attempt to appeal even more to a younger audience. The show's executive producer Ben Fox stated that the show was projecting a

> new image ... new values and goals. We're trying to capture the forward thrust of American youth. ... We're going much deeper into characterization. We're getting into the human frustrations and trials. And we're giving more emphasis to the light touch, to humor. There have to be laughs and love to make the show credible [Hogan "What Makes" 6].

Fox also said that writers were instructed to add "all kinds of little things into the scripts—phrases which might be identified with the language of today. We will use such terms as 'okay' and 'kids.' 'Kids' is better than young'uns. That is only one way we will seek to capture the feeling of living as it is today." Fox gave another example:

> There is a surprising similarity between the goals of teen-aged youth in 1967 to those of the same group back in 1876. Just as kids are interested in cars and souped-up hot rods today, so Clay Monroe and a young friend will be shown in an upcoming script as they devise ways to speed up their sulkies and wagons [Jones "It's a New Look" 10].

Fox was hopeful the show would pick up in the ratings when audiences saw the changes. He noted that *The Monroes* "jumped 7.5 Nielsen points since January 11. We have to assume that the points came from *The Virginian* and *Lost in Space* ... we have to assume that the audience has noticed the changes." But Fox knew that it would be an uphill climb for the network to agree to bring the show back for another season: "Our Nielsen right now is about 16.0. You usually need between 15 and 20 for renewal" (Hogan "What Makes" 6). According to Ron Soble,

> There's a 60–40 chance we'll go next year. Remember, we're dealing with a nervous network. CBS or NBC would have with us. [*sic*] As it is, we're firm for 24 shows and reruns, and they may do it. *The Big Valley* last year moved to a new time slot in the summer and built a new audience. If the same thing doesn't happen to us, we'll be just another of TV's many gravestones [Leonard "Soble on Indian" 42].

Ratings-wise, *The Monroes* did much better in England, thanks to Michael Anderson who *was* from England. The actor said, "At the start of the year, the BBC had announced they would present no more Westerns. But they made an exception with *The Monroes*. And now look—No. 1!" (Freeman "*Monroes* Star" 35).

The show added a dog, attempted to relate to a younger audience, was #1 in England, and had somewhat of an uptick in ratings in the States; but in March 1967, it was announced that *The Monroes* would not be picked up for another season ("Syndicators Have Pitches" 100). Letters reportedly flowed in to ABC-TV vice-president of programming Leonard Goldberg, protesting the cancellation (Peterson "Viewers Protest" 5). But they did not change anyone's mind and the last episode aired on March 15, 1967, after 26 episodes on the air. *The Monroes* was replaced by the historical Western *Custer*.

The Virginian

The Virginian, set in the fictitious town of Medicine Bow in the Wyoming Territory in the 1890s, revolved around the Shiloh ranch foreman who went by the name "The Virginian." The series was based on a 1902 novel by Owen Wister, which had reportedly sold over two million copies by time *The Virginian* debuted on NBC on September 19, 1962 ("*Virginian* Bowing" 133).

Prior to coming to television, the book *The Virginian* was made into four feature films, two silent in 1914 and 1923 and two with sound in 1929 and 1946. *The Virginian* was originally brought to TV on July 6, 1958, on the NBC anthology series *Decision* with James Drury in the title role. The half-hour black-and-white episode was to serve as a pilot episode for the series.

TV viewers had to wait nearly four years for the show to finally develop. It was picked up by NBC in the fall of 1962 and Drury was cast as a more rugged The Virginian than was in the pilot. Drury in the meantime had played various roles on the TV Westerns *Black Saddle, The Rebel* and *Wagon Train*, and in the film *Ride the High Country* (1962).

Other characters in the series included distinguished Shiloh Ranch owner Judge Garth (Lee J. Cobb) who hired the Virginian as foreman and was often described as a father figure to him; Judge Garth's daughter Betsy (Roberta Shore); Trampas (Doug McClure), a rowdy cowhand who often found himself in scrapes with the law, and Trampas and the Virginian's buddy Steve Hill (Gary Clarke).

When *The Virginian* premiered in color, it was called "the most ambitious and costly programming in network television history," due to its weekly 90-minute running time. Three production units were used; each unit had separate writer-producer and producer-director teams and were responsible for casting and filming of each episode's interwoven storylines of the series main characters ("*Virginian* Bowing" 133).

Universal brought in Alex Quiroga as *The Virginian*'s color coordinator. Mexican-born Quiroga wrote a column for the *Los Angeles Times* in 1963, saying that the U.S. was

> the most color-conscious country in the world. ... It's no wonder, therefore that this is the country in which color television has been pioneered and perfected. We not only have the necessary standard of living and technical skill to bring forth color TV. ... The people who have such a strong yen for color in their television also have a strong insistence that this color be nothing short of the best. They want their fire engines red, their trees green and, most important, their skin tones flesh colored.
>
> We could design a show exclusively for color that would look terrific, but we must remember that this show is still being viewed by many in black and white. Hence we must choose, for example, only those color contrasts that also produce good brightness contrasts on black and white sets [Quiroga 576].

The show's intro featured the cast on horseback while the theme by Percy Faith played. Instrumental mood music bandleader Faith may be best known for his song "Theme from *A Summer Place*" and the album *Themes for Young Lovers*.

Each episode featured a guest star from television, Hollywood or Broadway. Many noteworthy actors made appearances, including Leonard Nimoy, DeForest Kelley, William Shatner, Forrest Tucker, Robert Lansing, Patrick Macnee and Robert Culp, all of whom made a splash in the 1966–1967 TV schedule.

In *The Virginian*'s first year (1962–1963), it was the only color program in its time slot and it pulled in respectable ratings. But in the second year, ratings took off. *The Virginian* was reliably a top-25 show for the next several seasons (Brooks and Marsh).

In the meantime, the cast of characters grew: singing cowboy Randy Benton (Randy Boone), Deputy Sheriff Emmett Ryker (Clu Gulager) and Morgan Star (John Dehner). The latter ran the ranch after Judge Garth was named governor of Wyoming in the fourth season and written out of the show.

The Virginian was so popular that in the fall of 1965, NBC presented a spin-off, *Laredo*. The *Laredo* characters were introduced in the *Virginian* episode "We've Lost a Train," in which Trampas, en route to Mexico to pick up a bull, was saved by Company B of the Texas Rangers. These Rangers were later featured in *Laredo*.

In 1966–1967, *The Virginian* had very stiff (and, for the first time, all-color) competition in its 90-minute Wednesday 7:30 slot. ABC-wise, it aired opposite *Batman* and *The Monroes* and CBS-wise opposite *Lost in Space* and *The Beverly Hillbillies*. But *Batman* began dropping in the ratings, and *The Monroes* and *Lost in Space* failed to live up to expectation. Only *The Beverly Hillbillies* delivered: It rose to the seventh highest-rated show of the season (Brooks and Marsh).

The Virginian outdid expectations and became the tenth highest-rated show of the season, tying with *Gomer Pyle, U.S.M.C., The Lawrence Welk Show* and *The Ed Sullivan Show* with a 22.8 rating. It even pulled in good ratings early in the season when the initial excitement was still high for *Batman, Lost in Space* and *The Monroes* (Brooks and Marsh; "The Numbers Game" 60; "The Latest" 69).

That season, *The Virginian* saw some major changes in casting, after the Shiloh Ranch was purchased from Judge Garth by John Grainger (Charles Bickford). Along with Grainger came his grandchildren Stacey (Don Quine) and Elizabeth (Sara Lane). Notable guest stars included Angie Dickinson, George Kennedy, Jack Lord, Cloris Leachman and Andrew Prine.

In the 1966–1967 season, the Virginian dealt with cattle rustlers, tracked down a killer, fought with other ranch owners, was held up while on a stagecoach, got amnesia and was framed for a hold up.

At the end of the 1966–1967 season, Charles Bickford passed away at the age of 76 and was replaced by John McIntire, who played John Grainger's brother Clay. Clay became the owner of the ranch and, along with his wife Holly (Jeanette Nolan), looked after Stacey and Elizabeth.

The Virginian remained one of the top-20 highest-rated programs, despite the addition and subtraction of cast members, until the 1969–1970 season when it dropped in the ratings due to a strong CBS lineup which featured *The Glen Campbell Goodtime Hour, Hee Haw* and *The Beverly Hillbillies*. *The Virginian* was retooled for the 1970–1971 season and was renamed *The Men from Shiloh*.

The Men from Shiloh featured a new 1970s–style introduction and a new theme by famed composer Ennio Morricone, who also scored *A Fistful of Dollars* (1964), *The Good, the Bad and the Ugly* (1966) and *Once Upon a Time in the West* (1968). There were also more new cast members and plots. In *The Men from Shiloh,* the Shiloh ranch was purchased from the Graingers by Englishman Colonel Alan MacKenzie (Stewart Granger), who came to the ranch along with his valet Parker (John McLiam). The ranch also acquired a new hand, Roy Tate (Lee Majors). In the series, the remaining characters spent the season having a hard time adjusting to MacKenzie's formal style.

The show did pick up in ratings that season and was the season's 18th highest-rated show. In March 1971, MCA announced that *The Virginian/The Man from Shiloh*'s entire 249 color episode library would be sold into syndication, which at the time was typically a sign that a show was marked for cancellation ("'Name' in Syndication" 40).

In May 1971 came the announcement that *The Men from Shiloh* would be cancelled, but the network would be keeping Lee Majors under contract (Scheuer 48). Majors played on *Owen Marshall, Counselor at Law* (1971–1974) the next season, then took on the role of Steve Austin in his most notable series, *The Six Million Dollar Man* (1973–1978).

The Men from Shiloh's last episode aired on March 24, 1971, before the show's notice of cancellation by the network. In 1971, *The Virginian/The Men from Shiloh* was one of the longest running shows shot entirely in color (with the exception of the 1958 pilot episode), second only to fellow Western *Bonanza*. All nine seasons ran in the same Wednesday 7:30 slot.

James Drury, who played the Virginian throughout the show's run, felt that the cancellation was due to a cultural shift:

> The television Western is by no means dead but it's resting. I think it's because young people are so involved with social issues that they're bored with Westerns in which everything is

black and white, full of good guys and bad guys. ... I would have been happy to go on with the series. But nine years is far too long for an actor of my varied interests. ["TV Westerns Resting" 20].

In 1974, Drury did the ABC series *Firehouse* in which he played Captain Spike Ryerson for one season.

The Man from Shiloh's time slot was filled in the 1971–1972 season by the Jack Webb–produced police procedural *Adam-12* and *The NBC Mystery Movie*, which that season featured three shows, *McCloud*, *Columbo* and *McMillan & Wife* on a rotating basis. Both shows were a success for the network (Brooks and Marsh).

Laredo

The characters of NBC's *Laredo* were first introduced to TV audiences on the April 21, 1965, episode of *The Virginian*, "We've Lost a Train," which served as a backdoor pilot for *Laredo*. In the episode, Shiloh Ranch hand Trampas stopped at a Laredo, Texas, saloon where, after watching a woman sing and dance, he got into a fight with the woman's jealous boyfriend. Later in the episode, the boyfriend's gang came looking for Trampas, but he was saved by Company B of the Texas Rangers: Reese Bennett (Neville Brand), Joe Riley (William Smith), Peter Brown (Chad Cooper) and Captain Parmalee (Philip Carey).

The hour-long color Western *Laredo* premiered on September 16, 1965, and featured guest star Burgess Meredith as crooked prospector Grubstake "Grubby" Sully, who once double-crossed the Rangers. The show also featured Beverly Garland as Angie, a Laredo saloon owner. Future *Laredo* guest stars included George Kennedy, Bruce Dern, DeForest Kelley, Kurt Russell, Lyle Talbot, Lee Van Cleef, John Carradine and Doodles Weaver.

Most newspaper reviews for *Laredo* were far from kind:

> "One constructive step ought to be taken ... like using live ammunition on the writers."—Jack Anderson, *Miami Herald*

> "A complete disaster area."—Larry Wolters, *Chicago Tribune*

> "A full-hour travesty in color."—Ann Hodges, *Houston Chronicle*

> "Sharp improvement will be needed."—Bernie Harrison, *Washington Evening Star*

> "Passable enough for Western fans."—Rex Polier, *Philadelphia Evening Bulletin*

But the reviews were not all bad: James Flanagan of *The Cleveland Plain Dealer* called it a "Superior production" ("The Critics' View, Part 2" 66).

The Texas Rangers took on bandits, gangs, kidnappings, escaped convicts and murderers and regularly featured on-screen shootings and deaths.

The color on the program was coordinated by Robert Brower, who also worked on *The Virginian*, *Pistols'n'Petticoats* (1966–1967), *Tammy* (1965–1966) and *Wagon Train* (1957–1965) along with movies *Destination Moon* (1950), *When Worlds Collide* (1951) and Alfred Hitchcock's *Rope* (1948). It was given vivid color by both the wardrobe and set design. The wardrobe supervisor Vincent Dee also worked on *Run for Your Life*

(1965–1968), *Dragnet* (1967–1970), *Mr. Terrific* (1967) and *The Virginian* that season. Set decorator John McCarthy, Jr., also worked that season on *Run for Your Life, Pistols'n'Petticoats, Mr. Terrific* and *Bob Hope Presents the Chrysler Theatre.*

Unlike *The Virginian, Laredo* was never a ratings success and was the 43rd highest-rated show of the season—one of its lowest-rated shows ("TVs Vast" 55). NBC renewed it for another season despite its poor showing and moved it to Fridays at 10:00. There it competed with the English spy import *The Avengers* and the last hour of the *CBS Friday Night Movies.* The show also added a new character, rookie Texas Ranger Erik Hunter (Robert Wolders). But ratings failed to improve in the Friday slot.

In February 1967, NBC cancelled *Laredo* after two seasons and 56 episodes ("CBS Reshuffle" 26; "Television's 1966–1967" 180). The last episode aired on April 7. NBC replaced it in the Friday 10:00 slot with a rotating schedule of hour-long special programs.

The Road West

Set in the years following the Civil War, *The Road West* was the story of widower Benjamin Pride (Barry Sullivan), who moved his family from Ohio to a new homestead in the Kansas Territory, which had both fertile land and all the dangers of the wild west. His family consisted of sons Timothy (Andrew Prine) and Kip (Kelly Corcoran), daughter Midge (Brenda Scott) and his parents (Charles Steel, Katherine Squire).

TV critic Charles Witbeck wrote that the Prides were "ready to stand off marauders, Indians, land grabbers, floods and famine" (Witbeck "Drama in a Sod" 18). The family received help from brave friend Chance Reynolds (Glenn Corbett) and Ben's love interest Dr. Elizabeth Reynolds (Kathryn Hays).

Executive producer Norman Macdonnell, who had previously written for *Gunsmoke* and produced *The Virginian,* felt that many TV shows were "wholly lacking in human values" and explained how *The Road West* was different:

> Ben Pride is a man who is a simple farmer originally from Ohio. His main concern is for his family. He is willing to fight for them—die for them if need be—and hold the family together at all costs. But Pride doesn't wear a six-gun to do it. Neither did most of the early pioneers. Their main interest wasn't shooting but building. It is this idea—a return to basic moral and human values, a reflection on the basic dignity of man—for which we are striving in *The Road West* ["*Road West* Aims" 12].

The show's stars also felt that *The Road West* was very different. Kathryn Hays echoed Macdonnell's sentiment, stating, "Our show is really an hour-long dramatic series which happens to be set in the West. The people and their relationships are the important thing. ... Though each story will be separate and complete ... there will be continual development of all the major characters as the series progresses" (Coffey "TV to Take" 10).

Sullivan, who previously starred in the spy series *The Man Called X* (1956–1957), the dramatic adventure series *Harbormaster* (1957–1958) and the Western *The Tall Man* (1960–1962), believed that he would never do another TV series until he unintentionally accepted *The Road West*: "When I began filming the show, I thought it was a feature for '*Tuesday Night at the Movies.* Honest. When I heard it was going to be a pilot, I got a bellyache. And when I heard it had sold, I didn't know whether to run or check into a mental hospital" ("Sullivan Changes" 77).

The production on *The Road West* helped change Sullivan's mind about TV: "What a change from *Tall Man* where we never had a script until the day of shooting. It was murder—which, incidentally, is what a series is under the best of circumstances. With *Road West*, we have scripts weeks in advance plus the best of everything—producers, writers, directors and actors." Sullivan later praised the medium of TV: "Actors often talk of the lack of time for rehearsal in television. Nonsense! With pros, the time is found and utilized. With a professional crew, you can have a top TV show. ... There's plenty of time to do something worthwhile in television" ("Sullivan Changes" 77).

Sullivan later added, "After 50 Westerns, I consider the horse sort of a second home" but other actors on the show were not as confident about their riding skills. Kathryn Hays admitted that she preferred limousines and was just getting used to horseback riding. Andrew Prine stated that he was not in love with riding even though he learned on the series *Wide Country* (1962–1963). but was "always looking to improve." Brenda Scott was attempting to overcome her fear of horses ("Westerns Are Popular" 19).

Kathryn Hayes called Elizabeth Reynolds "an unusual female character for television, a very strong independent, almost defiant woman. In the pilot, she was an awfully good person, perhaps unrealistically so, but I think in recent episodes we've given her new dimensions and a more rounded human image" (Coffey "TV to Take" 10).

In March 1966, NBC vice-president of programs Mort Warner announced that the hour-long *Road West* would air in color on Mondays at 9:00 ("Barry Sullivan" 12).

The Road West suffered from an inconsistent schedule. The show was preempted five times in the 1966–1967 season in favor of *Perry Como's Kraft Music Hall*; host Como had been performing for 33 years and was still popular with audiences in every age demographic ("7 Perry Como" 49). The season marked *Kraft Music Hall*'s eighth season on NBC ("Perry Como Signs" 12). *Perry Como's Kraft Music Hall* aired a total of seven times that season, also preempting *Bob Hope Presents the Chrysler Theatre* on two Wednesday nights that season.

Even though *The Road West* did not feature a shootout every week like some Westerns, it had plenty of action. In the two-part premiere "This Savage Land," a band of bushwhackers led by Jud Barker (George C. Scott) and his henchman Stacey Daggart (John Drew Barrymore) confront the Pride family on their new Kansas homestead. The bushwhackers burn and badly injure Grandpa Tom Pride in a fire, kill Grandma Pride, and kidnap the rest of the family. When it looked like there was no hope for them, they were rescued by a bushwhacker who had a change of heart.

TV critics praised *The Road West* and felt that it would succeed in the ratings:

> "All the Western charm of an old William S. Hart boot."—Joseph T. Sullivan, *Boston Herald*
>
> "Looks like it will build up a steady audience."—Percy Shain, *Boston Globe*
>
> "We think [*The Road West*] will be taken to the hearts of viewers."—Kay Gardella, *New York Daily News*
>
> "Beamed with a surprising degree of effectiveness."—Bob Hull, *Los Angeles Herald–Examiner*
>
> "Had many moments which were rewarding."—Terrence O'Flaherty, *San Francisco Chronicle*

"Excellently cast and acted."—Jack E. Anderson, *Miami Herald* ("Critics' Views" 64)

Although critics may have been fond of the show, audiences felt differently. Possibly this traditional Western would have been more successful in 1956, when the Western genre was at its peak of popularity. *The Road West* lost in the ratings to the popular CBS series *The Andy Griffith Show* and the new ABC police drama *The Felony Squad* in the first half-hour and two very modern TV shows in the season half-hour, ABC's nighttime soap opera *Peyton Place* and the popular new CBS sitcom *Family Affair*.

After running into what Newspaper Enterprise Association writer Stan Maays called a "roadblock, manned by the Nielsen rating mob," the show added actress Jan Shepard, whom writer Paddy Cheyevsky nicknamed the "actress with the saddest eyes" because she was almost exclusively cast in emotional roles where inevitably she would cry her eyes out. On *The Road West*, she played recent widow Ellen Brewster, who accompanied the Prides on their move from their Kansas homestead as they forged further west (Maays "*Road West*, Cancelled" 35).

Shepard would have continued in her role as Ellen Brewster but in July 1967 it was announced that *The Road West* would be cancelled. The last of the show's 29 episodes aired on August 28, 1967, and it was replaced in the fall by the anthology series *The Danny Thomas Hour*.

In 1969, *The Road West*'s two-part premiere episode was released to movie theaters under the title *This Savage Land*. It played as a second feature at drive-ins throughout the U.S.

Rango

Coming into the 1966–1967 season, ABC had high expectations for the variety series *The Milton Berle Show*, starring "Mr. Television" Milton Berle. Berle was one of TV's earliest and most recognizable stars and signed with ABC after he requested his early release from a 30-year NBC contract he signed in 1951, reportedly worth a million dollars ("Milton Berle Signs" 243; "Networks Seek Sean" 20). Berle tirelessly promoted his new show and even appeared with ABC's two hottest characters, Batman and Robin, to promote *The Milton Berle Show* on ABC's *7 Nights to Remember* preview show.

The hour-long *Milton Berle Show*, which debuted on September 9, 1966, at 9:00, featured big-name guests throughout its run: Adam West, Van Williams, Bruce Lee, Steve Allen, Lucille Ball, Bette Davis, Bob Hope and Phyllis Diller, and musical acts Paul Revere and the Raiders, Peter and Gordon, the Yardbirds and Sam the Sham and the Pharaohs. But despite the hype, audiences largely rejected the show in favor of *The CBS Friday Night Movies*, the 17th highest-rated show that season, and the last half hour of *The Man from U.N.C.L.E.* and *T.H.E. Cat* on NBC (Brooks and Marsh).

ABC cancelled *The Milton Berle Show* and replaced the first half-hour with the Western comedy *Rango*, starring Tim Conway fresh off his role as bumbling Ensign Parker on ABC's *McHale's Navy* (1962–1966). Conway took on the title character of Rango, who was not much different than his previous role with one major exception: He traded in his Navy uniform for a Texas Ranger badge and cowboy hat.

The bumbling Rango believed he was the toughest Texas Ranger but he cannot shoot straight, ride a horse or catch a crook. Other characters included Rango's commanding officer, Captain Horton (Norman Alden), and a Native American sidekick, Pink Cloud (Guy Marks). Captain Horton continuously attempted to get Rango out of the Texas Rangers, but Rango had a powerful ally: his Uncle George, who happened to be head of the Texas Rangers.

Rango first aired, in color, on Friday the 13th of January 1967. Conway felt the starting date was appropriate "because Rango is such an unlucky guy. He means well. He tries hard, but everything he does turns out wrong—we hope, hilariously wrong" ("Tim Conway Fills" 25).

Rango bumbled his way through the take-down of gang members, outlaws and bandits. But *Rango*, like *The Milton Berle Show*, failed to impress audiences. In the show's first weeks, it lost out to *The CBS Friday Night Movies* and NBC's *The Man from U.N.C.L.E.* ("Second Season" 60; "CBS Edges" 60). ABC cancelled the show, and ten others, in early April 1967. New episodes ran until May 5. There were only 17 episodes (Dubé 15).

Chapter Eight

Spies

The first four films with Sean Connery as British MI6 Agent 007 James Bond—*Dr. No* (1962), *From Russia with Love* (1963), *Goldfinger* (1964) and *Thunderball* (1965)—kicked off a spy craze that swept the world. In 1965, *Thunderball* did record-breaking box office business, and retail stores reported "fantastic success" with James Bond–themed items such as pajamas and cologne. Merchants called James Bond toys "the hottest thing on the market" (Reiter "How Do Shore").

Movie companies all over the globe attempted to capitalize on the craze. America's answer to James Bond, *Our Man Flint* (1966), grossed over $16,000,000. Italy flooded the market with Bond clones in films such as *Super Agent Super Dragon* (1966), *Kiss Kiss ... Bang Bang* (1966) and *Last Man to Kill* (1966). El Santo, Mexico's real-life masked professional wrestler, comic book hero and cinema monster slayer, changed gears to appear in the Bond-inspired spy adventure *Operation 67* (1966). A string of spy flicks featuring super-spy Kommissar X were filmed and produced throughout Europe beginning with *Kiss Kiss ... Kill Kill* (1966). Spanish director Jess Franco directed two French-language super-spy films, starring movie tough guy Eddie Constantine, which paid homage to Bond films, *Residence for Spies* (1966) and *Attack of the Robots* (1966). From the Philippines came the low-budget *James Batman* (1966), exploiting the Bond *and* Batman crazes.

In music, Johnny Rivers had a hit (reaching #3 in 1966 on the Billboard Hot 100 charts) with the spy-themed "Secret Agent Man," which also served as a theme song for the British television show *Danger Man* (1960–1968). The Ventures and crooner Mel Tormé recorded cover versions of "Secret Agent Man" that same year (Brooks and Marsh).

Some felt that the spy craze was "a way for the public to escape the fears of the Cold War, and that they can voice their support for evil or good by watching Bond and friends." Some saw it as a passing fad. (Wigglesworth 2).

Regardless of the reason why people were interested, TV attempted to capitalize on the spy craze.

Get Smart

Get Smart, a satirical take on James Bond spy adventures, chronicled bumbling Agent 86 Maxwell Smart (Don Adams) of the counterintelligence organization CONTROL. Much like James Bond, Smart found himself fighting against an evil organization, part Red Flag Communist, part neo–Nazi and part paramilitary despot: KAOS.

Like Bond, Maxwell Smart had his fair share of colorful gadgets, most famously his shoe phone and the Cone of Silence, a device designed to prevent others from overhearing top secret conversations; it rarely worked, and sometimes even prevented the people using it from hearing each other. Other gadgets included Explosive Expando-Rice Ignitopaste Toothpaste, Exploding Birthday Cake, Cigarette Hand Grenades, Poison Phonograph Needle, Knockout Lipstick and Bazooka Broom.

Smart's partner was Agent 99 (Barbara Feldon). Other characters included the Chief of CONTROL (Edward Platt), his hapless assistant Larabee (Robert Karvelas), the humanoid robot Hymie (Dick Gautier) and KAOS agents Ludwig Von Siegfried (Bernie Kopell) and his sidekick Shtarker (King Moody).

Get Smart was created by Buck Henry and Mel Brooks. Buck Henry went on to write the films *The Graduate* (1967) and *Heaven Can Wait* (1978), and at the time, Mel Brooks was famous for writing for the TV sketch comedy series *Your Show of Shows* (1950–1954) and for his comedy album *The 2000 Year Old Man* (1960). Brooks later wrote and directed a score of comedic films such as *The Producers* (1967), *Blazing Saddles* (1974) and *Young Frankenstein* (1974).

When *Get Smart* was pitched to ABC, the network was less than kind when they rejected it. According to Henry, the network said the show was "creepy," "not funny," "un–American," and they asked, "Didn't the writers understand that people liked to eat while watching television and that a subplot about trash would turn their stomachs?" The network's comments were in reference to the pilot episode "Mr. Big" in which KAOS plotted to destroy the Statue of Liberty using a heat death ray called Enthermo. Smart and Agent 99 discover that the Enthermo was being hidden on a garbage scow covered in trash. Henry added that ABC executives told him that Americans wouldn't accept a cowardly dog: Max's shaggy sidekick Fang, who fled after being threatened by the bad guys; "and there was 'too long a list of things we can't foist on the American public'" (Smith "How Maxwell Smart").

NBC took a chance on *Get Smart,* despite the garbage and the cowardly dog. It debuted on September 18, 1965. Critics praised it on every level:

> "The ha-ha, and even ho-ho, quota is refreshingly high."—Harry Harris, *Philadelphia Enquirer*
>
> "The wackiest farce."—Martin Hogan, Jr., *Cincinnati Enquirer*
>
> "[Don Adams] almost succeeds in being the straight man to himself."—Jack Anderson, *Miami Herald*
>
> "Pure fun from start to finish."—Aleen MacMinn, *Los Angeles Times*
>
> "May be the best of the 30-minute comedies."—Allen Rich, *Hollywood Citizen-News*
>
> "Great Comic Possibilities."—Rick DuBrow, United Press International ("The Critics' View, Part 2" 69)

The pilot episode "Mr. Big" was shot in black-and-white but every subsequent episode was in color. In the fall of 1965, *Get Smart* aired on NBC on Saturdays at 8:30, right before the *NBC Saturday Night Movie.* The series' producers capitalized on the color broadcasts, most notably with Barbara Feldon's wardrobe. According to the actress:

> I wore my own clothes on the first few *Get Smart* episodes until we had time to shop and figure out just what Agent 99 would wear in her part. It's odd how the influence of the colors I

wear on the show has changed my wardrobe choices—along with the high colors that exist in California—the flowers and the pink and green houses. Color is everywhere....

Feldon added that her wardrobe was influenced by pop art, which was the rage in 1966 ("Agent 99 Gets Smart" 514). Set designers and producers also took advantage of color, giving Smart an apartment with colorful 1960s furniture. There was also an occasional psychedelic villain with a multi-colored hippie aesthetic, like the Groovy Guru (Larry Storch).

In its first season, *Get Smart* was TV's 12th most-watched show. Adams was not surprised by its success; in fact, he predicted it. "To predict is one thing, to see it happen is quite another," said Adams. "It's a tremendous satisfaction to discover that all the work involved in 39 weeks of shooting has not been in vain" (Brooks and Marsh; "*Get Smart*'s Don Adams" 13).

Get Smart's success was often credited to its multilevel humor that could be enjoyed by viewers of all ages, ranging from smart satire to gratuitous slapstick. An uncredited Joe Mikolas, best known for his roles on *The Ernie Kovacs Show* (1961–1962), provided *Get Smart* with many of its most memorable catchphrases: "Sorry about that, Chief," "Would you believe..." and "Gee, you really know how to hurt a guy." Henry said, "Everyone goes around sounding like Don Adams. The repetition is great for the show. Its value is very commercial, because it allows kids—adults—to play a character. And Maxwell Smart is perfect with ready-made dialogue." He later added, "We're always looking for the repeat line to help the show's identification. We can never hope to do anything as crazy as what happens in real life" (Scott "Smart Sayings" 32).

In time for the second season, a large array of items with the *Get Smart* name hit store shelves. Record stores carried a 1966 adventure album, *Get Smart*, where Don Adams as Maxwell Smart recalled his best TV adventures from the first two seasons. Barbra Feldon recorded a 7" 45 RPM single with the songs "Max" and the cult favorite "99." Bookstores stocked Dell Comics based on the show and several *Get Smart* novels by William Johnson. (He also wrote novels based on other 1966–1967 shows: *Gilligan's Island*, *Bewitched*, *The Monkees*, *F Troop* and *Iron Horse*.) Toy stores sold board games, trading cards, lunchboxes, jigsaw puzzles, coloring books and toy spy kits adorned with the *Get Smart* moniker.

In March 1966, NBC vice-president of programs Mort Warner unsurprisingly announced the show's renewal for the 1966–1967 season ("Get Smart Comedy" 12).

In the 1966–1967 season, *Get Smart* stayed in the Saturday 8:30 slot. Episodes that season spoofed Agatha Christie's *Ten Little Indians* and the films *Goldfinger* (1964), *Casablanca* (1942), *The Most Dangerous Game* (1932) and *How to Succeed in Business Without Really Trying* (1967). That season, *Get Smart* dropped to the 22nd highest-rated show while going against the long-running *The Lawrence Welk Show* on ABC and the poorly rated comedic Western *Pistols'n'Petticoats* on CBS (Brooks and Marsh).

Get Smart stayed in its Saturday slot for the show's remaining time on NBC, but never matched the ratings it got in its first two seasons. In 1969 when NBC cancelled the series, it was quickly picked up by CBS for the 1969–1970 season. Barbara Feldon stated that it was a "shock" to her when NBC cancelled *Get Smart*, despite good ratings. But the cast learned the very next day that CBS had picked up the show, which gave Feldon "a great sense of security" ("*Get Smart* Star Barbara" 16).

After the show's one season on CBS, *Get Smart* left the airwaves on May 15, 1970. But Don Adams was not finished with Maxwell Smart. In 1973, his voice was featured

Clips from *Get Smart* episodes on the *Don Adams: Get Smart* LP were "Washington 4—Indians 3," "School Days," "Satan Place," "Too Many Chiefs," "All In the Mind," "The Incredible Harry Hoo," "I'm Only Human," "Kisses for Kaos," and "Weekend Vampire" (Shubilla family archives).

in the animated *The New Scooby-Doo Movies* episode "The Exterminator." In the episode, his character has Maxwell Smart's distinctive cadence and incorporated many of Smart's catchphrases, such as "Would you believe…"

Adams again took on the role of Smart in the 1980 film *The Nude Bomb*. In the movie, KAOS invents a bomb which dematerialized clothing, thus giving KAOS and its fashion designer, Saint-Sauvage, the monopoly on the world's clothing industry. Although entertaining, the movie differed from the show in puzzling ways, with the most notable difference being that *The Nude Bomb* did not feature any other members of the original cast, with the exception of Robert Karvelas, who played the Chief's assistant Larabee. Inexplicably, Smart now works for the agency PITTS (Provisional Intelligence Tactical Service) instead of CONTROL. The movie makes no mention of Agent 99, the Chief, Hymie the Robot, Fang the dog or foes Siegfried and Shtarker.

Adams reunited with Barbara Feldon, Dick Gautier, Robert Karvelas, Bernie Kopell and King Moody in the ABC-TV movie *Get Smart, Again!* (1989). (Edward Platt had passed away in 1974.)

In the early 1990s, the original series started to air on the cable network Nick at Nite, which regularly featured *Get Smart* "Maximum Smart" marathons, sold "non-cellular/non-wearable" shoe phones, and even paraded 99 Agent 99 lookalikes around Times Square in 1991.

Nick at Nite reruns led to a 1995 reunion and a revival series. In the series, Smart has taken over as Chief of CONTROL. His son Zach Smart (Andy Dick) is, like his father, a bumbling CONTROL agent who takes on KAOS, still led by Siegfried. The series only aired on Fox for seven episodes.

Get Smart got a modern-day reimaging in 2008, with Steve Carell as Smart, Anne Hathaway as Agent 99 and Dwayne "The Rock" Johnson as Hymie the Robot. The movie utilized several of Smart's catchphrases and even featured a Bernie Kopell cameo. It was not well received by critics but was a profitable venture.

The Avengers

The Avengers originally aired in black-and-white in 1961 on the United Kingdom's ITV channel. In the first season, it showcased the exploits of well-dressed spies and proper English gentlemen John Steed (Patrick Macnee) and David Keel (Ian Hendry). In the second season David Keel was written off and Steed was given a new sidekick, Cathy Gale (Honor Blackman), memorable for her black knee-high boots. Once audiences were introduced to Cathy, they quickly forgot about Keel, and Blackman became an extremely popular character and the focal point on the show.

American viewers were not able to watch *The Avengers* until March 1966, but there was buzz about the series in the U.S. as early as 1964. *The New York Times* published a March 1964 article which mentioned the show: "Plots are preposterous and spiked with tongue-in-cheek humor, and the result is a kind of James Bond played strictly and stylishly for laughs." The article also stated that the plot was not the only reason why people watched the show in the U.K.; it was to see Honor Blackman. "About 20 million people spend the time between 10 p.m. and 11 p.m. each Saturday hoping to see [Cathy Gale] climb into her 'fighting suit' and hurl the heavies through plate glass windows," said Blackman. Blackman added that her fan mail was "98 percent male. ... Only about one percent is concerned with my acting ability." Blackman believed that if she turned most of the letters over to the police, "a sizable proportion of the male population of Britain would be liable to arrest." When asked the reason for her character's popularity, Blackman bluntly stated, "The explanation doesn't have to be complicated. It's quite simple. One three-letter word: sex." Blackman became known for her leather outfits and leather boots, which became known as "kinky boots." They quickly became a fashion trend in the U.K. (Carthew "All Honor").

Despite the big write-up in one of the largest and most widely read newspapers, Americans had to wait another two years to watch *The Avengers* on their TV sets.

Blackman left the show at the end of the 1964 season to appear in the James Bond movie *Goldfinger* (1964) as the villainous Pussy Galore. It was reported that she was cast by Bond producer Albert "Cubby" Broccoli despite primarily being known in Europe.

He said, "The Brits would love her because they knew her as Mrs. Gale, the Yanks would like her because she was so good—it was a perfect combination" (Moore 51).

Blackman was replaced in 1965 by a relative unknown, Shakespearean actress Diana Rigg, who took on the role of Emma Peel. Rigg proved to be even more popular than her predecessor; not simply based on her sex appeal and fighting skills but because the show was about to be seen by a much larger audience.

In January 1966, it was announced that two British shows, *The Avengers* and *Court-Martial* (a World War II drama about the judge advocate general's office), would be imported by ABC and start airing in March 1966 ("New ABC Programs" 24). *The Avengers* hit the U.S. airwaves on Monday, March 28, at 10:00, a summer replacement for the drama *Ben Casey* ("What the Networks" 58).

Airing on prime time network TV in the U.S. meant that the show had to go from being filmed using 405-line black and white video tape to 35mm black and white film. (Video was acceptable for broadcast in the U.K. but did not meet the picture quality standards for a prime time broadcast by a major U.S. TV network.)

Despite the fanfare, *New York Times* critic Vincent Canby wrote a mostly negative review of the newest ABC show, calling it "predictable and formulaic" (Canby 83). But the show did well enough as a summer replacement that ABC not only brought it back, they purchased the show from ITV, and so it was now produced by ABC Television Ltd. London.

ABC did not air *The Avengers* at the start of the 1966–1967 fall schedule. Instead they waited until January 1967 so that an entire season of new color episodes could air throughout the winter and summer months. The show made a time slot change as well, moving to Fridays at 10:00, replacing the cancelled World War II drama *12 O'Clock High*.

The Avengers, now in color, continued to be filmed on 35mm film which was also compatible with the United States' color broadcast standard, the NTSC system. With color came new opportunities for *The Avengers*. The show now featured exciting, colorful sets, a new opening title sequence, and new clothing for Emma Peel.

In 1965, England was yet to adopt a color TV standard; color TV would not arrive in English living rooms until 1967, when the PAL color system was introduced. But producers were looking across the Atlantic Ocean and to future broadcasts in syndication in the U.K., when putting together a wardrobe for Rigg. Her one-piece body suits became known as "Emma Peelers." According to *The Daily Mirror* (July 15, 1967), "The suit, made of stretch crimplene, is available in shops throughout the country, and designer Alun Hughes says that it is ideal for work or leisure." Other outfits for Emma Peel were designed by London fashion designer John Bates. Australian *TV Week* reported in January 1966,

> Gun-toting Emma Peel replaces Cathy Gale, the black-leather-girl who fought her way to fame alongside John Steed in ABC-TV's *The Avengers*. ... She's a fighting girl in the best Avengers tradition. But she's also a feminine girl—and even a funny girl. And her clothes! Mostly they're nothing short of sensational. When work began on this series, Emma wore the tailored leather-look which Cathy Gale made famous—at the request of American TV stations. Then world fashion changed—and to keep the avant-garde reputation of *The Avengers*, Emma Peel's wardrobe underwent a big change, also.

Bates focused on creating a design that gave Peel the ability to fight and look good:

> What man wouldn't be overcome by an Amazon in sex-kitten's clothing? Take Emma's white lace over flesh-fabric catsuit—what could be sexier? Only, perhaps, her blue lamé bra and

matching hipster trousers, which she wears for scenes in an old Scottish castle. Of course, she does wear clothes of a more 'butch' type. Like her black stretch jersey fighting suits for daytime. Or even a black leather fighting suit with a side-buckled waist and gun-pouch. But even the black-leather number is softened by a white crepe blouse. And it fits like a second skin.

TV Week predicted that "there'll be lots of Australian Emma Peels in the months to come. For John Bates clothes will be selling off-the-peg in countries where the series is shown." Even though official Emma Peel clothing was sold in stores, the designs were subject to knockoffs. According to the British tabloid *The People*, "Girls all over Britain want to look like Emma, actress Diana Rigg, and hundreds of copies of her outfits are being turned out. That is the cause of the battle, for most of the copies are by rag-trade 'pirates.'" The article stated that it was a test case to prevent future pirating of copyright merchandise and that ABC-TV, which got a percentage on sales of genuine *Avengers* clothes, "are sending warning letters to shops from their legal department" ("Emma Gives the Suit" 12–13; "Emma Gives the Suit" 12–13; Owen "Dressed to Kill"; "Now she's started").

The first episode in color, "From Venus with Love" kicked off the new *Avengers* season and featured a storyline about astronomers found dead with their hair bleached. They all belonged to the British Venusian Society, a group that was set to send a satellite to Venus. Peel and Steed investigate the crime.

On Friday night, *The Avengers* was pitted against the Western *Laredo* on NBC and the last hour of the very popular *CBS Friday Night Movie*. In the first week of the season, the *CBS Friday Night Movie*, which aired the Jerry Lewis film *The Delicate Delinquent* (1957), dominated the time slot, securing 51 percent of the viewing share and earning a 25.9 rating, *The Avengers* held its own, earning a 10.5 rating in the first half-hour and an 11.2 rating in the second half-hour, beating out *Laredo* by a little more than a ratings point in each of the half-hour time slots ("CBS Edges" 60).

Diana Rigg and Patrick Macnee appeared on the cover of the January 21, 1967, *TV Guide*, their first cover story Stateside. Seeing them on magazine covers would soon become commonplace in both the U.S. and the U.K.: *The Daily Mail*, *TV World*, *TV Times*, *Sunday American* and *TV Magazine*. In March 1967, *Playboy* magazine gave *The Avengers* a very positive review:

> It has taken America six years to discover *The Avengers*. Since 1961, the show's Mod mayhem has delighted a sophisticated British audience with its hip and slightly far-out antics. ... *The Avengers* has made a deserved return [in living color], because it is one of the small handful of consistently inventive, offbeat and thoroughly entertaining programs on television.

Of course, the publication could not go without mentioning Emma Peel's sex appeal but it also gave a nod to her fighting skills:

> "Mrs. Peel" is an erotic stylization, rather than a character, in pants suits, miniskirts and an incredibly kinky wardrobe. Her other great attribute is that she is one of the neatest brawlers anywhere: She karate-chops villains by the roomful, barely mussing her leather fighting suit. There are no holds barred for Miss Rigg or for the show's uproarious style ["*The Avengers*— Jolly Good"].

Like the actress she replaced, Diana Rigg left the *Avengers* to play in a James Bond film, *On Her Majesty's Secret Service* (1969). It starred George Lazenby as Bond and Rigg as his love interest, Countess Tracy di Vicenzo. Rigg left in October 1967, eight episodes into the 1967–1968 season, after a dispute about pay. Rigg, who made £150 a week, stated,

"If I go back to *The Avengers*, it will have to be for at least three times as much. The salary was a fair one when I started a year ago, but suddenly being Emma Peel is obviously worth a lot more" (Davis 3).

Before co-starring in *On Her Majesty's Secret Service*, Rigg first went in an entirely different direction: Shakespeare. On December 24, 1967, the *San Francisco Examiner and Chronicle* wrote about Rigg's departure from the show, "At the height of her success as 'Mrs. Peel,' she quit ... to return to the Royal Shakespearean Company for her first movie." Rigg played the role of Helena in the 1968 release *A Midsummer Night's Dream*. Rigg asserted, "For me it represented everything a film should be, working with actors and actresses who I admired and respected." She also reported that she would soon be filming the movie *The Assassination Bureau* (1969). Rigg stated that she took that role because it was the best film script she read in a long time and that she finds nothing unusual about her being a "Shakespearean actress, swinging spy and militant feminist." Rigg stated, "I am an actress and should be able to embrace every single medium and style and text" ("A Lanky, Long-haired").

Rigg was replaced on *The Avengers* by Canadian actress Linda Thorson as Tara King for the 1968–1969 season, which turned out to be the final season. In March 1969, ABC announced that *The Avengers* would not be returning (Shippy 19).

In the fall of 1976, ITV attempted to recreate the success of *The Avengers* and produced *The New Avengers,* a direct sequel to the original show. Patrick Macnee reprised his role as John Steed along with two new sidekicks, Mike Gambit (Gareth Hunt) and Purdey (Joanna Lumley). *The New Avengers* aired until December 1977 in the U.K. It was seen for the first time on American TV on CBS in September 1978 in the 11:30 p.m.–12:30 a.m. late night slot on Fridays. The show had limited success on both sides of the Atlantic.

The Avengers's cult following lasted long after the final new episode. Fanzines were self-published, including *The Diana Rigger* and *En Garde,* which featured fan art, fan fiction and interviews with the original cast and crew members. Officially licensed merchandise popped up over the years, starting with the 1977 action figures of Steed, Emma Peel, Cathy Gale and Purdy.

The 1998 movie *The Avengers* starring Ralph Fiennes as Steed and Uma Thurman as Emma Peel, was a box office bomb. Universally panned by critics, it is considered one of the worst films ever made (Cheshire; LaSalle; Maslin).

The Man from U.N.C.L.E.

The Man from U.N.C.L.E. was secret agent Napoleon Solo (Robert Vaughn), His Russian sidekick, with a mod Beatles-style haircut, was Illya Kuryakin (David McCallum), and their boss was U.N.C.L.E.'s New York bureau chief Alexander Waverly (Leo G. Carroll). The show was described by Vaughn as "James Bond on television" ("Robert Vaughn").

Unlike James Bond who worked for the British government's MI6, U.N.C.L.E. was an international organization. The narrator of the premiere episode (Monday, September 22, 1964, at 8:00), explained the concept of U.N.C.L.E. to viewers:

> In New York City, on a street in the East 40s, there is an ordinary tailor shop. Or *is* it ordinary? We enter through the agents' entrance and we are now in U.N.C.L.E.

headquarters—that's the United Network Command for Law and Enforcement. U.N.C.L.E. is an organization consisting of agents of all nationalities. It's involved in maintaining political and legal order anywhere in the world.

Episodes typically revolved around an innocent person unwillingly getting caught up in an international affair, often instigated by the evil organization THRUSH. The show never revealed what THRUSH stood for; according to novelizations, THRUSH stood for "Technological Hierarchy for the Removal of Undesirables and the Subjugation of Humanity" (McDaniel 89).

Vaughn described the basic premise as "a girl in Kansas gets swept up, taken away to Nova Scotia, then to Israel and she's suddenly for a mad week or two of her life in the middle of a giant international story of some kind with bad guys, good guys, weapons, everything—then she's put back in Kansas" ("Robert Vaughn").

The Man from U.N.C.L.E. quickly gained popularity and became a TV favorite. Its two stars soon found themselves on the covers of many magazines. Tabloid magazines such as *TV and Movie Screen* published reports of a feud between Vaughn and McCallum. Vaughn said, "Nothing could be further from the truth" and maintained that they were the best of friends ("Robert Vaughn").

The press also played up the sex appeal of the leading men. Vaughn said that to create Napoleon Solo, "I said to myself, what are the qualities in a person that would make a woman attracted to him? ... So I tried to figure out what it was that I had in terms of sex appeal in real life and transferred it into the character of Napoleon Solo on screen." He believed that the "oddness" of the show and the fact that they looked so starkly different and played such different characters helped create individual fan bases. Vaughn also claimed in an interview that between McCallum and himself, they were receiving 70,000 pieces of fan mail a month ("Robert Vaughn").

The conclusion of every show stated, "We wish to thank the United Network Command for Law and Enforcement without whose assistance this program would not be possible." This statement gave the show the air of believability and reality; *so* much that people would write the show on a regular basis seeking more information about the organization or how to join ("Robert Vaughn").

Fans who wanted to joint U.N.C.L.E. could instead buy their own U.N.C.L.E. identification badges, action figures, spy sets, model kits, toy gun sets, games, Gold Key comic books, novelizations and even a *Man from U.N.C.L.E.* magazine from Leo Margulies Corp. A *Man from U.N.C.L.E.* LP was released in 1965 and *More Music from* The Man from U.N.C.L.E. in 1966.

To kick off the second season in the fall of 1965, the show made the switch to color. It also became less serious and more of a spoof on the spy genre.

In the second season, *The Man from U.N.C.L.E.* was moved to Fridays at 10:00. Friday night was often seen as a death sentence for shows geared towards young adults, but the 1965–1966 season was the show's highest-rated season, pulling in an average of a 24.0 Nielsen rating, making it TV's 13th highest-rated show (Brooks and Marsh). It won a Golden Globe Award for Best TV Show in 1966 and was nominated for several Emmys and Golden Globes for acting, editing and music from 1965 to 1967.

Although the show saw success in the 10:00 slot, *The Man from U.N.C.L.E.* was moved to an earlier Friday slot (8:30 p.m.) for the 1966–1967 season. *Parents Magazine* published a report by the watchdog group the National Association for Better Broadcasting on what TV shows in the 1966–1967 season they felt were acceptable for children.

Hugo Montenegro recorded both *The Music from The Man from U.N.C.L.E.* and *More Music from The Man from U.N.C.L.E.*, and released a number of soundtrack albums for films including *A Fistful Of Dollars* (1964), *For a Few Dollars More* (1965), *The Good, the Bad and the Ugly* (1966), *Hang 'Em High* (1968) and *The Godfather* (1972) (Shubilla family archives).

The Man from U.N.C.L.E. was not one of them. According to the NABB, "Unfortunately [*U.N.C.L.E.*] has been switched to an earlier evening hour, for its vividly depicted horror make it unsuitable for children" (Leonard "What's Out" 78).

Man from U.N.C.L.E. may have done well in the 10:00 slot when young adults may have been getting in for the night, but the 8:30 slot was too early for many of its viewers. Another factor in the show's ratings drop may be that audiences were sick of the weekly "innocent person caught up in an international affair" storyline.

To make matters worse, *U.N.C.L.E.* faced stiff competition that season. In the first half-hour, it went up against the last half-hour of *The Time Tunnel* on ABC, and the season's 18th highest-rated show *Hogan's Heroes* on CBS. *U.N.C.L.E.* fared better in the second half-hour going against the poorly rated *The Milton Berle Show* on NBC and the *Friday Night Movie* on CBS (Brooks and Marsh; "Few Cheers" 58). *U.N.C.L.E.* dropped from being the 13th highest-rated show in 1965–1966 to the 46th in 1966–1967 (Spencer "TV's Vast" 64).

Perhaps another reason for the poor ratings: The show had a new producer each season and each season, every producer brought his own ideas, making it a different show than originally conceived. Vaughn stated. "It went from being a straight James Bond kind of show … by the third season it had become almost a farce because we were shooting cupcakes out of guns on the sides of cars. It was no longer James Bond. It was something very silly and it went off the air the fourth year for that very reason" ("Robert Vaughn").

After the 1966–1967 season, *U.N.C.L.E.* once again moved back to Mondays at 8:00. In November 1967, NBC announced the show would be ending its run on January 15, 1968, to be replaced by *Rowan & Martin's Laugh-In* ("New Season" 56). *New York Times* TV columnist George Gent wrote that the announcement came to "almost no one's surprise."

U.N.C.L.E. agents were not only seen on television but on bookshelves in a number of spy adventures (courtesy Kevin Daugherty collection).

The show went into syndication after the announcement of the cancellation and was particularly popular in the overseas market ("U.S. Programs" 76). Fifteen years later, *The Man from U.N.C.L.E.* returned to the small screen in the form of a TV movie, *The Return of the Man from U.N.C.L.E.: The Fifteen Years Later Affair* (1983). In it, Vaughn and McCallum finally defeat the evil THRUSH.

Director Guy Ritchie brought *The Man from U.N.C.L.E.* to the big screen in 2015 with Henry Cavill as Napoleon Solo, Armie Hammer as Illya Kuryakin and Hugh Grant as U.N.C.L.E. chief Alexander Waverly.

The Girl from U.N.C.L.E.

NBC announced in November 1965 that the network would be testing a pilot entitled *The Girl from U.N.C.L.E.*, a *Man from U.N.C.L.E.* spin-off ("Bumper Crop" 30). They aired a test episode of *Girl from U.N.C.L.E.*, "The Moonglow Affair," on Friday, February 25, 1966, with Mary Ann Mobley as rookie U.N.C.L.E. agent April Dancer ("N.B.C. Schedule Next" 67).

The Girl from U.N.C.L.E. was officially picked up by NBC in February 1966 but with Stefanie Powers in the title role. Powers was known for her performances in the movie *McLintock!* (1963), *Die! Die! My Darling!* (1965) and *Stagecoach* (1966), and guest starring roles on TV's *Bat Masterson, Bonanza* and *Route 66*. NBC soon began running *Girl from U.N.C.L.E.* promos stating, "She's bold, she's clever, she's tricky, and the evil forces of THRUSH have never had so gorgeous an enemy." The hour-long show replaced the half-hour sitcoms *My Mother the Car* and *Please Don't Eat the Daisies,* airing at 7:30 on Tuesdays ("N.B.C. Schedule Next" 67).

The Girl from U.N.C.L.E. would be a wonderful showcase for the new color TV landscape. The show featured many exotic locations such as rain forests and desert dunes, foreign cities, fast cars, spy gadgets and fight scenes that usually concluded with April Dancer knocking out THRUSH agents with a karate chop. Perhaps most notably, *The Girl from U.N.C.L.E.* was much more fashionable than the show's counterpart, *The Man from U.N.C.L.E.* April, an American, wore all the latest colorful mod British fashions and was influenced more by James Bond films. The fashion and Bond influence also led to the casting of British actor Noel Harrison as April's partner Mark Slate (Pfeiffer 27).

TV Guide's 1966–1967 Fall Preview edition stated, "*The Girl from U.N.C.L.E.* is a kissing cousin of *The Man from U.N.C.L.E.* … [It] has the same headquarters (behind the dry cleaning shop), the same enemy (THRUSH) and the same attitude toward international intrigue (irreverent and slightly cockeyed)" ("1966–1967 Fall Preview"). *The Girl from U.N.C.L.E.* also featured Leo G. Carrol as U.N.C.L.E. chief Alexander Waverly and in the third episode, "The Mother Muffin Affair," *The Man from U.N.C.L.E.*'s Napoleon Solo (Robert Vaughn) appeared alongside April Dancer.

The show debuted on Tuesday September 13, 1966, to mixed reviews:

> "Moves along nicely, thanks to some clever dialogue."—Walt Dutton, *Los Angeles Times*
>
> "The Man from U.N.C.L.E. in high heels."—Paul Molloy, *Chicago Sun Times*
>
> "Next season we'll be ready for a new series about the Jackass from U.N.C.L.E."—Laurence Laurent, *Washington Post*
>
> "Violent, sadistic and altogether repellent."—Harriet Van Horne, *New York World Journal Tribune* ("Critics Views" 67)

The show was detested by the National Association for Better Broadcasting, who called it

> an illustration of network television's irresponsibility to children. Explicit terror. Torture for fun. This is a worse show even than *Man from U.N.C.L.E.* … Ordinary violent death is too mild a form of entertainment for this show. It has to be accomplished with pits of boiling oil, with carnivorous fish, electricity or chemical solvents to reduce the body to dust. It has to be produced by people who delight in creating nightmares. … [C]ynical treatment and macabre humor make this violent suspense program unsuitable for young children" [Horn 10; Leonard "What's Out" 78].

The show started off strong in the ratings. *The Girl from U.N.C.L.E.*'s first week's Arbitron ratings indicated that it was the 13th highest-rated show in prime time—and the fourth highest-rated new show in its first season, behind only *It's About Time, The Rat Patrol* and *CBS Friday Night Movies,* averaging a 19.7 Arbitron rating. It beat out its time slot rivals, ABC's *Combat!* and CBS's *Daktari* ("ARB" 68).

In the second week, viewership dropped but to a respectable 18.2 average rating, which helped NBC claim victory in the prime time ratings battle early in the season ("Trendex Top 40" 58; "NBC Claims" 10). Ratings picked back up in the third week, to a 19.7 Nielsen rating, keeping *Girl from U.N.C.L.E.* queen of the Tuesday 7:30 slot ("Ratings Photo Finish" 68).

Stefanie Powers appeared on the cover of *TV Guide* in December 1966 wearing a metallic silver ensemble complete with a metallic background. *Girl from U.N.C.L.E.* also had a number of merchandising opportunities in late 1966, such as the "THRUSHER Buster" toy car, an age-inappropriate *Girl from U.N.C.L.E.* garter gun holster, and official *Girl from U.N.C.L.E.* Stefanie Powers doll. The soundtrack was also released in 1966 with music arranged and composed by pop singer Teddy Randazzo. From December 1966 to December 1967, a total of seven issues of *Girl from U.N.C.L.E.* magazine was published by Leo Margulies Corp., each edition featured a novelization, several short stories and biographical information about the show's actors. In addition, several *Girl from U.N.C.L.E.* Gold Key comic books and novelizations were published. The novelizations were straight espionage thrillers and not nearly as campy as the TV show.

Ratings gradually dropped after viewers' early love affair with the show, and time slot rival *Daktari* rose to become one of the season's top shows (Brooks and Marsh).

It did not help that *Girl from U.N.C.L.E.* continued to receive abysmal reviews. *TV Guide* on December 17, 1966, wrote, "Honestly, in one season how many spoofs can you take? If a spoof is going to be effective, it must surely have to begin with something serious to spoof off from. ... [*The Girl from U.N.C.L.E.* is] about as believable as women's wrestling. And it has as much wit as a roller derby." The reviewer also commented that the acting "is enough to make you cry aunt" (Armory 21).

Clearly there were too many agents from U.N.C.L.E. on TV and on February 28, 1967, it was announced *Girl from U.N.C.L.E.* was cancelled along with 11 other NBC shows. The show remained on the air until April 11, running for 29 episodes. It started off as one of the season's highest-rated shows, but then fell so far that it had the distinct displeasure of being one of the two least-watched shows of the season. The only show that did worse was CBS's Western comedy *Pistols'n'Petticoats*. In the fall of 1967, *The Girl from U.N.C.L.E.*'s time slot was taken over by the second season of *Star Trek* ("NBC to Cancel"; Spencer "TV's Vast" 54).

Clearly NBC did not want to continue with a show that was expensive to produce and was on such a sharp ratings decline.

Mission: Impossible

According to *TV Guide*'s 1966–1967 Fall Preview,

Mission: Impossible is exactly what it sounds like: An elite team of undercover agents hop from one hot spot to another, performing incredible feats. One week they're South of the Border swiping two nuclear warheads from an impenetrable vault. Another week they're behind the Iron Curtain breaking into and out of a maximum-security prison ["1966–1967 Fall Preview"].

Mission: Impossible was acquired by Lucille Ball's Desilu Productions in 1964 from creator Bruce Geller, put into production in 1965 and picked up by CBS for the 1966–1967 season. Desilu Productions also produced *Star Trek* and Ball's own *The Lucy Show* that season.

Each week on the show, Dan Briggs (Steven Hill), leader of the Impossible Mission Force (IMF), received a seemingly impossible mission: toppling governments, recovering Nazi gold, impersonating dictators, freeing political prisoners, stopping a deadly plague. Each week Briggs chose a team of undercover agents to assist him. Most often, the team consisted of model and actress Cinnamon Carter (Barbara Bain); electronics, mechanical and forgery expert Barney Collier (Greg Morris); strongman Willy Armitage (Peter Lupus), and master of disguise and impersonation Rollin Hand (Martin Landau). In every episode, Briggs was warned, "As always, should you or any of your IM Force be caught or killed, the secretary will disavow any knowledge of your actions."

Mission: Impossible also featured one of TV's most iconic themes. Composed by Argentinian pianist Lalo Schifrin, it reached #41 on the Billboard Hot 100 charts (Brooks and Marsh).

In the 1966–1967 season, the first half-hour of *Mission: Impossible* went up against ABC's long-running *The Lawrence Welk Show*. Welk had made a career out of more than playing his "Champaign Style" of music on his accordion. His show routinely beat out his competition, despite being torn apart by TV critics starting in the mid–1950s when it knocked Sid Caesar's *Caesar's Hour* (1954–1957) off its pedestal and right out of the TV airwaves. Caesar said he pulled the plug on *Caesar's Hour* because he was exhausted from being unable to beat Welk in the ratings (Gould "TV: Welk"; Barnes and Byrge).

In the Fall 1966 season, Welk was entering his 12th year on TV; the ABC Fall Preview, *7 Nights to Remember,* promised that it would be a "vintage year" for him. The prediction was not off. *The Lawrence Welk Show* had an average of a 22.8 rating, making it the 12th highest-rated show that season (Brooks and Marsh).

In the second half-hour, *Mission: Impossible* was opposite the slumping *Hollywood Palace*. Bu *Mission: Impossible* still managed to lose in the time slot week after week.

Mission: Impossible's NBC competitor, *NBC Saturday Night at the Movies,* featured *Robinson Crusoe on Mars* (1964), *The Joker Is Wild* (1957) and *The Buccaneer* (1958) that season. It averaged a 21.4 rating, beating *Mission: Impossible* by five or more percentage points each week ("The Latest" 68; "Few Cheers" 58; "ARB's Top 20" 68; "Second Season" 60; Brooks and Marsh).

Mission: Impossible received mostly positive reviews:

> "Level of suspense throughout the hour rarely achieved in television."—Don Page, *Los Angeles Times*
>
> "Very likely [will] catch on."—Jack Gould, *The New York Times*
>
> "A taut tale."—Bob Hull, *Los Angeles Herald Examiner*
>
> "Maybe be the best-of-breed of the new network series batch."—Bob Williams, *New York Post* ("How Critics Assess" 74)

But the show was too much for some critics:

> "Strained credulity will be beyond the breaking point."—Lawrence Laurent, *Washington Post*
>
> "It was virtually an impossible mission for the viewers to sort out the good guys from the bad guys and still keep track of the plot."—Bill Irvin, *Chicago's American* ("How Critics Assess" 74)

Although *Mission: Impossible* struggled in the ratings vs. *Lawrence Welk, Hollywood Palace* and *Saturday Night at the Movies,* CBS still had hope the show would catch on. The network announced in October 1966 that the series was "secure in the lineup" ("The Ratings" 68).

To help the show in January 1967, CBS moved it back a half-hour to 9:00. Although the swap put *Mission: Impossible* against a full hour of *Lawrence Welk* on ABC and *Get Smart* and the first half hour of *Saturday Night at the Movies* on NBC, the show "shot up into the upper third of the popularity list" (Lowry "Old-Timers" 7). It finished the season 51st in the ratings and was renewed by the network (Spencer "TV's Vast" 54).

CBS felt ratings would improve after *Mission: Impossible* was nominated for six Emmy Awards and took four awards; Martin Landau was nominated for Actor in a Leading Role in a Dramatic Series and Lalo Schifrin for Individual Achievements in Music-Composition. The show won for Best Dramatic Series, Outstanding Writing Achievement in Drama and Outstanding Achievement in Film and Sound Editing. Barbara Bain won for Actress in a Leading Role in a Dramatic Series

In the fall of 1967, the Emmy-winning series was moved to Sundays at 10:00 where there was not much competition: *The ABC Sunday Night Movie* and the NBC Western *The High Chaparral.* That season, Peter Graves replaced Steven Hill as star of the series. The change was believed to have been made, in part, due to Steven Hill (née Shlomo Hill) and his Jewish faith. Hill refused to work late on Friday and on Saturday in observance of the Sabbath, which caused problems with the show's tight shooting schedule ("Reb Shlomo Hill Z"L"; Gates 8).

Despite low ratings, CBS stuck with *Mission: Impossible.* The next season, it finally struck a chord with viewers and was the season's 11th highest-rated show, averaging a 23.3 rating. The 1968–1969 season was Landau's last. The actor was ostensibly replaced in the 1969–1970 season by Leonard Nimoy, in one of his first post–*Star Trek* roles, as IMF agent Paris.

Although *Mission: Impossible* never again reached the heights it did in the 1968–1969 season, it stayed on the air until 1973. In its final season, CBS moved the show from Saturdays at 10:00 to Fridays at 8:00, but the change did not help. In January 1973, it was reported that *Mission: Impossible* dropped from a 30.0 share to a 22.0 share, and in February its cancellation was announced, due to the show's low 12.5 rating ("CBS Ups" 48; "'Burnett' Gains" 44).

Mission: Impossible was sold into syndication by Paramount Television, which purchased the show from Desilu in 1967. Advertisements to TV station program directors called it a "unique solution for a self-destructing program schedule" and an "action-adventure in every suspense-filled hour," and touted the show's Emmys and that it was "All color" (advertisement for Paramount Television Sales, 18). At the time, most shows that ran long as *Mission: Impossible* would have at least one season of black-and-white episodes. In 1973, the only scripted weekly episodic shows that were 100 percent in color with more episodes were *Bonanza, The FBI* and *The Virginian.*

In 1988, Peter Graves reprised his Jim Phelps role in an ABC revival of the series that lasted two seasons. And starting in 1996, Tom Cruise starred in the highly successful and long-running *Mission: Impossible* film franchise loosely based on the TV show.

"Mission: Impossible" composer Lalo Schifrin also worked on a number soundtracks for films including *Cool Hand Luke* (1967), *Dirty Harry* (1971) and *Enter the Dragon* (1973), and television shows such as *Mannix* (1967–1975), *Starsky & Hutch* (1975–1979) (Shubilla family archives).

I Spy

Before playing Dr. Huxtable on *The Cosby Show* (1984–1992) and long before scandals and prison sentence, the notorious Bill Cosby co-starred in the NBC action-adventure series *I Spy* alongside top-billed Robert Culp. They played U.S. Intelligence agents Kelly Robinson (Culp) and Alexander "Scotty" Scott (Cosby), jet-setting around the country in the guise of international tennis bums.

In 1965 when Cosby was cast, *I Spy* became the one of the first weekly network TV shows to feature an African American star in an "integrated cast." At the time, NBC feared that some affiliate stations would not accept an integrated cast and reject *I Spy*, especially in the South which has a history of racial segregation. But 180 network affiliates carried the show. The only major media markets which could not pick up *I Spy* were Albany, New York; Savannah, Georgia; Daytona Beach, Florida, and Alexandria, Louisiana. The Birmingham, Alabama, NBC affiliate also refused the show but it was available on a Ultra-High Frequency station which was beamed into the market (Adams "*I Spy* with Negro" 7; "All Channel Television Receiver Law"). Cosby later thanked NBC "for having guts" for airing *I Spy* despite the risk (Adams "Bill Cosby of 'I Spy'" 68).

After the first season, Culp stated, "The fact that they—a white man and a Negro—work together as friends also carries an underlying message of the brotherhood of man, though there is never any preaching about it" (Thomas "Robert Culp Happy" 32).

The hour-long series debuted in color on Wednesday, September 15, 1965, at 10:00 and received positive reviews:

> "This could be the one to watch."—Bob Hull, *Los Angeles Examiner*
>
> "The best spy series we've ever encountered."—Jack O'Brian, *New York Journal-American*
>
> "There are tones of Bond ... a cross between *Espionage* and *Hong Kong*."—Louis Cedrone, Jr., *Baltimore Evening Sun*
>
> "Creditable cloak-and-dagger series."—Bill Irwin, *Chicago American*
>
> "A show in search of an attitude and also the style to go with it."—Jack Gould, *The New York Times*
>
> "A fast-moving, slick production."—Cynthia Lowry, Associated Press ("How Critics See" 39)

In the 1965–1966 season, *I Spy* aired against ABC's *Amos Burke, Secret Agent* (previously entitled *Burke's Law*, it morphed into a spy drama to cash in on the spy craze) and CBS's variety series *The Danny Kaye Show*. Although *I Spy* was not one of the most-watched shows of the season, it regularly dominated its 10:00 Wednesday time slot.

Most spy shows in the 1960s were greatly influenced by James Bond films, but *I Spy* attempted to keep its distance from Bond. Culp called Bond an "amoral figure who treats his enemies and women with equal cruelty." He felt that *I Spy* was different: "From the very beginning, Bill and I insisted that Robinson and Scott would be portrayed as fallacious men, full of foolishness and failure. ... And our heavies are not members of any vast network of evil, they are all individuals, and often on the silly side" (Thomas "Robert Culp Happy" 32).

Cosby and Culp's chemistry got attention. *The Chicago Tribune Service* wrote the actors "have been developing into a very sophisticated comedy team. Watching them cavort as secret agent heroes in their adventure-comedy series, *I Spy,* makes it clear they have become a natural and perfect comedy duo" ("*I Spy* Duo" 28). The series' stars also got attention for their clothing style: tennis sweaters, Polo shirts and boat shoes. This style became the archetype for the mid–Atlantic prep school or preppy style popular in the 1970s (Birnback).

Both actors were nominated for Outstanding Lead Actor in a drama series; the award went to Cosby (Handsaker 20). In its second season, *I Spy* finished 47th in the ratings, yet it continually won the time slot (Spencer "TV's Vast" 55). That season, it was up against *The Danny Kaye Show* and the ABC variety show *Stage 67.*

In the 1967–1968 season, spy shows were declared "all but dead" by TV critic Ric Du Brow: Most of the spy shows that premiered in the mid–1960s were off the air. *Mission: Impossible, The Man from U.N.C.L.E., The Avengers, Get Smart* and *I Spy* were the exceptions (Du Brow "Spy Series Slump" 36). *I Spy* was now seen on Mondays opposite *The Big Valley* on ABC and *The Carol Burnett Show* on CBS. Some critics felt that Carol Burnett was not likely to give its competition any cause for concern, but her series overshadowed both *I Spy* and *The Big Valley* ("Opinions Vary" 78C; "Specials Confuse" 77; "Few of TV's Virgin" 71).

I Spy was parodied in the 1968 *Get Smart* episode "Die Spy," with Maxwell Smart as an international table-tennis champion and African American actor Stu Gilliam (doing his best Bill Cosby impression) as his partner. Robert Culp made an uncredited cameo appearance as a drunk waiter at a Turkish restaurant.

Culp and Cosby were nominated for Outstanding Lead Actor in a Drama Series all three years that *I Spy* was on the air; Cosby won all three years. At one ceremony, Cosby said, "I extend my hand to a man by the name of Robert Culp. He lost this because he helped me" ("Van Dyke Show Triumphs" 20).

I Spy helped Cosby become a household name and one of the highest priced comedians in the world. He went on to many successful TV ventures while Culp starred in *The Greatest American Hero* (1981–1987). The two reprised their former roles in the 1994 TV movie *I Spy Returns,* where Scotty and Robinson come out of retirement to help their children (now secret agents themselves) pick up scientists defecting from the former Soviet Union.

In late 2014, Cosby was accused of sexual misconduct and TV stations pulled the plug on reruns of *I Spy* and most other Cosby series. The allegations led to Cosby being convicted and eventually imprisoned on multiple charges.

The Man Who Never Was

ABC's *The Man Who Never Was* shares the same name as a 1953 Ewen Montagu book and its 1956 movie adaptation. But as *Free Press* TV-radio writer Bettelou Peterson wrote, the show "takes one well-known title and grafts it on another plot. ... It has no relation to the true story of World War II intrigue which was a successful book and a hit movie" (Peterson *Batman* 14).

The TV series starred Robert Lansing as Peter Murphy, an American spy who is the spitting image of the richest man in the world, Mark Wainwright (also played by Lansing). In the first episode, Murphy ran into Wainwright in the midst of being chased by assassins in the vicinity of the Berlin Wall. The assassins mistake Wainwright for Murphy and kill him. After the assassination, Murphy assumes Wainwright's identity and even manages to obtain the cooperation of Wainwright's wife (Dana Wynter). It turns out to be the perfect cover for his covert European operations. Each episode, Murphy was given a new cloak-and-dagger assignment by Colonel Jack Forbes (Murray Hamilton).

A year earlier, Lansing was bumped from the ABC show *12 O'Clock High* because producers wanted the show to feature a more youthful star. But ABC was still high on Lansing and wanted him to star in another series. But *The Man Who Never Was* was not ABC's first choice for him. In early 1966, Desilu Productions went into production on the Western *The Long Hunt for April Savage* starring Lansing, and ABC placed it on the 1966–1967 schedule. But in late March, ABC announced that it was dropping *April Savage* after writer Sam Rolfe (*Have Gun, Will Travel, The Man from U.N.C.L.E.*) quit the production. ABC replaced *April Savage* with *The Man Who Never Was* with Lansing. A 20th Century–Fox production, it aired Wednesdays at 9:00 (Messina "*River Kwai*" 61).

In Berlin, the show took advantage of the abandoned subway system. Later episodes were shot in Munich, Germany; Nice, France, and Athens, Greece ("*Man Who Never*"; Peterson "*Batman*" 14).

ABC previewed *Man Who Never Was* (and 12 of the network's other 16 new shows) a week earlier than the official start of the season (September 7, 1966). Out of all the shows previewed, *The Man Who Never Was* was the lowest-rated: 38.6 ("Peek at Ratings" 35). To make matters worse, some review were disparaging:

> "A study in puzzlement."—Joseph E. Sullivan, *Boston Herald*

> "Pretty preposterous."—Bernie Harrison, *Washington Evening Star*

> "Poorly executed and scripted."—Don Page, *Los Angeles Times*

> "It makes the plots on *Batman* seem high drama."—Lawrence Laurent, *Washington Post*

But other critics enjoyed the show:

> "A cool and cleverly done espionage series."—Rex Polier, *Philadelphia Bulletin*

> "Has an impressive list of attributes which should make it appealing to spy buffs."—Clay Gowran, *Chicago Tribune*

And then there was this head-scratcher of a review:

> "If you can swallow the first episode, it may turn out exciting."—Dean Gysel, *Chicago Daily News* ("The Critics Review" 37)

In the show's second week, it had a decent 15.4 rating but then started slipping ("Critics' Views" 60). The series was overshadowed by its competition, *Green Acres* on CBS and *Bob Hope Presents the Chrysler Theatre* on NBC. That season, *Green Acres* was the sixth highest-rated show and *Chrysler Theatre* the 26th highest-rated (Brooks and Marsh).

In November 1966, ABC announced that *The Man Who Never Was* would not be back for the second half of the season. It had been cancelled after only 18 episodes. The series aired until January 4, 1967. That same year, *Man Who Never Was* episodes were pieced together to make two "movies," *The Spy with the Perfect Cover* and *Danger Has Two Faces*. Both were sold alongside *I Deal in Danger*, a recut of Larry Cohen's short-lived series *Blue Light* (O'Brian "The Voice" 5).

Chapter Nine

Southerners

The Southern portion of the United States and rural living was a subject of five shows in the 1966–1967 fall lineup: CBS's *The Beverly Hillbillies, Petticoat Junction, Green Acres, The Andy Griffith Show* and *Gomer Pyle, U.S.M.C.* Many critics considered the shows "corn" but they were five of TV's highest-rated shows—not just during that season, but in TV history.

The Beverly Hillbillies

Arguably the most popular of the five Southern CBS shows, *The Beverly Hillbillies* debuted on September 26, 1962. Its theme song, "The Ballad of Jed Clampett," tells viewers the story of Jed Clampett (Buddy Ebsen), a poor hillbilly widower who struck oil on his Limestone, Tennessee, property while hunting for food for his family.

Clampett was paid millions of dollars by the OK Oil Company to drill on his land and he was encouraged by his kinfolk to move to California with his newfound wealth. He brought along his animal-loving, cute, naïve, but tough tomboy daughter Elly May (Donna Douglas), his no-nonsense mountain doctor mother-in-law Granny (Irene Ryan) and his dimwitted nephew Jethro Bodine (Max Baer, Jr.), who pursued new activities in the Hills of Beverly: becoming a "double naught" spy, an airline pilot, a brain surgeon, and a streetcar conductor—all while pursuing a playboy lifestyle he read about in a swingers magazine.

Jed and his family, not "up" on modern society, had unique ways of spending their money, which was deposited in Commerce Bank managed by Milburn Drysdale (Raymond Bailey). To keep his depositors happy, Drysdale tried to make the Hillbillies' every outlandish request a reality, often with the help of his secretary Jane Hathaway (Nancy Kulp).

The show was created by writer Paul Henning, whose interest in hillbillies went back to his childhood:

> I always had a fondness for hillbillies.... [I]n my experience as a Boy Scout in the Ozarks, I found that there were pockets of historical places where the people resisted modernization and they resisted roads being built. So, this was the germ of the idea. You could find someone from a remote, protected spot ... they don't have radio, telephone, television or anything—to transplant them by some means into the modern world ... and that was the beginning of the thought of the Beverly Hillbillies ["Paul Henning"].

Henning did not want to place the Hillbillies in their own backwoods hometown of Limestone, because he felt that the setting would have been depressing. He originally had the idea of moving the Hillbillies to New York City, but realized that shooting there would be too expensive. So he decided on Beverly Hills, which he felt had the "same level of sophistication—maybe more" ("Paul Henning").

In the first two seasons, *The Beverly Hillbillies* was TV's highest-rated show, averaging a colossal 37.55 rating. It was one of the top 20 shows every season until its ninth season in 1971–1972 (Brooks and Marsh). The episode "The Giant Jackrabbit" (January 8, 1964) was not a season premiere, finale or a "very special" episode—it was a regular episode in the middle of the second season in which Granny mistakes a kangaroo for a jackrabbit. The episode is one of the most watched TV episodes of all time, watched by 23 million households. At the time, most households only had one TV, so it is estimated that that equals approximately 50 million viewers. In addition, the show earned a 65 share (Dalton "Most Influential").

President Lyndon Johnson's first State of the Union Address to Congress after assuming the office of the presidency preceded the episode, and some believe that this boosted the show's ratings. But the next week's episode "The Girl from Home" had a 42.8 rating and a 62 share of the audience. A total of 20 of the *Beverly Hillbillies* episodes were among the highest-rated episodes of the 20th century ("Top 100 TV Shows").

The Beverly Hillbillies was so popular that "The Ballad of Jed Clampett" by Lester Flatt and Earl Scruggs reached #44 on the Billboard Charts in 1962. There were also *Beverly Hillbillies* comic books which lasted as long as the series, a set of Topps Trading Cards, *Granny's Hillbilly Cookbook*, model kits, card games and a 1966 album featuring vocals of the entire main cast.

The Beverly Hillbillies switched from black and white to color to kick off the 1965–1966 season. There was one big difference between the show in color and the show in black and white: the Hillbillies' mansion. *TV Guide* had revealed the mansion's location and the owners were besieged by tourists asking to meet the Hillbillies. When the crew prepared to go to the mansion to shoot stock shots in color, the owner decided not to let the show use their house again. The producers had to find a new location. Henning understood the owner's decision, but he described it as a "mortal blow" to the show's production ("Paul Henning on The Beverly Hillbillies"). But it was not a mortal blow to the ratings, *The Beverly Hillbillies* was the seventh highest-rated show of the 1965–1966 season.

By the 1966–1967 season, the Hillbillies had been living in Beverly Hills for five years but were still dealing with culture shock and finding new ways to spend their money. Examples include Jed running for the office of Beverly Hills Smog Commissioner, joining the board of the OK Oil Company, and even trying an early version of computer dating. The Clampett family took dance instruction, Granny threw Elly a coming out party with hopes of landing her a husband, and Jethro continued to use his family money to impress women. That season, the show was once again the seventh most popular show on television with a 23.4 rating, which tied the show with *Daktari* and *Bewitched* (Brooks and Marsh).

The show's ratings stayed strong throughout eight seasons but fell off in the ninth and final season in 1971–1972. But after being cancelled, the stars were not finished being Hillbillies. *Beverly Hillbillies* reruns went into syndication in 1966 and aired in the morning on CBS under the title of *Mornin' Beverly Hillbillies*. It was pitched to TV stations as a show that could air in the late afternoons due to a high viewership with young housewives, aged 18–49, perfect for both stations and advertiser dollars ("Prize Catch" 1).

The Hillbillies re-emerged in 1981 in a *CBS Tuesday Night Movie* titled *Return of the Beverly Hillbillies*. In this TV movie, the Hillbillies solve America's energy crisis and dependence on oil, despite oil making them rich in the first place. Three years after the reunion, Nancy Kulp (Jane Hathaway) entered the political arena and ran for Congress as a Democrat against 12-year incumbent Republican Congressman E.G. "Bud" Shuster in Pennsylvania's 9th Congressional district. Although it was a high-profile race, Kulp did not get the support of her *Beverly Hillbillies* castmate Buddy Ebsen. On the show, Granny would have made Ebsen and Kulp box their differences out in the backyard, but Ebsen took a different approach. A Conservative Republican, he recorded a radio ad in support of Kulp's rival Shuster. Ebsen stated in the ad, "Hey, Nancy, I love you dearly but you're too liberal for me—I've got to go with Bud Shuster" ("Campaign Notes"). Kulp lost to Shuster in the rural, solidly Republican district. The Associated Press reported, "Shuster won 117,203 votes Tuesday in central Pennsylvania's Ninth District, while the Democratic challenger drew 59,449" ("Former 'Hillbilly' Loses").

Kulp later told the Associated Press that she did not blame Ebsen for the loss. She instead blamed her loss on the conservative nature of the district: "I was perceived to be an ultra-liberal. If that is their perception—even if they like me—then I can't win" (Barker "Former 'Beverly Hillbilly'").

In 1993 came a 20th Century–Fox film of the same name and with the same premise as the TV show, with Jim Varney as Jed. The one original Hillbilly making a cameo appearance was Buddy Ebsen. Although financially successful, the film got mixed reviews. According to *The Los Angeles Times,*

> This seems like potentially dangerous stuff, messing with people's TV memories. It's especially tricky when you're dealing with something as ingrained in American pop consciousness as the Beverly Hillbillies. ... This is a show that was No. 1 practically from the moment it premiered in September 1962, dominated the Nielsen ratings for nearly 10 years and still pops up on cable at least four times a day. There are millions of rerun-addicted hard-core Clampettologists out there who won't take kindly to much big-screen Hillbilly revisionism. ... [T]hese folks won't be easy to please [Rhodes].

For several decades, Max Baer, Jr., planned to build a *Beverly Hillbillies*–themed casino. Baer, who reportedly owned the rights to use the series name for casinos, hotels, theme parks, restaurants, cosmetics and consumables, was unable to complete the project for financial and zoning reasons ("Jethro Bodine's"). A *Beverly Hillbillies* casino was never built, but there are several *Beverly Hillbillies*–themed slot machines in casinos across the country, with such names as "The Bubblin' Crude," "The Moonshine Money" and "The Clampetts' Cash" ("Jethro Bodine's").

Petticoat Junction

A year after *The Beverly Hillbillies* hit the airwaves, another Paul Henning Southern comedy debuted on Tuesday, September 24, 1963, in black and white at 9:00. *Petticoat Junction* took place in the same television universe as *The Beverly Hillbillies*.

Between the fictitious towns of Hooterville and Pixley was the Shady Rest Hotel which was owned and operated by Kate Bradley (Bea Benaderet) and managed by Uncle Joe (Edgar Buchanan). The show's theme song promised "lots of curves" which the audience got with Kate's beautiful daughters, "The Petticoat Junction Girls": Billie Jo (played by three actresses through the show's run, Jeannine Riley in Seasons 1 and 2, Gunilla Hutton in Season 3 and Meredith MacRae in Seasons 4 through 7), Bobbie Jo (Pat Woodell in Seasons 1 and 2, Lori Saunders in Seasons 3 through 7) and Betty Jo (Paul Henning's daughter Linda Kaye Henning, who played her role for all seven seasons).

Throughout the show, Uncle Joe and Kate got involved with the three girls' personal and dating lives, all while dealing with problems with the hotel and with the Hooterville Cannonball, the train that shuttled passengers between Hooterville and Pixley. Its engineers Charley Pratt and Floyd Smoot were played by former cowboy Western stars Rufe Davis and Smiley Burnette.

Although *Petticoat Junction* was technically a spin-off of *The Beverly Hillbillies*, the show had a much different feel. Story consultant Don Quinn declared, "There's a touch of sophisticated frenzy about the whole show. One of my main problems as a dialogue specialist is to make the writers realize that not everyone who lives in the country speaks like Jed Clampett. They're not hillbilly types at all!" (Ashe "Gorgeous Girls" 16).

Despite the almost constant cast changes, especially when it came to the daughters, *Petticoat Junction* was one of the top 25 shows every year in the show's first four years. In its first season, it was the fourth most popular show, averaging a 30.3 rating (Brooks and Marsh).

Still shot in black and white, *Petticoat Junction* moved to 9:30 in 1964–1965. Like *The Beverly Hillbillies*, it switched to color for the 1965–1966 season. In its first season in color, the show became the 15th most-watched, an averaging a 25.2 Nielsen rating (Brooks and Marsh).

In 1966–1967, *Petticoat Junction* had a sluggish start against the very popular *NBC Tuesday Night at the Movies* and ABC's short-lived sitcom *Love on a Rooftop*. The latter scored high ratings early in the season and was then moved to Thursday and replaced by *Peyton Place*. The move was beneficial to *Petticoat Junction*: It jumped in the ratings and, despite the early ratings losses, was the 23rd highest-rated show of the season, tied with *The Rat Patrol* ("Critics' Views" 60; "The Latest Form Sheet" 69; Brooks and Marsh).

That season, Uncle Joe hosted a wedding-and-honeymoon contest to promote business, Hooterville residents took over operation of the Cannonball (which forced the crew to quit), the Shady Rest became a diet farm for an overweight girl, Billie Jo got a paid singing gig, and the hotel served as a temporary jail for the county.

Bea Benaderet explained the show's popularity: "Our show appeals to all ages. We have the train and dog for the children, the girls for the young people and the middle-age characters for the middle-aged people. All of us love 'corn.' I think this is one reason for the success of the show" (Herman 32).

Edgar Buchanan felt that the show gave people the sense of home: "The small community is a heritage of every American. Young people have heard stories passed down by their folks and their folks, in many cases, remember it well. It's this association that gives the show an interesting realism" ("*Petticoat Junction* Like" 3).

The show rode the high ratings train until the 1968–1969 season when it moved out of its normal Thursday time slot. Now running on Saturdays at 9:30, ratings fell (Brooks and Marsh). To make matters worse, the next season the show lost one of its stars. While viewers did not seem to mind the almost constant casting changes of "The Petticoat Junction Girls," they turned away from the show after the death of Bea Benaderet. The actress took time off in 1967–1968 so she could receive five treatments of radiation therapy after a lung cancer diagnosis and returned for the final episodes of the season. She received letters from fans wishing her well and was intent on answering them all. "It was just beautiful. Letters poured in from people of all ages. Some were addressed simply to 'Bea Benaderet, Actress,' but they got to me. And there were others mailed out as class projects" (Heisner "Bea Benaderet Remembered" 49).

Benaderet returned for the 1968–1969 season, but filmed only five segments in three episodes, because at the time she was still ill and even hospitalized after filming. Although her doctors were "delighted" with the progress she was making, on October 12, 1968, she lost her cancer battle ("Bea Benaderet Succumbs" 18). Throughout the remainder of the show's time on the air, when a character referred to Kate, it was stated that she was simply "out of town."

Ratings continued to fall despite the addition of June Lockhart as Dr. Janet Craig. Lockhart took on the mother role for the Petticoat Junction Girls. Lockhart was coming off two other popular mother roles: Ruth Martin on *Lassie* and Maureen Robinson on *Lost in Space*.

The show stayed in the Saturday 9:30 slot until it was cancelled in 1970 despite still capturing 32 percent of the viewing audience. It was scheduled for syndication later that year ("CBS-TV Affiliates" 38; "Chicago" 81).

Green Acres

For viewers who could not get enough Southern-based comedy, CBS's *Green Acres* debuted in 1965. A direct spin-off of *Petticoat Junction*, it took place in Hooterville—the town where the *Petticoat Junction* train, the Hooterville Cannonball, originated.

Green Acres and *Petticoat Junction* were originally going to have more crossover. Jay Sommers, *Green Acres*' creator, co-writer and producer, stated, "The original plan was to exchange performers with *Petticoat Junction*. We're getting away from that concept now. It's awfully hard to schedule when the actors will be available, and they are busy enough with their own shows. Besides, I think *Green Acres* should stand on its own feet" (Thomas "Don't Underestimate" 7).

Green Acres debuted in color on Wednesday, September 15, 1965, at 9:00. It aired for six seasons and was on the list of prime time TV's top 20 shows in its first four seasons, averaging a Nielsen rating of 23.4 during those seasons (Brooks and Marsh).

Green Acres' premise was derived from the radio program *Granny's Green Acres*. Thanks to the success of *The Beverly Hillbillies* and *Petticoat Junction,* Paul Henning brought the show to television.

According to the show's theme song, Oliver Wendell Douglas (Eddie Albert), successful New York attorney, brought his beautiful wife, the Hungarian-accented Lisa (Eva Gabor), to rural Hooterville to realize his dream of owning a farm. Lisa was less than enthusiastic about the move and would rather still be in New York City. To make matters worse, Oliver did not know the first thing about farming. To realize his dream of owning a working farm, Oliver had to rely on the less than reliable people of Hooterville: bungling farmhand Eb Dawson (Tom Lester), their elderly neighbors Fred Ziffel (Hank Patterson), Doris Ziffel (Barbara Pepper 1965–1968 and Fran Ryan 1969–1971) and their pet pig Arnold; forgetful county agricultural agent Hank Kimball (Alvy Moore), general store owner Sam Drucker (Frank Cady); the Monroe Brothers, carpenters who are actually brother and sister Alf (Sid Melton) and Ralph (Mary Grace Canfield) and industrious con man Mr. Haney (Pat Buttram).

In essence, *Green Acres* was a mirror image of *The Beverly Hillbillies*: The Hillbillies are out of place outside of the country, whereas Oliver and Lisa are out of place outside of an urban setting.

In 1966–1967, *Green Acres* had its most popular season, averaging a 24.6 rating, making it the sixth highest-rated show. It aired opposite *The Man Who Never Was,* an ABC spy drama that only lasted half a season, and NBC's *Bob Hope Presents the Chrysler Theatre.*

That season, Oliver rented a plane from Mr. Haney to crop dust, pig-sat for Arnold, fought unfair taxation, objected to Hooterville's law against owning a real Christmas tree, enrolled Lisa in homemaking classes at the high school, and turned to computers to help with his farming.

According to Jay Sommers, *Green Acres* "appeals to a basic human urge: Everyone would like to buy a farm. And we came up with a brilliant combination in Eddie Albert and Eva Gabor. They work together like a dream" (Thomas "Don't Underestimate" 7).

Green Acres would be a top show for another two seasons but dropped after CBS moved it to 9:00 on Saturdays in 1969. In an attempt to boost ratings, CBS next moved it to Tuesdays at 8:00 in the 1970–1971 season. But ratings never improved and *Green Acres* was cancelled.

Most of the surviving cast members, including Eddie Albert and Eva Gabor, reunited for a CBS telemovie, *Return to Green Acres* (1990).

The Hooterville Television Universe

The Beverly Hillbillies, Petticoat Junction and *Green Acres* will forever be linked, not only because they aired on CBS and were rural Southern shows, but due to the fact that all three resided in "The Hooterville Television Universe."

The town of Hooterville was first mentioned in the 11th *Beverly Hillbillies* episode, "Elly Races Jethrine." In the episode, the Hillbillies return to their hometown of Limestone, Tennessee, and Jethro's sister Jethrine (also played by Max Baer) is asked to a dance in Hooterville. *Petticoat Junction*'s Shady Rest Hotel is located between Hooterville and Pixley. *Petticoat* spin-off *Green Acres* takes place in Hooterville proper.

There has always been speculation on where Hooterville would be located. In the *Green Acres* episode "Flight to Nowhere," it was mentioned that Chicago was 300 miles away. In the episode "Music to Milk By," Eb listens to WPIXL radio. Radio stations west of the Mississippi begin with K; the fact that the station began with W would indicate the channel was located east of the Mississippi.

But *The Beverly Hillbillies* needs to be factored in as well. The Clampetts hailed from Limestone, Tennessee, where Hooterville was first mentioned. A real Tennessee town, Limestone is located in the northeastern portion of the state, which could easily place Hooterville in northeast Tennessee, southwest Virginia, northwest North Carolina or southeast Kentucky.

Although the town's location was intentionally vague, it is safe to put both shows in the South.

One of the main links between the shows was Drucker's General Store owner Sam

Drucker (Frank Cady), who appeared on both *Green Acres* and *Petticoat Junction* simultaneously. Drucker's General Store served as the main commerce hub for characters on both *Green Acres* and *Petticoat Junction*.

On November 27, 1968, the *Beverly Hillbillies* episode "The Thanksgiving Spirit" brought together characters from the entire Hooterville Universe: The Clampetts, along with Mr. Drysdale and Miss Jane traveled to Hooterville and had Thanksgiving dinner with the *Green Acres* and *Petticoat Junction* characters. Granny traveled to Hooterville in the December 1968 *Petticoat Junction* episode "A Cake from Granny."

Hogan's Heroes was also in the Hooterville Television Universe. In the *Green Acres* episode "Wings Over Hooterville," Oliver reveals that he met Lisa while he was a fighter pilot in World War II and was forced to bail out of his plane over Hungary. Oliver was captured by his future wife Lisa, head of the Hungarian Underground. In the episode, Oliver was told of Colonel Hogan and Stalag 13, which were featured on *Hogan's Heroes*.

The Andy Griffith Show

CBS had two other, equally famous Southern-based shows in its lineup in 1966: *The Andy Griffith Show*, set in the town of Mayberry in rural North Carolina, and *Gomer Pyle, U.S.M.C.*, whose title character hailed from Mayberry.

The Andy Griffith Show, which debuted on October 3, 1960, tells the story of small-town sheriff Andy Taylor, played by the show's namesake, Andy Griffith. Andy Taylor was a widower; other characters included his son Opie (Ronny Howard), Andy's Aunt Bea (Frances Bavier) and Andy's bumbling deputy Barney Fife (Don Knotts).

Before the show hit the air, Andy stated,

> The emphasis of the show will be comedy.... In the series, I'm just an ordinary small-town type of fella. I tell a joke once in a while. Kind of a rural character—not a rube though. I'm the sheriff and Don Knotts plays my deputy. But that's just our job. You won't see a lot of slambang action on the show. It's a comedy. Every once in a while, I'll even play the guitar a little [Stern "Andy Given" 19].

Previous to *The Andy Griffith Show*, Knotts appeared with Griffith in the film *No Time for Sergeants* (1958) and was a longtime sidekick to comedian Steve Allen.

The Andy Griffith Show also had a revolving cast of supporting characters: Floyd the barber (Howard McNear), gas station attendants Gomer Pyle (Jim Nabors) and Goober Pyle (George Lindsey), town drunk Otis Campbell (Hal Smith) and Aunt Bea's friend Clara Edwards (Hope Summers).

The New York Times called *The Andy Griffith Show* "only mildly entertaining," but in the show's first several weeks it had an extremely high average rating of 41.8. Griffith stated, "I'm mighty happy about it, of course, but it might just have been curiosity. Hope not. Time will tell" ("How Critics Described" 17; Andersen "Manhattan Interlude," 120).

Clearly it was not just curiosity that made viewers tune in. *The Andy Griffith Show* appealed to audiences who lived in the small and rural towns of America and those who *wanted* to ... or at least were nostalgic for a simpler way of living, when town sheriffs did not have to carry guns. And much like shows in the Hooterville Universe, *Andy Griffith* also appealed to the small-town community heritage that Edgar Buchanan of *Petticoat Junction* talked about when he said, "The small community is a heritage of every

American. Young people have heard stories passed down by their folks and their folks, in many cases, remember it well. It's this association that gives the show an interesting realism" ("*Petticoat Junction* Like" 3).

Aside from nostalgia for small-town living, *Andy Griffith*'s humor appealed to audiences no matter where they lived. Griffith credited this to the fact that everyone on the show, besides the young Ron Howard, had a long show business background and knew how to make scripts humorous. "I guess you could call us surgeons," said Griffith. "We cut up the script. Figure out which lines are funny ... odd thing. A script can read just hilariously. But when you go to play it, it falls down like a tired puppy. And that's when we start to rewrite and cut and revise" (Silden 12).

In the first season, *Andy Griffith* was the fourth highest-rated show, averaging a 27.8 rating—and ratings would not decline. The show was one of America's top ten shows, averaging a rating of 28.0, in all eight seasons (Brooks and Marsh). *Andy Griffith* switched from black and white to color in 1965. That season, it was the sixth highest-rated show with a 26.9 rating (Brooks and Marsh).

But one of the show's stars would not transition to color. Don Knotts got a chance to star in his own feature film, *The Incredible Mr. Limpet* (1964), when *Andy Griffith* shooting wrapped for the season in 1964. The film was so successful, Knotts received an offer to leave *Andy Griffith* and make more movies. Knotts accepted. He left the show and went on to star in 15 films, play many supporting film roles, and continued to appear on TV until his death in 2006.

When it was announced that Knotts was leaving the show, Griffith stated, "This show might not have ever lasted if it wasn't for Don. ... Don is the best comedy actor in the country. I never considered him a second banana on the show. I never considered him anything but an equal or more than equal" (Leonard "Don Knotts Leaving" 54).

Rumors circulated that Knotts was leaving because he was irritated that Jim Nabors got a spin-off show, *Gomer Pyle, U.S.M.C.*, before *he* did. But Griffith assured viewers that Knotts was leaving because of his desire to make movies: "Don could have a spin-off series. It was in his contract" (Leonard "Don Knotts Leaving" 54). Knotts made occasional appearances on *Andy Griffith* after leaving.

In 1966, *Andy Griffith* aired on Monday nights at 9:00, the same time as the police drama *The Felony Squad* on ABC and the Western *The Road West* on NBC. *Andy Griffith* was the third highest-rated show of the season, losing out only to *Bonanza* and *The Red Skelton Hour* (Brooks and Marsh).

Although Nabors and Knotts left *The Andy Griffith Show*, the show's supporting cast picked up the slack and larger roles were written for Opie, Floyd the barber, Goober, Aunt Bea and Andy's girlfriend Helen Crump (Aneta Corsaut). That season, the show also added Jack Dodson in the role of county clerk Howard Sprague. In a *Chicago Tribune* interview, Dodson talked about the character: "We've all known somebody like him, I should imagine—kind of a good-natured, warm-hearted guy who is too introverted and unsure of himself to have any real social life or ever progress in the world, yet the kind of person you can always depend on in a pinch. I like him, and I like playing him" (Gowran "31 Million" 24).

Andy Griffith was on the air for one more season and went out on top. In the 1967–1968 season, it was TV's highest-rated show, averaging a 27.6 rating (Brooks and Marsh). Andy Griffith had decided to step away from the show to pursue other acting roles, something that he had been hinting at doing for several years. Griffith's character Andy Taylor got married and moved with his Helen and Opie to Charlotte, North Carolina (Leonard "Don Knotts Leaving" 54).

The other Mayberry residents remained and the show morphed into *Mayberry R.F.D.* starring Ken Berry, whose character was introduced toward the end of the 1967–1968 season. Berry played Sam Jones, a young farmer with political potential who moved to town with his son Mike (Buddy Foster). Frances Bavier's Aunt Bea stayed on the show for another season and then semi-retired from acting; she was ostensibly replaced by Alice Ghostley as Alice Cooper. Goober, Howard Sprague, Clara Edwards and handyman Emmett Clark (Paul Hartman) were also regularly seen on *Mayberry R.F.D.* Andy Griffith made occasional appearances and produced *Mayberry R.F.D.*

Mayberry R.F.D. was also a hit. In its three seasons, it never left the top 15 shows of the year, averaging a 24.0 rating (Brooks and Marsh). *Mayberry R.F.D.* left the air in 1971. Many of the cast members reunited for the TV movie *Return to Mayberry* (1986).

Gomer Pyle, U.S.M.C.

The Andy Griffith Show was such a success that in 1964, Jim Nabors' character got his own spin-off show *Gomer Pyle, U.S.M.C.*—which also became a hit.

In the third and fourth seasons of *The Andy Griffith Show,* Nabors played the sometimes incompetent gas station attendant Gomer Pyle. The character became a fan favorite, so CBS gave him his own show. Pyle was recruited by the Marine Corps, thus creating the spin-off show *Gomer Pyle, U.S.M.C.*, which revolved around Gomer, now a Marine private, and his bumbling and good, wholesome nature that often clashed with his hardnosed Sergeant Carter (Frank Sutton).

Nabors's character was well-defined on *Andy Griffith* and audiences anticipated his catchphrases "Gooollllly" and "Shazam!," but the character of Sergeant Carter needed some work. Sutton stated, "Carter was too heavy. He was a brick wall for Gomer to bounce against. But there can be no heavies in this series. It must be light" (Witbeck "His Best Friend" 31).

Not only was the Gomer character familiar to audiences, the plot of *Gomer Pyle* was familiar to audiences due to its similarity to the 1958 Andy Griffith–Don Knotts film *No Time for Sergeants. New York Times* critic Jack Gould assured audiences there were some differences between *No Time for Sergeants* and *Gomer Pyle*: "Mr. Nabors conveys a particular mood of attractive awkwardness and naiveté, a contagious quality of special poignancy rooted in laughter. The premise of *Gomer Pyle* has the virtue of delightful simplicity and credibility; the recruit merely assumes that everyone in the Marines is as friendly as the folks back home" (Gould "Freshness in Old").

Debuting in black and white on September 25, 1964, *Gomer Pyle* aired Fridays at 9:30. It took place on fictitious military bases—originally Camp Wilson, North Carolina, then Camp Henderson, California. *Gomer Pyle* appealed to the same audience *The Andy Griffith Show* did. Critics were dismissive, as they were toward many of TV's rural shows, but *Gomer Pyle* got high ratings, regularly besting time slot rivals *12 O'Clock High* on ABC and *The Jack Benny Show* on NBC. *Gomer Pyle* was that season's third highest-rated show, averaging an impressive 30.7 rating (Brooks and Marsh).

In the second season, *Gomer Pyle* joined the ranks of color television and ended up the second highest-rated show, even overshadowing *Andy Griffith* which came in third (Brooks and Marsh).

Jim Nabors did not want the #1 spot: "If you get to the top, there's only one direction to go, down. Just anywhere in the top five is nice and comfortable. It gives you a little room to move around in" (Scott "Gomer Pyle Finished Year" 21).

On October 7, 1965, CBS aired (in color) *The Andy Griffith–Don Knotts–Jim Nabors Special*. The three actors sang, danced, told stories and performed together in a courthouse sketch. A year before the show, Griffith and Nabors had put on a similar performance at Lake Tahoe's Harrah's Club. Prior to the show's airing, Nabors' manager Dick Linke stated, "We've embellished the nightclub show a little. ... You see, in the past year, the gap between the talents of Andy and Jim Nabors has closed considerably. Nabors has emerged as a full-blown star and can hold his own. ... Wait until you hear Jim sing 'Rockabye Your Baby,' and then you see him dance like a pro. You forget all about the goofball Marine character" (Witbeck "Folkey Trio" 34).

The special and *Gomer Pyle* were so popular that CBS gave Nabors his own special in October 1966, *Friends and Nabors*. It showcased Nabors' unique singing talent but still featured Andy Griffith as well as country singer Tennessee Ernie Ford.

Jack Gould wrote an October 13, 1966, article about how CBS was capitalizing on its many Southern shows. He remarked that it was atypical for someone in New York to hear a Southern accent, even on TV. "Since [CBS] has made several fortunes from country and folk television, it follows logically that the network would fashion a special around such homespun stars as Jim Nabors, Andy Griffith, and Ernie Ford. ... The rural diversion came last night on Channel 2 with a heap of accents unlikely to be confused with speech in areas east of the Hudson River." Gould predicted that the ratings for *Friends and Nabors* would be high, and he was not wrong (Gould "TV: A Homespun Trio").

That week CBS scored a massive 33.0 rating with *Friends and Nabors*, beating out NBC's *Bonanza*, a Bob Hope special, *Walt Disney's Wonderful World of Color* and even CBS's *The Andy Griffith Show*, *The Red Skelton Hour*, *The Lucy Show*, *The Beverly Hillbillies*, *The Jackie Gleason Show* and *The CBS Friday Movie* that week ("The Nielsen's").

In 1966–1967, *Gomer Pyle* moved to 9:30 on Wednesdays, airing opposite *Peyton Place* and *Bob Hope Presents the Chrysler Theatre*. It was the season's tenth highest-rated show, tying with *The Virginian* and *The Lawrence Welk Show* (Brooks and Marsh).

In 1966, Associated Press movie–TV writer Bob Thomas wrote, "[S]ome observers of the television scene drew this lesson from the first Nielsen ratings of the 1966–1967 season: Never underestimate the value of corn. " He also called out the sophisticates who sniff at that fact that among the ten top-rated shows were *Gomer Pyle, Green Acres, The Andy Griffith Show* and *The Beverly Hillbillies* (Thomas "Don't Underestimate" 7).

Although seen by some as "nothing but corn," *Gomer Pyle* was constantly in the top 20 prime time shows and had an average of a 26.82 rating in the show's five seasons.

After five seasons, Nabors was finished with his Gomer Pyle character and looking to future endeavors. "You can't reach another rung on a ladder unless you let loose of the one you're on," said Nabors. *Gomer Pyle* left the air in May 1969. By letting loose of *Gomer Pyle*, Nabors got the opportunity to host his own weekly CBS variety series, *The Jim Nabors Hour*, starting in the fall of 1969. On his show, Nabors showed off his unique singing talent, performed skits and welcomed guest stars. *The Jim Nabors Hour* picked up where *Gomer Pyle* left off in the ratings: It was the 12th highest-rated show in the 1969–1970 season, with an average 22.4 Nielsen rating (Brooks and Marsh).

The Rural Purge

CBS aired all five very popular and long-running Southern rural-based shows, thereby gaining the reputation of being the Southern rural network. But by the 1970–1971 season, most Southern rural shows were gone from CBS's prime time lineup, including *Green Acres*, *The Beverly Hillbillies*, *Mayberry R.F.D.* and *The Jim Nabors Hour*. CBS also cancelled any show that had an older audience or anything seen as unsophisticated such as *The Original Amateur Hour*, *Hee Haw*, *Lassie*, *Hogan's Heroes*, *The Red Skelton Hour* and *The Johnny Cash Show*. The cancellation of these shows became known as the Rural Purge.

Who at CBS was responsible for the Rural Purge? Most often, the network's chairman and chief executive officer William Paley was blamed due to simply being the head of the company and the belief that his marriage to New York socialite Barbara "Babe" Cushing Mortimer influenced his decision to woo a more sophisticated viewership. During Paley's tenure, he labeled the network "The Tiffany Network"—in reference to the channel being the jewel of broadcast television, as one would find in famed jewelers Tiffany and Company, and interestingly because the first local public demonstrations of color TV were held by CBS in the Tiffany and Company Building at 401 Fifth Avenue in Manhattan ("C.B.S. to Present").

But the Museum of Broadcast Television wrote that CBS president Robert Wood was to blame:

> [Wood's] strategy in 1970 was to cancel rural and older-skewing classic series [*Green Acres*, *The Beverly Hillbillies*, *Petticoat Junction* and *Hee Haw*], and established stars [*The Red Skelton Hour*, *The Jackie Gleason Show*, *The Ed Sullivan Show*], in favor of more contemporary urban-oriented programming. ... Rather than farcical situation comedies [sitcoms], these shows built on issues affecting characters as interacting persons, thus becoming "character comedies" instead [Brown "Robert Wood"].

Wood was quoted as saying that CBS was committed to a "new look," that the network was "playing the numbers game"; and that although the network could play it safe for the 1970–1971 season, it would mean the network would be "stringing along with those shows that might still deliver respectable ratings for another season, even though we had concluded, reluctantly, that they had no long-term future on our schedule." A Wood assistant stated. "We're going from the county to the city" (Gould "C.B.S. Line-Up for Fall Omits"; "CBS-TV Affiliates" 38).

Wood's decision was not malicious. He called the move a "soul-searching decision," stating that "neither past performance nor present popularity is sufficient any longer to guarantee future pulling power." Wood believed that the network had to look forward rather than to the past when he stated,

> The days are gone in programming when we can afford to be imitative rather than innovative. ... We have to hold the audiences we have; we have to broaden our base; we have to attract new viewers of every generation, reflecting the educated and sophisticated in American life, people who live in every part of the county. ... We are taking a young, fresh new approach to programming.

He added that CBS would be giving new shows a chance and were not afraid to try something new ("CBS-TV Affiliates" 38).

Regardless of who was to blame, the Rural Purge was seen as an assault on Southern conservative values in the form of cancelling shows that high society New York liberals saw as unintelligent or unsophisticated.

But in 1970, the ratings for rural-themed shows were slipping, and the average age of viewers who tuned in for that type of programming was getting older; CBS was looking to start the process of cancelling shows that catered to an older audience as early as the end of the 1966–1967 season when they almost cancelled *Gunsmoke*, but eventually caved to audience backlash and brought it back (Lowry "Mature Programs" 24).

Additionally, the Federal Communications Commission started to require all three major networks to give three and a half more hours of programming a week to local affiliates to "provide greater programming diversity." This forced networks, including CBS, to cut out more shows in prime time and make difficult programming decisions (Gent "Welk Show Among 11").

Some did not accept the changes without a fight. To protest the Rural Purge, country music singer Roy Clark released the novelty song "The Lawrence Welk–Hee Haw Counter-Revolution Polka" in 1972. The song reached the Billboard Top 100 country music charts.

In the next several seasons, CBS rolled out new urban- and suburban-based programs and shows with humor seen as more sophisticated by CBS executives; for example, *All in the Family* and *The Mary Tyler Moore Show*. CBS also presented movies four nights a week, which displaced many more series.

CHAPTER TEN

Situation Comedies

It is argued that *Mary Kay and Johnny* (1947–1950), which aired on the DuMont Network and later NBC and CBS, was TV's first situation comedy. It is also reportedly the first show to have a married couple sleeping in the same bed and to deal with the subject of pregnancy, both taboo for 1948 television.

But the fall of 1966 saw a shift in the sitcom landscape. A number of long-running and iconic sitcoms left the airwaves—most notably *The Dick Van Dyke Show*, the 16th highest-rated show the previous season, averaging a 23.6 rating (Brooks and Marsh).

In its five seasons, *Dick Van Dyke* was never in color. Its creator and head writer Carl Reiner recalled that color would cost an additional $7000 an episode at a time when an average show cost approximately $40,000 to produce. Reiner also wanted the show "to have a consistent look when reruns appeared in syndication," and he believed that shooting in color would have killed the show's profit margin. Then, too, he wanted to go out on top. "We had already done almost every premise that we knew of ... we wanted to go out strong. We all felt the same way," said Reiner (Battaglio). And the show did just that.

Several other sitcoms that never made the jump to color vanished from the network airwaves just before the 1966–1967 season: *The Munsters* (1964–1966), *The Addams Family* (1964–1966), *The Patty Duke Show* (1963–1966), *McHale's Navy* (1962–1966) and *The Donna Reed Show* (1958–1966). And some long-running sitcoms that did make the leap to color were cancelled: *The Adventures of Ozzie and Harriet* (1952–1966), *My Favorite Martian* (1963–1966) and *Hazel* (1961–1966).

This paved the way for a new crop of situation comedies which made up 33 percent of all new shows on the air. In addition to new shows, several long-running sitcoms stuck around and contributed to the colorful 1966–1967 season.

The Monkees

In the mid–1960s, Beatlemania was running high. Not only were the Beatles arguably the biggest band in the world, their movies *A Hard Day's Night* (1964) and *Help!* (1965) were successful both critically and at the box office. They even had a popular ABC Saturday morning cartoon (1965–1967). Columbia wanted to take advantage of the craze and reproduce Beatlemania by creating an American version of the Beatles and build their fame around an NBC-TV show. Instead of finding an existing band, producers held auditions to create a new band whose image and music they could control and cultivate. Columbia went as far as using a similar intentional misspelling of the band's name: the Monkees.

An ad ran in *Variety* and *The Hollywood Reporter* on September 8, 9 and 10, 1965, which read, "Madness!! Auditions. Folk & Roll Musicians—Singers for acting roles in new TV series. Running Parts for 4 insane boys, age 17–21. Want spirited Ben Frank's-types. Have courage to work. Must come down for interview" ("Advertisement for *The Monkees*"; Larson 3).

In total, 437 young men auditioned, including the four ultimately cast: guitarist Mike Nesmith, drummer Micky Dolenz, singer Davy Jones and bassist Peter Tork. All four acted in scenes with other potential Monkees, showed off their musical ability and pantomime skills, and talked about their life experiences.

Also among the 437 young men: Steven Stills, who went on to play in Buffalo Springfield and Crosby, Stills, Nash and Young; Paul Petersen, former star of *The Donna Reed Show* and future Academy Award–winning composer; and Danny Hutton of Three Dog Night (Bronson).

An urban legend circulated that cult leader Charles Manson, who at the time of the auditions was 31 years old and in prison, tried out for the group. Davy Jones reportedly took credit for originating the rumor (Brioux 74).

Mike Nesmith and Peter Tork, both accomplished musicians, were plucked from relative obscurity. Micky Dolenz and Davy Jones already had show business experience. Dolenz had been in other bands and was a child actor on NBC's *Circus Boy* (1956–1958): In that show, billed as Micky Braddock, he played Corky, a young boy whose parents died in a trapeze accident; he was adopted by a circus family and was the waterboy for a baby elephant named Bimbo. In his audition, Dolenz was at one point referred to as "Elephant Boy." Jones acted in the Broadway play *Oliver!* as the Artful Dodger and appeared on *The Ed Sullivan Show* on February 9, 1964, to promote the play—the same episode in which the Beatles made their American TV debut. Jones later stated, "I watched the Beatles from the side of the stage, I saw the girls going crazy, and I said to myself, this is it, I want a piece of that" (Nachman).

Jones went on to pursue that rock'n'roll career as a solo artist and, prior to *The Monkees,* he even had a song, "What Are We Going to Do?," on the Billboard Hot 100. He performed it on ABC's musical showcase show *Shindig!* in 1965.

The soon-to-be Monkees proved they had everything necessary: humor, good looks and personalities that could connect with and represent 1960s teens. Musical talent was not a must.

Tork said in an interview that Berkeley Schneider and Bob Rafelson, the idea men behind the show, hoped to "get enough musicianship out of the band" so they could play gigs but certainly put an emphasis on acting over music. Dolenz and Tork confirmed that the music on the Monkees' first album was recorded before they were cast, and the band later recorded the vocals ("The Wrecking Crew!").

In November 1965, the industry magazine *Broadcasting* announced 90 new potential projects for all three major networks. *The Monkees*, which was misspelled as *The Monkeys,* was listed but very few details were given other than that it was a half-hour comedy in color from Screen Gems ("Bumper Crop" 30).

Soon after the show was announced, David Gordon, director of public relations for United Artists Television, and David Yarnell, an RKO Studios executive, claimed that *The Monkees* was a "carbon copy" of a program they presented to Screen Gems in 1964, *Liverpool, U.S.A.* Gordon and Yarnell retained former NBC lawyer James A. Stabile to represent their case and sought approximately $3,500,000 in damages. The lawsuit was not settled until October 1970, when the Supreme Court of New York, Appellate Division, ruled in Gordon and Yarnell's favor for an undisclosed amount of money (Messina "ABC to Scrap" 50; "Supreme Court").

TV Guide wrote in their 1966–1967 Fall Preview issue,

> The Monkees is coming. And win, lose or draw, it's a series, which at least is different. The premise is conventional enough: A rock'n'roll quartet romps through miscellaneous cornie misadventures, pausing to sing things like "I wanna be free-ee-ee like the bluebirds…" and to say things like "She's a groovy kid" and "You must be out of your bird." The difference is in the way the show is done. Just four leading men patterned on the Beatles, its production techniques are borrowed in large measure from the Beatles' movies. The whole thing is played with a nonrealistic framework, with frantic changes of costume and scene, slapstick chases, photographic pranks of all sorts ["1966–1967 Fall Preview"].

The NBC show debuted on Monday, September 12, 1966, in the 7:30 time slot, and competed with CBS's *Gilligan's Island* and ABC's *Iron Horse*. According to that week's Arbitron ratings, *The Monkees* lost out to both shows ("Critics' Views" 59).

Despite a disappointing first week's ratings, the show got several very promising reviews from newspaper critics:

> "Could be the first comedy hit of the season."—Jack Gould, *The New York Times*
>
> "Moments of wonderful, wild humor."—Harriet Van Horne, *New York World Journal Tribune*
>
> "Extraordinary laugh-maker."—Bob Hull, *Los Angeles Herald Examiner*
>
> "Adults will scream in outrage. … [It] will delight the young."—Lawrence Laurent, *Washington Post*
>
> "A delectable treat."—Bob Williams, *New York Post* ("Critics' Views" 63)

The band's music, image and show were closely monitored by producer Don Kirshner, head of music at Screen Gems, the TV production arm of Columbia, which distributed the show. Initially, most songs performed by the band were written by famed songwriters Tommy Boyce and Bobby Hart, who previously wrote songs such as "Come a Little Bit Closer" by Jay and the Americans and "(I'm Not Your) Steppin' Stone" by Paul Revere and the Raiders. The Monkees' albums and singles were released by Colgems, also owned by Columbia. Although the Monkees provided vocals on the tracks, the musical instruments were played by studio musicians—most notably the famed Wrecking Crew who played on recordings by the Beach Boys, Frank Sinatra, Nancy Sinatra, Sonny and Cher, Jan and Dean, Gary Lewis and the Playboys, Ricky Nelson and Johnny Rivers, and did numerous sessions with infamous music producer Phil Spector ("The Wrecking Crew!").

Although the show was never a ratings success, the Monkees boasted two Billboard #1 hits in 1966 on the band's self-titled album, "Last Train to Clarksville" and "I'm a Believer." The show's ratings were inconsequential to Columbia as long as the show bolstered the Monkees' album sales ("The Monkees Chart History").

Much like Batmania and Beatlemania; Monkeemania began sweeping the nation and Screen Gems was ready to capitalize on the merchandising opportunities. The Monkees' faces were slapped on all kinds of merchandise: lunch boxes, T-shirts, board games, model kits, trading cards, pins, puzzles, books and more.

Color played a role in *The Monkees*' popularity. On the show, the boys drove around in a bright red, open engine Dean Jeffries–designed Pontiac GTO Monkee-mobile, lived in a colorful house, and wore vibrant and trendy clothes. The band's colorful wardrobe was created by designer Gene Ashman. Their outfits became "popular with teens around the world," who began sporting similar styles. Monkees Halloween costumes were a popular trick-or-treating choice in 1966 (Welch "Why the Monkees Matter" 105).

In the October 1967 issue of *16* magazine, costume designer Ashman talked about coming up with the Monkees' signature look:

> We wanted to avoid the Carnaby Street look, the "Mod" look, or any other well-established look. Ultimately, I decided that ... all the Monkees' clothes would be derived from basically the same design. ... I was worried about their opinions. I shouldn't have worried at all—they flipped over my first design. When Davy looked at me and said, "Man, that's definitely in our bag"—it was one of the greatest compliments I've ever received [Ashman].

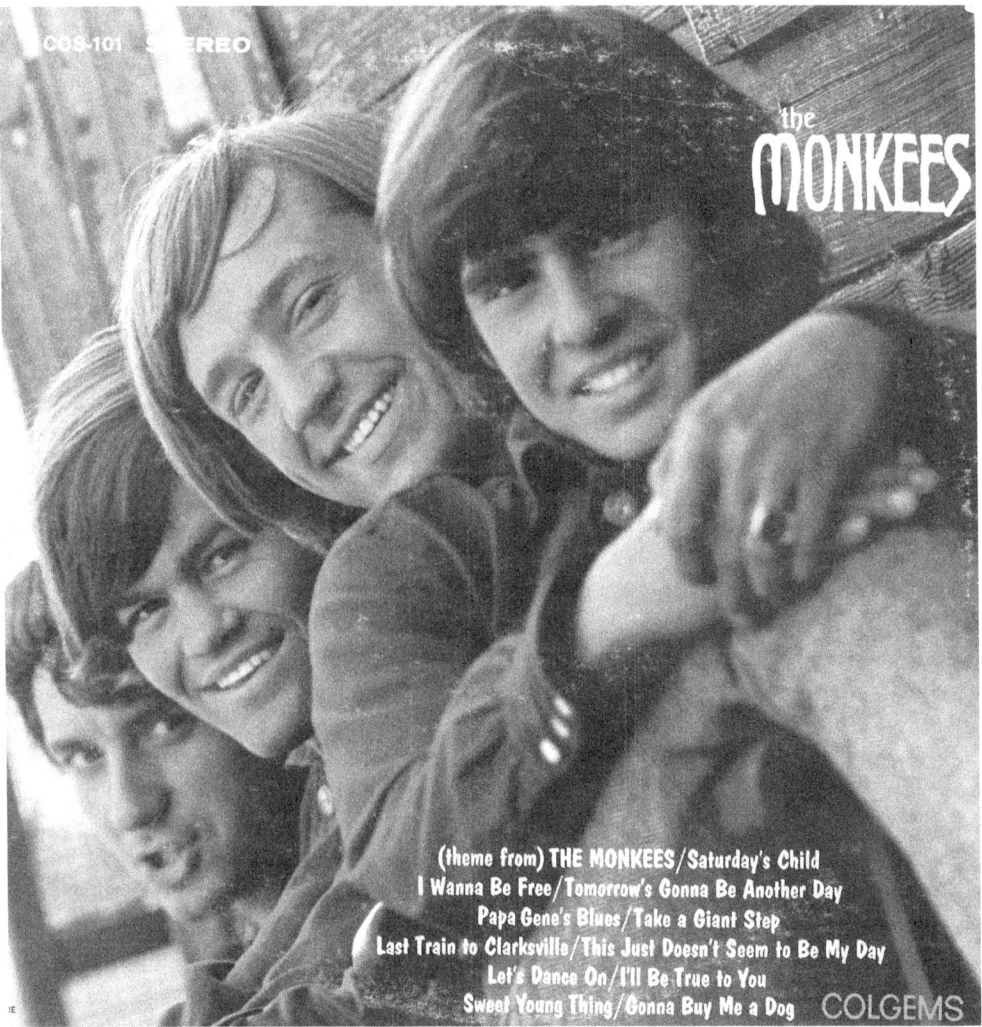

Above and opposite page: The first two albums released *The Monkees* on the Colgems label. Both albums were multi-platinum selling LPs for the band (Shubilla family archives).

Chapter Ten. Situation Comedies 169

The *Monkees* TV show was more than just mindless fluff made for young teens in order to make a profit. The show was named the best comedy show of the 1966–1967 season by the Academy of Television Arts and Sciences, and nominated for two Emmys—one for best comedy series, the other for best comedy direction for James Frawley's work on the episode "Royal Flush." Perhaps the smart writing is part of the reason why the show's popularity has lasted throughout the years (Brooks and Marsh).

There was even the question if the Monkees were more popular than the artists they emulated, the Beatles. KBZY radio deejay Clayton Henry in Salem, Oregon, was quoted in the newspaper *Capital Journal* on December 2, 1966, "The Beatles are dead, long live the Monkees!" He added, "That seems to be the cry of the trade papers and record sales reports lately." He also alleged that "in one East Coast city poll," the Monkees outpolled the Beatles three to one (Henry).

In a world without the internet or 24/7 entertainment news, not everyone knew the truth about how the Monkees were formed; many assumed that their formation was as organic as that of the Beatles. But there were rumblings. Clayton Henry also reported on the band's prefabricated nature: "Unlike the Beatles, who had a background in music long before their big hits, the Monkees' previous experience as a group is no doubt limited and in fact a well-kept secret. There are stories circulating that they were formed especially for the series and that even now their instrumental backing is by another group" (Henry).

Once the public learned that the Monkees did not write their own songs, play their own instruments, there was a backlash. The band became known as the "Prefab Four," a takeoff on the Beatles' nickname "The Fab Four." But the Beatles were not as judgmental. Micky Dolenz claimed that Beatle John Lennon once stated, "I like the Monkees, they're like the Marx Brothers" (Sullivan "Tork Death").

Even though the Monkees' musical ability was low on the producer's list of priorities, they actually had musical talent and wanted to break free and show it off—not just be a band that plays one on TV. *Monkee Spectacular* magazine featured the article "Do They Play Their Own Instruments" in April 1967, and it stated that the band's acting schedule was the reason that they were not able to play on their own records:

> At first the boys didn't play all their album band tracks. Not because they did not know how to play their instruments, but because they just did not have the time. Imagine shooting a television show from seven in the morning until seven at night every day and having enough energy left over to go into a recording studio for several more hours! ... During the entire month of November, they had even less time because they were rehearsing their stage act every night from 8 to 11 o'clock!

The article went on to ask, "Are the Monkees just a product of other people's talents?" The answer: "[C]onsidering that they ad-lib much of their TV show, and they sing and play their music (some of which they have written) and they have developed their own, original and sensational stage act, what do you think. Right!" ("Do They Play").

On December 3, 1966, the Monkees began a 14-city U.S. tour starting in Honolulu, proving that they had their own talent and that they could play their own instruments. But they still wanted more creative freedom.

While on tour, the LP *More of the Monkees,* released by Colgems contained B-sides and tracks not heard on the band's first album. Much to the chagrin of the Monkees, the album was released without the band's knowledge or consent. Michael Nesmith called a press conference where he stated, "We're being passed off as something we're not. We all play instruments but we haven't on any of our records. Furthermore, our company doesn't want us to and won't let us." He also threatened to quit the band unless the Monkees were given more control over their product. To appease the band, Don Kirshner was relieved of his duties and the band was able to hire their own music producer, the Turtles' bassist Chip Douglas (Massingill "Total Control").

In 1967, the Monkees released *Headquarters,* their first album after taking over creative control and hiring Douglas. The band played their own instruments on the record and were the principal writers on much of the album. That same year, they also released the LP *Pisces, Aquarius, Capricorn & Jones Ltd.,* which featured the #1 single "Pleasant Valley Sunday." It stayed on the charts for four weeks but was the band's last #1 hit. Nesmith began writing for other artists after Linda Ronstadt recorded his song "Different Drum" with her band Stone Poneys in 1967.

Although the band achieved success in the charts and record sales, the second season of *The Monkees* did not meet expectations, so it was the show's last. The last episode of *The Monkees* aired on March 25, 1968, after 58 episodes in two seasons. An Associated Press article quoted Nesmith as saying, "The second season was just the first season rehashed. ... We felt that we had become more proficient, but we were only given the same stuff to do. Most people thought that we were cancelled. The fact is that we told NBC that we didn't only want to do the same thing. And so, the series came to an end. I can't really say that I'm sorry." The Associated Press claimed that the Monkees were earning $1250 per segment of the series, "a mere pittance of what they can collect elsewhere. Such are the rewards of instant fame that the lads made between four and five million dollars last year." The Associated Press also reported that Nesmith personally made $2,500,000 "since he originated much of the musical material used by the Monkees on their shows and albums" (Thomas "Monkees Lose").

The Monkees released the album *The Birds, the Bees & the Monkees* in April 1968. It was the band's first album *not* to reach #1, but it did feature two successful and iconic singles, "Daydream Believer" and "Valleri."

The Monkees also continued to act. The psychedelic movie *Head* (1968), co-written by Jack Nicholson, starred the four members of the band. A sharp contrast to the TV show, it was full of social commentary, drug references, counterculture themes, attacks on consumerism, and anti-war sentiment. At the time *Head* was a commercial and critical failure. Paulina Kael of *The New Yorker* wrote,

> The movie might have worked for bored kids at kiddie matinees, but the filmmakers got ambitious. The by-now standard stuff of girls squealing as pop idols perform is not even convincing when they're squealing for the Monkees, and when this is intercut with documentary footage of the suffering and horror of war, as if to comment on the shallowness of what the filmmakers are manufacturing and packaging and desperately trying to sell, the doubling up of greed and pretensions to depth is enough to make even a pinhead walk out.

Famed critic Stanley Kauffmann said the Monkees were "virtually devoid of charm ... but they are vigorous and willing," and Renata Adler wrote in *The New York Times* that the film "takes subversive styles and covers them in mediocrities" (Knight and Roberson). Dolenz stated that he believed the movie helped the band seem less like "establishment products" than what they were portrayed as in the TV show ("Monkee Mickey Says" 8).

The *Head* soundtrack was a flop as well. Since the show's release, *Head* has found a cult following, and critics have taken a more positive look at both the film and soundtrack.

NBC aired a *Monkees* variety show special, *33⅓ Revolutions Per Monkee*, on April 14, 1969; it featured Jerry Lee Lewis, Fats Domino, Little Richard and the Monkees both individually and as a group. The show marked the end of Tork's run with the Monkees, who went on to form the short-lived rock band Release.

The Monkees carried on as a trio for a year, making appearances on *The Glen Campbell Goodtime Hour* and *The Johnny Cash Show,* and embarking on a 47-show North American tour. Reviews for the latter were positive and critics began to accept that the Monkees were more than a cookie cutter made-for-TV band. *The Tampa Tribune* wrote, "The stage show the Monkees have developed promises to be different from the clown act they used to have. With a strong revival of stage acts and hard music, the Monkees have a chance to prove they can get into the front line of rock music" ("'New' Monkee" 38).

After the band's final show of the tour in Salt Lake City, Utah, on December 6, 1969, Nesmith quit the Monkees and was released from his contract with Colgems. In a December 1969 *Rolling Stone* interview, Micky Dolenz revealed that Nesmith was leaving the band to start his own country-western band. He also declared,

> *The Monkees* is the name of a TV show. I was hired to play the part of a rock'n'roll drummer, but what I am is an entertainer trying to reach an audience of eight-year-old girls. I'm no more a *Monkee* than Lorne Greene is a Cartwright [in reference to TV's *Bonanza*]. ... There'll be *Monkee* records in the future, done by Davy and me [Ward "Monkees" 10].

In 1970, Dolenz and Jones briefly attempted to continue the Monkees as a duo, making appearances throughout the U.S. and releasing the moderately successful album *Changes*, their last album for Colgems. The two men again joined forces in 1975, forming another incarnation of the band which included the Monkees' original songwriters Bobby Hart and Tommy Boyce, and they performed as Dolenz, Jones, Boyce and Hart. The group performed classic Monkees songs along with songs written by Boyce and Hart: "I Wonder What She's Doing Tonight?," "A Teenager in Love" and "Come a Little Bit Closer" ("Monkee's Chart History").

For the next ten years, Tork and Nesmith concentrated on their own music careers and Dolenz and Jones focused on acting, and little was heard about the Monkees. But in 1986, the *Monkees* TV show had a second life when it began airing on MTV, which introduced the series to a new generation. It was one of the cable channel's first non–music video–based regular programs, along with British the sitcom *The Young Ones* (1982–1984).

The New York Times reported in June 1986 that scripted programming was being added to MTV, due to the slumping ratings of the all–music video channel. *The Chicago Tribune* wrote that on February 23, 1986,

> things really took off when MTV broadcast their "Pleasant Valley Sunday" tribute—22½ consecutive hours of Monkeemania, comprising 45 episodes of their 1966–68 TV series. A month-long daily showcasing of episodes followed on MTV. Then another month of cable-casts was added because the audience reaction proved so positive for the Monkees' time-less combination of bubble rock and irreverent, Marx Brothers–inspired slapstick humor. ... More than 140 TV stations throughout the nation will be broadcasting the *Monkees* episodes daily. Then in September, the video simians move their hijinks over to the Nickelodeon cable channel [Takiff].

MTV's airing of *The Monkees* led to the Monkees reuniting, minus Michael Nesmith, and a tour featuring special guests Gary Puckett and the Union Gap, Herman's Hermits and the Grass Roots. The Monkees also released a 20th anniversary "best of" record with a new Arista Records single of the same name, "That Was Then, This Is Now." The single had a feel of *The Monkees*' hit "Pleasant Valley Sunday." A year later, 1987, the Monkees released a new album, *Pool It!* (again minus Nesmith), through Rhino Records. Nesmith did play with the band during their encore at a concert at the Greek Theater in Los Angeles on September 7, 1986, performing "Pleasant Valley Sunday" and "Listen to the Band."

Anecdotally, when MTV first aired *The Monkees*, many younger fans thought it was a new show and were disappointed when they learned that their new favorite band and/or celebrity crushes were no longer 20-somethings but instead men in their 40s.

But not all was well in Monkee world.

Although MTV brought *The Monkees* to a new audience and heavily played the video for the single "That Was Then, This Is Now," the station refused to play the single from *Pool It!,* "Heart and Soul," reportedly because the Monkees "broke a commitment to make a special appearance on MTV's Super Bowl special" due to Jones reportedly being out of the country, as reported in the "Cheers and Jeers" section of *TV Guide* in 1987. *TV Guide* went on to state, "MTV maintains the group's popularity has evaporated—despite the fact that the Monkees have scored well on the channel's call-in request show. MTV should respond to its viewers, not its own apparent need for petty revenge" (Diltz "Cheers").

Of course, this greatly upset Monkees fans. The *Monkee Business Fanzine*, published in 1987, wrote a strongly worded open letter to MTV executives about leaving the Monkees off the station and broke down the call-in request show numbers. The newsletter also claimed they were sent by an anonymous source the number of call-in votes the song received on September 1 and 2, 1987. According to the source, the Monkees' "Heart and Soul" was one of the ten most requested videos but MTV did not honor the requests. The newsletter invited fans to continue to request "Heart and Soul" and the band's second single, "Every Step of the Way," to MTV and local radio stations ("MTV vs. the Monkees?").

"That Was Then, This Is Now" peaked at #20 on the Billboard Hot 100, and "Heart and Soul" peaked at #87.

MTV stopped airing *The Monkees* in 1987, but the show began airing on MTVs sister station Nickelodeon during the channel's late-night block of classic programming known as "Nick at Nite." Since then, the show has lived on in reruns on cable and nostalgia-based stations and The Monkees have played as a band on and off since the 1986 reunion, with members leaving and rejoining at various points in time. The only constant member of *The Monkees* was Micky Dolenz.

In 1995, Dolenz, Jones and Tork appeared on the ABC show *Boy Meets World* (1993–2000). That same year, Dolenz, Jones and Tork appeared in a Pizza Hut commercial along with the Beatles' drummer Ringo Starr.

The last album on which all four Monkees recorded together was *Justus*, released in 1996 by Rhino Records. The Monkees waited 20 years to release another album, *Good Times!* (2016). *Good Times!* featured all four original members on vocals with the inclusion of a posthumous release of a recording by Davy Jones, who died in 2012. The group did the same with Jones on vocals on their 2018 album *Christmas Party*. *Good Times!* and *Christmas Party* were put out by Rhino Records. Nesmith and Dolenz continued to perform as the Monkees, even after the death of Peter Tork in 2019, until their 2021 farewell tour.

At a press conference for the Monkees' arrival in Great Britain on July 3, 1967, Dolenz was asked if the group was going to continue with their pop careers. He responded, "It's impossible to get out of the pop world when you're in it because you take it along with you and 40 years from now the people that I'm playing to now, I'll be playing to then. If I'm popular, they'll still be my fans and it'll be 'pop' to them." Little did Dolenz know that it would not be just 40 years—it would be seven decades of the Monkees. They proved that even though the band's formation was not organic, their music, TV series and movie had staying power and proved to be influential to future artists (British Movietone).

That Girl

In November 1965, ABC announced the production of 14 of their newest potential shows, including a show (originally titled *Miss Independence*), created by former *Dick*

Van Dyke Show writers Sam Denoff and Bill Persky. According to the industry magazine *Broadcasting*, "New York is the backdrop for Marlo Thomas, who plays a small-town girl coming to the city with ambitions as an actress" ("Bumper Crop" 28).

The project title was later changed to *That Girl*.

That Girl was the story of the quirky Ann Marie (played by Marlo Thomas, daughter of actor-producer Danny Thomas), who moves from suburban New York to New York City to make it on her own and try her hand at a career in acting, much to the chagrin of her parents Lew (Lew Parker) and Helen (Rosemary DeCamp). Although she occasionally gets a role, Ann Marie has to take various temp jobs to make ends meet. Also featured was Ann Marie's boyfriend, *Newsweek* writer Donald Hollinger (Ted Bessell) and his friend and co-worker Jerry Bauman (Bernie Kopell).

Critics gave mostly positive reviews:

> "If bounce, energy and abundance of lighthearted naivete can provide the spark of success, Marlo Thomas ... is on the right track."—Bill Irwin, *Chicago's American*

> "A tasteful blend of the usual elements of situation comedy."—Lawrence Laurent, *Washington Post*

> "A delight."—Ben Gross, *New York Daily News*

> "Consistently entertaining and risible."—Percy Shain, *Boston Globe* ("Critics' Views" 59)

Ann Marie, unlike other single women on TV at the time, was fine with simply dating Donald and was not desperate to marry him. Thomas later explained,

> I think the legacy of *That Girl* is the fact that, as Billy Persky always says, we threw the grenade into the bunker. We opened up the window for young women. You did not have to be the wife or the daughter of somebody or the secretary of somebody, but that you could be somebody. The story could be about you and what you wanted in life. Once that happened, I think that really paved the way for a lot of other shows ["Marlo Thomas"]

To help protect the show's reputation and the goodwill built up with viewers, Thomas did not want any merchandise: "I was very afraid of that. Batman was in the year before ... and there was a lot of things in stores with people's faces hanging from dresses and stuff. I thought, 'Oh God. I don't want to do this'" ("Marlo Thomas").

That Girl debuted on September 8, 1966, in the Thursday 9:30 slot and, like every other show during the 1966–1967 season, in color. But *That Girl*'s first broadcast in Alaska, 11 days later, was special for Alaskan television. Although the NTSC color TV system was approved by the Federal Communication Commission in 1953 and was widely available throughout the continental U.S. by the early 1960s, Alaska and Hawaii had to wait a little longer. Hawaii did not get color broadcasts until 1965 and Alaska on September 19, 1966, when it broadcast *That Girl*'s debut episode "Don't Just Do Something, Stand There!" in color ("About KTUU-TV").

In the fall of 1966, *That Girl* had time slot competition with NBC's new short-lived and low-rated *The Hero* and the very popular *CBS Thursday Night Movie* which that season featured the color movies *The Music Man* (1962), *Breakfast at Tiffany's* (1961), *Bye Bye Birdie* (1963), *Die! Die! My Darling!* (1965) and *Jason and the Argonauts* (1963). Although the *CBS Thursday Night Movie* dominated the evening time slots, *That Girl* managed respectable ratings and was featured on the cover of the November 12, 1966, *TV Guide*. ("Critics Views"; "The Latest"; "ARB's Top-20 Programs Sept. 25–Oct 1" 59; "ARB Top-20 Programs Oct. 2–8" 68; "Top-20 Arbitrons Oct. 9–15" 56 "Top-20 Arbitron's Oct. 16–22" 64; "Top-20 Arbitrons Oct. 23–29" 56 "Top-20 Arbitrons Oct. 30–Nov 5" 72; "The Arbitrons Nov 13–19" 84).

In January 1967, ABC swapped *That Girl* with fellow sitcom *Love on a Rooftop*, which had previously preceded *That Girl*, putting the show in competition with the first half-hour of the *CBS Thursday Night Movie* and *Star Trek* on NBC, with the seventh most-watched show that season in the 9:00 slot (Brooks and Marsh).

The move sunk *That Girl* in the ratings and it finished at the bottom of the time slot week after week and finished the season a dreadful 57th most-watched show. It was one of the lowest-rated shows renewed by the network ("Second Season" 60; "CBS Edges" 60; "More Ratings" 69; Spencer "TV's Vast" 54).

Despite the inability to score high ratings, ABC stuck with *That Girl* and brought the show back season after season. For the 1970–1971 season, *That Girl* was moved to Friday nights at 9:00, where it aired immediately after the very popular *Partridge Family*, the 25th highest-rated show that season. Despite the strong lead-in, *That Girl* was still unable to make a dent in the ratings (Brooks and Marsh).

After five seasons, ABC announced that *That Girl* would not be back for the 1971–1972 season after the Federal Communications Commission decreed that all three major networks needed to give three and a half more hours a week to local affiliates to "provide greater programming diversity." ABC also cancelled the game shows *Let's Make a Deal*, *The Newlywed Game* and *The Reel Game*; the musical variety series *The Lawrence Welk Show*, *The Pearl Bailey Show* and *The Johnny Cash Show*; the scripted programs *The Young Lawyers* and *Make Room for Granddaddy* (a series starring Marlo's father Danny Thomas), and *The ABC Monday Night Movie*. Meanwhile, *That Girl* reruns were sold into syndication, insuring that the show would remain on TV for the foreseeable future ("ABC-TV's Revamped" 9; MPC Syndicates 77).

Soon after the show's cancellation, a Gothic novel featuring Thomas' *That Girl* character was published. Written by Paul W. Fairman, it was very loosely based on Ann Marie, who was cast in a play based on the novel *Wuthering Heights*; but the play was not yet written and the show's fanatical playwright hypnotized and drugged the actors. The book's cover claimed, "She's a frightened young maiden pursued on a haunted moor by a wrathful wraith." Other than the Ann Marie character being an aspiring actress and a drawing of Thomas on the cover, any connections to the show were purely coincidental.

In 1973, animation studio Rankin-Bass Productions, creators of the Christmas specials *Rudolph the Red-Nosed Reindeer* (1964) and *Frosty the Snowman* (1969), released the ABC Superstar Movie *That Girl in Wonderland*. Unlike previous Rankin-Bass productions, it was cheaply animated but it brought back Marlo Thomas to voice Ann Marie. In this special, Ann Marie apparently gave up her dream to become an actress and took a job as an editor for a publishing company. As her first assignment, she was tasked with writing a Christmas book and came up with the idea of rewriting *Snow White*, *The Wizard of Oz*, *Cinderella* and *Sleeping Beauty* with a Christmas twist on each of them. *That Girl in Wonderland* became a popular Saturday morning children's special, airing regularly over the next several years.

Gilligan's Island

Gilligan's Island was the story of five seafaring tourists and two crew members of the boat *S.S. Minnow*, who took a three-hour Pacific Ocean tour but instead found themselves caught in a storm and then marooned on an uncharted desert island: Gilligan (Bob Denver), "The Skipper" Jonas Grumby (Alan Hale, Jr.), millionaire couple Thurston Howell III (Jim Backus) and Lovey (Natalie Schafer), Professor Roy Hinkley (Russell Johnson), Hollywood movie star Ginger Grant (Tina Louise) and farm girl Mary Ann (Dawn Wells).

The Skipper and his first mate Gilligan had experience on the high seas and the Professor had scientific ingenuity, but the castaways could never find a way off the island, more often than not due to Gilligan's reckless antics. So the castaways make themselves at home on the island but often cope with unwanted visitors: gangsters, wayward pilots, witch doctors, mad scientists, radio contestants and a hunter looking to hunt human beings. All of them failed to disclose the castaways' location after they returned to civilization.

Along with being one of *the* most iconic TV shows, *Gilligan's Island* has one of the most iconic theme songs in TV history, "The Ballad of Gilligan's Isle." However, the unaired 1964 pilot featured different lyrics with a calypso-style melody. Producer Sherwood Schwartz did not feel the song was right because the show was set on a Pacific island, not in the Caribbean. So Schwartz enlisted his friend, songwriter George Wyle, to help with the theme song. Schwartz stated, "We had a couple of meetings, and we arrived at the song you now know ... which has a sea shanty rhythm" ("Sherwood Schwartz").

Gilligan's Island's spent its first year on the airwaves, 1964–1965, at 8:30 on Saturdays. The show quickly rose to become one of the season's top shows, even regularly beating out the long-running *Lawrence Welk Show* ("CBS Takes Lead" 52; "Stability and Shifts" 42; "ABC Riding High" 10; Brooks and Marsh).

Gilligan's Island was the 18th highest-rated show in its debut season, tying with the sitcom *The Munsters*.

Some viewers may have taken the comedy a little too seriously. Schwartz claimed that the Coast Guard was being sent telegrams asking them to help rescue the castaways; he said that a typical message was: "For a couple of months now we've seen several Americans on an island and they are going to die. Why can't we spare one vessel to save these people?" Schwartz wondered if those people considered where the laugh track and commercials were coming from ("Sherwood Schwartz").

Gilligan's Island's popularity chagrinned TV critics who almost universally panned it. Hal Humphrey of *The Los Angeles Times* called it the worst sitcom of the year, "the kind of thing one might expect to find running for three nights at some neighborhood group playhouse" (Humphrey "The Low Men" 69).

The very next season, *Gilligan's Island* began broadcasting in color along with several other formerly black-and-white CBS shows. There was also a change to the theme song and time slot.

In the first season, "The Ballad of Gilligan's Isle" named Gilligan, the Skipper, the Howells and Ginger but failed to mention the Professor and Mary Ann; the song simply referred to them as "the rest." Russell Johnson later said, "How you could do a show about seven people on an island and throw two of them out?" The two characters were added to the theme song in the second season (Herman "Russell Johnson").

With an updated theme song and color, CBS moved the show to Thursdays at 8:00 opposite the pioneer Western *Daniel Boone* on NBC and the soon-to-be-cancelled *Donna Reed Show* on ABC. *Gilligan's Island* was the 22nd highest-rated show of the season (Brooks and Marsh).

In the 1966–1967 season, *Gilligan's Island* got another time slot change, moving to Mondays at 7:30. It was the lead-in for *Run, Buddy, Run* in the fall of 1966 and the superhero spoof *Mr. Terrific* in the winter of 1967.

After three time slot changes in three years, *Gilligan's Island*'s ratings fell off. It ended the season 49th. When the show wrapped at the end of the season on April 17, 1967, the actors were reportedly assured that it would be picked up for a fourth season; in the last episode of the third season, "Gilligan, the Goddess," the castaways had yet to be rescued. *Gilligan's Island was* placed on the 1967–1968 CBS schedule, but that schedule did not include the long-running Western *Gunsmoke* (Gent "Marshal Dillon Gunned"). One month later, *Gunsmoke* was put back on the schedule and CBS cancelled the new half-hour sitcom *Doc* before the show aired and cancelled *Gilligan's Island* before viewers could see the castaways get rescued.

After *Gilligan's Island*'s cancellation, its 92 episodes (62 in color) never left the airwaves. It went into syndication in April 1967 ("UA Syndicates" 50) and stayed on the air for years to come due to increased demand for color programming. Due to its popularity in reruns, a TV movie reunion was produced by Sherwood Schwartz: Set 15 years after the show went off the air, *Rescue from Gilligan's Island* (1978) found the Professor finally figuring out how to get off the island after retrieving a barometer from a crashed Soviet satellite. The castaways made it back to civilization but found it difficult to get accustomed to life in 1978. In the sequel *The Castaways on Gilligan's Island* (1979), the Howells and the others started a hotel and island resort on Gilligan's Island. In both made-for-TV movies, the original cast reunited with the exception of Tina Louise, who declined to return. In both movies, the role of Ginger was played by Judith Baldwin. The last official reunion of the *Gilligan's Island* characters was *The Harlem Globetrotters on Gilligan's Island* (1981), in which the island resort is under attack by evil robots but saved by basketball's Harlem Globetrotters. This time, Ginger was played by Constance Forslund. *Harlem Globetrotters* also featured *Mission: Impossible* stars Barbara Bain and Martin Landau (1966–1973). Denver, Hale, Wells and Johnson reprised their *Gilligan's Island* roles in a 1987 episode of *ALF* (1986–1990).

Two *Gilligan's Island* cartoons were also produced. *The New Adventures of Gillian* (1977) followed the same story arc as the original series. In *Gilligan's Planet* (1982), the Professor attempts to get the castaways off the island by building a spaceship—but the castaways soon find themselves marooned in space. Both cartoon adaptations featured the voices of the original cast members with the exception of Dawn Wells in *New Adventures* and Tina Louise in both.

In 1986, the Ted Turner–owned Turner Entertainment Company purchased United Artists for $1.5 billion. This included the syndication rights to *Gilligan's Island* and it began to air on Turner channels such as TNT and TBS ("TFE '67" 68; Delugach and Crook).

Turner announced they would be colorizing many of their film properties, much to the dismay of many filmmakers and traditionalists. For example, although unsubstantiated, it was reported by colleague of Orson Wells, Henry Jaglom, that Wells' dying request was "I want you to make sure you stop Ted Turner from coloring my movie with his crayons" in 1985 in reference to Turner's plan to colorize Citizen Kane (Masters "Turner Won't"). Ted Turner, asked about the controversy in a *Los Angeles Times* article, stated "The last time I checked, I owned the films that we're in the process of colorizing. … I can do whatever I want with them, and if they're going to be shown on television, they're going to be in color. … All I'm trying to do is protect my investment in MGM." said Turner. The article also pointed out that advertising rates for black-and-white movies were lower than the rates for color movies (Voland "Turner Defends"). Turner did not stop at films: The 30 black-and-white *Gilligan's Island* episodes also underwent the process. At the time, digital colorization was yet to be perfected, so the colorized episodes had a much different look and feel to them than the episodes that were filmed in color.

TBS aired the *Gilligan's Island* pilot for the first time on October 16, 1992, in its original black-and-white format. Both the black-and-white and color versions of *Gilligan's Island* have been staples of cable and nostalgia television stations since leaving the airwaves.

The Tammy Grimes Show

In the mid–1960s, Tammy Grimes, star of the 1961 Tony Award–winning Broadway musical comedy *The Unsinkable Molly Brown,* began to move from the stage to the world of film and TV. As early as 1960, she was guesting on TV shows such as *Route 66, The Virginian* and *Burke's Law.*

Grimes made an error in her career in 1963 when she turned down the role of suburban housewife and witch Samantha Stephens on *Bewitched.* The series was an instant success and made its star Elizabeth Montgomery a household name (Javna 60).

Grimes was also not cast in the title role of the big screen adaptation of *The Unsinkable Molly Brown* (1964): It went to Debbie Reynolds. The leading male character, Johnny Brown, was played by the Broadway play's star Harve Presnell.

The New York Times reported on March 12, 1965, that Grimes was attacked on the street by "four white youths in black leather jackets" while walking in New York City. It was believed that the attackers were related to her association with African-American entertainers, most notably Sammy Davis, Jr. ("Tammy Grimes Hurt").

Grimes was still looking to break through as a star, and in March 1966 it was announced that she had signed with MGM to make her movie debut, alongside *Man from U.N.C.L.E.* star David McCallum, in the movie *Three Bites of the Apple* ("Metro Signs"). The film was released in 1967.

Grimes also signed with 20th Century–Fox to do *The Tammy Grimes Show*. The TV series was produced for Fox by William Dozier's Greenway Productions, the same company that produced *Batman* and *The Green Hornet* that season. *The Tammy Grimes Show* was Dozier's third show on the TV schedule in the fall of 1966. ABC announced on July 11, 1966, that *The Tammy Grimes Show* would air Thursdays at 8:30 ("What the Networks" 58).

George Axelrod, writer of *The Seven Year Itch* (1955) and *Will Success Spoil Rock Hunter?* (1957), came up with the idea for a show that revolved around "madcap heiress" Tammy Ward (Grimes), who inherits a bank yet cannot touch her fortune ("Post-Mortem" 15). The *TV Guide* 1966–1967 Fall Preview described the series this way:

Chapter Ten. Situation Comedies

Photo of Tammy Grimes from the press kit of her Tony Award winning musical *The Unsinkable Molly Brown* (Shubilla family archives).

"Tammy's persistent attempts to get her hands on an inheritance so she can do all the uninhibited things madcap heiresses want to do—wear bizarre clothes, keep a roomful of tropical birds, frug the night away, buy a baseball player with a credit card, fly away to a ski lodge at the drop of a yodel." It went on to state that in the show, Tammy and her money were under the watchful eye of her "skinflint Uncle Simon" ("1966–67 Fall Preview"). The show also starred Dick Sargent as Tammy's uptight, square twin brother Terence.

With its first episode, *The Tammy Grimes Show* did okay in the ratings, earning a Trendex rating of 14.7, beating out a CBS rerun of *My Three Sons* but losing out the premiere of NBC's *Star Trek* ("Critics' Views" 59).

Critical reviews were horrendous and far from what Grimes was used to:

> "May not be the most inane and the most insipid half-hour in television, but offhand we can't think of one that would better qualify."—Bill Irvin, *Chicago American*
>
> "Talented comedienne is absolutely wasted."—Don Page, *Los Angeles Times*
>
> "Unhappy Ordeal."—Jack Gould, *The New York Times*
>
> "The worst yet."—Ann Hodges, *Houston Chronicle* ("Critics' Views" 58)

By the second episode, the series was at the bottom of the ratings barrel along with ABC's *Hawk*; both averaged a 10.7 rating. That week, *Tammy Grimes* lost out to the *My Three Sons* season premiere and the second episode of *Star Trek* ("The Latest Form Sheet" 69). *Tammy Grimes'* ratings continued to sink. On September 28, 1966, less than a month after its premiere and after only four episodes on the air, *The New York Times* reported that the show was being cancelled and replaced with a color prime time version of *The Dating Game*. The reason given: The show received "unfavorable critical reaction and poor ratings" ("A.B.C.-TV Ax Falls"). The next day, Associated Press Television-Radio writer Cynthia Lowry stated that it was "an extremely short run for a prime-time network show"; series are typically allowed to stay on the air for at least 13 weeks (Lowry 16).

TV Guide estimated that 20th Century–Fox lost approximately a million dollars on *The Tammy Grimes Show* and many people connected with the show did not have kind words for its star ("Post-Mortem" 16).

In early 1967, Dozier recalled his experience with the show and talked about what went wrong. He called it an "organized disaster," admitting, "It was the wrong idea for her. ... I'm from the Midwest and out there we'd call her a ritzy dame." Dozier also felt that audiences just could not relate to Grimes. "She played an heiress about to inherit a bank, and with that peculiar accent [Grimes had a mid–Atlantic prep school accent], she alienated an awful lot of viewers. ... It was the wrong idea for the wrong person at the wrong time" (Leonard 82).

Dozier seemed to have a problem with demographics in all three of his 1966 TV series: *Batman* because, as Dozier put it, "it wasn't delivering a big enough audience of the right kind, it wasn't delivering enough adults who buy things"; *The Green Hornet,* attempting to appeal to a young adult audience, was on the wrong night and at the wrong time, and *Tammy Grimes*' story was not appealing to the average American (Eisner 11).

The Tammy Grimes Show co-producer Alex Gottlieb felt that Grimes herself was to blame. "There was no rapport between Tammy and the audience. ... She has a brittle quality which doesn't work on TV. You've got to be warm on that cold tube." Gottlieb also believed that if Grimes were "one-tenth as warm and likable on film as Dick Sargent was, the show would have been a hit" ("Post-Mortem" 19).

Cynthia Lowry wrote, "Miss Grimes, a fine stage comedienne, has a distinctive style but it does not seem to adapt itself very well to television" (Lowry "Jericho Looks" 9).

Dick Sargent went on to replace Dick York as Darrin Stephens on *Bewitched* in 1969 and Grimes continued to appear on TV and in films throughout her life. She also continued her successful Broadway career. But she never made the leap to stardom as she had once hoped.

Bewitched

Throughout late 1963 and early 1964, details began surfacing about Screen Gems' newest pilot, *Bewitched.* It was created by TV writer Sol Saks and loosely based on the 1942 film *I Married a Witch*, the 1941 Thorne Smith novel *The Passionate Witch*, and the play *Bell, Book and Candle* ("Her 'Witch Twitch'" 42).

The role of the show's good-natured newlywed witch, Samantha Stephens, was originally offered to Broadway actress Tammy Grimes, who turned it down (see the chapter on *The Tammy Grimes Show*). Elizabeth Montgomery was subsequently cast as "Sam" (Javna 60).

Montgomery was not new to television. She first appeared on her father Robert Montgomery's Emmy-winning anthology series *Robert Montgomery Presents,* at the age of 18 in 1951. She then appeared in numerous films, Broadway plays and TV dramas.

Several actors auditioned for the role of Samantha's mortal husband, advertising agent Darrin Stephens before Dick York was cast. Week after week, Darrin attempted to get her to stop using her powers and become a typical suburban housewife—usually until using her powers was beneficial to him.

Agnes Moorehead, who did the *Bewitched* pilot in between stops on her one-woman show "The Fabulous Redhead," was cast as Samantha's domineering mother Endora, who does not want Samantha to give up on witchcraft, especially for Darrin. In fact, Endora encourages her to use her powers more and would prefer she leave her mortal husband (Hopper "Levant" 28).

Screen Gems brought on Harry Ackerman, who previously produced *Bachelor Father* (1957–1962), *Leave It to Beaver* (1957–1963) and *Dennis the Menace* (1959–1963), as *Bewitched*'s executive producer. The show was then picked up by ABC and was given the coveted Thursday 9:00 slot (Fanning "Nets' Fall Line-Up" 39).

The Newspaper Enterprise Association's Hollywood writer Erskine Johnson described *Bewitched* as a "supernatural domestic comedy" with Montgomery starring as "a new bride who can transform herself into a witch" (Johnson "Runaway" 4).

Samantha could cast spells and transform her surroundings with a twitch of her nose—a move known as "The Witch Twitch." According to *Bewitched* producer-director William Asher, "The viewers wait for that twitch. But we save it until Samantha is so sorely tempted to use her witchery that the audience is usually saying, 'Do something!'" ("Her 'Witch Twitch'" 42).

Bewitched premiered on September 17, 1964, and shot up to the top of the ratings early in the season, getting almost twice as many weekly viewers as the game show *Password* on CBS and the medical drama *Dr. Kildare* on NBC ("CBS Still" 9). It was the second highest-rated show of the 1964–1965 season, second only to *Bonanza* (Brooks and Marsh). Throughout the season, Darrin and Samantha navigated their way through typical domestic newlywed situations, with the added twist of Samantha's witchcraft—which she inevitably used every episode to get out a jam or to improve the couple's situation, much to Darrin's chagrin. Samantha also felt pressure from her mother Endora, who complicated situations by introducing witchcraft (often to spite Darrin). Both Darrin and Samantha also worked to keep the truth about Samantha's powers from Darrin's boss Larry Tate (David White), the couple's nosey neighbor Gladys Kravitz (Sandra Gould) and Darrin's parents Phyllis (Mabel Albertson) and Frank (a role alternated between Robert F. Simon and Roy Roberts).

At the beginning of the second season, it was announced that Samantha and Darrin were having a child. On January 13, 1966, in the episode "And Then There Were Three…" Tabitha (Erin Murphy) was born. To complicate matters, the episode also introduced Samantha's identical cousin Serena, also played by Montgomery, a free-spirited brunette. In the episode, Darrin, who was previously unaware of Serena, assumed that Serena was actually Tabitha, transformed into an adult by Endora. *Bewitched* was the seventh highest-rated show of the 1965–1966 season, tied with CBS's *The Beverly Hillbillies,* and the highest-rated black-and-white program that season.

Bewitched writers managed to keep storylines fresh, adding characters like Sam's mischievous Uncle Arthur (Paul Lynde), Dr. Bombay (Bernard Fox) and bumbling Aunt Clara (Marion Lorne). The show also added yearly Halloween and Christmas episodes, and continued to find new situations for the cast. The show had a crossover episode with ABC's prime time cartoon comedy *The Flintstones*: "Bewitched" (October 22, 1965) guest-starred Samantha and Darrin (voiced by Montgomery and York) as the

Flintstones' new neighbors. *Bewitched*'s intro featured animation from Hanna-Barbera, the same company that produced *The Flintstones* (1960–1966).

Before the 1966–1967 season, *Bewitched* producers announced that the show would make the jump from black and white to color. Head cameraman Robert Tobey said he had to be "especially watchful" to make sure items in the background like sheeting, towels, tablecloths and napkins were matching colors—something he did not have to worry about when the show was shot in black and white ("Color Premiere" 48). Perhaps no one benefited more from the transition to color than Sam's cousin Serena, who now wore colorful psychedelic outfits, giving her a sharp contrast to the more conservatively dressed Samantha. *Bewitched* was also given a new color animated introduction.

Bewitched now aired opposite the first half-hour of the *CBS Thursday Night Movie* and the last half-hour of NBC's *Star Trek*. It once again took over in the ratings battle every week. In the winter of 1967, *Bewitched* was moved to the 8:30 slot, replacing the unpopular prime time edition of *The Dating Game*. The sitcom *Love on a Rooftop* was put in *Bewitched*'s 9:00 slot in hopes of jumpstarting its lagging ratings. *Love on a Rooftop* lasted only one season.

Bewitched, now competing with the long-running *My Three Sons* and the first half hour of *Star Trek*, continued to be a ratings winner and was again the season's seventh highest-rated show, tying with the CBS shows *Daktari* and *The Beverly Hillbillies* with a 23.4 average Nielsen rating (Brooks and Marsh).

That season, Tabitha discovered her witchcraft powers (and Samantha attempted to hide this from Endora and Darrin), Serena tried computer dating, Samantha had her powers taken away by the Witches' Council, Endora used her powers to calm Darrin's nerves, and a wood nymph carried out a curse put on the Stephens family for crimes the family committed four centuries ago. The show even explained the Northeast Blackout of 1965: According to the episode "The Short Happy Circuit of Aunt Clara," it was caused by Aunt Clara, whose witchcraft was not as reliable as it used to be, when she was tried to use her powers to move a grand piano (Lowry "*Bewitched* Explains" 17).

The show rode high in the ratings all the way through to 1969 and was the 11th highest-rated show in both the 1967–1968 and 1968–1969 seasons. Audiences may have noticed that Dick York was featured less prominently in the latter season. His absence was due to problems stemming from an old back injury. They led to an overdependence on painkillers and ultimately caused him to leave in 1969 ("Dick York" 10).

Starting in the next season, Darrin was played by Dick Sargent, who was considered for the role of Darrin several years earlier, when *Bewitched* was initially being cast. Sargent had previously appeared in the second season episode "Divided He Falls" as a different character. His movie credits included *Operation Petticoat* (1959), *The Great Imposter* (1960), *That Touch of Mink* (1962), *The Ghost and Mr. Chicken* (1966) and *Love a Little, Live a Little* (1968). Rumors began swirling that Sargent would take over the Darrin role, due to York's back injury, as early as 1965. So the casting was obvious (Page "Dick Sargent Joins" 309; "TV Mailbag" 33).

Bewitched did not provide any on-screen explanation as to why Darrin looked different. Don Page of *The Los Angeles Times* told readers his theory: "The transition will be simple ... since Miss Montgomery is a witch in the series, she has the magic to change her husband's face, right? It's an advantage a lot of housewives would relish" (Page "Dick Sargent Joins" 309).

Sargent credited producer William Asher with making the casting work. "His casting is brilliant," said Sargent. "This sounds egotistical, but I'm not speaking of myself. Asher knows when the show is starting to lag and he'll interject something to pep it up." Sargent also believed that most people would not mind the change. "You can't really change Darrin; His reactions will be about the same. I don't think I'll bother anyone who enjoyed the show before. However, as a human being, I suppose some of myself will change him a little" (Page "Dick Sargent Joins" 309).

Sargent was first seen as Darrin in "Samantha and the Beanstalk" (September 18, 1969), the new season's premiere episode.

The show also added a clumsy witch maid to the Stephens household, Esmeralda (Alice Ghostley). Esmeralda ostensibly replaced Aunt Clara (Marion Lorne died in May 1968).

The Stephenses welcomed a second child, Adam (twins David and Greg Lawrence), in the October 16, 1969, episode "And Then There Were Four..." Adam was originally thought to be mortal like his father Darrin, but the family later discovered that the powers were deep within him and that he was indeed a warlock, Esmeralda brought Julius Caesar to 1969, Uncle Arthur changed Tabatha's pet bunny into a Playboy Bunny, famed songwriters Boyce and Hart made an appearance, and Santa Claus was brought to the Stephens house for the Christmas episode.

That season, ratings took a tumble: *Bewitched* fell to the 24th highest-rated show of the season. Perhaps audiences were not bewitched by the new Darrin. The show had robust competition from the 12th highest-rated show, the CBS variety series *The Jim Nabors Hour*, and the 15th highest-rated show, the NBC crime drama *Ironside* (Brooks and Marsh).

The next season, 1970–1971, ratings plunged even further, despite the fact that some of the show's most interesting episodes were shot on the location of the 1692 Salem Witch Trials Salem, Massachusetts. Once again *Bewitched* lost out to *Jim Nabors* and *Ironside*. In the fall of 1971, ABC moved *Bewitched* to Wednesdays at 8:00. The shows' producers attempted to vary storylines by taking the characters to Europe, but it consistently lost out to CBS's *The Carol Burnett Show*, the season's 23rd highest-rated show (Brooks and Marsh). The Associated Press' Cynthia Lowry wrote in October 1971, "[*Bewitched*] is beginning to look threadbare after eight years. It is the same old combination of magic tricks and wrangling between the witches and the mortal husband" (Lowry "ABC's Wednesday" 4).

Although the show had been getting low ratings for the past three seasons, Harry Ackerman and William Asher were reported to have been in talks with ABC about doing seasons 9 through 12 (Mark "Witch World" 13). When ratings failed to improve in the fall of 1971, ABC moved the show to Saturdays at 8:00, where *Bewitched* again lost to a CBS show: the top-rated show of the season, *All in the Family* (Brooks and Marsh).

In April 1972, ABC announced that *Bewitched* would not be returning for a ninth season and went into syndication immediately after cancellation. Both Ackerman and Asher were still under contract to ABC for another year so they agreed to make two new half-hour sitcoms for the network, *Temperatures Rising* and *The Paul Lynde Show* ("The Other Two" 27).

Due to continued popularity in reruns, Samantha and Darrin's children, Tabitha and Adam, were the subject of two TV projects. The first premiered on Saturday, December 2, 1972: the Hanna-Barbera *The ABC Saturday Superstar Movie* "Tabitha and Adam and the Clown Family." In this cartoon, Tabitha and Adam spend the summer with their

Aunt Georgia and her children, who are members of a traveling rock band-circus act, the Clown Family. In 1977, ABC again attempted to recreate the success of *Bewitched* with the show *Tabitha,* starring Lisa Hartman as the now teenage witch Tabitha Stephens and David Ankrum as her now inexplicably *older* brother Adam. Like Darrin, Adam attempted to get Tabitha not to use her magic. Bernard Fox reprised his role as Dr. Bombay. The show suffered from low ratings in its Saturday 8:00 time slot and was cancelled in early 1978. It lasted 11 episodes.

In 2005, the film *Bewitched* starred Nicole Kidman and Will Farrell as actors cast in a reboot of the *Bewitched* TV series—but with the twist of Kidman's character being a *real* witch. That same year, a statue of Elizabeth Montgomery as Samantha Stephens, wearing a pointed witch hat and sitting on a broom, was erected in Salem, Massachusetts.

I Dream of Jeannie

NBC's *I Dream of Jeannie* was one of only four shows to debut in black and white in the 1965–1966 season, the others being *F Troop, Lost in Space* and *Convoy.* The show's star Barbara Eden revealed the reason: "[T]he executives behind *I Dream of Jeannie* did not want to spend the extra $400 per episode. ... [Sidney Sheldon, the show's creator] was so outraged that he offered to invest his own money in having the show shot in color, but the executives still refused to budge" (Eden and Leigh).

Seen by many as NBC's answer to *Bewitched, I Dream of Jeannie* debuted on September 18, 1965. Returning from a space flight, astronaut Tony Nelson (Larry Hagman) splashes down outside his target area and is stranded on a deserted desert island. There he finds a bottle in which a genie named Jeannie (Eden) has been trapped for 2000 years. Jeannie falls in love with Tony and sneaks into his bag before he's rescued. Jeannie spends the first season breaking up Tony and his fiancée. Tony keeps Jeannie a secret from his NASA co-workers such as Roger Healey (Bill Daily) and Colonel Alfred Bellows (Hayden Rorke). Jeannie can grant Tony's wishes with a blink of her eyes but, like Darrin on *Bewitched,* Tony discourages this.

Jeannie's provocative genie costume did not expose her navel. It has been long reported that in 1965, there was media coverage and viewer outrage over the prospect of Jeannie showing her belly button on TV. Eden later called this situation "the silliest thing in the whole world," adding, "It wasn't an issue until the media hyped it" (Howard "Barbara Eden"). But Eden and news outlets may have been repeating television lore. There are very few articles written before 1968 which even mention Eden's belly button; the first reports of "outrage" in the 1960s appeared in the 1980s, when the show started to air on cable television. However, there are test photos of Eden, taken before the show aired, in a Jeannie outfit that exposed her navel. Marilyn Beck, writer of the syndicated newspaper column "Close-Up TV Time," asked readers in 1968, "Have you ever noticed Barbara Eden has no navel? At least it's disguised so that she looks belly buttonless on *I Dream of Jeannie.* Love to know why the producers ever decided on that sort of deceit" (Beck "Close-Up TV Time" 9). Clearly there was an attempt by the network and producers to mitigate the belly button issue and they used an alternative outfit that covered her navel.

Media outcry may not have been the real reason that Eden covered up her belly button. The National Association of Radio and Television Broadcasters Television Code of 1952 was a self-imposed code by TV stations to "maintain a level of television programming which gives full consideration to the educational, informational, cultural, economic, moral and entertainment needs of the American public to the end that more and more people will be better served" ("The Television Code" 8). Among many other restrictions (profanity, obscenity, sex, violence, drug use), the Code called for all performers' costuming to be "within the bounds of propriety, and shall avoid such exposure or such emphasis on anatomical detail as would embarrass or offend home viewers." Shows that followed the Code would display a "Seal of Good Practice" during the closing credits ("The Television Code" 3, 8).

The year the Television Code was introduced, *The Quarterly of Film Radio and Television* called the Code "a completely un–American type of censorship over the public-owned television channels," and said that the code had a "neo–Victorian sense of morality" (Orme 404–13). By the mid–1960s, the standards in the Code were liberalized and what most Americans viewed as embarrassing or offensive changed.

Even when *I Dream of Jeannie* jumped to color and Eden donned colorful new outfits, Jeannie still did not expose her navel. Yet in the third season, in the December 19, 1967, episode "Jeannie Goes to Honolulu," several bikini-clad women displayed their belly buttons; and previous to this, women's navels were exposed on shows such as *Star Trek, Batman, The Monkees, The Man from U.N.C.L.E.* and *The Girl from U.N.C.L.E.*

It is theorized by some *I Dream of Jeannie* fans that because Jeannie was a genie, who was not born but rather created, she would not have a belly button.

Eden stated in several interviews that she was approached by George Schlatter to expose her belly button on *Rowan & Martin's Laugh-In* but NBC rejected the idea (Howard "Barbara Eden").

Making a 1981 appearance on *The Tonight Show Starring Johnny Carson* to promote her show *Harper Valley P.T.A.*, Eden stated that producers are very careful and would constantly remind her about "anatomical detail" (Eden "Episode 78"). By that time, female belly buttons had become commonplace on broadcast TV and were no longer viewed as a Code violation.

The National Association of Radio and Television Broadcasters Television Code of 1952 was in effect until 1983. It was abandoned due to TV deregulation and several First Amendment violation claims. Since then, over-the-air broadcast channels adopted a practice of self-regulation and developed a system of standards and practices for network programming. Several programs continued to display the Seal of Good Practice until the mid–1980s.

Sheldon also realized that on top of a provocative outfit, the show could easily have provocative storylines:

> The network had given me a completely free hand. In 30 years of show business, I don't think I've ever been so free of restriction and it's a wonderful feeling. ... You realize that the basic premise of *Jeannie* could be provocative if we allowed it to be. After all, we have a situation where an attractive bachelor is living in a house with a scantily clad girl. Even if she is a genie who pops in and out of a bottle, it could be a touchy situation.

Jeannie and Tony living together, outside of wedlock, would also be in violation of the Television Code which called for respect for the sanctity of marriage and the value of the home, and warned: "Illicit sex relations are not treated as commendable."

Sheldon claimed that the show never received one letter of complaint from viewers ("Writer-Producer on Job" 10; "The Television Code" 2).

Mort Werner, NBC's vice-president of programming, announced in March 1966 that *I Dream of Jeannie* would be now shot and broadcast in color ("Color Added" 9). The September 24, 1966, *TV Guide* reported that the show was making the most out of broadcasting in color thanks to special effects man Richard Albain and his team. Tasked with creating colorful smoke during time lapses and scene dissolves, they reportedly "spent weeks inventing a process to create a cloudy effect which would seemingly waft the beautiful Barbara across TV screens. … After many experiments, the special effects men settled on a system of colored lights, dry ice and steam to produce the desired cloud formations" ("Watch Jeannie's Smoke" 7). Sheldon stated, "It's just great. We're going to have Jeannie disappearing in different-colored puffs of smoke, depending on her mood: green for jealousy, blue for sad, and so forth" ("He Taps Universal" 26).

The switch to color and smoke did not come without problems. Eden said, "After two hours around those lights it got pretty hot. Not only that but my expensive silk-chiffon pants shrank" ("Watch Jeannie's Smoke" 8).

Along with the color smoke and new purple bottle, which was actually a 1964 December 25 bottle of Beam's Choice, the show now also featured a new color introduction and closing credits, orange NASA outfits and plenty of colorful and unique genie outfits.

In the 1966–1967 season, *I Dream of Jeannie* was moved to Mondays at 8:00, right after *The Monkees*. It did not have much competition, scheduled against the second half of the ABC Western *Iron Horse* and the short-lived CBS sitcom *Run, Buddy, Run* in the fall and then the superhero spoof. With the exception of the first several *Mr. Terrific* episodes, none of those shows had particularly high ratings (Brooks and Marsh).

In the second season, Jeannie and Tony finally recognized their love for one another and got engaged. The two waited to get married until the show's last season in 1969, so of course Jeannie remained in her bottle at night until they finally wed. Throughout the season, Jeannie and Tony did battle with the evil genie who imprisoned Jeannie in her bottle 2000 years ago, went back to the Old West, cloned Sammy Davis, Jr., and met Napoleon Bonaparte. Tony even found himself in trouble with the IRS.

Along with color, *I Dream of Jeannie* now featured an iconic theme song by Hugo Montenegro.

I Dream of Jeannie was never a ratings hit in its time, but it was a hit in reruns and even found a new audience: children. A 1975 report by the Congressional House Committee on Interstate and Foreign Commerce indicated that more than 50 percent of the members of *I Dream of Jeannie*'s audience were children under 12, with more than six million children viewers throughout the country ("Broadcast Advertising" 99). The show became a staple of daytime TV and connected with a generation that may not even have been alive during its initial run. In *Ferris Bueller's Day Off* (1986), Bueller (Matthew Broderick) faked an illness, skipped school and spent part of his morning dancing to the *I Dream of Jeannie* theme on television.

To capitalize on *Jeannie*'s success in reruns, NBC produced two reunion movies, *I Dream of Jeannie … Fifteen Years Later* (1985) and *I Still Dream of Jeannie* (1991). Eden reprised Jeannie role in both movies but Larry Hagman was unable to participate due to his commitment to his role on the long-running *Dallas* (1978–1991). In both movies, it was explained that Tony Nelson was away on a top-secret NASA mission.

The Jean Arthur Show

Debuting on September 12, 1966, the CBS sitcom *The Jean Arthur Show* marked the return of actress Jean Arthur after 13 years of retirement from show business. Arthur was best known for her roles in a trio of Frank Capra films, *Mr. Deeds Goes to Town* (1936), *You Can't Take It with You* (1938) and *Mr. Smith Goes to Washington* (1939), and for being Oscar-nominated for *The More the Merrier* (1943). Arthur reportedly retired due to stage fright, and in subsequent years became more reclusive. But she was convinced to come out of retirement by Lucille Ball, whose *Lucy Show* was also on CBS at the time. Ball conscripted the help of "spellbinding verbal hypnotist" Jay Richard Kennedy to help convince Arthur to return to show biz. Kennedy stated, "I think [Arthur] was right to stay away from acting during our period of negativism and nothingness. … But now the time is ripe for a change. It's the bright side of the moon again, I believe Miss Arthur feels it in her bones" ("TV Lures" 18).

Arthur agreed to take on the role of successful yet zany lawyer Patricia Marshall, who accepts her son Paul (Ron Harper), a recent law school graduate, into her law practice. Other characters included Patricia's chauffeur Morton (Leonard Stone) and her on-again-off-again boyfriend Richie Wells (Richard Conte), a gangster. *The Jean Arthur Show* also featured a weekly guest star; they included Mickey Rooney, Wally Cox and Raymond Burr (Penton "Jean Arthur Returns" 61).

Before it hit the airwaves, ads ran in newspapers with the tagline: "A female legal eagle joins forces with her son to give a fresh twist to the barrister business. In color." Most newspaper critics objected to the legal comedy:

> "Promises very little in the way of sound comedy."—Joseph T. Sullivan, *Boston Herald*

> "What this series needs is a good defense."—Kay Gardella, *New York Daily News*

> "Put the blame on one of the most frightful, triteful scripts."—Dwight Newton, *San Francisco Examiner*

Two critics viewed the show less harshly:

> "A class production in scenery, costumes and talent."—Aleene MacMinn, *Los Angeles Times*

> "A triumph."—Jack E. Anderson, *Miami Herald* ("Critics' Views" 64)

The half-hour *The Jean Arthur Show* ran opposite ABC's Western *The Big Valley* and NBC's man-on-the-run drama *Run for Your Life* on Mondays at 10:00. It soon found itself with lower ratings than both competitors ("TV's Vast 67"). By early October 1966, less than a month into the show's run, CBS was growing weary of *The Jean Arthur Show*'s low ratings and marked it for "replacement or reshuffling." They cancelled the show two weeks later ("NBC Claims" 10; "The Ratings" 68).

TV critic Cynthia Lowry called *The Jean Arthur Show* a "major disappointment of the new season" and the Associated Press' Bob Thomas reported that it wound up 65th among 90 shows in the Nielsen ratings (Lowry "Nabors Puts" 11; Thomas "Jean Arthur" 11).

Ron Harper described the show as a "disaster area from the onset" and that the show "spent $100,000 on scripts [in which] we spent a half-hour defending an iguana or a chicken. It was a children's animal show. ... [Arthur] had some bad advisers. She was terribly conscious of her former reputation of being unpredictable. I was unaware of it. She never opened her mouth. Consequently, at crisis points, no one assumed responsibility for the show." Harper also criticized the show for focusing on guest stars rather than the development of the regular characters (Gysel "*Garrison's Gorillas*" 21).

Arthur said of the series' cancellation, "I'm relieved that I don't have to read any more of those awful scripts." She also said that she believed that the producers did not listen to her script input. "I tried to make myself heard. But I guess the machine is so big that they can't be bothered with the human element" (Peterson "Jean Arthur" 10).

The Jean Arthur Show's last episode aired on December 5, 1966, after only 12 episodes, and the next week it was replaced by the color prime time edition of the game show *To Tell the Truth*.

Although the show failed, Arthur began looking for a new project, stating, "If someone offered me a feature, I'd go to work tomorrow. I'd like to do another series. But if it happens, I would make sure I had authority" (Peterson "Jean Arthur" 10).

Arthur never got the call to do another feature film *or* series and the notoriously reclusive actress once again left the public eye. The one exception: an August 14, 1973, appearance on *The Merv Griffin Show*, appearing on the talk show alongside Frank Capra.

Hey Landlord!

In NBC's *Hey Landlord!*, aspiring writer Woody Banner (Will Hutchins) inherits a dilapidated New York brownstone from his uncle. To make ends meet, he took in many wacky tenants and worked odd writing jobs. Fans of *Hey Landlord!* waited all week to see what tenants would be featured; they included struggling comedian Chuck Hookstratten (Sandy Baron); photographer Jack (Michael Constantine); TV weathergirl Theresa (Pamela Rodgers); an airline stewardess (Miko Mayama), and two little old ladies (Ann Morgan Guilbert and Kathryn Minner).

Will Hutchins was best known for his role on the Western *Sugarfoot* (1957–1961). *Hey Landlord!* was produced and written by Jerry Belson and Garry Marshall, who were coming off their gig writing for the *Dick Van Dyke Show* (1961–1966). The *Dick Van Dyke* audience skewed toward mature and sophisticated; *Hey Landlord!* was aimed at young adults. Hutchins said, "We figure the young-marrieds will look at us and say 'Hey, remember when we lived like that?' And the teenagers dream of this kind of life, when they can move out of the house and be on their own" (Ashe "Stars, Writers Add" 44).

Before hitting the airwaves, *Hey Landlord!* received a substantial amount of press. There were full-page write-ups in newspapers, perhaps due to the connection to the popular *Dick Van Dyke Show*. *Hey Landlord!* debuted on Sunday, September 11, 1966, at 8:30. Critics were less than amused:

> "A lightweight comedy."—Bob Hull, *Los Angeles Herald-Examiner*
>
> "Can't last long."—Bob Williams, *New York Post*
>
> "Meager half-hour."—Hal Humphrey, *Los Angeles Times*
>
> "I wasn't overcome with laughter."—Millie Budd, *Houston Post*

Even the positive reviews were lukewarm:

"Better than the title suggests."—Harriet Van Horne, *New York World Journal Tribune*

"A gentle situation comedy."—Lawrence Laurent, *Washington Post*

The one thing that got positive reviews: the sex appeal of Pamela Rodgers. Ed Misurell, writer of the syndicated "TV Cameos" column, wrote, "Pamela stands five feet eight inches tall without heels and weighs 118 pounds. Her vital statistics are 35½–22–35½, and these are usually topped off by an infectious smile. … [H]er flowing titian tresses were set off spectacularly by a purple dress with a mini-skirt that stopped at mid-thigh. Mod boots brought her somewhat close to six feet in height" (Misurell 13).

Hey Landlord! was the only show that season shot in front of a live studio audience and the only show without canned laughter. "It's like playing a nightclub," said Sandy Baron. "You know you're dying with people out there when you hear the band behind you give out with a Haaaaaaaaa!!!!! Here [at Desilu Studios] when we hear those people in the bleachers laughing at us, we know we're getting our point across" (Ashe "Stars, Writers Add" 44).

Its first week, *Hey Landlord!* lost to time slot rival *The Ed Sullivan Show*, which received a 27.0 Arbitron rating. It beat out *7 Nights to Remember*, an ABC Fall Preview show hosted by Batman and Robin, by 6.4 ratings points with a 16.8 ("The Numbers Game" 59). Despite floundering ratings, *Hey Landlord!* continued to get good press and lengthy write-ups through November 1966. But in February 1967, NBC finally evicted *Hey Landlord!* from the prime time premises after 31 episodes ("CBS Reshuffle" 26). The last episode aired on April 23, 1967. Producers Marshall and Belson went on to bigger and better things: the film *How Sweet It Is* (1968) and TV's *The Odd Couple* (1970–1975). Marshall produced *Happy Days* (1974–1984), *Laverne & Shirley* (1976–1983) and *Mork & Mindy* (1978–1982) while Belson wrote for *Love, American Style* (1969–1974) and *The Tracey Ullman Show* (1987–1990).

Please Don't Eat the Daisies

Hitting the airwaves in the 1965–1966 season, *Please Don't Eat the Daisies* was a sitcom based on the bestselling Jean Kerr book and a same-name 1960 movie starring Doris Day and David Niven, about a suburban family with four young boys and their 150-pound sheepdog.

Before a pilot episode was shot, production hit several snags. It was reported that Patricia Crowley, slated to star in the pilot, was "out" in early January 1965: MGM had cancelled her contract after she failed to report to the set for three consecutive days (Gross "Around the Dials" 12). *Please Don't Eat the Daisies* was reportedly in the works for a year and Crowley's firing was going to put the show off another year (Doan "The Week That Was" 14). Making matters worse, Crowley announced she would be filing a "million dollar libel suit against MGM" over the matter, asserting that she did not appear on set at her agent's request because of "unresolved issues" in her contract (Barrett "The Chatterbox" 3). Five days later, Crowley and MGM patched up their differences and Crowley came to the set. It was reported that Crowley no-showed because she was upset that she could not bring her own hair stylist, George Masters, to the set (Hopper "Actress Loses Job" 10). An MGM official was quoted as saying, "Maybe Liz Taylor and one or two other big-timers could get away with such a thing but that sort of pampering for the average performer had been out of bounds for as long as I can remember." Crowley came to work without her private hairdresser (Heffernan 14).

A month later came the announcement that *Daisies* would be airing on NBC Tuesdays at 8:00 in the fall 1965–1966 season. April brought the news that it would be in color (Kleiner "Star Shirley Booth" 8; Doan "Familiar Faces" 18; Fanning "4th Network" 39).

The show, often referred to as a "sophisticated" situation comedy, starred Crowley as Joan Nash, a journalist who works from home. *Daisies* also featured Joan's college professor husband Jim (Mark Miller), their four boys Kyle (Kim Tyler), Joel (Brian Nash), Trevor (Jeff Fithian) and Tracy (Joe Fithian); and their old English sheepdog, Ladadog.

Please Don't Eat the Daisies debuted on September 14, 1965, and received a very high 21.5 Trendex rating, making it the week's seventh highest-rated show, easily beating out the long-running Western *Rawhide* on CBS and the World War II action series *Combat!* on ABC ("First Returns" 32). When the TV series bowed, the 1960 *Daisies* movie was still making the rounds at drive-ins and second-run movie theaters. By May 1965, the novel had sold 2,500,000 copies, bringing the upcoming TV show more attention then most new shows ("*Daisies* Gobbled Up" 25).

Despite the high ratings, critics were unenthusiastic:

> "The sheep dog gives a radiant, luminous performance."—Harriet Van Horne, *New York World Telegram and Sun*
>
> "Needs a lot of work."—Arthur E. Fetridge, *Boston Herald*
>
> "The show may be a hit with children and dogs."—Dwight Newton, *San Francisco Examiner*
>
> "Just another in a long list of domestic situation comedies."—Paul Molloy, *Chicago Sun-Times*
>
> "The premiere was not reassuring."—Jack Gould, *The New York Times*
>
> "Should be the laughingest of the new series."—Donald Kirkley, *Baltimore Sun* ("How Critics" 34)

Although the show could not keep up the extremely high ratings it received in its first week, it did manage to continue to beat out *Rawhide* and *Combat!* throughout the first half of the season. In January 1966, *Daisies* was featured on the cover of *TV Guide*. Inside, readers learned that the show "has not set the TV world aflame, but ratings have been good enough to give it at least an even money chance to continue" (De Roose 17).

That same month, CBS cancelled *Rawhide,* which was falling in ratings the last three seasons, and replaced it with thew drama *Daktari,* which that season scored very high ratings and became one of TV's most watched shows (Brooks and Marsh). In July 1966, NBC announced that *Daisies* would move to Saturdays at 8:00 ("New *Daisies*" 60). There it played opposite the new Western *Shane* with David Carradine and the variety–sketch comedy series *The Jackie Gleason Show*. That season, the latter series would feature newly produced *Honeymooners* skits for the first time since 1956, making it a must-see for Gleason fans and *Honeymooners* fans.

Week after week, *The Jackie Gleason Show* punched *Daisies* "pow, right in the kisser" when it came to ratings: It was TV's fifth highest-rated show, averaging a 25.3 rating (Brooks and Marsh). This did not give *Daisies* much opportunity to gain viewers ("The Latest" 68; "Few Cheers" 58; "Second Season" 60).

Daisies had connections to two other shows airing at the time, *The Man from*

U.N.C.L.E. and *The Girl from U.N.C.L.E.* In the *Daisies* episode "Say UNCLE," Robert Vaughn and David McCallum appeared as their *Man from U.N.C.L.E.* characters Napoleon Solo and Illya Kuryakin. Stefanie Powers appeared as her *Girl from U.N.C.L.E.* character April Dancer in the February 1967 *Daisies* episode "Remember Lake Serene."

Daisies was plucked from the NBC lineup in March 1967 ("NBC Fills" 52). Several days later it was announced that *Daisies*' 58 half-hour episodes would be sold into syndication. MGM Television highlighted the fact that the show was in color: "Here's the best new off-network comedy for all-family viewing. Top-rated in color homes. Top appeal for those 35 and under. Top attraction for TV's largest spot advertisers" (advertisement for *Please Don't Eat* 117). This made the show very attractive to station managers, who were reportedly "demanding" color programs in 1967 ("TFE '67" 68).

Please Don't Eat the Daisies last episode, "The Day the Play Got Away," aired on April 22, 1967. In the episode, Jim takes a sabbatical from his college professor gig to write a play and learns that his replacement at the college seemed to be doing better at his job than Nash did.

Please Don't Eat the Daisies was replaced by the action-adventure series *Maya* with Jay North. Unlike Jim Nash's replacement on the last *Daisies* episode, *Maya* did not fare better than its predecessor and was cancelled after 18 episodes.

Run, Buddy, Run

Leonard Stern, producer of the spy spoof *Get Smart*, produced another spoof in 1966, this one a send-up of the "man on the run" shows then on the air (*The Fugitive*, *Run for Your Life*). CBS's *Run, Buddy, Run* revolved around New Orleans jazz trumpet player Buddy Overstreet, played by real-life trumpeter and comedian Jack Sheldon. In a Turkish bath, Buddy overhears notorious Chicago gangster Mr. Devere (Bruce Gordon) discussing secret information. He takes his story to the police and asks for their protection. But the police do not believe him, and Buddy is forced to go on the lam: He moves from city to city and takes different odd jobs: bartender, farm hand, welder, boxing sparring partner, horse trainer. The gangsters put a bounty on Buddy's head and even start a "Buddy Overstreet Fund" to help nab him.

When CBS announced their 1966–1967 fall lineup, *Run, Buddy, Run* was scheduled to air on Monday at 8:00 p.m. There it was in good company, sandwiched between *Gilligan's Island* (the 22nd highest-rated show the previous season) and *The Lucy Show* (the third highest-rated show the previous season) (Brooks and Marsh).

The newspapers reviews were mixed:

> "Has possibilities."—Jack E. Anderson, *Miami Herald*
>
> "Dialogue is painfully shallow."—Don Page, *Los Angeles Times*
>
> "A deadpan lampoon of *The Fugitive*."—Harriet Van Horne, *New York World Tribune*
>
> "Runs out of steam."—Joseph P. Sullivan, *Boston Herald*
>
> "Doesn't seem to have the staying power to click as a weekly entry."—Percy Shain, *Boston Globe*
>
> "Out of Hollywood's bottomless bin of trivia."—Jack Gould, *The New York Times*

"Personally, I shall run from Buddy."—Lawrence Laurent, *Washington Post*

"Smartly done."—Bernie Harrison, *Washington Evening Star* (Critics' Views 64).

The show was given a jazzy bongo drum–driven theme, heard under this exposition:

This is Buddy Overstreet. He's wanted by the most powerful crime syndicate in the country. In a steam room, Buddy overheard their vital secret and the mysterious words "Chicken Little." Now he knows too much. These are the orders given to all members of the syndicate, from one end of the country to the other: "Get him! Get him! Get him!"

The theme was featured on trumpeter Al Hirt's album "The Horn Meets the Horn," which also featured covers of *The Green Hornet, Batman, Tarzan, Run for Your Life, The Monkees, Tarzan* and *T.H.E. Cat* themes.

Reviewers often commented that the show's humor harkened back to the days of Laurel and Hardy and even the Keystone Cops, Buster Keaton and Charlie Chaplin (Ashe "Run, Buddy, Run" 2; Gardella "TV Hoods" 31).

Although the show had decent reviews and a sizable amount of press coverage, by late October, it was rumored that CBS was thinking of pulling the plug. In mid–November, they did just that. There was a total of 13 episodes, the last playing on January 2, 1967.

Syndicated television columnist Cynthia Lowry questioned the move, stating that shows that were much worse than *Run, Buddy, Run* stayed on the air (Lowry "Short-Lived Series" 5).

Run, Buddy, Run was replaced by *Mr. Terrific*, which spoofed the superhero genre ("Second Season" 56; "Two More" 72; "Bumper Crop" 29). Perhaps *Run, Buddy, Run* was sacrificed to make room for *Mr. Terrific* so the network could capitalize on the *Batman* craze. But *Mr. Terrific* also failed to take flight. Other theorize that *Gilligan's Island*'s sharp decline in the ratings hurt the show that followed it.

Sheldon had a connection to two other series in the 1966–1967 season: *The Hero* and *Dragnet*. He played trumpet in *The Hero*'s orchestral scoring and played various roles on *Dragnet* (Ashe "Run, Buddy, Run" 2).

But Sheldon's most famous role was yet to come. Throughout the 1970s, he provided vocals on the popular educational animated series *Schoolhouse Rock!* (1973–2009) for songs such as "I'm Just a Bill" and "Conjunction Junction."

Interestingly, NBC had considered a very similar show for the 1966–1967 season: *Run, Jack, Run*. It was about two waiters (David Astor and Adam Keef) who shot a Mafia boss with a camera they did not know was actually loaded with bullets. The pair then made their way around the country working different jobs, much like Buddy Overstreet. *Run, Jack, Run* was not picked up by the network but in July 1970, the pilot aired as a NBC *Monday Theater* episode ("Bumper Crop" 30; "Run, Jack Run").

In *Run, Buddy, Run*'s final episode, Buddy Overstreet's arch-nemesis Mr. Devere gave up his chase after he himself had to go on the run from IRS tax auditors.

The Pruitts of Southampton aka *The Phyllis Diller Show*

In 1962, CBS introduced *The Beverly Hillbillies*, the rags-to-riches story of a Tennessee hillbilly family that strikes oil and moves to Beverly Hills. ABC's *The Pruitts of Southampton* is the contrasting story of a wealthy family that loses their fortune.

Chapter Ten. Situation Comedies

Based on the Patrick Dennis book *Hour Party, Pruitts* was the story of the wealthy Pruitt family from Long Island, New York, who went broke due to years of unpaid taxes. The IRS let the family, headed by Phyllis Pruitt (Phyllis Diller), keep their mansion and Rolls-Royce because they felt that if the American public discovered that the Pruitts were bankrupt, it would lead to an economic depression. Supervised by IRS agent Mr. Baldwin (Richard Deacon), the Pruitts close down 52 rooms of their vast mansion and live in eight, fire the servants and do their own cooking and chores. For the first time in her life, Phyllis has to live in the real world and learn how to do things like use kitchen appliances.

ABC saw the success of *The Beverly Hillbillies,* a consistently top-rated show, and attempted to put their spin on the genre. The two shows were made by the same production company, Filmways Productions (Brooks and Marsh). The network went so far as to say in a commercial, "This year ABC has its very own poverty program." The promo also proudly proclaimed that the show is was color. Diller described *Pruitts* as "grand, chic and low comedy" (Graham "Nothing but Money" 28).

The show was seen as a starring vehicle for comedienne Diller, who attained fame by touring extensively throughout the country for ten years and starring in *Boy Did I Get a Wrong Number* (1966) alongside Bob Hope and Richard Deacon (Thomas "Phyllis Laughs" 26).

After the show debuted (September 6, 1966), the critics had their say:

> "A lot of disastrous kitchen slapstick comedy."—Bob Williams, *New York Post*

> "It disappointed."—Bernie Harrison, *Washington Post*

> "Puerile parade of primitive japes."—Harry Harrison, *Philadelphia Inquirer*

> "A very, very bad show. … Let's hope Miss Diller will soon return to the nightclub circuit."—Win Fanning, *Pittsburgh Post-Gazette*

> "Atrociously executed."—Kay Gardella, *New York Daily News*

> "The show's premise is thin and its gags are timeworn and predictable. But the show does have some powerful canned laughter and this occasionally drowns out the dialogue."—Laurence Laurent, *Washington Post*

> "Predictable but hopefully forgettable comedy."—Bob Hull, *Los Angeles Herald-Examiner*

> "For Phyllis Diller fans. I thought I was among them until last night."—Bill Barrett, *Cleveland Press* ("The Critics Review" 36)

Although *Pruitts* was ridiculed by critics, audiences gave it a chance. In the first week, it had a 29.7 rating and a 54.5 audience share, even besting *Batman* which aired the next night. But the show was still in previews and aired against reruns from the previous season on the other networks ("Peek at Ratings" 35).

The half-hour sitcom, which aired on Tuesdays at 9:00, held its own against *The Red Skelton Hour* on CBS and *NBC Tuesday Night at the Movies* in its first several weeks. Then audiences tired of its basic format of Phyllis learning how to live like common people while selling off her family artwork, and the ratings plummeted.

The network still believed in the show but felt that it needed a makeover. On January 19, 1967, it became *The Phyllis Diller Show.* Along with the name change, it was moved to Fridays at 9:30, away from *The Red Skelton Hour* which rose to become the season's second highest-rated show (Brooks and Marsh).

The Phyllis Diller Show's executive producer David Levy explained, "Changes are underway to make the series lighter and to give it more youthful feeling" ("'Renovation' Slated" 8).

The show also added new comedic actors: Paul Lynde as Phyllis' deadbeat brother Harvey; former *Addams Family* (1964–1966) star John Astin as Phyllis' brother-in-law Rudy Pruitt; and former *I'm Dickens … He's Fenster* (1962–1963) star Marty Ingels as Norman Krump, a handyman owed money by the Pruitts; he becomes a houseguest in lieu of payment.

The Phyllis Diller Show aired opposite NBC's *T.H.E. Cat* and *The CBS Friday Night Movie*. Despite the restructuring, it was squashed in the ratings by the latter. By February 1967, ABC executives felt that it "will struggle and get nowhere" so it was not picked up for a second season ("Second Season Is" 64). *The Phyllis Diller Show* was replaced by the legal drama *Judd, for the Defense*, which took the Friday 9:30 slot.

Two years later, Diller starred in her own short-lived variety show, NBC's *The Beautiful Phyllis Diller Show*. It did even worse than her previous series and was cancelled by mid-season.

Diller never had a successful TV vehicle; however, she continued to do stand-up comedy and regularly appeared on TV and films throughout her career.

The Hero

The Dick Van Dyke Show took a look at a family man who works behind the scenes in show business. NBC's *The Hero* took a look at a family man who worked in front of the camera.

The Hero chronicled fictitious Western star Sam Garret, who starred on the *Gunsmoke*-like show *Jed Clayton: US Marshal*. Garret was nothing like the tough, square-jawed character he played on TV: He could not shoot a gun, was afraid of horses, and had allergies. Garret was played by character actor Richard Mulligan, then a relative unknown; he went on to star on *Soap* (1977–1981) and the *Golden Girls* spin-off *Empty Nest* (1988–1995). Possibly the best description of *The Hero* came from Associated Press TV critic Cynthia Lowry: "[It's] a series about a Western star who is dashing on camera but at home is one of those dopey husbands and fathers that used to dominate most TV situation comedies" (Lowry "Jericho Looks" 9).

The Hero first aired on September 8, 1966, in the Thursday 9:30 slot. Critics, impressed, gave it positive reviews:

> "Has plenty of potential."—Harry Harris, *Philadelphia Inquirer*
>
> "Strikes me as believable."—Percy Slain, *Boston Globe*
>
> "Another winner."—Aleene MacMinn, *Los Angeles Times*
>
> "NBC may have a 'sleeper' in this one."—Paul Molloy, *Chicago Sun-Times*
>
> "The premise is funny and so is the star, Richard Mulligan."—Bill Irvin, *Chicago American* ("Critics' Views" 59)

The critics may have been positive but audiences certainly were not: The show was consistently in the bottom one-third of the ratings and was surpassed each week by *That Girl* on ABC and *The CBS Thursday Night Movie* ("The Ratings" 68).

Less than a month into the show's run, advertisers indicated that they were watching *The Hero* "closely for new rating indicators—up or down." NBC had *The Hero* on its list of "most questioned" shows of the season and may have been looking to cancel it at mid-season ("Second Season" 56; "Casualty Report" 5).

But the show did have allies. NBC and *The Hero*'s sponsors received a wire from the National Association for Better Broadcasting which thanked them for sponsoring *The Hero* and urged the sponsors to help "keep the show on the air so that it could attract the audience it deserves." But the NABB cautioned the network and sponsors that if the show was cancelled mid-season, it would "reaffirm the belief that only ratings determine which program lives or dies" ("Wire About" 30).

Despite that plea, in early November 1966 NBC cancelled *The Hero*. NBC originally considered replacing it with the British import *The Saint* or the unrealized William Dozier project *Dick Tracy*. Ultimately *The Hero* was replaced by the reboot of the iconic Jack Webb series *Dragnet*, which scored much higher ratings ("The Ratings" 68; "ABC 2d" 56).

The show's 16th and last episode aired on January 5, 1967. Amusingly, the next season, Richard Mulligan went on to guest star in "Wonder," an episode of the series he satirized on *The Hero*: *Gunsmoke*.

The Lucy Show

Lucille Ball's follow-up to the iconic and incredibly popular *I Love Lucy* (1951–1957) and *The Lucy-Desi Comedy Hour* (1957–1960) was *The Lucy Show*.

In the early 1960s, Ball went through a lot of personal and professional changes. She divorced her real-life and on-screen husband Desi Arnaz and married to comedian Gary Morton. Arnaz and Ball still had a working relationship, and they still owned the largest independent studio in Hollywood: Desilu. Arnaz continued to propose projects on behalf of Ball. On January 16, 1962, he proposed a new Ball series, *The Lucy Show*, to CBS. It was based on the novel *Life Without George*, about a divorced suburban woman ("Keeping Lucy's" 145).

Just five days later, CBS agreed to air *The Lucy Show* and began a publicity campaign to promote the show (Adams "CBS Still Loves").

Because *I Love Lucy* was such a beloved and highly rated show, there was great anticipation for *The Lucy Show*. At first everyone was tight-lipped about it, including executive producer Arnaz. "We are going to keep it a secret until a few weeks before the show goes to air," he said. "I can't tell you anything" ("Keeping Lucy's" 145). The casting of Vivian Vance, who played Lucy's neighbor and best friend Ethel Mertz on *I Love Lucy*, was announced in mid–April 1962 (Lowry "Oscar Awards" 18; Lowry "Season of TV" 29).

Debuting on October 1, 1962, *The Lucy Show* aired Mondays at 8:30. An instant success, it averaged a 29.8 Nielsen rating each week and became the year's fourth highest-rated show (Brooks and Marsh). Ball played Lucy Carmichael, a widow (not a divorcee as in *Life Without George*) living in Connecticut with her children Chris (Candy Moore) and Jerry (Jimmy Garret). Sharing the home are recent divorcee Vivian Bagley (Vance) and her son Sherman (Ralph Hart).

Viewers welcomed the reunion of Ball and Vance, but tensions arose behind the scenes. Vance reportedly wanted to spend more time with her family and left after the 1964–1965 season (Lowry "Next Year's" 22).

Lucy's deceased husband left her a trust fund that was managed by banker Mr. Barnsdahl (Charles Lane). In the second season, Lane was replaced by Gale Gordon who played banker Mr. Mooney.

The show debuted in black and white; in the second season, episodes were shot in color but not broadcast in color. CBS waited another year to broadcast new episodes in color; the episodes previously shot in color were finally seen in color in reruns and syndication. Audiences could finally see Lucille Ball's signature red hair in all its glory.

But the color broadcasts almost did not happen. In February 1964, Ball and CBS president James T. Aubrey announced that the series would be discontinued. Ball said this was due to her desire to devote more time to Desilu. But one month later, she changed her mind and announced that *The Lucy Show* would continue (Adams "C.B.S. Lucy"; Adams "C.B.S. Continuing").

Later came some major changes: By 1965, Lucy had moved to Hollywood; shipped both her children off to school (and never mentioned them again); found a new best friend, Mary Jane Lewis (Mary Jane Croft), and now worked at a bank with Mr. Mooney. Guest stars included Milton Berle, Art Linkletter, Mickey Rooney, Dean Martin, Bob Crane, Danny Thomas and even a team of trained dolphins (Lowry "Some Old" 9).

In the first official week of the 1966–1967 season, Monday, September 12, at 8:30, *The Lucy Show* kicked off its fifth season. Hopes were obviously high for *The Lucy Show*, which was in the top ten shows every year and was the third highest-rated show in the 1965–1966 season. But in 1966, *The Lucy Show* had a fight on its hands. That season, it aired opposite ABC's World War II action-adventure series *The Rat Patrol* and NBC's music-variety series *The Roger Miller Show* (Brooks and Marsh).

The Lucy Show began the season in its typical spot as one of the top-rated shows, earning a 21.4 rating. But *The Rat Patrol*, while not getting much network support, was on *The Lucy Show*'s heels: It scored a 19.8 rating ("The Numbers Game" 59; "ARB Top-20 Programs Sept. 11–17" 68).

The following week, *The Rat Patrol* shot up to the top of the ratings heap, becoming the fifth highest watched show of the week. Its 22.7 Arbitron rating beat out *The Lucy Show*, which received a 19.3 rating. CBS started hitting the proverbial panic button, as *The Lucy Show* was considered a "bread and butter" show (DuBrow "*Rat Patrol* Hits Lucy" 21; "'*Rat Patrol*' Rates High" 48).

Television critics covering the ratings anomaly wondered if audiences were getting tired of Ball. *The Lucy Show* continued to lose in the ratings to *The Rat Patrol* early in the season, but the tables soon turned: *The Lucy Show* gradually going up and *The Rat Patrol* down. On October 31, with an episode guest-starring Carol Burnett, *The Lucy Show* overtook *Rat Patrol* and stayed on top the rest of the season ("ARB's Top-20 Programs Sept. 25–Oct 1" 59; "ARB Top-20 Programs Oct. 2–8" 68; "Top-20 Arbitrons Oct. 9–15" 56 ; "Top-20 Arbitron's Oct. 16–22" 64; "Top-20 Arbitrons Oct. 23–29" 56). *The Lucy Show* ended the season as the fourth highest-rated show with a 26.2 Nielsen rating and *The Rat Patrol* the 23rd highest-rated show with a 20.9 rating. *The Roger Miller Show* was one of the season's lowest rated shows (Brooks and Marsh; Fredericks "New Shows" 76).

That season, *The Lucy Show* featured guest stars George Burns, Ed Begley, Paul Winchell, John Wayne, Phil Silvers, Tennessee Ernie Ford, Sheldon Leonard and Jim Nabors (in a crossover episode with *Gomer Pyle, U.S.M.C.*) and Lucy was up to her usual antics such as being a part of a nightclub act, getting stuck in a submarine and babysitting a baby chimp. Ball also won a Primetime Emmy for Outstanding Lead Actress in a Comedy Series.

By the fall of 1966, Ball was the sole owner of Desilu Productions, having bought out Arnaz. That season, Desilu was producing *The Lucy Show*, *Star Trek* and *Mission: Impossible*, and a number of shows were being filmed on the Desilu lot: *Gomer Pyle, U.S.M.C.* (1964–1969), *I Spy* (1965–1968), *Hogan's Heroes* (1965–1971), *That Girl* (1966–1971) and *Family Affair* (1966–1971).

The Lucy Show went off the air after its successful 1967–1968 season. In its last year, it was the second highest-rated show. There were more than enough episodes for a proper run in syndication.

That same year, 1968, Ball sold her stake in Desilu to Gulf+Western. The Desilu moniker was dropped and it was renamed Paramount Television.

Ball was not finished with television. In 1968, she began starring as Lucy Carter in *Here's Lucy* alongside her real-life teenage children Lucie Arnaz and Desi Arnaz, Jr. Lucy once again brought in Gale Gordon to co-star as her brother-in-law, who owns Carter's Unique Employment Agency and employs Lucy there. Like *I Love Lucy* and *The Lucy Show*, *Here's Lucy* was quite popular, was one of the most-watched shows on the air. It even survived CBS's Rural Purge, the 1971 cancellation of traditional comedies and Westerns. But in late February 1974, Ball announced the end of *Here's Lucy*. According to the TV industry journal *Broadcasting*,

> [T]here has been a steady erosion of *Here's Lucy's* ratings, *NFL Monday Night Football* on ABC and NBC's *Monday Night at the Movies* have scooped out fairly large hunks of Miss Ball's audience in recent years, turning what was once a perennial top-10 show into one that new hovers between 30th and 35th place each week. ... Some commentators have attributed Miss Ball's declining popularity to the new situation comedies format, particularly those by Norman Lear, who has insisted on presenting topics such as menopause, impotency, alcoholism and abortion. ... In this changed context, Miss Ball's continued reliance on knockout, slapstick farce has seemed tame and old-fashioned to the 18–49-year-old audiences that sponsors are particularly eager to attract ["End" 31].

Ball did not return to TV until the Fall of 1986 with CBS's *Life with Lucy*. Gale Gordon co-starred as a widower who owns half a stake in a hardware store. Unlike Ball's TV ventures in the 1950s and 1960s, *Life with Lucy* was not a ratings success; in fact, it was one of TV's least watched shows. It was cancelled after only eight episodes ("NBC Goes" 63; "Four" 96; "Mets-Sox" 54).

Family Affair

Originally entitled *My Family Right or Wrong* when piloted by CBS, *Family Affair* was created by Edmund L. Hartman and Don Fedderson. It was originally described as a "comedy in which the hero, a successful mining engineer, has his life altered when a young orphaned relative comes to live with him" ("Bumper Crop" 29).

The original premise of one orphan grew to three by time the show hit the air on September 12, 1966: 15-year-old Cissy (Kathy Garver) and five-year-old twins Jody (Johnny Whitaker) and Buffy (Anissa Jones). Brian Keith, who previously starred on NBC's short-lived *The Westerner* (1960) and the Walt Disney film *The Parent Trap* (1961), was cast as wealthy bachelor Bill Davis, who must now raise his brother's orphaned children in his upscale New York apartment. Helping Davis is his longtime valet, proper Englishman gentleman Giles French (Sebastian Cabot), who reluctantly took on the role of a nanny rather than worrying about being suave and refined. At the time, Cabot was best known for co-starring in the detective series *Checkmate* (1960–1962). French grew fond of the children as the show progressed.

Every show opened with a colorful jeweled kaleidoscopic pattern under the credits in lavish cursive writing, along with the theme written by Academy Award–nominated composer Frank De Vol.

Critics gave the sitcom mostly positive reviews:

> "Should have it made for at least a season or two."—Hal Humphrey, *Los Angeles Times*

> "It's all as cute as a puppy's behind and if [you] dig this blarney, be my guest."—Jack E. Anderson, *Miami Herald*

> "It's easy to take."—Joseph T. Sullivan, *Boston Herald*

> "Has wonderous warmth, subtle humor and flashes of slapstick cemented in realism."—Dwight Newton, *San Francisco Examiner*

> "I may tune in each week just to watch [Anissa Jones] pout."—Harriet Van Horne, *New York World Journal Tribune* ("Critics' Views" 64).

That season, the half-hour *Family Affair* aired on Mondays at 9:30 p.m., opposite NBC's Western *The Road West* and ABC's prime-time soap opera *Peyton Place*. The latter was the top-rated show in the Monday 9:30 slot early in the season ("The Numbers Game" 60; "The Latest" 69). By mid-season, *Family Affair* jumped over *Peyton Place* and rose to be the 14th highest-rated show by the end of the season. It averaged a 22.6 rating ("2d Season" 51; Brooks Marsh).

Indianapolis Star TV Scene writer Julia Inman wrote about why *Family Affair* connected with audiences:

> It's not just that *Family Affair* avoids the obvious in slapstick and broad comedy. It's having Keith as the "father" *pro tem* that makes all the difference. ... After years of bumbling weak-kneed paternal figures on the small screen, Keith comes through as rugged, nonchalant and real. Following his lead, Sebastian Cabot also underplays but hits every laugh involved in a "gentleman's gentleman" forced by circumstances into being a "well-upholstered middle-aged housekeeper" [Inman "Keith Puts Starch" 15].

Family Affair also had a fresh, modern look. The photography was handled by a diverse and experienced team headed by Stanley Cortez, the cinematographer on the film classics *The Magnificent Ambersons* (1942), *The Night of the Hunter* (1955) and *Shock Corridor* (1963). Paul Ivano was most popular for his work in the film noir–detective genre. Philip Tannura was famous for his work on the Fred Astaire-Rita Hayworth musical *You'll Never Get Rich* (1941). And relative unknown Michael P. Joyce went on to shoot *The Streets of San Francisco* (1972–1977).

Family Affair did even better in the 1967–1968 season, rising to become the fourth highest-rated show of the year (tied with the long-running Westerns *Gunsmoke* and *Bonanza*), with an average 25.5 rating. *Family Affair* was the fifth highest-rated show in 1968–1969 and 1969–1970 seasons.

Each character received almost an equal number of episodes dedicated to them,

Anissa Jones, whose character Buffy was rarely seen without her doll Mrs. Beasley, was clearly the series' breakout star. She was almost immediately the subject of newspaper write-ups and she even started making personal appearances at department stores. Just in time for Christmas 1968, Mattel Toy Company released a 6" Buffy Doll with detachable Mrs. Beasley Doll and an 11" "Talking Mrs. Beasley Doll" programmed to say ten phrases from the show. She also had her own cookbook, various coloring books, and a *Family Affair* series novelization.

Even with the children getting older, writers continued to produce episodes as if Jody and Buffy were the same age as when the show started, and audiences began to notice. The show fell out of favor by the 1970–1971 season when it played opposite NBC's hip new variety show *The Flip Wilson Show*, which scored massive ratings in its first season and became TV's second highest-rated show (Brooks and Marsh).

Family Affair went off the air on March 4, 1971, after 138 episodes. It was replaced by the notoriously unsuccessful, short-lived and critically panned *The Chicago Teddy Bears* (1971), a sitcom set in the Prohibition era.

Like many child actors, Anissa Jones could not break out of the role that made her famous. Although considered for various roles, she never landed another steady acting gig. Five years after *Family Affair* was cancelled, on August 28, 1976, at the age of 18, Jones died of an overdose of barbiturates, cocaine, angel dust and quaaludes. Orange County, California, coroner Robert Creason called it one of the worst overdose cases he had ever seen ("Buffy–Drugs" 1). Obituaries did not feature a picture of Jones as an 18-year-old but as the seven-year-old child that people most closely associated her with … the image Jones was trying to break free from.

My Three Sons

After his wife's death, aviation engineer Steve Douglas (Fred MacMurray) must raise their boys Mike, 18 (Tim Considine), Robbie, 14 (Don Grady), and Chip, seven (Stanley Livingston). Steve has the help of his father-in-law Bub O'Casey (William Frawley), who serves as the boys' *de facto* nanny.

Fred MacMurray, who starred in dozens of films, agreed to take on the *My Three Sons* role of Steve but as per MacMurray's contract, he was only obligated to work 65 non-consecutive days of shooting. To accommodate his light schedule, most of his scenes were written and filmed in advance and producers had to account for MacMurray not being available for the majority of filming dates. This created several continuity errors throughout the years. This became known as "The MacMurray Method" (Brooks "The American Family" 59).

The show had accomplished actors to work around MacMurray's schedule and do a lot of the heavy lifting. Frawley was fresh off his role as Fred Mertz on *I Love Lucy*. Considine starred in the Disney TV productions *Spin and Marty* (1955–1957) and *The Hardy Boys* (1956–1957) and also appeared in Disney films, including *The Shaggy Dog* (1959) with MacMurray. Grady was previously a Mickey Mouse Mouseketeer. The youngest of the TV brothers, Stanley Livingston, played on *The Adventures of Ozzie and Harriet* from 1958 to 1963 and in the movies *Please Don't Eat the Daisies* (1960) and *How the West Was Won* (1962).

When this series premiered on ABC on September 29, 1960, many sitcoms revolved around the family unit, but *My Three Sons* was unique due to its all-male cast. Even the family Briard dog, Tramp, was male. Most advertisements revolved around there not being a lady in the entire household.

The opening credits featured a theme written by Academy Award–winning composer Frank De Vol, who also did the *Family Affair* theme, and iconic artwork of three pairs of shoes representing the ages of the three: sneakers for the youngest Chip, penny loafers for middle son Robbie, and wingtips for the eldest Mike. The infectious theme was so popular that in 1961, bandleader Lawrence Welk's version of it hit reached #55 on the Billboard Hot 100 charts.

My Three Sons was an instant success. Though never a top ten show, it was always one of the top 30 and became a cornerstone of the ABC prime time lineup (Brooks and Marsh). In 1965, CBS announced that it had purchased the rights to *My Three Sons* and that it would become a highlight of their prime time lineup. *Broadcasting* magazine reported that CBS paid "over $6 million to acquire the program rights from Producer Gregg-Don Inc." and that the network also secured the rights to the 184 black-and-white episodes which already aired. The episodes would be sold into syndication and aired on CBS in the daytime. That year, CBS also purchased the NBC sitcom *Hazel* ("CBS-TV Acquires" 75).

CBS president Jack Schneider described *My Three Sons* and *Hazel* as "free balls," meaning they did not have network affiliation and were free to sign with any network that wanted them. Schneider felt that picking up the already established shows, rather than developing new ones, made more economic sense. "They were free market commodities which we wanted on our network so we bought them," said Schneider ("Schneider Comes On" 60). In May 1965, CBS announced that they would make *My Three Sons* in color ("CBS-TV Adds" 59).

"The addition of color hasn't changed things much," said MacMurray. "Oh, I've got to be a bit more careful about what I wear. And we had to spruce up the set a bit; we didn't realize how dowdy it looked until we saw it on color film. The scenes take a little longer to light but otherwise we just keep rolling along" (Thomas "*My Three Sons*" 6). *My Three Sons* fans did not have to rearrange their schedules to watch the show on CBS: It remained on Thursdays at 8:30.

There were other changes: One of the three sons, Tim Considine, left at the end of the 1964–1965 season, Story-wise, his character, Mike, married his girlfriend Sally Morrison (Meredith MacRae) and they were written off the show. MacRae went on to play the third Billie Jo Bradley on *Petticoat Junction* (1963–1970).

The role of the eldest son was ostensibly taken over by middle son Robbie. In order to keep focused on three sons, Barry Livingston, real-life brother of Stanley, was made a full-time cast member. Barry had been on the show since 1963, playing Chip's buddy Ernie, but after Considine's departure, it was written into the story that Ernie's parents were actually his foster parents and their jobs were being transferred to "The Orient," so the Douglas family adopted Ernie.

Considine, who was 24, left to pursue bigger and better acting roles and hoped to do some writing and directing. Like many other former Disney child actors, he never became the star he wanted to be (McLain "TV Star Considine" 30).

William Frawley also did not transition to CBS. In ill health, he left the show in January 1965 when his character Bub went to Ireland for his aunt's 104th birthday. Frawley was replaced by character actor William Demarest, who played Bub's brother Charley ("Old Friends" 11).

When asked about replacing Frawley, Demarest replied "We didn't make a big thing over it and the reviews were all good. ... A switch like this can be touchy. A man is on a show for five years and then he disappears. People do care. Bub was a lovable character" (Witbeck "Demarest Replaces" 97).

Robbie's storylines began to revolve around girls and dating, as Considine's character Mike's once did, Twelve-year-old Chip took on the role of the middle son, and ten-year-old Ernie was now the youngest.

In the 1965–1966 season, *My Three Sons* picked up where it left off in terms of popularity and was the 15th highest-rated show. Its rivals on the other networks were the NBC Western *Laredo* and ABC's ratings duds *O.K. Crackerby!* with Burl Ives in the fall and *The Double Life of Henry Phyfe* with Red Buttons in the spring (Brooks and Marsh). By the 1966–1967 season, ratings fell but it still managed a respectable 31st highest-rated (Spencer "TV's Vast" 54).

In the spring of 1967, its competition included ABC's highly rated sitcom *Bewitched* and NBC's *Star Trek*. Although *My Three Sons* beat *Star Trek* in the ratings, each week was a fight for the share of the audience not taken by *Bewitched,* which consistently won the time slot and was the season's seventh highest-rated show (Spencer "TV's Vast" 54).

That season, Robbie started a cake business, made an underground movie for a film class, worked part-time selling houses, learned to become a bullfighter, and was almost forced into marriage due to an old Italian custom. Chip had girl troubles seemingly throughout the entire season. Ernie failed a school science fair, went on a fishing trip with his dad, saw a UFO, and learned that he was allergic to the family dog Tramp. Steve did poorly in a quiz game against Chip and Ernie, fell for the same woman as Chip, and ran a cross-country race against other fathers. And Charlie, a former sailor, almost left the family for the sea once again, and attempted to pick up one of Ernie's teachers with tales of the sea. The 1966–1967 season also featured storylines involving the entire family: a band of gypsies camp out in the Douglases' front yard, an meter maid (Yvonne Craig) gets aggressive, a trip to Hawaii is undertaken.

In the next season, *My Three Sons* was moved from its traditional 8:30 Thursdays slot to 8:30 Saturdays. Not only that, but the TV family moved from their fictitious midwestern town of Bryant Park to Los Angeles. Ratings picked up (Brooks and Marsh).

Storylines would constantly evolve and change to accommodate the boys' ages and even Steve Douglas. Eventually, Steve married widow Barbara Harper (Beverly Garland) and adopted her daughter Dodie (Dawn Lyn). Robbie got engaged and eventually married Katie Miller (Tina Cole), and at the end of the 1970–1971 season, the couple added baby triplets to the family, Robert, Steven and Charles—a new generation of "Three Sons." Robbie was written out after his character moved to San Francisco with his wife and children. The move was designed to set up a spin-off series which was to be entitled *Three of a Kind* or *Robbie,* but it was never picked up by a network.

Even Chip, at the age of 18, would elope with his high school sweetheart Polly Williams (Ronne Troup), and was seen less and less.

In the 1971–1972 season, CBS moved *My Three Sons* to Mondays at 10:00. That season, the show introduced the storyline of Steve's identical cousin Lord Fergus McBain Douglas of Sithian Bridge, also played by MacMurray. Improbable plots, a time slot change, the abandonment of the unique storyline of an all-male household all led to decline in ratings and eventual cancellation.

The last episode of *My Three Sons,* "Whatever Happened to Ernie?," was shot before the series was cancelled. In it, the Douglases helped one of Ernie's classmates, a drug addict. The story was in sharp contrast to the wackier storylines seen that season. When "Whatever Happened to Ernie?" was being produced, CBS was listing *My Three Sons* as a "cancellation candidate," so the episode was an attempt to stay relevant with what *Broadcasting,* an industry magazine, called "the 18–49-year-old audiences that sponsors are particularly eager to attract." (The Norman Lear sitcoms *All in the Family* and *Sanford and Son* were then dominating the ratings with stories that dealt with more serious subject matter.) The last *My Three Sons* aired on April 13, 1972, and the series left the air after 12 seasons and 360 episodes ("The Other Two" 27; "End" 31; "Who Will Survive" 45).

The *My Three Sons* cast returned to ABC in 1977 in a Thanksgiving special along with the Partridge Family in an *ABC Family Reunion.*

Occasional Wife

In February 1966, newspaper TV columns reported on the start of production of the new NBC color sitcom, *Occasional Wife*. On the show, young corporate executive Peter Christopher (Michael Callan) cannot move up the ladder because his boss Max Brahms (Jack Collins) believes that every man should have a wife. Christopher is also being pressured to get married by his overbearing mother (Sara Seegar). She even asks Christopher if he is "eccentric" (with the implication Peter was secretly gay).

To advance in the workplace and appease his mother, Peter marries struggling artist Greta Patterson (Patricia Harty). It was far from a conventional marriage. Patterson was simply hired to play the role of his wife when it was convenient, such as when the boss came over for dinner or when Peter went to his mother's house. Peter moved Greta into a separate but attached apartment in his building and provided her with art lessons. Throughout the series, the couple keep up the ruse, *and* learn to work well together as a team.

It was unclear how close Peter and Greta actually got. Harty was once asked about whether or not she felt her character had ever consummated her marriage to Peter, and she said it was up to the audience to decide. She did offer: "I think Greta is a mature woman who is very intelligent and realistic and knows exactly what she wants." Asked if she believed her character was a virgin, Harty exclaimed, "Of course not!"—and then added, "But she doesn't fool around" (Stone "From Ingénue").

After the first episode aired on September 13, 1966, at 8:30, *New York Times* TV columnist Jack Gould said that Harty had "winning appeal" and added, "[I]t was Miss Harty who primarily made last night's outing palatable" (Gould "TV: Patricia"). The other critics were mostly negative:

> "May amuse your dotty old Aunt Susie but its ineptitude will be painful for the rest of the family."—Harriet Van Horne, *New York World Journal Tribune*

> "Light-hearted, potential sophisticated comedy."—Bob Hull, *Los Angeles Herald-Examiner*

> "It will also have an occasional life."—Paul Molloy, *Chicago Sun-Times*

> "A laundered bedroom farce."—Mary Wood, *Cincinnati Post & Times-Star*

Perhaps the most vicious reviews came from Lawrence Laurent of the *Washington Post*: "A sure cure for insomnia. It beats sleeping pills and is guaranteed not to be habit-forming" ("Critics' Views" 64).

At the start of the 1966–1967 season, the new series' ratings regularly beat out the new ABC Western *The Rounders* and matched those of CBS's long-running *The Red Skelton Hour* ("The Numbers Game" 60; "The Latest" 69; "ARB's top 20" 68). By mid-season, *Occasional Wife* was one of only nine new shows that were "in the upper half of the Nielsen-rated programs" along with *The Rat Patrol, Family Affair, Tarzan, The Felony Squad, Iron Horse, Run, Buddy, Run, Star Trek* and *The Dating Game*. The other two dozen new programs were in the lower half ("Two More" 72).

By January 1967, *Occasional Wife*'s honeymoon was over: Viewers tuned out and ratings dropped. *The Red Skelton Hour* picked back up in the ratings; the low-rated *The Rounders* was cancelled and replaced with the science fiction thriller *The Invaders*, which did considerably better in the ratings (Brooks and Marsh; Spencer "TV's Vast" 54).

Occasional Wife had a unique concept but only so many storylines that can be hatched about Peter and Greta almost being discovered by gawking neighbors, snooping family members and prying co-workers. By season's end, it had dropped from being one of the highest-rated new shows to one of the season's lowest-rated shows (Spencer "TV's Vast" 54).

NBC clearly did not see much future in *Occasional Wife* and in February 1967 announced their divorce from the show, as well as *Hey Landlord!, The Andy Williams Show, Captain Nice, The Road West, The Girl from U.N.C.L.E., Bob Hope Presents the Chrysler Theatre, T.H.E. Cat, Laredo, Please Don't Eat the Daisies* and *Flipper* ("CBS Reshuffle" 26). After one season and 30 episodes, *Occasional Wife* was replaced by the sitcom *Julia* in the fall of 1967. Peter and Greta's secret was never discovered.

Love on a Rooftop

In late 1965, Screen Gems and producer Harry Ackerman announced their newest TV project: *Love on a Rooftop*, a comedy about a young married couple living in a small rooftop apartment in San Francisco, attempting to make ends meet on David's apprentice architect's salary of $85.37 a week. Julie and David Willis also feel pressure from her wealthy parents, who do not like their daughter living in such a small apartment and married to someone making so little (Laurent "Ackerman Has Most" 27).

The lead dancer on NBC's dance show *Hullabaloo* (1965–1966), Donna McKechnie, was originally considered for the role of Julie. But the role went to English-born actress Judy Carne, while Pete Duel, best known for his role as John Cooper on the sitcom *Gidget* (1965–1966), was cast as David. Julie's parents Fred and Phyllis were played by Herb Voland and Edith Atwater, and the couple's neighbors Carol and Stan were played by Barbara Bostock and "Man of a Thousand Voices" Rich Little. Little described his character as a "zany, far-out nut" who keeps coming up with "screwy ideas for making money" (Daley "Canadian Entertainer" 39).

According to *TV Guide*,

> *Love on a Rooftop* is this year's newlywed comedy. The lovebirds are Julie and David. Their nest is a barely furnished, windowless flat with rooftop privileges affording them a glorious

view of San Francisco. Julie calls the roof their "patio." David, however, views things more realistically. "Honey," he says, "where I come from, any place with 14 TV antennas and pigeons is a roof" ["1966–1967 Fall Preview"].

Love on a Rooftop's first episode aired at 9:30 on Tuesday, September 6, 1966. It drew a 56.8 share with little competition ("Peek at Ratings" 35). Mostly positive reviews flowed in:

> "Proved to have the touch of the great situation comedies."—Win Fanning, *Pittsburgh Post-Gazette*
>
> "It has possibilities, thanks to appealing people, reasonably amusing lines and wry comments by offscreen narrator."—Harry Harris, *Philadelphia Inquirer*
>
> "Has lighthearted appeal."—Bill Barrett, *Cleveland Press*
>
> "It has all been said before but [the show] is a cute little situation comedy."—Martin Hogan, Jr., *Cincinnati Enquirer*
>
> "View from this rooftop is lovely."—Aleen MacMin, *Los Angeles Times*

Perhaps the most prophetic review:

> "Funny lines ... and some lovely moments about a young couple in love. ... [S]till the show is in for trouble."—Lawrence Laurent, *Washington Post* ("The Critics Review" 36–37)

The following week, *Love on a Rooftop* scored a 17.9 Arbitron rating, beating out the season premiere of CBS's rural show *Petticoat Junction* and coming close in the ratings of *NBC Tuesday Night at the Movies*' airing of the Elvis Presley film *Blue Hawaii* (1961). The latter was the top-rated show in the time slot with a 18.6 rating ("Critics' Views" 60; Brooks and Marsh).

Love on a Rooftop ratings took a hit when ABC moved the show to Thursdays at 9:00. Making matters worse, ABC moved it once again in the spring to 9:30. Clearly, *Love on a Rooftop* was not high on ABC's priority list and they were looking to put other shows in better positions to succeed, even if it meant sacrificing shows like *Love on a Rooftop*.

By March 1967, Judy Carne was already looking for her next job:

> I'd love to do a movie, but I'm kind of not quite the movie type. ... You know they are making another movie, starring Dick Van Dyke with the same writers and the same composers that did *Mary Poppins*, and they're looking for an unknown English girl who sings and dances. It's a Julie Andrews sort of thing, and if I could get a part like that I would never look back. I wouldn't have to [Mead "Judy Looking" 70].

The movie Carne was referencing was *Chitty Chitty Bang Bang* (1968), and she was not cast in it. She did guest star on *The Man from U.N.C.L.E.* the following season, and then became famous as the "Sock It to Me" girl on *Rowan & Martin's Laugh-In* (1968–1970).

In the April 6, 1967, episode of *Love on a Rooftop*, the Willises were convinced that their neighbors, Stan and Carol, were having a baby and they threw the couple a surprise baby shower. It turns out that Carol was not pregnant, and Julie and David revealed that *they* may soon need the baby supplies purchased for the shower. The baby storyline was never realized because *Love on a Rooftop* was cancelled that month. The network announced the news at their annual affiliates meeting in Chicago ("ABC Cancels" 16).

F Troop

Richard K. Doan, a newspaper writer on radio and TV affairs, wrote in late 1964 that Warner Brothers was attempting to combine two "tried-and-true formats, the Western and the situation comedy," and announced that Forrest Tucker would take on the starring role in a series entitled *F Troop* (Doan "Silent Comedy" 5).

Before the first episode of the ABC series aired on September 14, 1965, at 9:00, *Los Angeles Times* TV writer Hal Humphrey declared, "*F Troop* looks like a winner" and reported that Tucker had stated, "I've been around a while and I think I know what audiences like. *F Troop* will be a big success, believe me" (Humphrey "*F Troop* Looks" 18).

Audiences learned the premise of *F Troop* as the theme song played during the opening credits: In the post–Civil War West, Fort Courage is commanded by bumbling Captain Wilton Parmenter (Ken Berry), who was promoted to captain after a sneezing fit caused him to accidentally call for a charge toward enemy soldiers and giving him the nickname "The Scourge of Appomattox." Other characters included Sergeant Morgan O'Rourke (Tucker) and his sidekick Corporal Randolph Agarn (Larry Storch), who have struck a clandestine business deal with a local Native American tribe, the Hekawis. Chief Wild Eagle (Frank de Kova) and Crazy Cat (Don Diamond) specialized in bootleg items for visitors, townspeople and soldiers Also stationed at Fort Courage were soldiers unfit for other assignments: the dreadful bugler Dobbs (James Hampton), legally blind lookout Vanderbilt (Joe Brooks) and elderly Trooper Duffy (Bob Steele). Also featured was cowgirl Wrangler Jane (Melody Patterson), who was as tough as she was beautiful.

F Troop's guest stars included Henry Gibson as Trooper Wrongo Star (his name a takeoff on Ringo Starr), Don Rickles as Hekawi wild man Bald Eagle, Milton Berle as Native American Wise Owl, Harvey Korman as a Prussian balloonist, Zsa Zsa Gabor as the gypsy Marika, and two actresses who played Catwoman on *Batman*: Lee Meriwether as potential saloon owner Lily O'Reilly and Julie Newmar as the long-lost Hekawi Indian known as Yellow Bird.

Syndicated columnist Charles Witbeck compared the show to another ABC military-themed comedy, *McHale's Navy*, but "on horseback played in the dry West." Newspaper critics instantly fell in love with *F Troop*.

> "Should be the laughingest of the new series."—Donald Kirkley, *Baltimore Sun*
>
> "Find a soft spot on the floor ... on which to roll."—Bob Hull, *Los Angeles Herald Examiner*
>
> "It's Laurel and Hardy time in the Old West."—Bernie Harrison, *Washington Evening Star*
>
> "Could be a top winner this season."—John Marshal Cuno, *Christian Science Monitor*
>
> "Could tickle the fancy of the entire family."—John Horn, *New York Herald-Tribune*
>
> "May be the best of [Tuesday] night's entries, but definitely not a woman's show."—Harriet Van Horne, *New York Telegram and Sun* ("How Critics See" 34)

F Troop was one of only four shows that debuted in the 1965–1966 season in black and white (the others were *I Dream of Jeannie*, *Convoy* and *Lost in Space*); and it was the only new black-and-white show on ABC. In this season, *F Troop* aired opposite the last hour of the long-running color *Red Skelton Hour* on CBS and *NBC's Tuesday Night at the Movies* which featured mostly color films such as *The Savage* (1952), *Secret of the Incas* (1954), *The Birds* (1963), *Funny Face* (1957) and *G.I. Blues* (1960) (Coffey "TV Movie Night" 18).

Although ratings started off high, *F Troop* ended the season as the 40th most watched show and lost out in the ratings to both *The Red Skelton Hour* and *NBC's Tuesday Night at the Movies* ("First Returns" 20 Spencer "TV's Vast" 55).

In April 1966, ABC announced that *F Troop* was renewed for another season, now in color, and moving to a new night, Thursdays at 8:00. There it aired opposite the first half-hour of CBS's World War II series *Jericho* and NBC's Western *Daniel Boone*. ("TV Topics: TV Tidbits" 10).

Forrest Tucker saw a bright future for *F Troop*:

> There's no stopping us now. We're good for five years at least. Maybe ten. In the first place, they pitted us against *Red Skelton* and *NBC's Tuesday Night Movies*. You should get clobbered in a spot like that, but we survived. Also, they put us on at nine o'clock, which knocked out a lot of our kid audience. But we still got plenty of them.
>
> The worst thing was that we were in black-and-white against two color shows. ... *F Troop* had uniforms, Indians, wigwams, trees, mountains, everything that cried out for color. But we had to go in black-and-white. Whoever made that decision has got to be stupid. And our [new 8:00 time slot] makes more sense. We're opposite *Daniel Boone* and a new show that nobody knows anything about, *Jericho*. And we're on earlier in the evening, to catch the kids We can't fail [Thomas "*F Troop* Will Go" 18].

In the fall of 1966, Warner Brothers replaced *F Troop* producer William T. Orr with Hy Averback, a specialist in "over-the-top satirical slapstick comedy." According to Averback, "*F Troop* is one of the very few shows on television today that can take full advantage of this classic comedy form. Most series are handicapped because their formats preclude the strictly physical joke—or because their performers aren't capable of handling this sort of humor."

Averback credited casting as the key, especially the slapstick comedy of Berry, Tucker and Storch, and noted, "Quite often our scripts carry this notation: 'Physical business to be worked out by cast and director.' This means they are working out a new way to fall from a horse, a different way to walk blindly into a flagpole, to fall down the well, or yet another way to step into a bear trap" (Averback "*F Troop* Will Go" 18).

The second season featured a shortened instrumental version of the theme along with an introduction illustrated by famed cartoonist Jack Davis. The new season's kick-off episode "The Singing Mountie" guest-starred Paul Lynde as Canadian Mountie Sergeant Ramsden, who falsely accuses Sergeant Agarn's identical French-Canadian cousin Pierre (also played by Storch) of being the infamous Burglar of Banff. The season also featured mayoral candidates from Agarn's hometown of Passaic, New Jersey, coming west to court Agarn's absentee vote to break a tie in the election, a Prussian balloonist operating at Fort Courage to the amazement of the Hekawis, a white-faced Transylvanian played by horror legend Vincent Price, and O'Rourke and Agarn needing to convince a 147-year-old Hekawi Chief not to invade Fort Courage.

F Troop was expecting big ratings, especially considering the fact that the show had Thursday night's edition of *Batman* as a lead-in. But *Batman* began falling out of favor with audiences; its ratings tumbled and the Thursday night edition fell to 37th in the ratings ("The Numbers Game" 59–60; "The Latest" 69; Spencer "TV's Vast" 54). In late March 1967, ABC announced that *F Troop*'s 65 episodes (34 in black and white, 31 in color) would be sold into syndication. Soon after, despite Forrest Tucker's prediction of another five years of *F Troop*, the network announced the show's cancellation ("Syndication for *F Troop*" 115).

The cancellation, dubbed the "*F Troop* Massacre" by *San Francisco Examiner* TV writer Dwight Newton, was not due to low ratings. In early March 1967, *F Troop* was averaging a 21.4 rating and was the 26th highest-rated show, and the fifth highest-rated ABC show—losing out only to *Bewitched*, *Lawrence Welk*, *The Big Valley* and a half-hour special, *Mini-Skirt Rebellion*. Newton suspected that *F Troop*'s cancellation was due in part to ABC's deteriorating relationship with Warner Brothers. ABC once aired many Warner Brothers series such as *Sugarfoot* (1957–1960), *77 Sunset Strip* (1958–1964), *Bourbon Street Beat* (1959–1960) and *Surfside 6* (1960–1962). But by 1967, ABC only aired two shows that were shot at Warner Brothers: *F Troop* and *The F.B.I.* And *The F.B.I.* was not produced by Warners, it was produced by Quinn Martin who simply rented space at Warners. Newton surmised it was "studio rejection" that killed *F Troop*. Newton stated that traditionally if a show had ratings above a 19.7 it was believed that show was "axe-proof."

Ken Berry was upset with the show's seemingly undeserved cancellation. "I don't dig it. Shows are supposed to die only because of bad ratings. Just check them." Berry later asked, "Do you have to be No. 1 to be renewed?" (Newton "The *F Troop* Massacre" 27).

The last episode of *F Troop* (April 6, 1967) was appropriately titled "Is This Fort Really Necessary?"

Undeterred by the cancellation, Tucker, Storch and Berry turned *F Troop* into a stage act and performed it in the Headliner Room at Harrah's Casino in Reno, Nevada, for three weeks in April 1967.

Berry went on to star in the *Andy Griffith Show* spin-off *Mayberry R.F.D.* Storch and Tucker continued to appear together on TV specials throughout the late 1960s and 1970s and starred in the CBS children's show *The Ghost Busters* (1975), in which they contended with classic monsters and villains. Storch and Tucker's characters, Kong and Spencer, were very similar to their characters on *F Troop*.

Works Cited

"ABC Cancels 10 Shows, Cuts 'Batman' in Half." *Indianapolis Star* [Indianapolis, Indiana], 4 Apr. 1967. p. 16.

"ABC Moves Up." *Broadcasting*, 22 Jan. 1968. p. 9.

"ABC OK's Production of QM's 'Invaders.'" *Broadcasting*, 26 Sept. 1966. p. 76.

"ABC Premiere Press Release 17 Aug. 1966." William Dozier Papers, American Heritage Center, University of Wyoming. Box 19, Press Releases dated 27 Feb. 1952 through 11 Feb. 1969.

"ABC 2d Season All but Set." *Broadcasting*, 7 Nov. 1966. p. 56.

"A.B.C. to Replace 6 of Its TV Shows with 5 New Ones." *The New York Times*, 14 Nov. 1968.

"The ABC West Is Going Thataway." *The World* [Coos Bay, Oregon], 3 Dec. 1965. p. 22.

"ABC-TV Affiliates Told of Firm Fall Lineup." *Broadcasting*, 1 Apr. 1963. p. 104.

"A.B.C.-TV Ax Falls on 'Tammy Grimes.'" *The New York Times*, 28 Sept. 1966.

"ABC-TV gives walking papers to 'Tammy Grimes.'" *Broadcasting*, 3 Oct. 1966. p. 58.

"ABC-TV Renews Show." *Broadcasting*, 2 Nov. 1964. p. 62.

"ABC-TV Reveals Fall Schedule." *Broadcasting*, 6 Apr. 1964. p. 59.

"ABC-TV Sets Its Fall Plans." *Broadcasting*, 3 Apr. 1967. p. 114.

"ABC-TV's Revamped Fall Schedule." *Broadcasting*, 22 Mar. 1971. p. 9.

"ABC's 'Second Season' hikes, ratings shares." *Broadcasting*, 17 Jan. 1966. p. 9.

"About KTUU-TV." www.ktuu.com/aboutus/. History.

"Adam West: Batman Unmasked." *E! True Hollywood Story*, E! Channel, 1999. Television.

"Adam West, Bruce Lee, and Van Williams Press Conference." *ABC News*. 1966.

Adams, Val. "A.B.C. Picks 16 New Fall TV Shows." *The New York Times*, 22 Mar. 1966.

Adams, Val. "A.B.C. Prepares Innovations for Its Venture into Baseball." *The New York Times*, 8 Apr. 1965.

Adams, Val. "ABC's Fall Schedule to Omit 19 Present Shows." *The New York Times*, 28 Feb. 1966. p. 53.

Adams, Val. "Bill Cosby of 'I Spy' Set." *The New York Times*, 23 May 1966. p. 68.

Adams, Val. "'Bonanza' Leads Nilsen TV Poll." *The New York Times*, 12 Oct. 1965.

Adams, Val. "C.B.S. Continuing 'The Lucy Show.'" *The New York Times*, 4 Mar. 1964.

Adams, Val. "C.B.S. Fall Slate Omits 14 Shows." *The New York Times*, 4 Feb. 1965.

Adams, Val. "C.B.S. 'Lucy Show' in Last Season; Comedienne to Devote More Time to Desilu in '64–65." *The New York Times*, 1 Feb. 1964.

Adams, Val. "C.B.S. Still Loves Lucy, May Bring Her Back in a New Weekly Comedy Show—Other Items." *The New York Times*, 21 Jan. 1962.

Adams, Val. "Friday's Friend on the Felony Squad." *The New York Times*, 17 Jul. 1966.

Adams, Val. "'Gunsmoke' Plans Hour-Long Shows." *The New York Times*, 19 Jan. 1961.

Adams, Val. "'I Spy' with Nergo Is Widely Booked." *The New York Times*, 10 Sept. 1965. p. 71.

Adams, Val. "People Just Keep Running on TV." *Shreveport Journal* [Shreveport, Louisiana], 11 Mar. 1966. p. 46. New York Times News Service.

Adams, Val. "76 Pilot Films Contend for TV Places." *The New York Times*, 23 Dec. 1964.

Advertisement for ABC Films. *Broadcasting*, 3 Apr. 1967. p. 41.

Advertisement for Christmas RCA Victor. 1952.

Advertisement for MGM Television. *Broadcasting*, 27 Oct. 1969. p. 3.

Advertisement for Monkees Audition. *Hollywood Reporter*; *Variety*, 8–10 Sept. 1965.

Advertisement for Paramount Television Sales, Inc. *Broadcasting*, 12 Feb. 1973. p. 18.

Advertisement for *Please Don't Eat the Daisies*. *Broadcasting*, 27 Mar. 1967. p. 117.

Advertisement for *The Big Valley*. *Broadcasting*, 17 Mar. 1969. pp. 62–63.

Advertisement for *The Hawk*. *The Charlotte Observer* [Charlotte, North Carolina], 15 Sept. 1966. p. 20.

"Affiliates Hear ABC-TV's Plans." *Broadcasting*, 22 Mar. 1965. p. 86.

"Agent 99 Gets Smart About Color in Clothes." *Chicago Tribune*, 13 Nov. 1966. p. 14.

Amory, Cleveland. "Review—The Girl from U.N.C.L.E." *TV Guide*. 17 Dec. 1966. p. 21.

Andersen, Viggo H. "Manhattan Interlude Andy Griffith." *Hartford Courant* [Hartford, Connecticut], 23 Oct. 1960. p. 120.

"Annual Chess Game Starts." *Broadcasting*, 20 Feb. 1967. p. 64.

"ARB Top-20 Programs." *Broadcasting*, 26 Sept. 1966. p. 68.

"ARB Top-20 Programs Oct. 2–8." *Broadcasting*, 17 Oct. 1966. p. 68.

"ARB Top-20 Programs Sept. 11–17." *Broadcasting*, 26 Sept. 1966. p. 68.

"ARB Top-20 Programs Sept. 18–24." *Broadcasting*, 3 Oct. 1966. p. 59.

"The Arbitrons Nov. 13–19." *Broadcasting*, 28 Nov. 1966. p. 84.

"ARB's Top-20 Programs Sept. 25–Oct. 1." *Broadcasting*, 10 Oct. 1966. p. 59.

Ashe, Isobel. "Gorgeous Girls Inhabit 'Petticoat Junction.'" *The Post-Crescent* [Appleton, Wisconsin], 27 Oct. 1963. p. 16.

Ashe, Isobel. "'Run, Buddy, Run' Has a Fast Track." *The Daily Intelligencer* [Doylestown, Pennsylvania], 20 Aug. 1966. p. 2.

Ashe, Isobel. "Stars, Writers Add New Touch to 'Landlord.'" *The Ogden Standard-Examiner* [Ogden, Utah], 20 Nov. 1966. p. 44.

Asherman, Allan. "Special Effects." *Castle of Frankenstein*, no. 11, 1967. pp. 8–11.

Ashman, Gene. "I Make The Monkees Clothes." *16 Magazine*, Oct. 1967.

"At 'Batman' Premiere It Will Be Exciting and Glamorous." *Austin American Statesman* [Austin, Texas], 23 Jul. 1966.

"Austin Aqua Pre-Festival Events." *Austin American Statesman* [Austin, Texas], 26 Jul. 1966.

"The Avengers—Jolly Good Show." *Playboy*, Mar. 1967.

Averback, Hy. "F Troop Will Go on for Years." *The Times Herald* [Port Huron, Michigan], 23 Jul. 1966. p. 18.

Bachor, Kenneth. "See the Trippy Look of the Long-Buried Original Star Trek Pilot." *Time*, 7 Sept. 2016, time.com/4480743/star-trek-pilot-gallery/.

Barker, Jeff. "Former 'Beverly Hillbilly' Says She Didn't Play the Political 'Game.'" *Associated Press News*, 18 Feb. 1985.

Barnes, Mike, and Duane Byrge. "Sid Caesar Dead: Comedy Titan Was 91." *The Hollywood Reporter*, 12 Feb. 2014, www.hollywoodreporter.com/news/sid-caesar-dead-comedy-titan-679817.

Barnum, Michael. "Van Williams: Green Hornet and Surfside 6 Star." *Classic Images*, 8 Jan. 2007.

Barrett, Rena. "The Chatterbox." *The Daily Reporter* [Dover, Delaware], 15 Jan. 1965. p. 3.

"Barry Sullivan to Take Road West." *Biddeford-Saco Journal* [Biddeford, Maine], 12 Mar. 1966. p. 12.

"Batchief Producer of Flick Hardly Newcomer to the Trade." *Austin American Statesman* [Austin, Texas], 26 Jul. 1966.

"Batman and Robin to Become Texans." *Austin American Statesman* [Austin, Texas], 29 Jul. 1966.

"Batman: Hoopla Over Visit Probably Record Here." *Austin American Statesman* [Austin, Texas], 31 Jul. 1966.

"Batman Meets Godzilla." William Dozier Papers, American Heritage Center, University of Wyoming, Box 45. Story Outlines Movies.

"Batman Roars into Arena at Shrine Circus Shows." *The Herald* [Jasper, Indiana], 2 Nov. 1977. p. 36.

"Batman's' TV Spot Going, to 'Second Hundred Years.'" *The New York Times*, 14 Feb. 1968.

Battelle, Phyllis. "Barbara Stanwyck Has No Stage Yen." *Cumberland Evening Times* [Cumberland, Maryland], 8 Jan. 1965. p. 4.

Baxter, Brian. "Burt Reynolds Obituary." *The Guardian*, 6 Sept. 2018.

"Bay Area Going 'Ape' Over Batman, Clubs Turn Latest Gimmick Into $$." *The Argus* [Fremont, California], 16 Feb. 1966.

"Bea Benaderet Succumbs." *The Times* [Shreveport, Louisiana], 14 Oct. 1968. p. 18. United Press International.

Beck, Calvin T. "Star Trek Forever: An Endorsement." *Castle of Frankenstein*, no. 11, 1967.

Beck, Marilyn. "Hollywood Close-Up TV Time." *Calgary Herald* [Calgary, Alberta, Canada], 5 Jan. 1968.

Bender, Jack. "Goodbye Iron Horse, Hello Avengers." *The Courier* [Waterloo, Iowa], 10 Nov. 1967. p. 36.

Berman, Ruth. "A Mid-Spring's Night's Dream, or, Journey to Backstage." *Plak-Tow*, Issue 8. 30 June 1968.

"Bill Mumy." *Television Academy Interviews*, Television Academy Foundation. 3 Sept. 2013. https://interviews.televisionacademy.com/interviews/bill-mumy.

Birnback, Lisa, et al. *The Official Preppy Handbook*. edited by Lisa Birnbach. Workman Publishing, New York. 1980.

"Bjo Trimble: The Woman Who Saved Star Trek." *Startrek.com*. 31 Aug. 2011, www.startrek.com/article/bjo-trimble-the-woman-who-saved-star-trek-part-1.

"Bob Weatherwax: The Elite Family of Hollywood Dog Trainers." *Weatherwax Trained Dogs*, 2019, http://weatherwaxtraineddogs.com/Weatherwax_Legacy.html.

Boley, Gary. "Old Batman Is Dying, Long Live The Green Hornet, Merchants Say." *The Greenville News* [Greenville, South Carolina], 11 Sept. 1966.

"The Boom in Color—TV Ads." *Broadcasting*, 5 Sept. 1966. p. 40.

Boutenko, Irene A., and Kirill Emilevich Razlogov. "Recent Social Trends in Russia 1960–1995." *McGill-Queen's Press*, 22 Jul. 1997. p. 237.

Bowman, Harry. "NBC 'Sneaks' Three New Series." *The Dallas Morning News* [Dallas, Texas], 9 Sept. 1966.

Brioux, Bill. *Truth and Rumors: The Reality Behind TV's Most Famous Myths*. Praeger, 2008. p. 42.

British Movietone. "Monkees Arrival and Press Conference." *British Movietone*, 3 Jul. 1967.

"The British (Programs) Are Coming." *Broadcasting*, 31 Jan. 1966. p. 23.

"Broadcast Advertising and Children." *Hearings*

Before the Subcommittee on Communications of the Committee on Interstate and Foreign Commerce House of Representatives Ninety-Fourth Congress First Session, 1975. p. 99.

Broeske, Pat H. "Man Behind the Mask." *Los Angeles Times*, 14 May 1989.

"Bronislau Kaper Scores 'FBI.'" *San Antonio Express* [San Antonio, Texas], 8 Aug. 1965. p. 101.

Bronson, Fred. *The Billboard Book of Number One Hits*. Billboard Books, 1988.

Brooks, Marla. *The American Family on Television: A Chronology of 121 Shows, 1948–2004*. McFarland, 2005.

Brooks, Tim, and Earle Marsh. *The Complete Directory to Prime Time Network TV Shows: 1946–Present*. Ballantine Books, 1979.

Brown, James A. "Robert Wood." *The Museum of Broadcast Communications*, N.D. http://www.museum.tv/archives/etv/W/htmlW/woodrobert/woodrobert.htm.

Brown, Les. "CBS Will Drop 'Gunsmoke' and Introduce Nine Series for the Fall." *The New York Times*, 30 Apr. 1975.

Browning, Ricou. "Show Director Explains How He Teaches 'Flipper.'" *Fond Du Lac Commonwealth Reporter* [Fond Du Lac, Wisconsin], 18 Jul. 1966. p. 11.

Buchwald, Art. "The Appointment of Lassie." *The Decatur Herald* [Decatur, Illinois], 9 May 1967. p. 6.

Buck, Jerry. "'Star Trek' Engenders Cult in U.S., England." *Youngstown Vindicator* [Youngstown, Ohio], 14 Mar. 1972.

Buck, Jerry. "There's No Death Knell for Bonanza with 14 Years' Worth of Color Reruns." *The Robesonian* [Lumberton, North Carolina], 24 Dec. 1972. p. 6A. Associated Press.

"Buffy-Drugs." *The York Dispatch* [York, Pennsylvania], 14 Sept. 1976. p. 1. Associated Press.

"Bumper Crop of Network Pilots." *Broadcasting*, 29 Nov. 1965. pp. 27–32.

"Burnett Gains in Rescheduling." *Broadcasting*, 5 Feb. 1973. p. 44.

Busch, Noel F. "America's Oomph Girl." *Life*, 24 Jul. 1939. p. 64.

"Business Briefly...." *Broadcasting*, 18 Jan. 1964. p. 52.

Bustin, John. "Stars Reluctantly End Austin Visit." *Austin American Statesman* [Austin, Texas], 1 Aug. 1966.

Bustin, John. "This Is the Day 'Batman' Invades City for Premiere." *Austin American Statesman* [Austin, Texas], 30 Jul. 1966.

Byers, Bill. "Burt Reynolds, Star of 'Hawk' Indian With Gags." *North Adams Transcript* [North Adams, Massachusetts], 6 Aug. 1966. p. 17.

"Cable's Story." *NCTA (Internet & Television Association)*, www.ncta.com/cables-story.

"CAMPAIGN NOTES; Actress in Pennsylvania to Run for Congress." *The New York Times*, 2 Feb. 1984.

"Can 'Peyton Place' Find Happiness Off-Network?" *Broadcasting*, 26 May 1969. p. 58.

Canby, Vincent. "TV: 'Avengers' Is Unveiled by A.B.C." *The New York Times*, 29 Mar. 1966. p. 83.

"Carradine to Star in 'Shane.'" *Reno Gazette-Journal* [Reno, Nevada], 13 May 1966. p. 36.

Carthew, Anthony. "All Honor Honor." *The New York Times*, 1 Mar. 1964.

"CBS, ABC Race into the Season." *Broadcasting*, 11 Sept. 1967. p. 45.

"CBS Doesn't Plan to Rest on Its Laurels." *Broadcasting*, 5 May 1975. p. 26.

"CBS Edges Ahead in 8th Nielson." *Broadcasting*, 30 Jan. 1967. p. 60.

"CBS Leads Latest Nielsen." *Broadcasting*, 13 Feb. 1967. p. 66.

"CBS Reshuffle, Emphasis on Youth." *Broadcasting*, 27 Feb. 1967. pp. 25–26.

"CBS Still High on Thursday." *Broadcasting*, 5 Oct. 1964. p. 9.

"C.B.S. TO PRESENT TV COLOR TO PUBLIC; Demonstrations Open Tuesday at Old Tiffany Building, Day R.C.A. Suit Will Begin Adapter Needed for Black, White R.C.A. Suit to Open." *The New York Times*, 9 Nov. 1950.

"CBS Ups Shares." *Broadcasting*, 15 Jan. 1973. p. 48.

"CBS-TV Acquires 'Sons' for '65–66 Season." *Broadcasting*, 8 Feb. 1965. p. 75.

"CBS-TV Adds More Color." *Broadcasting*, 31 May 1965. p. 59.

"CBS-TV Affiliates Strike a Harmonious Chord." *Broadcasting*, 11 May 1970. p. 38.

"Celebrating 40 Years Since Trek's 1st Convention." *Star Trek*. 20 Jan. 2012. https://www.startrek.com/article/celebrating-40-years-since-treks-1st-convention.

"Changes in Cast." *Honolulu Star-Bulletin* [Honolulu, Hawaii], 13 Apr. 1966. p. 24.

"Chart: Number of Program Hours by Month & Broadcast Source (Studio, Film, Outside)." *Electronics Magazine*, Mar. 1940.

Cheshire, Godfrey, III. "The Avengers—Sputtering Spies: Steed and Peel Lack Appeal." *Variety*, 17 Aug. 1998.

"Chicago: Opener for a Big Film Sales This Year." *Broadcasting*, 30 Mar. 1970. p. 81.

Coffee, Jerry. "Exciting New Features Planned for 'The Fugitive.'" *Fort Worth Star-Telegram* [Fort Worth, Texas], 16 Apr. 1966. p. 22.

Coffey, Jerry. "TV Movie Night Boasts Full Run of First-Timers." *Fort Worth Star-Telegram* [Fort Worth, Texas], 14 Aug. 1965. p. 17.

Coffey, Jerry. "TV to Take 'Road West.'" *Fort Worth Star-Telegram* [Fort Worth, Texas], 13 Jul. 1966. p. 10.

Cole, Stephen. "Francks for the Memories." *CBC News*, 12 Dec. 2007. web.archive.org/web/20120109024936/https://www.cbc.ca/arts/film/francks.html.

"Color Added to I Dream of Jeannie." *Biddeford-Saco Journal* [Biddeford, Maine], 12 Mar. 1966. p. 9.

"Color on All the Networks: Well on Way to 100%." *Broadcasting*, 3 Jan. 1966. pp. 76–78.

"Color Premiere." *Lancaster New Era* [Lancaster, Pennsylvania], 28 Jul. 1966. p. 48.

"Color TV Demand Still Outruns Supply." *Business Week*, McGraw-Hill. 4 June 1966. p. 44.

Comerford, Sherna, and Davra Michele Lanstam, editors. "Spockanalia." *Garlic Press Publications #1*. 1 Sept. 1967. Cushing Memorial Library and Archives, Texas A&M University Libraries.

Conner, Jim. "Naming the Space Shuttle." Memo to President Ford, 7 Sept. 1976. The memorandum recommended naming the first space shuttle "Enterprise" as a response to appeals by supporters of the television show "Star Trek." https://history.state.gov/historicaldocuments/frus1969-76ve03/d133.

Conrad Prange. "Comes the Dawn." *Statesman Journal* [Salem, Oregon], 9 Jul. 1958. p. 4.

"Converting TV Set to UHF Not Costly." *Chicago Daily News*, 4 Jan. 1966.

"'Coronet Blue' Series to Go Before Cameras Soon." *The San Bernardino County Sun* [San Bernardino, California], 3 May 1965. p. 25.

Correll, John T. "The Real Twelve O'Clock High." *Air Force Magazine*, Jan. 2011. Vol. 94. No. 1.

"'The Cowboy's Cowboy' Now Riding Iron Horse." *The Pocono Record* [Stroudsburg, Pennsylvania], 19 Sept. 1966. p. 12.

Crawford, Linda. "Break Says Big Valley's Ranch Is Actually Run by Barbara's Sons." *Chicago Tribune*, 19 Feb. 1967. p. 184.

Cray, Douglas W. "ABC, TV's Question Mark, Pins Much on New Season." *The New York Times*, 21 Sept. 1969.

"The Creation's Eddie Phillips on Rushmore, Little Richard, and Being Copied by Oasis." *Bandcamp Daily*, 21 Mar. 2017, daily.bandcamp.com/2017/03/21/the-creation-making-time-interview/.

"The Critics Review the Season's First Previews." *Broadcasting*, 12 Sept. 1966. pp. 36–37.

"The Critics' View, Part 2." *Broadcasting*, 27 Sept. 1965. p. 69.

"Critics Views of Hits, Misses." *Broadcasting*, 19 Sept. 1966. pp. 58–63.

Crosby, Joan. "Rounders Kicks It Off." *The Pittsburgh Press*, 6 Sept. 1966. p. 63.

Crosby, Joan. "Tube Moves Boobs." *The Desert Sun* [Palm Springs, California], 30 May 1969. p. 14.

Crowther, Bosley. "'Dragnet' Has Debut at Victoria Theatre." *The New York Times*, 21 Aug. 1954.

"Curses!!! 'Batman' Meets His Master: Television's Ratings." *The New York Times*, 26 Jan. 1968.

"'Daisies' Gobbled Up." *The Daily Item* [Sunbury, Pennsylvania], 28 May 1965. p. 25.

Daley, Frank. "Canadian Entertainers Lack Desire to Succeed—Little." *The Ottawa Journal* [Ottawa, Ontario, Canada], 8 Jan. 1966. p. 39.

Dalton, John. "The Most Influential Television Episodes by Decade: The 1960s. The Beverly Hillbillies." *Television Academy Foundation: The Interviews*, Academy of Television Arts & Sciences, 25 Jan. 2018, interviews.televisionacademy.com/news/the-most-influential-television-episodes-by-decade-1960s. *The Interview Project News*.

Danson, Tom E. "CBS Guide 15 Years Ago Is Now Producer-Director." *The San Bernardino County Sun* [San Bernardino, California], 9 Dec. 1952. p. 23.

Danson, Tom E. "Show Has Cows, but No Corn." *News-Pilot* [San Pedro, California], 28 May 1952. p. 5.

David Dortort. "Television Academy Interviews." *Television Academy Foundation*, 8 Aug. 2002. https://interviews.televisionacademy.com/interviews/david-dortort.

"David McCallum—Bob Vaughn: The Truth About Their Feud." *TV and Movie Screen*, Jan. 1966. Vol. 13, no. 2. p. 24.

Davis, Clifford. "Diana May Quit the Avengers." *Daily Mirror*, 25 Jan. 1966. p. 3.

"Davy Crockett Elected." *The New York Times*, 19 May 1955.

De Roos, Robert. "Daisies Grow Better with Pepper." *TV Guide*, 29 Jan.–4 Feb. 1966. p. 17.

Delugach, Al, and David Crook. "$1.5-Billion Turner Deal for MGM Reported Near." *Los Angeles Times*, 6 Aug. 1985.

Dern, Marian. "Will Time Tunnel Stand the Test of Time." *Valley Times* [North Hollywood, California], 1 Oct. 1966. p. 15.

"Dick York, 63, Actor Who Was Husband In TV's 'Bewitched.'" *The New York Times*, 22 Feb. 1992. p. 10. Associated Press.

DiLego, Carmen. "The Cable TV View." *The Gazette* [Cedar Rapids, Iowa], 2 Mar. 1965. p. 19.

Diltz, Henry. "Cheers and Jeers." *TV Guide*, 1987.

"Distribution of Receivers Geographically and by Type of Establishment. Data Received by Questionnaires Circulated to the Audience." *Electronics Magazine*, Mar. 1940.

Doan, Richard. "Between Channels." *The Salem News* [Salem, Ohio], 14 Mar. 1966. p. 3.

Doan, Richard K. "Familiar Faces Next Season on NBC." *The Kokomo Morning Times* [Kokomo, Indiana], 18 Feb. 1965. p. 18.

Doan, Richard K. "Silent Comedy." *The Marion Star* [Marion, Ohio], 8 Dec. 1964. p. 5.

Doan, Richard K. "The Week That Was." *The Gazette* [Cedar Rapids, Iowa], 14 Jan. 1965. p. 14.

"Donna Sings, Dances Into Screen Test." *Muncie Evening Press* [Muncie, Indiana], 1 Jan. 1966. p. 23.

Dozier, William. "Dozier to Bruce Lee." 17 Feb. 1965. William Dozier Papers, American Heritage Center, University of Wyoming, Box 6. Correspondence.

Dozier, William. "Dozier to Trendle." 16 Nov. 1966. William Dozier Papers, American Heritage Center, University of Wyoming, Box 7. Correspondence.

Dozier, William. "Dozier to Trendle." 3 Jan. 1967. George W. Trendle Papers, Detroit Public Library, Burton Historical Collection, Box 38, Folder 5. Correspondence.

Dozier, William. "Dozier to Van Williams." 7 Mar.

1967. William Dozier Papers, American Heritage Center, University of Wyoming, Box 7. Correspondence.

"Drat! Adam West Zapped by Keaton for Batman Job." *The Spokesman-Review Spokane Chronicle* [Spokane, Washington], 28 May 1989. p. 35. Associated Press.

Du Brow, Rick. "Aging Parents of Monroes Leave New TV Show Early." *Lancaster Eagle-Gazette* [Lancaster, Pennsylvania], 10 Sept. 1966. p. 14.

Du Brow, Rick. "Batman Is Not as Hip as Advertised." *Tucson Citizen* [Tucson, Arizona], 13 Jan. 1966. p. 29.

Du Brow, Rick. "'Coronet Blue' Tagged 'Pseudo.'" *The Hanford Sentinel* [Hanford, California], 30 May 1967. p. 7.

Du Brow, Rick. "Spy Series Slump in New TV Season." *Honolulu Star-Bulletin* [Honolulu, Hawaii], 27 Jul. 1967. p. 36.

Du Brow, Rick. "Television in Review." *The Town Talk* [Alexandria, Louisiana], 8 Dec. 1964. p. 22.

Du Brow, Rick. 'Television Review." *New Castle News* [New Castle, Pennsylvania], 3 Sept. 1964. p. 29. *United Press International.*

Du Brow, Rick. "'Mission: Impossible' Beats CIA." *The Capital Times* [Madison, Wisconsin], 19 Sept. 1966. p. 7.

Dutton, Walt. "Hawk: Flying High." *Los Angeles Times*, 18 Sept. 1966. p. 566.

"Ears Today...." *The Guardian* [United Kingdom], 12 June 1976.

"Ed McMahon on Ed Ames Tomahawk Gag on *The Tonight Show Starring Johnny Carson*." *Television of American Television*, 15 Aug. 2002. https://interviews.televisionacademy.com/interviews/ed-mcmahon.

Eden, Barbara. "Episode 78." Interviewed by Johnny Carson. *The Tonight Show Starring Johnny Carson*, 5 Feb. 1981.

Eden, Barbara, and Wendy Leigh. *Jeannie Out of the Bottle*. Biography and Autobiography, 2011.

Edwards, Owen. "How 260 Tons of Thanksgiving Leftovers—Gave Birth to an Industry." *Smithsonian.com*, Smithsonian Institution, 1 Dec. 2004. www.smithsonianmag.com/history/tray-bon-96872641/.

"800,000 Video Sets Given as '48 Output." *The New York Times*, 5 Aug. 1948.

Eisner, Joel. *The Official Batman Batbook*. Contemporary Books, Inc., 1986. pp. 10, 11, 31, 114, 163.

"Emma Gives the Suit Cat Appeal." *Daily Mirror*, 15 Jul. 1967. pp. 12, 13.

"End of an Institution." *Broadcasting*, 4 Mar. 1964. p. 31.

"The Enterprise Needs Your Help." Flyer, Unknown. 1976.

Entertainment Weekly: The Ultimate Guide to Star Trek. Time, Inc. Books, 2016.

"Expensive Rerun." *Broadcasting*, 2 Sept. 1968. p. 5.

"The Extent of the Service: Number of Program Hours by Months and Percentages of Origination from Studio Film, and Outside Pick Up." *Electronics Magazine*, Mar. 1940.

"Fall Preview 1966–1967 Shows." *TV Guide*, 10–16 Sept. 1966.

"Fall Schedule Announced by CBS." *Broadcasting*, 27 Feb. 1967. p. 26.

"Family Pet." Advertisement by Telesynd for Timmy & Lassie. *Broadcasting*, 2 Jan. 1967. p. 16.

Fanning, Win. "'4th Network' Held Distinct Possibility." *Pittsburgh Post-Gazette*, 15 Apr. 1965. p. 39.

Fanning, Win. "Nets' Fall Line-Ups Include 32 Debuts." *Pittsburgh Post-Gazette*, 30 Jan. 1964. p. 39.

Farber, Stephen. "The Coloring of Classic TV Shows." *San Francisco Examiner*, 21 June 1987. p. 255.

"Federal Communications Commission Eighteenth Annual Report." *Federal Communications Commission*, 1953.

"Federal Communications Commission Fifteenth Annual Report." *Federal Communications Commission*, 1949.

"Felony Squad' Rates High Among Viewers." *Standard-Speaker* [Hazleton, Pennsylvania], 15 Dec. 1966. p. 31. Associated Press.

"Few Cheers for New Shows." *Broadcasting*, 3 Oct. 1966. p. 58.

"Few of TV's Virgin Shows Look Like Hits." *Broadcasting*, 25 Sept. 1967. p. 71.

"50 Years on National Television: The Lawrence Welk Show." *Lawrence Welk Show Musical Family News 1*, no. 1: n.d., 1–5. *Germans from Russia Heritage Collection. North Dakota State University Archives.*

"First Returns in New Season." *Broadcasting*, 20 Sept. 1965. pp. 20–32.

Fisher, Ginny. "Little Big Horn Results Confirmed—Custer Loses." *Sunday Journal and Star* [Lincoln, Nebraska], 26 Nov. 1967. p. 68.

"Flipper Flips." *Delaware County Daily Times* [Chester, Pennsylvania], 17 Sept. 1966. p. 11A.

"Flipper Will Take to Air; He'll Get a Playmate, Too." *Chicago Tribune*, 17 Jul. 1966.

"Former 'Hillbilly' Loses." *The New York Times*, 8 Nov. 1984. Associated Press.

"Four in a Row for NBC." *Broadcasting*, 27 Oct. 1986. p. 96.

Fredricks, Jay. "New Shows Bringing Up the Rear." *Sunday Gazette-Mail* [Charleston, West Virginia]. 23 Oct. 1966. p. 76.

"The Freebies Go to Color." *Broadcasting*, 3 Jan. 1966. p. 90.

Freeman, Alex. "'Animals' Returning for 4-Week Tour." *The Hartford Courant* [Hartford, Connecticut], p. 8.

Freeman, Donald. "Fugitive Gains Backers as David Janssen Flees." *Fort Worth-Telegram* [Fort Worth, Texas], 30 Oct. 1963. p. 21.

Freeman, Donald. "Monroes Star Finds Show Big Hit in Native England." *The Press Democrat* [Santa Rosa, California], 1 Jan. 1967. p. 35. *Copley News Service.*

"Fugitive Captured, Grabs Top Rating." *The Tennessean* [Nashville, Tennessee], 10 Sept. 1967. p. 107.

"The Fugitive Finally Stops Running." *Chicago Tribune*, 30 Jul. 1967. p. 14.

Gardella, Kay. "Dems to Join Ike on ABC." *Daily News* [New York, New York]. p. 442.

Gardella, Kay. "Network Control of Shows Okay with TV Producer." *Daily News* [New York, New York], 19 Mar. 1966. p. 11.

Gardella, Kay. "TV Goes Out of This World." *Daily News* [New York, New York], 18 Sept. 1966. p. 46S.

Gardella, Kay. "TV Hoods Will Give Buddy Hatful of Pain for Laughs." *Daily News* [New York, New York], 12 Aug. 1966. p. 31.

Gardner, Paul. "A.C.L.U. Lifts Bars to Pay-Television." *The New York Times*, 8 Mar. 1965.

Gates, Anita. "Steven Hill, Who Starred on 'Law & Order' and 'Mission: Impossible,' Dies at 94." *The New York Times*, 23 Aug. 2016. p. 8. sec. B.

Gent, George. "'All in the Family' Takes First Place in Nielsen Ratings." *The New York Times*, 25 May 1971.

Gent, George. "'Bonanza' Faces Showdown at 9." *Broadcasting*, 14 Feb. 1967. p. 87.

Gent, George. "Campy Batman Flying High on TV." *The New York Times*, 15 Jan. 1965.

Gent, George. "Coonskin Parker Fights Kentucky." *The New York Times*, 5 Mar. 1966.

Gent, George. "'Gunsmoke's Doc Hails a Reversal." *The New York Times*, 11 Mar. 1967.

Gent, George. "In Order to Bet Better ABC's 'Batman' Must Get Worse." *The Decatur Review* [Decatur, Illinois], 24 Jan. 1966. p. 6. *The New York Times*.

Gent, George. "'Man from U.N.C.L.E.' Goes to Spy Limbo." *Arizona Republic* [Phoenix, Arizona], 18 Nov. 1967. p. 119.

Gent, George. "Marshal Dillon Gunned Down in C.B.S. Fall Line-up." *The New York Times*, 23 Feb. 1967.

Gent, George. "N.B.C. to Cancel 11 Shows in Fall." *The New York Times*, 28 Feb. 1967.

Gent, George. "Pravada Meets 'Batman' Head On." *The New York Times*, 30 Apr. 1966.

Gent, George. "TV Show to Take Secret to Grave." *The New York Times*, 15 Jul. 1967.

Gent, George. "Welk Show Among 11 Programs Dropped from A.B.C. Fall Slate." *The New York Times*, 20 Mar. 1971.

"Get Smart Comedy Series Is Renewed."*Biddeford-Saco Journal* [Biddeford, Maine], 12 Mar. 1966. p. 12.

"'Get Smart' Star Barbara Feldon Likes Show's Mood." *The Charlotte Observer* [Charlotte, North Carolina], 11 Jul. 1969. p. 16.

"Get Smart Switches Networks, Nights." *Broadcasting*, 24. Feb. 1969. p. 64.

"'Get Smart's' Don Adams Yearns to Be a Villain." *The Daily Record* [Long Branch, New Jersey], 29 Aug. 1966. p. 13.

"G.I's in Vietnam Get a TV Station." *The New York Times*, 26. Sept. 1966. p. 6.

Goodman, Jessica. "Aquatic Tale Led Hendersonville Man to Co-Write 'Flipper.'" *Times-News* [Hendersonville, North Carolina], 30 Nov. 2010.

Gorog, William F. "Naming the Space Shuttle." *Memo to President Ford*. 3 Sept. 1976. Ford Library, Presidential Handwriting File, Subject File, Box 34, Outer Space. No classification marking. Ford initiated his approval. The September 7 document reporting the reactions of White House staff is attached to the memorandum. The decision in favor of "Enterprise" was announced on September 9, one day after the meeting with NASA officials. https://history.state.gov/historicaldocuments/frus1969-76ve03/d133.

Gould, Jack. "'Batman': Nothing (Pow!) for Everyone." *The Courier-Journal* [Louisville, Kentucky], 23 Jan. 1966. p. 93. *New York Times News Service*.

Gould, Jack. "C.B.S. Line-Up for Fall Omits Once-Prized Country Comedies." *The New York Times*, 17 Mar. 1971.

Gould, Jack. "Freshness in Old Military Tale." *The New York Times*, 26 Sept. 1964.

Gould, Jack. "Television in Review: N.B.C. Color; Tournament of Roses Parade Is Sent Over 22-City Network." *The New York Times*, 4 Jan. 1954.

Gould, Jack. "TV: A Homespun Trio." *The New York Times*, 13 Oct. 1966.

Gould, Jack. "TV: Crisis in Middle East Is Given Full Coverage." *The New York Times*, 30 May 1967.

Gould, Jack. "TV: N.B.C. Tarzan, He Urbane and Sophisticated." *The New York Times*, 9 Sept. 1966.

Gould, Jack. "TV: Patricia Harty, an Appealing 'Occasional Wife.'" *The New York Times*, 14 Sept. 1966. p. 95.

Gould, Jack. "TV: 'Rat Patrol' Takes on Rommel." *The New York Times*, 20 Sept. 1966. p. 93.

Gould, Jack. "TV: Spies, Space and the Stagestruck." *The New York Times*, 16 Sept. 1966.

Gould, Jack. "TV: Welk, a Surprise Hit; Band Leader's Show Follows Old Formula." *The New York Times*, 10 Feb. 1956.

Gould, Jack. "TV: Why a 'Bonanza'?" *The New York Times*, 21 Jul. 1965. p. 75.

Gould, Jack. "Why 'Kwai' KO'd 'Bonanza' and Ed Sullivan." *The New York Times*, 2 Oct. 1966. p. 135.

Gowran, Clay. "31 Million Sold on Andy Griffith." *Chicago Tribune*, 27 Nov. 1966. p. 24.

Graham, David A. "Picture of the Day: A Vulcan, and a 'Star Trek' Actress." *The Atlantic*, 4 Apr. 2012.

Graham, Glen. "TV People Coming Out with Three Dimensions." *Petaluma Argus-Courier* [Petaluma, California], 6 Jan. 1965. p. 6.

Graham, Sheila. "Nothing but Money Pouring In for Pyllis Diller." *Des Moines Tribune* [Des Moines, Iowa], 16 Feb. 1966. p. 28. *North American Newspaper Alliance*.

Grams, Jr., Martin. *The Time Tunnel: A History of the Television Series*. Bear Manor, 2013.

Grant, Hank. "TV News Beat." *The Daily Reporter* [Dover, Delaware], 12 Oct. 1964. p. 6.

Grant, Hank. "TV News Beat." *Hartford Courant* [Hartford, Connecticut], 30 Aug. 1964. p. 129.

"Green Hornet Series Budget: Twentieth Century Fox." 25 May 1966. William Dozier Papers, American Heritage Center, University of Wyoming, Box 2. Budgets.

"Green Hornet William Dozier promo." *ABC Affiliate Network Convention*, Summer 1966.

Greenwood, Peter. "In the Original 'Star Trek' Pilot, It Wasn't Easy Being Green." *MeTV*, 21 Oct. 2016, www.metv.com/stories/star-trek-original-pilot-green-slave-girl-wrong-color.

Gross, Ben. "Around the Dials." 9 Jan. 1965. *Daily News* [New York, New York]. p. 12.

Grossman, Gary H. *Saturday Morning TV*. Dell Publishing, 1981. pp. 8–21.

Gysel, Dean. "Ben Alexander Sounds Like Policeman Even Over Phone." *The Corpus Christi Caller-Times* [Corpus Christi, Texas], 19 Feb. 1967. p. 67. *Chicago Daily News*.

Gysel, Dean. "Garrison's Gorillas Get Top Banana." *The Salt Lake Tribune* [Salt Lake City, Utah], 8 Jul. 1967. p. 21. *Chicago Daily News*.

Gysel, Dean. "Ratings KO Berle, Others." *The Charlotte News*, 5 Nov. 1966. p. 40. *Chicago Daily News*.

Hall, Isabelle. "Group Files Test Against TV Violence." *The Tennessean* [Nashville, Tennessee], 13 Nov. 1970. p. 15.

Handsaker, Gene. "Van Dyke Show Triumphs Again; Pathos Dramatized Emmy Awards." *The Journal Times* [Racine, Wisconsin], 23 May 1966. p. 20.

Hart, Ron. "Batman Concert Facing and Inquiry." *The New York Times*, 8 Jul. 1966.

Hartmetz, Alijean. "New 'Star Trek' Plan Reflects Symbiosis of TV and Movies." *The New York Times*, 2 Nov. 1986.

"'Hawk' Reynolds Still Flying." *Press and Sun-Bulletin* [Binghamton, New York], 26 Nov. 1966. p. 34.

"Hawk' to 'Lassiter.'" *Indianapolis News*, 15 Nov. 1966. p. 7.

Hayde, Michael J. *My Name's Friday: The Unauthorized but True Story of Dragnet and the Films of Jack Webb*. Langara College, 1 June 2001. p. 48.

"'Hazel' and 'Sons' Added to 1965–1966 Color Season." *The Parsons Sun* [Parsons, Kansas], 4 June 1965. p. 13.

Heffernan, Harold. "Fired for Beautician Demand, Pat Repents, Is Back in Series." *The Times-Tribune* [Scranton, Pennsylvania]. 22 Jan. 1965. p. 14.

Heiman, Roberta. "Shrine Circus Is a Smash: Batman Is a Flop." *Evansville Press Metro* [Evansville, Indiana], 25 Nov. 1977.

Heisner, John. "Bea Benaderet Remembered." *Democrat and Chronicle* [Rochester, New York], 15 Oct. 1968. p. 48.

Heisner, John. "More Honest Than Batman." *Democrat and Chronicle* [Rochester, New York], 29 Jan. 1967. p. 3.

Heisner, John. "A Talk with Van Williams: He's an Old 'Green Hornet' Fan." *Democrat and Chronicle* [Rochester, New York], 27 Nov. 1966.

Henderson, Hubert D. *Supply and Demand*. Harcourt, Brace and Company, 1922.

Henry, Clayton. "Who's on Top—The Monkees or the Beatles?" *Capital Journal* [Salem, Oregon], 2 Dec. 1966.

"Her 'Witch Twitch' Is a Far Cry from Salem's." *The Des Moines Register* [Des Moines, Iowa], 27 Dec. 1964. p. 42.

Herman, Edna Mae. "Petticoat Junction Star Likes Activity." *Daily Independent* [Kannapolis, North Carolina], 13 Aug. 1967. p. 32.

Herman, Karen. "Russel Johnson." Television Academy Foundation, *Television Academy Interviews*, 8 Feb. 2004. https://interviews.televisionacademy.com/interviews/russell-johnson.

Hinson, Sandra. "'Monroes' Position 'Iffy.'" *The Orlando Sentinel* [Orlando, Florida], 9 Mar. 1967. p. 16.

Hinson, Sandra. "TV Lures Jean Arthur Out of Retirement." *The Orlando Sentinel* [Orlando, Florida], 15 Jul. 1966. p. 18.

"History to Be Used on Bonanza." *Daily Reporter* [Dover, Ohio], 19 Sept. 1959. p. 16.

Hobson, Dick. "The War in the Desert." *TV Guide*, 3 Dec. 1966. pp. 14–18.

Hogan, Jr., Martin. "What Makes 'The Monroes' Tick?" *The Cincinnati Enquirer* [Cincinnati, Ohio], 21 Feb. 1967. p. 6.

"'Hogan's Heroes' Readies for Fall." *Standard-Speaker* [Hazleton, Pennsylvania], 29 May 1965. p. 21.

"Holy Shea Stadium! The Batman's Saved." *The New York Times*, 25 June 1966.

Hopper, Hedda. "Actress Loses Job Over Hairdresser." *Los Angeles Times*, 14 Jan. 1965. p. 10. *Chicago Tribune–N.Y. News Syndicate Inc.*

Hopper, Hedda. "Levant 'Can't Afford' a Nervous Breakdown." *Hartford Courant* [Hartford, Connecticut], p. 28.

Hopper, Hedda. "Zimbalist Will Star in TV Series About FBI." *Chicago Tribune*, 18 Mar. 1965. p. 31.

Horn, John. "Rating Shows on Quality." *The Marion Star* [Marion, Ohio], 31 Mar. 1967. p. 10.

"House-Cleaning Time Comes to Television." *Fort Lauderdale News* [Fort Lauderdale, Florida], 1 Jan. 1968. p. 6.

"How Critics Assess New Shows—Part 3." *Broadcasting*, 26 Sept. 1966. p. 74.

"How Critics Described Some New Shows." *The New York Times*, 9 Oct. 1960. p. 17.

"How Critics Rate New Shows." *Broadcasting*, 16 Jan. 1967. pp. 50–51.

"How Gutsy of Him to Live Like That!" *Independent Star-News* [Pasadena, California], 26 June 1966. p. 64.

Howard, Jennifer. "Barbara Eden." Television Academy Foundation, *Television Academy Interviews*. 25 Apr. 2000. https://interviews.televisionacademy.com/interviews/barbara-eden. Bob Hope Collection.

Humphrey, Hal. "Dragnet Returns to Fill Social Need." *Los Angeles Times*, 8 Dec. 1966.
Humphrey, Hal. "'Fugitive' Pauses for a Rest Stop." *Los Angeles Times*, 10 Jul. 1967. p. 18.
Humphrey, Hal. "Gary May Be No.1 Rat in 'Rat Patrol.'" *The Marion Star* [Marion, Ohio], 22 Feb. 1967. p. 12. *Television and Radio*.
Humphrey, Hal. "The Low Men on TV's Totem Pole." *Los Angeles Times*, 1 Jan. 1965. p. 69.
Humphrey, Hal. "Monroes Go to a Dog to Get Higher Ratings." *The Miami Herald* [Miami, Florida], 1 Nov. 1966. p. 19.
Humphrey, Hal. "A New Race of Men, the 'Audiments,' Play TV's Numbers Game." *Arizona Republic* [Phoenix, Arizona], 27 Sept. 1967. p. 16. *Los Angeles Times Service*.
Humphrey, Hal. "Out of the Air: Timmy Leaves, but Lassie Lives On." *The Evening Review* [East Liverpool, Ohio], 18 May 1964. p. 15.
Humphrey, Hal. "Twin Faces of J. Edgar Hoover." *Los Angeles Times*, 14 Jul. 1965. p. 59.
Humphrey, Hal. "The Year They Went to Color." *Los Angeles Times*, Aug. 1965.
Humphrey, Hal. 'F Troop' Looks Like a Winner." *Oakland Tribune* [Oakland, California], 13 Sept. 1965. p. 18.
"I Spy Duo's Style Blends into Comedy." *The Daily Oklahoman* [Oklahoma City, Oklahoma], 19 Aug. 1966. p. 28. Chicago Tribune Service.
"Income of Families and Persons in the United States: 1948." *United States Census Bureau*, 14 Feb. 1950. Report Number P60-06. Revised: 4 Sept. 2018.
"Industry: Faded Rainbow." *Time*, 22 Oct. 1956.
Inman, Julia. "Keith Puts Starch into 'Family Affair.'" *Indianapolis Star*, 20 Sept. 1966. p. 15.
Inman, Julia. "New Violence Study May End 18-Year-Old Video Standoff." *The Indianapolis Star*, 18 Apr. 1969. p. 25.
Javna, John. *The Best of TV Sitcoms: The Critics' Choice: Burns and Allen to the Cosby Show, The Munsters to Mary Tyler Moore*. Harmony Books, 1988. p. 60.
"Jethro Bodine's Beverly Hillbillies Mansion & Casino." http://www.jethroscasino.com.
Johnson, Erskine. "Johnathan Harris Is Having a Ball." *Star-Gazette* [Elmira, New York], 19 Feb. 1966. p. 28.
Johnson, Erskine. "Roy Thinnes Coming Jan. 10 on The Invaders." *North Adams Transcript* [North Adams, Massachusetts], 31 Dec. 1966.
Johnson, Erskine. "'Runaway' Production Still a Problem." *The Akron Beacon Journal* [Akron, Ohio], 7 Dec. 1963. p. 4. Newspaper Enterprise Association (NEA).
Johnson, Erskine. "U.N.C.L.E.S.'s Man Has Political Eye." *Abilene Reporter-News* [Abilene, Texas], 3 June 1966. p. 21.
Johnson, James E. "'Batman' World Premiere at the Paramount." *Austin History Center: Austin Public Library*, Super 8 film. Published 20 Jul. 2017. Recorded 20 Jul. 1966.
Jones, Paul. "Hawk Is Above the Average but Will Vanish in Shakeup." *The Atlanta Constitution*, 20 Oct. 1966.
Jones, Paul. "It's a New Look for The Monroes." *The Atlanta Constitution*. 15 Feb. 1967. p. 10.
Jones, Paul. "New Batman Show Is So Bad, It's Good." *The Atlanta Constitution* [Atlanta, Georgia], 12 Jan. 1966. p. 10.
Jones, Paul. "TV's 'Iron Horse' Called a Sleeper." *The Atlanta Constitution* [Atlanta, Georgia], 26 Dec. 1966. p. 70.
Jordan, Turner. "Politicos, Election Special with Share Video Spot Here." *The Birmingham News* [Birmingham, Alabama], 28 Mar. 1963. p. 52.
"June Lockhart Is Still Lost in Space." *The Ithaca Journal* [Ithaca, New York], 13 Aug. 1967. Associated Press.
"Justice Will Out on Batman, Green Hornet." *TV Channels*, 21–27 Aug. 1966.
Keating, Micheline. "Smoke Will Linger as Matt Dillon Rides Off." *Tucson Citizen* [Tucson, Arizona], 6 May 1975. p. 13.
"Keep America Beautiful Poster Presentation." *The White House Historical Association*, 3 Sept. 2018.
"Keeping Lucy's Show a Secret." *The Des Moines Register* [Des Moines, Iowa], 11 Mar. 1962. p. 145.
Kesler, Susan E. *The Wild, Wild West: The Series*. Arnett Press, 1988.
Kimball, Trevor. "Batman TV Show: 1972 PSA, Yvonne Craig Last Batgirl." *Canceled TV Shows—TV Series Finale*, 19 Dec. 2008, tvseriesfinale.com/tv-show/batman-the-unusual-story-of-yvonne-craigs-final-appearance-as-batgirl/.
King, Susan. "Robert Clary a Survivor in Life and Entertainment." *Los Angeles Times*, 24 Mar. 2013.
Kleiner, Dick. "Bonanza Faces Up to Family Death." *Times Leader* [Wilkes-Barre, Pennsylvania], 13 Aug. 1972. p. 15B. Newspaper Enterprise Association (NEA).
Kleiner, Dick. "Hollywood Making Reappraisal." *Star-Phoenix* [Saskatoon, Saskatchewan, Canada], 10 Jul. 1968. p. 30.
Kleiner, Dick. "Series 'Purrfect' to T.H.E. Cat." *Orlando Evening Star* [Orlando, Florida], 22 Dec. 1966. p. 6.
Kleiner, Dick. "Star Shirley Booth Also Television Fan." *The Daily Telegram* [Eau Claire, Wisconsin], 12 Feb. 1965. p. 8.
Knight, Arthur, and Pamela Roberson. "Soundtrack Available: Essays on Film and Popular Music." *Duke University Press*, 3 Dec. 2001.
Kreiling, Ernie. "Actors, Sets Aid 'Monroes' Honesty." *Salina Journal* [Salina, Kansas], 18 Nov. 1966. p. 6.
Kristen, Marta, and Mark Goddard, panelists. Q&A. Moderated by Thomas Shubilla. *Monster Bash Conference*, 19 Oct. 2019. Marriott, Pittsburgh/North, Cranberry Township-Mars, PA.
"A Lanky, Long-haired Lass Is Leaving Miss Peel Behind." *San Francisco Examiner and Chronicle: Datebook*, 24 Dec. 1967.
Lardine, Bob. "A Show Made for a Fin." *Daily News* [New York, New York], 11 Oct. 1964. p. 8.

Larsen, Douglas. "Color Television Hangs in Doubt." *The Plain Speaker* [Hazelton, Pennsylvania]. 24 Sept. 1953. p. 14.

Larson, John. "The Monkees—Masters of Madness." *Nashua Telegraph*. [Nashua, New Hampshire], 1 Oct. 1966. p. 3.

LaSalle, Mick. "'Avengers' Is a Crime." *San Francisco Chronicle*, retrieved September 25, 2009. 15 Aug. 1998.

"Latest from the Sheet." *Broadcasting*, 26 Sept. 1966. pp. 66–69.

Laurent, Lawrence. "Ackerman Has Most Screen Gems TV Shows." *Arizona Republic* [Phoenix, Arizona], 5 Nov. 1965. *Washington Post Service*.

Laurent, Lawrence. "Can 'Monroes' Survive in the Low Nielsens?" *The Courier-Journal* [Louisville, Kentucky], 8 Sept. 1966. p. 28. *Los Angeles Times–Washington Post Service*.

Laurent, Lawrence. "'Coronet Blue' a Good Show." *The Des Moines Register* [Des Moines, Iowa], 31 May 1967. p. 10. *The Washington Post*.

Le Zotte, Jennifer. "The Invention of Vintage Clothing." *The Smithsonian Magazine*, 8 Feb. 2017.

Lee, Bruce. "Lee to William Dozier." 21 Feb. 1965. William Dozier Papers, American Heritage Center, University of Wyoming, Box 6. Correspondence.

Leonard, Vince. "Because of 'Batman' Life's Rosier for Bill Dozier." *The Pittsburgh Press*, 11 Jan. 1967. p. 82.

Leonard, Vince. "Don Knotts Leaving Griffith Show." *The Pittsburgh Press*, 7 May 1965. p. 54.

Leonard, Vince. "'Gleeps! It's Batman' (A Smash)." *The Pittsburgh Press*, 13 Jan. 1966. p. 50.

Leonard, Vince. "Time Tunnel Goes to the Well." *The Pittsburgh Press*, 3 Oct. 1966. p. 52.

Leonard, Vince. "What's Out for Children." *The Pittsburgh Press*, 25 Jan. 1967. p. 78.

Lew, Richard Warren. "New Girl in Town." *TV Guide*, 3 Dec. 1966. pp. 25–26.

Lewis, Jerry D. "The General Died at Dusk." *TV Guide*, 15–21 May 1965. p. 24.

Lewis, Richard Warren. "It Shouldn't Happen to an Ape Man." *TV Guide*, 26 Nov. 1966. pp. 23–25.

Liebenson, Donald. "How The Fugitive's Heart-Pumping Finale Changed TV Forever." *Vanity Fair*, 29 Aug. 2017.

"Life' Begins Its Second Run." *Broadcasting*, 18 Mar. 1968. p. 56.

LoBrutto, Vincent. "TV in the USA: A History of Icons, Idols, and Ideas." *ABC-CLIO*, 4 Jan. 2018. p. 315.

Lowry, Cynthia. "ABC's Wednesday Lineup Suffers from Low Ratings." *The Shreveport Journal* [Shreveport, Louisiana], 21 Oct. 1971. p. 4. Associated Press.

Lowry, Cynthia. "Ben Playing Cop Again with the Felony Squad." *Press and Sun-Bulletin*, [Binghamton, New York], p. 8-C. Associated Press.

Lowry, Cynthia. "'Bewitched' Explains Blackout." *Tucson Daily Citizen* [Tucson, Arizona], 11 Nov. 1966. p. 17. Associated Press.

Lowry, Cynthia. "'Gunsmoke' Back in the Saddle Again." *Lancaster New Era* [Lancaster, Pennsylvania], 8 Mar. 1967. Associated Press.

Lowry, Cynthia. "Jericho Looks Like Leftovers." *The Ithaca Journal* [Ithaca, New York], 16 Sept. 1966. p. 9. Associated Press.

Lowry, Cynthia. "Job Jeopardy Is Theme for FBI series." *Morning News* [Wilmington, Delaware], 18 Aug. 1965. p. 21. Associated Press.

Lowry, Cynthia. "Loss of Lucille Ball Is Painful for CBS." *Wilkes-Barre Times Leader* [Wilkes-Barre, Pennsylvania], p. 12. Associated Press.

Lowry, Cynthia. "Mature Programs Dying as TV Woos Young Folks." *Northwest Magazine Sunday*, weekly insert of *Oregonian* [Portland, Oregon], 19 Mar. 1967. p. 24. Associated Press.

Lowry, Cynthia. "'Mission: Impossible' Long on Time, Short on Plot." *Lancaster New Era* [Lancaster, Pennsylvania], 19 Sept. 1966. p. 19. Associated Press.

Lowry, Cynthia. "Nabors Puts on Really Good Show." *The Daily Advertiser* [Lafayette, Louisiana], 14 Oct. 1966. p. 11. Associated Press.

Lowry, Cynthia. "New TV Season, with 34 Shows, Not Likely to Cause Much Excitement." *Paducah Sun* [Paducah, Kentucky], 1 Sept. 1966. p. 22. Associated Press.

Lowry, Cynthia. "Next Year's 'Lucy Show' May Be Without Vivian." *The South Bend Tribune* [South Bend, Indiana], 12 June 1965. p. 18. Associated Press.

Lowry, Cynthia. "Old-Timers Survive '66–67 Video Year." *The Ogden Standard-Examiner* [Ogden, Utah], 6 May 1967. p. 7. *TV Revue and Prevue*. Associated Press.

Lowry, Cynthia. "Oscar Awards Took Too Long, as Usual." *The Sandusky Register* [Sandusky, Ohio]. 10 Apr. 1962. p. 18. Associated Press.

Lowry, Cynthia. "Season of TV Repeat Shows Nears." *The Capital Times* [Madison, Wisconsin]. 16 Apr. 1962. p. 29. Associated Press.

Lowry, Cynthia. "Short-Lived Series: 'Run, Buddy, Run,' Face Quick Halt." *Cumberland Evening Times* [Cumberland, Maryland], 15 Nov. 1966. p. 5. Associated Press.

Lowry, Cynthia. "Some Old TV Shows Will Be Greatly Revised." *Rushville Republican* [Rushville, Indiana], 1 Sept. 1965. p. 9. Associated Press.

Lowry, Cynthia. "Tammy Grimes Show Being Dumped." Associated Press/*Ocala Star Banner* [Ocala, Florida], 29 Sept. 1966. p. 16. Associated Press.

Lowry, Cynthia. "The Television Year in Review." *Sunday News* [Lancaster, Pennsylvania], 1 Jan. 1967. p. 8. Associated Press.

Maays, Stan. "'Road West, Canceled, but Jan Isn't Worried." *The Ithaca Journal* [Ithaca, New York], 8 Jul. 1967. p. 35.

Maksian, George. "'Star Trek' Will Become Movie Scheduled for Release in 1976." *Miami Herald*, 4 Mar. 1975. *New York News Service*.

"The Man Behind TV's Batman." *Telescope with Fletcher Markle*, 1966. CBC Archives.

"Man Who Never Was Filming in Berlin." *Sunday News* [Lancaster, Pennsylvania], 10 Jul. 1966.

"Many New Color Programs on CBS." *San Antonio Express*, 10 Sept. 1965. p. 35.

Mark, Norman. "Witch World an Adult Favorite Too." *The Parsons Sun* [Parsons, Kansas], 15 Oct. 1971. p. 13. *Chicago Daily News*.

"Marlo Thomas." *Television Academy Interviews*, Television Academy Foundation. 26 Mar. 2003. interviews.televisionacademy.com/interviews/marlo-thomas. Interview by Karen Herman.

Maslin, Janet. "'The Avengers': Shh! They're Trying Not to Be Noticed." *The New York Times*, 15 Aug. 1998.

Massingill, Randi L. "Total Control: The Monkees Michael Nesmith Story." *FLEXquarters.com Limited*, Jul. 1997. p. 59.

Masters, Kim. "Turner Won't Colorize 'Kane.'" *Washington Post*. 15 Feb. 1989.

McDaniel, David. *The Dagger Affair*. Ace Books, Inc. New York, 1964. p. 89.

McMahon, Ed, and David Fisher. *When Television Was Young: The Inside Story with Memories by Legends of the Small Screen*. T. Nelson, 2007. p. 25.

Mead, Mimi. "Burt (Hawk) Reynolds Haunted by Indians." *The Evening Sun* [Baltimore, Maryland], 20 Oct. 1966. p. 45.

Mead, Mimi. "Het Taps Universal Mind." *The Morning Call* [Patterson, New Jersey], 3 Aug. 1966. p. 26.

Mead, Mimi. "Judy Looking for Different Role After Love on a Rooftop Folds." *Calgary Herald* [Calgary, Alberta, Canada], 17 Mar. 1967. p. 70.

Mead, Mimi. "Lost in Space Can Be Rough, Says June." *Star-Gazette* [Elmira, New York], 16 Jan. 1966. p. 10B. *TV Time*.

Meech, Shirley. "Con Report." *Plak-Tow*, Issue 9. 19 Aug. 1968.

Meech, Shirley. "Encouragement to Write Letters." *Plak-Tow*, Issue 3. 29 Jan. 1968.

Meech, Shirley. "From the Editor." *Plak-Tow*, Issue 1. 13 Dec. 1967.

Meech, Shirley. "FunCon Planning." *Plak-Tow*, Issue 4. 21 Feb. 1968.

Meeker, Ward. "Noted Guitarist Neil LeVang Passes." *Vintage Guitar® Magazine*, 30 Jan. 2015, www.vintageguitar.com/20094/noted-guitarist-neil-levang-passes/.

Messina, Matt. "ABC to Scrap Stevens Show." *Daily News* [New York, New York], 15 Feb. 1966. p. 50.

Messina, Matt. "Action, No Gimmicks for Cool Cat Loggia." *Daily News* [New York, New York], 14 Aug. 1966. p. 256.

Messina, Matt. "River Kwai Film for TV." *Daily News* [New York, New York], 28 Mar. 1966. p. 61.

"Metro Signs Tammy Grimes." *The New York Times*, 3 Mar. 1966.

"Mets-Sox Deliver NBC Another Win." *Broadcasting*, 3 Nov. 1986. p. 54.

"Millions at ABC-TV." *Broadcasting*, 18 Mar. 1963. p. 9.

Misurell, Ed. "One of TV's Most Appealing Tenants." *The Cumberland News* [Cumberland, Maryland], 1 Oct. 1966. p. 13.

Mitchel, Dennie. "Latest Film News." *Castle of Frankenstein*, edited by Bhob Stewart. Feb. 1967. p. 42.

Mohbat, Joseph E. "TV Programs Found Fostering Violence." *Arizona Daily Star* [Tucson, Arizona], 25 Sept. 1969. p. 38.

"The Monkees Chart History." *Billboard*, 2019. www.billboard.com/music/the-monkees/chart-history/hot-100/.

Montgomery, Paul L. "'Star Trekkie' Show Devotion." *Lakeland Ledger* [Lakeland, Florida], 11 Mar. 1973. *New York Times*.

Moore, Sir Roger. *Bond on Bond: Reflections on 50 Years of James Bond Movies*. Rowman & Littlefield, 17 Sept. 2013.

"More Ratings on the Second Season." *Broadcasting*, 6 Feb. 1967. p. 69.

Morris, Bruce B. *Prime Time Network Serials*. McFarland, 1997.

Mosby, Aline. "Stagebrush Hero Speaks for TV." *The Baytown Sun* [Baytown, Texas], 1 Jan. 1955. p. 6.

"Movies Are Viewers' Favorites." *Broadcasting*, 31 Oct. 1966. p. 74.

"Moving Up to a Black Beauty." *The New York Times*, 19 June 1966.

"MPC Syndicates Specials and 'That Girl' Series." *Broadcasting*, 22 Mar. 1971. p. 77.

"MTV vs. The Monkees?" *Monkee Business Fanzine*, Issue #43. Dec. 1987.

Nachman, Gerald. "Right Here on Our Stage Tonight!: Ed Sullivan's America." University of California Press, 5 Nov. 2009.

"Name in Syndication, Finds Top-Market Buyers." *Broadcasting*, 15 Mar. 1971. p. 40.

"NASA-Wide Survey and Evaluation of Historic Facilities in the Context of the U.S. Space Shuttle Program: Roll-Up Report." NASA, Feb. 2008, revised Jul. 2008.

"NBC Claims It's Leading in Weekly Ratings Race." *Broadcasting*, 10 Oct. 1966. p. 10.

"NBC Claims Sweep, Not Counting Bridge." *Broadcasting*, 3 Oct. 1966. p. 10.

"NBC Fills Final Hole for 1967–1968." *Broadcasting*, 6 Mar. 1967. p. 52.

"NBC Goes 2 for 2 in Primetime." *Broadcasting*, 13 Oct. 1986. p. 63.

"N.B.C. Schedule Next Season Eyes a 'Girl from U.N.C.L.E.'" *The New York Times*, 18 Feb. 1966. p. 67.

"NBC Takes 6 of 7 in NTI rankings." *Broadcasting*, 7 Oct. 1967. p. 58.

"NBC-TV Aims for the Young." *Broadcasting*, 4 Mar. 1968. p. 28.

"Network Program Gears Grind." *Broadcasting*, 17 Feb. 1966. p. 76.

"Networks Start Race for Sales." *Broadcasting*, 26 Feb. 1968. p. 23.

"New ABC Programs Will Be British Imports." *Broadcasting*, 31 Jan. 1966. p. 24.

"New 'Daisies' Time." *Fort Lauderdale News* [Fort Lauderdale, Florida], 1 Jul. 1966. p. 60.

"'New' Monkees Features Own Music, Stage Show." *The Tampa Tribune* [Tampa, Florida], 19 Jul. 1969. p. 38.

"The New NBC-TV Weekly Series." *Broadcasting*, 28 Sept. 1959.

"New-Season TV Casualties Light." *Broadcasting*, 20 Nov. 1967. p. 56.

"New Shows Get No Brass Ring." *Broadcasting*, 7 Oct. 1967. p. 60.

"The New Shows: Souped Up, Slicked Up, Colored Up." *Television Magazine*, June 1966. p. 37.

"A New Space Craft Is Named Enterprise." *The New York Times*, 9 Sept. 1976. Associated Press.

Newton, Dwight. "Comedy in a War Prison." *San Francisco Examiner*, 3 Jul. 1965. p. 38.

Newton, Dwight. "The F Troop Massacre." *San Francisco Examiner*, 4 Apr. 1967. p. 27.

Newton, Dwight. "Rat Patrol Fooled 'Em." *San Francisco Examiner*, 16 Oct. 1966. p. 37.

Newton, Dwight. "Requiem for Storekeeper." *San Francisco Examiner*, 8 Nov. 1967. p. 45.

Nichols, Nichelle. *Beyond Uhura: Star Trek and Other Memories*. G.P. Putnam's Sons, 1994, p. 188.

"The Nielsens." *Broadcasting*, 14 Nov. 1966.

"1967 TV Set Buyers Guide." *TV Guide*, 17 Sept. 1966.

"1966-TV Drenched in Color." *The Cincinnati Enquirer*, 7 Sept. 1966.

"Now She's Started a SHOP WAR Too!" *The People*, 23 Jan. 1966.

"Numbers Game, Part One." *Broadcasting*, 19 Sept. 1966. p. 59.

"The Numbers Game, Part One." *Broadcasting*, 19 Sept. 1966. pp. 58–64.

O'Brian, Jack. "The Voice of Broadway." *Wilkes-Barre Times Leader, The Evening News, Wilkes-Barre Record* [Wilkes-Barre, Pennsylvania], p. 5.

"Old Friends Return on New TV Programs." *Longview News-Journal* [Longview, Texas], 2 Aug. 1965. p. 11.

"On Television." *The New York Times*, 22 Mar. 1956. p. 71.

"On the Networks This Spring." *Broadcasting*, 5 Apr. 1965. p. 119.

"Opinions Vary on TV Shows." *Broadcasting*, 18 Sept. 1967. p. 78C.

Orme, Frank. "The Television Code." *The Quarterly of Film Radio and Television*, vol. 6, no. 4, 1952, pp. 404–413. JSTOR, www.jstor.org/stable/1209951.

"The Other Two Put, Take and Shuffle." *Broadcasting*, 10 Apr. 1972. p. 27.

Owen, Roslyn. "Dressed to Kill." *TV Week* [Australia], 8 Jan. 1966.

Pack, Harvery. "NBC Signs Britain's 'The Saint.'" *The Journal News* [White Plains, New York], 10 Jan. 1966. p. 22.

Page, Don. "Dick Sargent Joins the Comedy Caldron on ABC's Bewitched." *Los Angeles Times*, 31 Aug. 1969. p. 309.

Page, Don. "Star Trek Is Costly Sci Fi Epic." *Los Angeles Times*, 21 Sept. 1966.

Pareles, Jon. "MTV Makes Changes to Stop Rating Slump." *The New York Times*, 12 June 1986.

Parsons, Louella O. "Tiff Between Jill St. John, Producer Rose Nipped in Bud." *Albuquerque Journal* [Albuquerque, New Mexico], 26 Feb. 1963. p. 10.

"Paul Henning." *Television Academy Interviews*, Television Academy Foundation, 12 Sept. 2012, https://interviews.televisionacademy.com/interviews/paul-henning#interview-clipsdaniels.

"Peek at Ratings—ABC View." *Broadcasting*, 12 Sept. 1966. p. 35.

Penton, Edgar. "Iron Horse Chugs Along TV Rails." *Fort Lauderdale News* [Fort Lauderdale, Florida], 1 Aug. 1967. p. 18.

Penton, Edgar. "Jean Arthur Returns as an 'Unorthodox' Lady Lawyer on TV." *Green Bay Press-Gazette* [Green Bay, Wisconsin], 31 Jul. 1966. p. 61.

"Perry Como Signs for 19th Season." *Biddeford-Saco Journal* [Biddeford, Maine], 12 Mar. 1966. p. 12.

Peterson, Bettelou. "'Batman' and the Quality Fad's First." *Detroit Free Press*, 31 Aug. 1966. p. 14.

Peterson, Bettelou. "Jean Arthur Agrees: Ugh!" *Detroit Free Press*, 15 Oct. 1966. p. 10.

Peterson, Bettelou. "Viewers Protest Cancellation of 'Monroes.'" *Detroit Free Press*, 17 Mar. 1967.

Petira of R' Shlomo (Steven) Hill Z'L." *The Yeshiva World*, 23 Aug. 2016.

"'Petticoat Junction' Like My Home." *The Daily Herald* [Provo, Utah], 2 Dec. 1963. p. 3.

"'Peyton Place'—A Show 'for All the Family.'" *Clovis News-Journal* [Clovis, New Mexico], 6 Sept. 1964. p. 14. *United Press International*.

Pfeiffer, Lee. "Making the Baddies Cry 'U.N.C.L.E." *Cinema Retro*, Apr./May 2019. Issue #44. p. 27.

"Plautus May Have Five Shows on CBS-TV." *Broadcasting*, 25 Jan. 1965. p. 74.

Poletika, Nicole. "Philo T. Farnsworth: The Father of Television." *Indiana Historical Bureau*, Indiana Historical Bureau, 14 Feb. 2014, www.in.gov/history/4230.htm.

"Post-Mortem on an 'Organized Disaster.'" *TV Guide*, 31 Dec. 1966. pp. 15–19.

Potts, Kimberly. *The Way We All Became The Brady Bunch*. Grand Central Publishing. Dec. 2019.

Powers, Forrest. "'Gunsmoke' Shift Saves 'Iron Horse.'" *The Minneapolis Star* [Minneapolis, Minnesota], 6 Apr. 1967. p. 89.

"Preview for Reviewers 'Batman' Greeted by Raves." *Austin American Statesman* [Austin, Texas], 22 Jul. 1966.

Prideaux, Tom. "The Whole County Goes Supermad." *LIFE*, 11 Mar. 1966. pp. 19–23.

"Prize Catch: Viacom advertisement for The Beverly Hillbillies." *Broadcasting*, 12 Feb. 1972. p. 1.

"Producing It's About Time." *Television Academy Interviews*, Television Academy Foundation. 17

Sept. 1997. https://interviews.televisionacademy.com/interviews/sherwood-schwartz.

"Public May Lose Interest. Will 'Batman' Fad Fizzle?" *The Charlotte News*, 29 Jan. 1966. p. 31. Associated Press.

"QM to Make ABC Movies." *Broadcasting*, 22 Jan. 1968. p. 48.

Quiroga, Alex. "There's Secord Side to This Color Coin." *Los Angeles Times*, 20 Oct. 1963. p. 567.

Raddatz, Leslie. "Banker with a Sting." *TV Guide*, 29 Oct. 1966.

"Rat Patrol' Rates High Lucille Ball Show Has Shaky Feeling." *Fort Lauderdale News*, 1 Oct. 1966. p. 48. United Press International [UPI].

"The Ratings: A Photo Finish." *Broadcasting*, 17 Oct. 1966. pp. 66–69.

"Red Viewers Dig Popular Video Shows." *Chicago Tribune*, 27 Aug. 1967. p. 10.

Reiter, Ed. "How Do Shore Psychiatrists Rate 007, Batman?" *Asbury Park Press* [Asbury Park, New Jersey], 30 Jan. 1966.

"The Relaxed One Is Back—One More Time." *Valley Times* [North Hollywood, California], 24 Nov. 1967. p. 57.

"'Renovation' Slated for The Pruitts." *Sunday News* [Lancaster, Pennsylvania], 1 Jan. 1967. p. 8.

"Richard Long's Hunch Pays Off in 'Big Valley.'" *The Daily Item* [Sunbury Pennsylvania], 14 Jan. 1966. p. 20.

Rittereiser, Susan. "Holy Superlatives, Batman! The Movie." Austin Public Library, 9 Aug. 2017, library.austintexas.gov/blog-entry/holy-superlatives-batman-movie-398478.

"Road West Aims for Human Values."*Biddeford-Saco Journal* [Biddeford, Maine], 1 Oct. 1966. p. 12.

Robert Vaughn interview. Interview conducted by Ron Simon. *Academy of Television Arts & Sciences*. New York, New York. 18 May 2007. https://interviews.televisionacademy.com/interviews/robert-vaughn.

Roberts, Nancy B. "Star Trek Fans Attend Convention." *The Portsmouth Herald* [Portsmouth, New Hampshire], 28 Mar. 1972.

Roddenberry, Gene. "Publicity Release from Gene Roddenberry." *Star Trek Enterprises*, 1968.

Roddenberry, Gene. *Star Trek Pitch*. 11 Mar. 1964.

Roddenberry, Gene. "Star Trek—TVs Newest." *TV Week*, 25 June 1966.

"Role Plugs Women, Negros." *Ebony Magazine*, Jan. 1967.

Rosenstein, Elyse, and Steven Rosenstein. "The End of the Five Year Mission...." *1976 Star Trek Lives! Program Book*, 1976.

Royal, Don. "An Out-Of-This-World Interplanetary Cliffhanger." *The Levittown Times* [Levittown, Pennsylvania], 7 Aug. 1965. p. 9.

Royal, Don. "Time Bothered Him, So He Abolished It." *Green Bay Press-Gazette* [Green Bay, Wisconsin], 23 Oct. 1966. p. 13.

"Run, Jack Run on Monday Theater Show." *The Press Democrat* [Santa Rosa, California], 19 Jul. 1970. p. 66.

"Russians Call Batman 'Idealized F.B.I. Agent.'" *The New York Times*, 12 Sept. 1966. *United Press International*.

Sanders, Charles H. "Moline's Ken Berry, Star of TV's F Troop, Returns Home." *The Rock Island Argus* [Rock Island, Illinois], 19 Feb. 1966. p. 19.

Santo, Avi. "'Batman' Versus 'The Green Hornet': The Merchandisable TV Text and the Paradox of Licensing in the Classical Network Era." *Cinema Journal*, vol. 49, no. 2, winter 2010, pp. 63–85. JSTOR, www.jstor.org/stable/25619771.

Sawyer, James. "A Collector's Trek #5: Lincoln Enterprises Merchandise." *Star Trek*, 13 Apr. 2019, www.startrek.com/article/a-collectors-trek-5-lincoln-enterprises-merchandise.

Scheuer, Steven H. "TV Key Mailbag." *The Shreveport Journal* [Shreveport, Louisiana], 14 May 1971. p. 48.

Schneider Comes on Strong at CBS-TV." *Broadcasting*, 15 Mar. 1965. pp. 60–61.

Scott, Vernon. "ABCs Batman So Square He's TVs Greatest Hippy" *The Arizona Republic* [Phoenix, Arizona], 16 Jan. 1966. p. 60. United Press International [UPI].

Scott, Vernon. "'Gomer Pyle' Finished Year 2nd in Ratings." *The Odessa American* [Odessa, Texas], 13 Sept. 1966. p. 21. United Press International [UPI].

Scott, Vernon. "Jack Benny Is Happy About His New Show." *Muncie Evening Press* [Muncie, Indiana], 22 Nov. 1966. p. 14. United Press International [UPI].

Scott, Vernon. "Smart Sayings Enter Dialogue." *Arizona Republic* [Phoenix, Arizona], 27 Feb. 1966. p. 32. United Press International [UPI].

"Second Season Is 'Sickening.'" *Broadcasting*, 6 Feb. 1967. p. 64.

"Second Season Loses to Movies." *Broadcasting*, 23 Jan. 1967. p. 60.

"Second Season to Exceed First?" *Broadcasting*, 24 Oct. 1966. p. 56.

Sedgeman, Judy. "Fan of Star Trek Works at Getting TV Show Returned." *St. Petersburg Times* [St. Petersburg, Florida], 29 May 1972.

Seitz, William. *The Responsive Eye*. Museum of Modern Art MOMA, 27 Jan. 1965.

"7 Perry Como Specials on Way." *Press and Sun-Bulletin* [Binghamton, New York], 18 Sept. 1966. p. 49.

The '72 Star Trek Con." *The Monster Times*. Sci-fi Super TV Special Issue 1, 1973.

Shaba, Theodore. "Lion of Daktari' Roams Soviet's Televisionland." *The New York Times*, 25 June 1973. p. 16.

Sharbutt, Jay. "Network to Broadcast Last Bonanza of Old Westerns." *Anderson Daily Bulletin* [Anderson, Indiana], 16 Jan. 1973. p. 14. Associated Press.

Sherman, Robert. "Batman to the Rescue in Shea Stadium Caper." *The New York Times*, 26 June 1966.

"Sherwood Schwartz" *Television Academy Interviews*, Television Academy Foundation. 17 Sept.

1997. interviews.televisionacademy.com/interviews/sherwood-schwartz. *Bob Hope Comedy Collection.*

Shippy, Dick. "Overhaul at ABC!" *The Akron Beacon Journal* [Akron, Ohio], 3 Mar. 1969. p. 19.

"Shock Appeal of Some TV Shows Noted." *Honolulu Star-Bulletin* [Honolulu, Hawaii],1 Feb. 1967. p. 44.

Shull, Richard K. "Converse Applauded for 'Coronet Blue.'" *The Record* [Hackensack, New Jersey], 1 Aug. 1967. p. 8.

Shull, Richard K. "Dragnet Is Back with Teen-Age LSD Shocker." *Indianapolis News*, 13 Jan. 1967.

Shull, Richard K. "Fading 'Bonanza Near End of Trail." *The Baltimore Sun*, 10 Dec. 1972.

Shull, Richard K. "Shull's Mailbag: The Following." *Indianapolis Times*, 3 Sept. 1969. p. 19.

Shult, Doug. "Cult Fans, Reruns Give 'Star Trek' and Out of This World Popularity." *The Milwaukee Journal*, 3 Jul. 1972. Los Angeles Times Service.

Silden, I. "The Andy Griffith Show Based on Everyday Humor." *The Brattleboro Reformer* [Brattleboro, Vermont], 8 Oct. 1960. p. 12.

"A Slot on the Network May Be Hard to Get." *Broadcasting*, 19 Jul. 1965. p. 29.

Smith, Cecil. "Jim Nabors Finished with Gomer." *Toledo Blade* [Toledo, Ohio], 31 Jan. 1969. p. 16.

Smith, Kyle. "How Maxwell Smart and His Shoe-Phone Changed TV." *Wall Street Journal Online*, 21 Mar. 2008, web.archive.org/web/20081123105044/http://online.wsj.com/public/article_print/SB120606471734053849.html.

"Some Network O&O's Fill Prime-Time Holes." *Broadcasting*, 29 Mar. 1971.

"Specials Confuse Ratings in Second Week." *Broadcasting*, 18 Sept. 1967. p. 77.

Spencer, Walter. "TV's Vast Grey Belt." *Television*, Aug. 1967. pp. 54–55. XXIV No. 8.

Stanley, John. "The Day Hoover Pinched Public Enemy Number One." *San Francisco Examiner*, p. 255.

"Star Trek and Space Science Convention." Flyer. Oakland Municipal Auditorium, 7–8 Aug. 1976.

"Star Trek Lives!" *The Monster Times*, Jul. 1975. pp. 4–6.

"Star Trek Lives!" Star Trek Convention program. 21–23 Jan. 1972.

Star Trek Promoters Out to Make a Fast Buck." *The New York Times*, 22 Feb. 1976.

"Star Trek' Real Science Fiction; 'It's About Time' Seen as Success." *Standard Speaker* [Hazleton, Pennsylvania], 19 Sept. 1966. Newspaper Enterprise Association (NEA).

"Status of Color Television." *RCA Radio Age*, 1947.

Steinberg, Cobbett. *TV Facts*, Facts on File, Inc., 1985. pp. 142, 144.

Stellwag, Ted. "This Is One Cat Who Is Really Cool." *Courier-Post* [Camden, New Jersey], 17 Sept. 1966. p. 59.

Stephen, Andy. "Andy Stephen Looks at TV." *Times Colonist* [Victoria, British Columbia, Canada], 26 Oct. 1966. p. 37.

Stern, Harold. "Andy Given Sheriff's Role for Fall Comedy." *Lansing State Journal* [Lansing, Michigan], 23 Aug. 1960. p. 16.

Stone, Judy. "From Ingenue to Other Woman to Occasional Wife." *The New York Times*, 16 Oct. 1966.

"Strong Start." *Broadcasting*, 26 May 1969. p. 3.

"Sullivan Changes His Mind About Television." *Clarion-Ledger* [Jackson, Mississippi], 18 Dec. 1966. p. 77.

Supreme Court of New York, Appellate Division, First Department. *David Gordon and David Yarnell, Plaintiffs-Respondents V. Screen Gems, Inc., Et Al., Defendants-Appellants, And Kellogg Company, Defendant. Records & Briefs New York State Appellate Division.* Vol. 178. 18 Sept. 1970.

"Suspicion Another Coronet Blue; M.A.N.T.I.S Another Science Fiction Fantasy." *The Courier* [Waterloo, Iowa], 11 Sept. 1994. p. 144. Associated Press.

"Syndication for F Troop." *Broadcasting*, 3 Apr. 1967. p. 115.

"Syndicators Have Pitches Ready." *Broadcasting*, 27 Mar. 1967. pp. 99–100. Special Report: Television Syndication '67.

Takei, George. Interview by Howard Stern. *The Howard Stern Show*. 9 Mar. 2015.

Takiff, Johnathan. "Made-for-TV Monkees Are Being Made a Hot Item Again." *Chicago Tribune*, 20 June 1986.

"Tammy Grimes Hurt in Street Attacks." *The New York Times*, 12 Mar. 1965.

Tan, Monica. "Life After Batman: How Adam West Built a New Career by Being Himself." *The Guardian*, Guardian News and Media, 29 Nov. 2014, www.theguardian.com/culture/2014/nov/29/beyond-batman-how-adam-west-built-a-new-career-by-just-being-himself.

"Television: Chasing the Rainbow." *Time Magazine*, 30 June 1958.

"The Television Code." The National Association of Radio and Television Broadcasters, 1 Mar. 1952. pp. 2, 3, 8.

"Television Field Seen." *The New York Times*, 18 Mar. 1948.

"Television Pilot Program Might be Filmed in Moab." *The Times-Independent* [Moab, Utah], 19 Nov. 1964. Vol. 69, no. 47.

"Television Prices." *Saturday Review*, 26 Feb. 1949.

"Television's 1966–1967 Scoreboard." *The Akron Beacon Journal* [Akron, Ohio], 9 Apr. 1967. p. 180.

"Ten Shows to Get the Axe on CBS This Fall." *Broadcasting*, 27 Feb. 1967. p. 25.

Terrace, Vincent. *Encyclopedia of Television Shows, 1925 through 2007*. McFarland, 2009.

"TFE '67: No Carnival This Year." *Broadcasting*, 10 Apr. 1967. p. 68.

"There's No Sunshine in Dodge City." *The Times* [San Mateo, California], 9 Jul. 1966. p. 5.

"They Wanted Star Trek." *The Calgary Herald* [Calgary, Alberta, Canada], 22 Jul. 1969.

Thomas, Bob. "Acting 'Rookie' Stars in 'The Big

Valley.'" *Lancaster New Era* [Lancaster, Pennsylvania], 18 Dec. 1965. p. 7. Associated Press.

Thomas, Bob. "Barbara Stanwyck Stars in 'The Big Valley' Series." *Nashua Telegraph* [Nashua, New Hampshire], 15 Sept. 1965. p. 34. Associated Press.

Thomas, Bob. "Batman, Zorro Not Necessarily Stereotyped." *The Kingston Daily Freeman* [Kingston, New York], 5 May 1966. p. 10. Associated Press.

Thomas, Bob. "Don't Underestimate Corn; 'Green Acres' Ranks High." *Moberly Monitor-Index* [Moberly, Missouri], 22 Oct. 1966. p. 7. Associated Press.

Thomas, Bob. "F Troop Will Go on for Years." *The Times Herald* [Port Huron, Michigan], 23 Jul. 1966. p. 18. Associated Press.

Thomas, Bob. "'Fugitive' Janssen Gets Lots of 'Help.'" *San Francisco Examiner*, 20 Dec. 1964. p. 2. Associated Press.

Thomas, Bob. "Fugitive Janssen Keeps Running." *The Indianapolis News*, 7 Mar. 1964. p. 9. Associated Press.

Thomas, Bob. "Gunsmoke in Color Uses Same Sets." *Star-Phoenix* [Saskatoon, Saskatchewan, Canada], 26 Sept. 1966. p. 10. Associated Press.

Thomas, Bob. "It's About Time Undergoing Changes." *Ocala Star-Banner* [Ocala, Florida], 28 Dec. 1966 p. 24. Associated Press.

Thomas, Bob "Jean Arthur Relieved That Show Is Canceled." *The Daily Advertiser* [Lafayette, Louisiana], 14 Oct. 1966. p. 11. Associated Press.

Thomas, Bob. "Monkees Lose Space on TV." *Public Opinion* [Chambersburg, Pennsylvania], 12 Jul. 1968. Associated Press.

Thomas, Bob. "My Three Sons Still Has Chuckles." *Fort Worth Star Telegram* [Fort Worth, Texas], 30 Aug. 1965. p. 6. Associated Press.

Thomas, Bob. "Phyllis Laughs All the Way from Alter." *Fort Worth Star-Telegram* [Fort Worth, Texas], 9 Feb. 1966. p. 26. Associated Press.

Thomas, Bob. "Plots in 'Felony Squad' Touch Reality by Accident, Innocent Producer Says." *The Ogden Standard-Examiner* [Ogden, Utah], 4 Dec. 1966. p. 62. Associated Press.

Thomas, Bob. "Plots on 'Felony Squad' Anticipate Real Events." *The Herald-News* [Passaic, New Jersey], 26 Nov. 1966. p. 29. Associated Press.

Thomas, Bob. "Robert Culp Happy Many Off James Bond Bandwagon." *The Indiana Gazette* [Indiana, Pennsylvania], 28 Feb. 1967. p. 32. Associated Press.

Thomas, Bob. "'Run for Your Life' Has Been Vindicated." *The Gazette* [Cedar Rapids, Iowa], 3 May 1967. p. 52. Associated Press.

Thomas, Bob. "TV's Peyton Place Offers Bold Concept." *Asbury Park Press* [Asbury Park, New Jersey], 11 Jul. 1964. p. 6. Associated Press.

Thompson, Ruth. "Basehart Pleased by Colorful Additions to 'Voyage.'" *Gettysburg Times* [Gettysburg, Pennsylvania], 13–20 Nov. 1965. *View TV Magazine*.

"Thursday Night Still Literally in the Air." *Broadcasting*, 12 Oct. 1964. p. 10.

"Top 100 TV Shows of All Time." *Variety*, 6 Aug. 2000.

"Top 10 Network TV Programs During August." *Broadcasting*, 19 Sept. 1966. p. 91.

"Top-20 Arbitron's Oct. 16–22." *Broadcasting*, 24 Oct. 1966. p. 64.

"Top-20 Arbitrons Oct. 23–29." *Broadcasting*, 7 Nov. 1966. p. 56.

"Top-20 Arbitrons Oct. 30–Nov. 5." *Broadcasting*, 14 Nov. 1966. p. 72.

"Top-20 Arbitrons Oct. 9–15." *Broadcasting*, 24 Oct. 1966. p. 56.

Torre, Marie. "Jack Berry Now in Fragrance Line." *Tampa Bay Times* [St. Petersburg, Florida], 10 Feb. 1960. p. 45.

The Toys That Made Us: Star Trek. Directed by Stern, Tom and Brian Volk-Weiss. The Nacelle Company, 25 May 2018. *Netflix*.

"Trendex Top 40 Programs." *Broadcasting*, 3 Oct. 1966. p. 58.

Trendle, George. "Trendle to Dozier." 13 May 1966. William Dozier Papers, American Heritage Center, University of Wyoming, Box 7. Correspondence.

Trendle, George. "Trendle to Dozier." 2 June 1966. William Dozier Papers, American Heritage Center, University of Wyoming, Box 7. Correspondence.

Trendle, George. "Trendle to Dozier." 21 Jul. 1966. William Dozier Papers, American Heritage Center, University of Wyoming, Box 7. Correspondence.

Trendle, George. "Trendle to Dozier." 22 Sept. 1966. William Dozier Papers, American Heritage Center, University of Wyoming, Box 7. Correspondence.

Trendle, George. "Trendle to Dozier." 26 Nov. 1965. George W. Trendle Papers, Burton Historical Collection. Detroit Public Library. Box 38, Folder 13. Correspondence.

Trimble, Bjo, and John Trimble. "Save Star Trek." 11 Dec. 1967.

"TV Has 'New' Star in Barbara Stanwyck." *Tampa Times* [Tampa Bay, Florida], 22 Sept. 1965. p. 19.

"TV Mailbag." *Pittsburgh Post-Gazette*, 24 Aug. 1965. p. 33.

"TV Networks Hurry Plans for Fall." *Broadcasting*, 12 Feb. 1968. p. 50

"TV Notes and Gossip." *St. Louis Post-Dispatch*, 4 Feb. 1964. p. 34.

"TV Sets." *The New York Times*, 4 May 1952.

"TV Shows Biting Dust." *The Montana Standard* [Butte, Montana], 1 Mar. 1971. p. 1.

"TV Topics: TV Tidbits." *Standard Speaker* [Hazelton, Pennsylvania], 16 Apr. 1966. p. 10.

"TV Violence Continues." *Herald and Review* [Decatur, Illinois], 22 Oct. 1968. p. 8.

"TV Westerns Resting, Not Dead, Actor Says." *The Monitor* [McAllen, Texas], 7 Jul. 1971. p. 20.

"12th Season 'Gunsmoke' Adds Color." *The Daily Times* [New Philadelphia, Ohio], 17 Sept. 1966. p. 9.

"Two More Shows Axed." *Broadcasting*, 14 Nov. 1966. p. 72.

"UA Syndicates Two More." *Broadcasting*, 24 Apr. 1967. p. 50.

United States. Congress. Senate. Committee on the Judiciary. "Juvenile Delinquency: Hearings Before the Subcommittee to Investigate Juvenile Delinquency of the Committee on the Judiciary, United States Senate, Eighty-sixth Congress 91st Congress." *U.S. Government Printing Office*. 1959. Part 2; Part 10. p. 1898.

"Universal Is Still the Hottest Studio." *Broadcasting*, 10 Apr. 1972. p. 30.

"Urge Reduction of Television Crime Violence." *The Columbus Telegram* [Columbus, Nebraska], 26 Aug. 1955. p. 1.

"U.S. Programs Hot Items Overseas." *Broadcasting*, 18 Dec. 1967. p. 76.

Van Gelder, Lindsy. "Roger Moore: 'The Saint's' Halo Is Almost Apparent." *The Times Recorder* [Zanesville, Ohio], 25 June 1967. p. 10. Section D.

Vartain, Vartanig G. "Batman Fad Aids Stock Rise…." *The New York Times*, 20 Mar. 1966.

Verba, Joan Marie. *Boldly Writing: A Trekker Fan and Zine History, 1967–1987*. FTL Publications, 1996.

"'Virginian' Bowing Wednesday with Many Television Firsts." *Fort Worth Star-Telegram* [Fort Worth, Texas], 16 Sept. 1962. p. 133.

Voland, John. "Turner Defends Move to Colorize Films." *Los Angeles Times*, 23 Oct. 1986.

"'Voyage' Lacking Beautiful Girls for the Skipper." *The Sandusky Register* [Sandusky, Ohio], 26 Feb. 1966. p. 20.

Walker, Virginia. "One Small Step, One Giant Step." *A Piece of the Action*, issue 39. Mar. 1976.

Walker, Virginia, and Helen Young, editors. "A Piece of the Action." *Star Trek Welcomittee*, issue #24, Mar. 1975.

Walson, John. "Oral History Interview with Cable Television Pioneer John Walson." Interviewed by Mary Alice Mayer, The Cable Center, Barco Library, 21 Jul.1970, http://www.cablecenter.org/barco-library-hauser-oral-history/item/walson-john.html.

Ward, Ed. "The Monkees: 'Ho-ho-ho, Just Wait & See!" *Rolling Stone*, 27 Dec. 1969. p. 10.

"Watch Jeannie's Smoke." *TV Guide*, 24 Sept. 1966. pp. 7–8.

Watkiss, Mike. "Blowup Over the Batguys." Producer Audrey Lavin. *A Current Affair*, 1989.

"Weatherwax Collies Gains AKC Registration." *Weatherwax Trained Dogs*, 4 Nov. 2013, http://www.weatherwaxtraineddogs.com/.

Webbink, Douglas W. "The Impact of UHF Promotion: The All-Channel Television Receiver Law." *Law and Contemporary Problems*, vol. 34, no. 3, 1969. pp. 535–561. JSTOR, www.jstor.org/stable/1190898.

Weiss, Ron. "The Monster Explosion." *Quasimodo's Monster Magazine*, vol 1, no 3. Jul. 1974.

"Westerns Are Popular: Notes on Television Shows." *The Baytown Sun* [Baytown, Texas], 25 Sept. 1966. p. 19.

"What Kind of 'Top 10' Is This." *Broadcasting*, 12 Oct. 1964. p. 15.

"What Television Offers You." *Popular Mechanics*, Nov. 1928. pp. 820–825.

"What the Networks Are Showing This Summer." *Broadcasting*, 11 Jul. 1966. p. 58.

"When You're the First in Color TV, There's Got to Be a Reason.'" RCA Victor advertisement. 1966.

White, Frank A. "Teen-Age Crime Grows Congress Prove Finds." *Rushville Republican* [Rushville, Indiana], 23 Mar. 1955. p. 1.

Whitfield, Stephen E., and Gene Roddenberry. *The Making of Star Trek*. Titan Books, 1991. p. 78; pp. 249–251.

Whitney, Dwight. "Batty Over Batman?" *TV Guide*, 26 Mar. 1966.

"Who Will Survive on the Networks?" *Broadcasting*, 6 Mar. 1972. p. 44.

Wigglesworth, Zeke. "TV 007's Agents Falsify Spying." *The Ottawa Herald* [Ottawa, Kansas], 15 Jan. 1966. p. 2.

"William Daniels." *Television Academy Interviews*, Television Academy Foundation, 29 Aug. 2017, interviews.televisionacademy.com/interviews/william-daniels.

Williams, Tony. *Larry Cohen: The Radical Allegories of an Independent Filmmaker*. McFarland. 1997.

Williamson, Clarke. "Top View." *Colorado Springs Gazette-Telegraph* [Colorado Springs, Colorado], 5 Aug. 1967. p. 35.

Winchell, Water. "Hubert's Big Role." *The Cincinnati Enquirer*, 9 Apr. 1965. p. 5.

Winfrey, Lee. "Movie Planned, but 'Star Trek Cartoon Canceled." *Knight Newspaper*, N.d1974.

Winston, Joan. "STAR TREK LIVES! Program Book." 1974.

"Wire About 'The Hero' Confuses Agency." *Broadcasting*, 24 Oct. 1966. p. 30.

Wister, Emery. "It's a Colorful Race." *The Charlotte News* [Charlotte, North Carolina], 22 May 1965. p. 38.

Witbeck, Charles. "Comic Book Heroes Zoom, Zap to Top." *The Herald Statesman* [Yonkers, New York]. p. 14.

Witbeck, Charles. "Demarest Replaces Frawley Quietly." *The Minneapolis Star* [Minneapolis, Minnesota], 13 May 1965. p. 97. *King Features Syndicate*.

Witbeck, Charles. "Dials Light Up on This Voyage." *Press Sun-Bulletin* [Binghamton, New York], p. 4. *King Features Syndicate*.

Witbeck, Charles. "Drama in a Sod House—'Road West' Is Down to Earth." *Press and Sun Bulletin* [Binghamton, New York], 23 Jul. 1966. p. 18. *King Features Syndicate*.

Witbeck, Charles. "F Troop Mission: Beat: Skelton." *Press and Sun-Bulletin* [Binghamton, New York], 25 Sept. 1965. p. 19. *King Features Syndicate*.

Witbeck, Charles. "'FBI' After Sullivan." *The Morning Call* [Allentown, Pennsylvania], 25 Sept. 1965. p. 16. *King Features Syndicate*.

Witbeck, Charles. "Felony Squad Not Armed with Gimmicks, Heroics." *Sunday News* [Lancaster,

Pennsylvania], 11 Dec. 1966. p. 126. *King Features Syndicate*.

Witbeck, Charles. "Flipper Learns Fast." *The Morning Call* [Allentown, Pennsylvania]. 31 Oct. 1964. p. 20. *King Features Syndicate*.

Witbeck, Charles. "Folksy Trio Special." *The Morning Call* [Allentown, Pennsylvania], 6 Oct. 1965. p. 34. *King Features Syndicate*.

Witbeck, Charles. "His Best Friend Is His Sargent." *The Winona Daily News* [Winona, Minnesota], 13 Dec. 1964. p. 31. *King Features Syndicate*.

Witbeck, Charles. "Rat Patrol Premieres Saturday." *Shreveport Journal* [Shreveport, Louisiana], 16 Sept. 1966. p. 41. TV Key Writer. *King Features Syndicate*.

Witbeck, Charles. "Small Fry Love 'Lost in Space." *The Rockland County Journal-News* [Nyack, New York], 9 Apr. 1966. p. 8. *King Features Syndicate*.

Witbeck, Charles. "Texas Tall-Talk Tale." *The Morning Call* [Allentown, Pennsylvania], 3 Aug. 1966. p. 32. *King Features Syndicate*.

Witbeck, Charles. "TV-Radio Chatter." *The Minneapolis Star* [Minneapolis, Minnesota], 25 Apr. 1967. p. 61. *King Features Syndicate*.

Witbeck, Charles. "'Voyage' Had High Adventure Flavor." *Tampa Tribune* [Tampa, Florida]. 25 Oct. 1964. *King Features Syndicate*.

"Without Cape, 'Batman' Adam West Looking for New Job." *The Star Press* [Muncy, Indiana], 4 Apr. 1975. p. 24. United Press International [UPI].

Wolfe, Sheila. "Alas, Fugitive Now Runs Backwards." *Chicago Tribune*, 19 Apr. 1967. p. C8.

Wolters, Larry. "Stars Give Critics Glimpses of Fall Fare." *Chicago Tribune*, 16 Aug. 1965. p. 8.

"The Wrecking Crew!" Directed by Denny Tedesco. Magnolia Pictures, 11 Mar. 2008.

"Writer-Producer on Job Alone." *The Daily Times* [New Philadelphia, Ohio], 30 Apr. 1966. p. 10.

Yenkin, Johnathan. "Non-Color TV Sales Becoming a Thing of Past: Technology: Sets with Black-and-White Screens Are Rarely Seen Even in Discount Stores Any More." *Los Angeles Times*, 31 Aug. 1992.

"Young Britons Told Not to Copy Batman." *The New York Times*, 24 Aug. 1966. Reuters.

"Zooming Batboat." *Austin American Statesman* [Austin, Texas], 27 Jul. 1966.

Index

Numbers in **_bold italics_** indicate pages with illustrations

ABC 4, 7, 8, 11, 13, 14, 16, 20, 21, 22, 23, 26, 27, 28, 32, 34, 35, 36, 37, 39, 40, 41, 42, 44, 50, 53, 54, 55, 56, 57, 59, 60, 61, 62, 63, 68, 69, 73, 81, 85, 88, 90, 91, 92, 93, 94, 95, 96, 97, 98, 99, 100, 101, 102, 103, 104, 107, 108, 110, 111, 113, 114, 116, 119, 120, 121, 123, 124, 126, 127, 129, 132, 133, 135, 136, 138, 139, 140, 143, 145, 147, 148, 150, 151, 152, 156, 158, 160, 161, 165, 166, 167, 173, 175, 176, 177, 178, 179, 180, 181, 183, 184, 186, 187, 189, 190, 192, 193, 194, 195, 196, 197, 198, 199, 200, 201, 202, 203, 204, 205, 206, 207
The ABC Saturday Superstar Movie 183
The ABC Sunday Night Movie 108, 148
Ackerman, Harry 181, 183, 203
Adam-12 67, **_129_**
Adams, Don 134–**_137_**
Adams, Val 57
The Addams Family 13, 21, 165, 194
Adventure at Scott Island see Harbormaster
The Adventures of Ozzie and Harriett 13, 163, 199
The Adventures of Superman 6, 11, **_12_**
Air Force Magazine 99
Al Caiola and His Orchestra 108
The Alaskans 46
Albert, Eddie 123, 157, 158
Albertson, Mabel 181
Aletter, Frank 84
Alexander, Ben 64, 68, 69
The Alfred Hitchcock Hour 57
All in the Family 110, 119, 164, 183, 202
Allen, Irwin 86, 87, 89, 90, 92, 94
Allen, Steve 52, 132, 159
American Football League (AFL) 30
Ames, Ed 114
Amos Burke, Secret Agent 150
André Jean and the Pharaohs 17
Anderson, Michael, Jr. 124, 126

Anderson, Warner 40
The Andy Griffith–Don Knotts–Jim Nabors Special 126
The Andy Griffith Show 69, 85, 104, 132, 153, 159, 161, 162, 207
The Andy Williams Show 37, 47, 203
Ankrum, David 18v4
Arbitron Rating 37, 44, 85, 103, 145, 167, 189, 196, 204
The Archer (Batman villain) 21
Armed Forces Television 98, 109
Arnaz, Desi 195
Arnaz, Desi, Jr. 197
Arnaz, Lucie 197
Arness, James **_117_**, 119
Arnold, Jack 36
Arthur, Jean 187
Asher, William 181, 182, 183
Associated Press 39, 81, 82, 86, 110, 111, 150, 155, 162, 170, 171, 180, 183, 187, 194
Astaire, Fred 198
Astin, John 13, 194
Attack of the Robots (1966) 134
Atwater, Edith 203
Aurora (model kits) 104
Austin American-Statesman 20
The Avengers 7, 100, 130, 138–141, 150
Averback, Hy 206

B. Bumble and the Stingers 31
Bachelor Father 181
Backus, Jim 176
Badge 714 64
Baer, Max, Jr. 153, 155, 158
Bailey, Raymond 153
Bain, Barbara 147, 148, 177, 186
Baird, John Logie 3, 6
Baker, Lavern 189
Bakula, Scott 96
Baldwin, Judith 177
Ball, Lucille 70, 132, 146, 187, 195–197
Baltimore Sun 91, 96, 124, 150, 190, 205
Bankhead, Tallulah 14
Banner, John 100, 111
Baron, Sandy 188, 189

Barrett (Roddenberry), Majel 72, 73, 81, 84
Barris, George 112
Barrymore, John Drew 131
Basehart, Richard 87, 88
Bat-boat 20
Bat-copter **_17_**, 20, 48
Bat-mania 14, 15, 19, 20, 91
Bat Masterson 145
The Batboys (band) 18, **_19_**
Batgirl **_22_**, 23
Batman (1943 serial) 13
Batman (1989) 25
Batman and Robin (1949 serial) 13
Batman Meets Godzilla 20, 22, 26
Batman: The Movie (1966) **_17_**, 20, 21, 93
Batman 2 11–26, 27, 28, 29, 30, 31, 32, 33, 34, 35, 36, 37, 38, 48, 49, 50, 64, 69, 91, 92, 99, 102, 111, 115, 127, 128, 132, 134, 152, 167, 174, 178, 180, 185, 189, 192, 193, 205, 206
Batmen, Los (band) 17
Batmobile 14, 16, 17, 25, 27
Battle of the Bulge (1965) 102
Batusi 15, 16, 17
Bavier, Frances 159, 161
BBC 104, 126
The Beach Boys 167
Beast of Hollow Mountain (1956) 85
The Beatles 14, 23, 64, 141, 165, 166, 167, 169, 170, 173
Before I Hang (1940) 13
Begley, Ed 95, 108, 196
Bell, Book and Candle 180
The Bell Telephone Hour 42, 54, 88
Belson, Jerry 188
Benaderet, Bea 155, 156, 157
Berle, Milton 7, 21, 23, 27, 32, 54, 132, 133, 143, 196, 205
Berry, Ken 161, 205, 207
The Beverly Hillbillies 98, 101, 109, 125, 127, 128, 153–157, 158, 159, 162, 163, 181, 182, 192, 193
Bewitched 2, 71, 73, 117, 136, 154, 178, 180–184, 201, 207

The Big Valley 57, 58, 120–122, 126, 150, 151, 207
Billboard 16, 17, 32, 64, 108, 112, 113, 134, 147, 154, 164, 166, 167, 173, 200
Billy the Kid Versus Dracula (1966) 20
The Birds (1963) 206
Bissell, Whit 93
black and white (television) 6, 9, 20, 46, 52, 54, 90, 97, 99, 100, 114, 123, 127, 129, 139, 154, 155, 156, 160, 161, 182, 184, 196, 205, 207
Black Beauty (The Green Hornet car) 27, 28, 29, 32, 33
The Black Saddle 120, 126
Black Widow (Batman villain) 14
Blackman, Honor 138, 139
Blake, Amanda 117
Blake, Madge 13
Blazing Saddles (1974) 135
Blocker, Dan *107*, 108, 109
Blondie 115
Bloomfield, Harry 16
Blue Light 94, 152
Bob Hope Presents the Chrysler Theater 37, 121, 130, 131, 152, 158, 162, 203
Bonanza 2, 63, 98, 102, 106–110, 117, 121, 128, 145, 148, 160, 162, 172, 181
Boone, Randy 127
Bostock, Barbara 203
Boston Globe 38, 50, 60, 62, 72, 103, 124, 131, 174, 191, 194, 198
Boston Herald 62
The Boston Pops 17
Bound for Glory (1976) 120
Bourbon Street Beat 27, 120, 207
The Bowery Boys 49
Boy Did I Get the Wrong Number (1966) 193
Boy Meets World 37, 173
Boyce and Hart 172, 183
Bracken's World 47
Brand, Nevill 129
Branded 60
Bray, Robert 41
Bread (band) 18
Breakfast at Tiffany's (1961) 63, 174
Breck, Peter 120, 121
Bridge on the River Kwai (1957) 109
Broccoli, Albert "Cubby" 138
Broderick, Matthew 186
Brodkin, Herbert 51, 52, 53, 120
Brooks, Joe 205
Brooks, Mel 135
Browning, Ricou 47, 48
Brubaker, Robert 118
The Buccaneer (1958) 147
Buchanan, Edgar 155, 156, 159
Buck Rogers 11
Buffalo Springfield 166
Buono, Victor 14, 111
Burnette, Smiley 156

Burns, George 196
Burns, Michael 64
Burr, Raymond 187
Business Week 8
Buttons, Red 201
Buttram, Pat 42, 158
Bye Bye Birdie (1963) 174

C.A Swanson & Sons 5
Cabot, Sebastian 198
Cady, Frank 157
Caesar, Sid 84, 147
Callan, Michael 202
Cameo Records 17
Camp Runamuck 111
The Camps 17
Canfield, Mary Grace 158
Capra, Frank 187
Captain Midnight 11
Captain Nice 1, 35–38, 203
Captain Video and His Video Rangers 11
Car 54 Where Are You? 84
Carey, Philip 129
Carlin, George 21
Carne, Judy 203, 204
Carney, Art 21, 120
The Carol Burnett Show 25, 53, 150, 183
Carradine, David 120, 190
Carradine, John 120, 129
Carrol, Leo G. 141, *143*, 145
Carson, Johnny 4, 56, 114, 185
Cartwright, Angela 90, 92
Casey, Lawrence 103
Cash, Johnny 108, 163, 171, 175
Cassidy, Ted 21
Castle of Frankenstein 30, 31, *34*, 73, *74*, 75
Catwoman (Batman villain) 20, 21, 26, 31, 93, 205
Cavalcade of Sports 4
Cavill, Henry 144
CBS 4, 7, 8, 11, 22, 25, 30, 35, 37, 41, 42, 44, 47, 49, 50, 51, 52, 53, 54, 55, 56, 57, 58, 60, 61, 63, 67, 70, 71, 73, 76, 77, 81, 82, 84, 85, 86, 88, 89, 90, 91, 92, 96, 98, 99, 100, 101, 102, 104, 107, 109, 110, 111, 112, 113, 114, 115, 116, 117, 118, 119, 120, 121, 122, 123, 125, 126, 127, 128, 130, 132, 133, 136, 140, 141, 143, 145, 146, 148, 150, 152, 153, 154, 155, 157, 158, 159, 161, 162, 163, 164, 165, 167, 174, 175, 176, 177, 179, 181, 182, 183, 186, 187, 189, 190, 191, 192, 193, 194, 195, 196, 197, 200, 201, 202, 203, 204, 206, 207
The CBS Friday Night Movies 54, 130, 132, 133, 145
CBS News Hour 55
CBS Thursday Night Movie 63, 67, 71, 74, 175, 182, 194
Chamberlain, Richard 52
Chandell (Batman villain) 21
Charles, Ray 21
Chase 67

Checkmate 198
The Checkmates 16
Chicago American 57, 101, 147, 150, 174, 179, 194
Chicago Daily News 38, 69, 116, 120, 124, 152
Chicago Sun-Times 38, 190, 194
Chicago Tribune 55, 91, 95, 125, 129, 150, 152, 160, 172
The Chiffons 16
Chitty Chitty Bang Bang (1968) 204
The Christian Science Monitor 111, 205
Cimarron Strip 115
Cincinnati Enquirer 8, 124, 135, 204
Cincinnati Post & Times-Star 202
Cinema Journal 33
Circus Boy 166
The Cisco Kid 6, 106
Clarence, the Cross-Eyed Lion (1965) 44
Clark, Dick 21
Clark, Roy 164
Clarke, Gary 127
Clary, Robert 100, 101, 102
Clayton, Jan 41
Cleef, Lee Van 129
Cleveland, George 41
Cleveland Plain Dealer 129
Close Encounters of the Third Kind (1977) 93
Clyde, Andy 41
Cobb, Lee J. 127
Coca, Imogene 84
Cohen, Larry 51, 52, 53, 94, 96, 124, 152
Colbert, Robert 92
Cole, Nat King 18, 21
Cole, Tina 201
Colgems 167, *168*, 170, 171, 172
Coliseum 99
Collins, Garry 115
Collins, Jack 202
Collins, Joan 23
Colonel Gumm (Batman villain) 30
color (television) 1, 2, 5, 6–11, 13, 14, 20, 21, 22, 30, 33, 35, 40, 42, 44, 45, 47, 49, 52, 55. 57, 58, 60, 62, 64, 70, 71, 73, 86, 87, 97, 98, 100, 101, 102, 106, 107, 108, 111, 112, 114, 115, 117, 118, 119, 121, 122, 123, 124, 127, 128, 129, 131, 133, 135, 136, 139, 140, 142, 145, 148, 150, 154, 156, 157, 160, 161, 162, 163, 165, 166, 168, 174, 176, 177, 179, 182, 184, 185, 186, 187, 188, 190, 191, 193, 196, 200, 202, 206, 207
Columbo 129
Combat! 7, 44, 96, 97–98, 109, 190
The Combo Kings (band) 17
"Come a Little Bit Closer" (*Jay and the Americans* song: written by Boyce & Hart) 167, 172

Index

Connally, John (Texas Governor) 20
Connors, Chuck 48
Conrad, Robert 110, 112
Conrad, William 117
Considine, Tim 199, 200, 201
Constantine, Eddie 134
Constantine, Michael 95, 188
Converse, Frank 51, 52, 53
Convoy 7, 90, 184, 205
Conway, Tim 132, 133
Cooper, Chad 129
Cooper, John 203
Corbett, Glenn 130
Corcoran, Kelly 130
Coronet Blue 51–53
Corsaut, Aneta 160
Cosby, Bill 149, 150, 151
The Cosby Show 149
Court-Martial 139
Courtleigh, Stephen 114
Cowboy in Africa 96
Cox, Wally 187
Craig, Yvonne 22, 23, 110, 201
Crain, Jeanne 68
Crane, Bob 100, 102, 196
The Creation 17
Creature from the Black Lagoon (1954) 36, 48
Creature of Destruction (1967) 17
The Creature Walks Among Us (1956) 48
Crosby, Stills, Nash and Young 166
Crowley, Patricia 189, 190
Culp, Robert 127, 149, 150, 151
Curtis, Sony 17
Custer 126
CW Network 26

The D.A. 67
Daily Mirror 139
Daktari 2, 44–47, 76, 92, 117, 145, 146, 154, 182, 190
Dallas 56, 186
Dan August 63
Danger Man 134
Daniel Boone 22, 99, 113–115, 177, 206
Daniels, William 37
The Danny Kaye Show 150
The Danny Thomas Hour 132
Danny Thomas's Make Room for Granddaddy see *Make Room for Granddaddy*
Dark Shadows 40
Darren, James 92
The Dating Game 120, 179, 182, 203
Davis, Chili 122, 123, 125
Davis, Jack 206
Davis, Rufe 156
Davis, Sammy, Jr. 21, 178, 186
Davy Crockett 113, 114
Dawson, Richard 100, 157
Day, Doris 109, 189
DC Comics 13, 24, 26, 33
Deacon, Richard 193

Dead End Kids see *The Bowery Boys*
The Dean Martin Show 63
Death Race 2000 (1975) 120
DeCamp, Rosemary 174
Decision (anthology series) 126
The Defenders 62, 94, 120
Dehner, John 127
de Kova, Frank 205
The Delicate Delinquent (1957) 140
Deliverance (1972) 63
Demarest, William 200, 201
Dennis the Menace 181
Denoff, Sam 174
Denver, Bob 112, 176
Dern, Bruce 129
Desilu 70, 73, 74, 78, 146, 147, 148, 151, 189, 195, 196, 197
Detective Comics see DC Comics
Detective Story (1951) 62
Detour (1945) 113
Diamond, Don 205
The Diana Rigger (zine) 141
The Dick Clark Show 107
Dick Tracy 22, 195
The Dick Van Dyke Show 121, 165, 188, 194
Dickinson, Angie 128
Die! Die! My Darling! (1965) 145, 174
Diller, Phyllis 192, 193, 194
Dinosaurus! (1960) 85
Dixon, Ivan 100, 101
Dr. Goldfoot and the Bikini Machine (1965) 84
Dr. Jekyll and Mr. Hyde 4
Dr. Kildare 45
Dr. No (1962) 134
Dodson, Jack 160
Dolenz, Micky 166, 170, 171, 172, 172, 173
Dolenz, Jones, Boyce and Hart 172
Domino, Fats 170
Donahue, Troy 52
The Donna Reed Show 100, 114, 165, 166, 177
Don't Call Me Charlie 97
Doohan, James 72, 79, 80, 81, 83, 84
Dortort, David 106, **107**, 108
Double Indemnity (1944) 120
The Double Life of Henry Phyfe 201
Douglas, Donna 153
Douglas, Kirk 62
Dowdell, Robert 87
Dozier, William 11, 20, 21, 22, 23, 26, 27, 28, 29, 30, 32, 33, 34, 178, 180, 195
Dragnet (1987 movie) 67
Dragnet (TV show) 63, 64, 65, 66, **67**, 68, 69, 104, 112, 130, 192, 195
Dragon: The Bruce Lee Story (1993) 35
Drury, James 126, 128, 129

DuBrow, Rick 14, 26, 135
Duel, Pete 203
Duff, Howard 68
DuMont Network 4, 11, 165
Dunn, Michael 111

East Side Kids see *The Bowery Boys*
Ebony (magazine) 72
Ebsen, Buddy 153, 155
The Ed Sullivan Show 14, 28, 60, 61, 109, 128, 163, 166, 189
Eden, Barbara 184, 185
Egghead (Batman villain) 14, 21, 24
Electronics Magazine 4
Ely, Ron 40
Emergency! 67
Emmy Awards 56, 148
Empty Nest 194
En Garde (zine) 141
Ensign O'Toole 97
The Ernie Kovacs Show 136
Evans, Dale 21
Evans, Linda 120, 121
Evans, Ray 108

F Troop 1, 7, 49, 50, 90, 99, 136, 184, 205–207
Faith, Percy 127
Family Affair 40, 69, 104, 115, 132, 197–199, 200, 203
Farnsworth, Philo T 3
Farrow, Mia 40
The F.B.I. 59–61, 95, 207
Federal Communications Commission (FCC) 6, 42, 164, 175
Feldon, Barbara 135, 136, 138
Felix the Cat 4
Fell, Norman 95
Felony Squad 57, 59, 64, 68–69, 132, 160, 203
Ferrell, Will 184
Filmways Productions 193
Firehouse 129
Fithian, Jeff 190
Fithian, Joe 190
Five Weeks in a Balloon (1962) 86
Flash Gordon 11
Flatt, Lester 154
"Flight of the Bumblebee" (Nikolai Rimsky-Korsakov composition) 31
The Flintstones 40, 111, 114, 181, 182
The Flip Wilson Show 115, 119
Flipper 2, 37, 45, 47–49, 203
The Flying Horse Big Band 16
The Flying Nun 115
Flynn, Errol 53
Fonda, Henry 122
Forbidden Planet (1956) 90
Ford, Gerald (United States President) 82
Ford, Glen 122
Ford, Harrison 56
Ford, Tennessee Ernie 113, 162, 196

Forslund, Constance 177
Fowley, Douglas 112
Fox, Bernard 181, 184
Franco, Jesús (Jess Franco) 134
Franks, Don 98, 99
Frawley, William 199, 200
Friends and Nabors 162
From Russia with Love (1963) 134
Frosty the Snowman (1969) 175
The Fugitive 7, 52, 54–59, 94, 95, 96, 191
Funny Face (1957) 206

Gable, Clark 63, 109, 121
Gabor, Eva 157, 158
Gabor, Zsa Zsa 23, 205
Gale, Gordon 196, 197
Gallant Men 97
Gallo, Lew 99
Garfield, John 62
Garland, Beverly 129, 201
Garner, James 100, 109, 116
Garret, Jimmy 195
Garrison's Gorillas 44, 98, 188
The Garry Moore Show 54, 98
Garver, Kathy 197
Gary Lewis and the Playboys 167
Gary Puckett and the Union Gap 172
Gates, David 18
Gautier, Dick 23, 36, 135, 138
Gaye, Lisa 110
Gazzara, Ben 57, 58
General Electric 5, 7
General Hospital 40, 95
Gent, George 14, 37, 53, 86, 95, 119, 114
George, Christopher 103
Get Smart 1, 2, 23, 31, 36, 37, 112, 113, 117, 134–**137**, 138, 148, 150, 151, 191
Get Smart (1995 TV series) 138
Get Smart (2008 movie) 138
Get Smart, Again (1989) 138
Getz, Stuart 49
Ghost and Mr. Chicken (1966) 182
Ghost and Mrs. Muir 115
Ghost Busters (1975 TV Show) 207
Ghostley, Alice 161, 183
G.I. Blues (1960) 206
Gibson, Henry 205
Gidget 203
Gilliam, Stu 151
Gillette Cavalcade of Sports 4
Gilligan's Island 37, 84, 85, 101, 114, 116, 119, 136, 167, 176–178, 191, 192
The Girl from U.N.C.L.E. 37, 44, 144–146, 185, 191, 203
The Glen Campbell Goodtime Hour 44, 128, 171
God Told Me to (1976) 96
Goddard, Mark 86, 90, 91, 92
Goldberg, Leonard 23, 56, 126
The Golden Girl 194
Golden Globes 56, 142
Golden Records 17

Goldfinger (1964) 134, 136, 138
Gomer Pyle U.S.M.C. 73, 76, 86, 99, 128, 153, 160, 161–163, 196, 197
The Good Guys 112
The Good, the Bad and the Ugly (1966) 128
Gordon, Bruce 191
Gordon, David 166
Gordon, Gale 196, 197
Gore, Leslie 21
Gorshin, Frank 16, 18, 24, 25
Gould, Jack 7, 14, 26, 29, 50, 52, 60, 62, 85, 98–99, 103, 107–108, 109, 147, 150, 161, 162, 167, 190, 191, 202
Gould, Sandra 181
The Graduate (1966) 37, 135
Grady, Don 199
Granger, Stewart 128
Grant, Hugh 144
Grass Roots 172
Grauman, Walter 68
Graves, Peter 95
The Great Escape (1963) 98, 102
The Great Imposter (1960) 182
The Greatest American Hero 151
Green, Lorne **107**, 108, 172
Green Acres 2, 28, 42, 109, 121, 152, 153, 157–158, 159, 162, 163
The Green Hornet 1, 21, 26–**32**, 33, **34**–37, 50, 93, 96, 102, 111, 178, 180, 192
The Green Hornet (1940 serial) 26
The Green Hornet Strikes Again (1941 serial) 26
Greenway Productions 20, 22, 26, 27, 178
Griffith, Andy 159, 160, 161, 162, 207
Grimes, Tammy 16, 178, **179**, 180
The Guardian 25, 80
The Guiding Light 40
Guilbert, Ann Morgan 188
Gulager, Clu 127
Gulf+Western 197
The Gunfighter (1950) 117, 119, 120
Gunsmoke 38, 61, 97, 104, 116, **117**, 118, 119, 130, 164, 177, 194, 195, 198

Hackman, Gene 95
Hagman, Larry 35, 56, 184, 186
Hale, Alan, Jr. 176, 177
Half-Hour on Broadway (1931) 4
Hall, Huntz 49
Halpin, Luke 48
Hamilton, Murray 151
Hamilton, Neil 13
Hammer, Armie 144
Hampton, James 205
Hank 111
Hanna-Barbera 24, 182, 183
Happy Days 189
Harbormaster 130
The Hardy Boys 199
Harper, Ron 187
Harris, Johnathan 89, 90

Harry (Batman villain) 21
Hart, Ralph 195
Hartman, Lisa 184
Hartman, Paul 161
Harty, Patricia 202
Hathaway, Anne 138
Have Gun, Will Travel 151
Hawaiian Eye 110
The Hawk 59, 61–63, 179
Hayes, Ron 44, 122, 123
Head (1968) 171
"Heart and Soul" (Monkees Song) 172, 173
Heaven Can Wait (1978) 135
Hedison, David 87, 88
Hee Haw 128, 163, 164
Hefti, Neal 16
Hendry, Ian 138
Henning, Linda Kaye 156
Henning, Paul 153, 154, 155, 156, 157
Henry, Buck 37, 135
Henry, Mike 49
Herbert, Tim 22
Here's Lucy 197
Herman's Hermits 172
The Hero 174, 192, 194–195
Hershey, Barbara 124
Hey Landlord 37, 188–189, 203
The High Chaparral 51, 148
Hill, Steven 147, 148
Hippodrome 123
Hirt, Al **31**, 51, 54, 57, 192
Ho, Don 21
Hoagland, Dick 82
Hogan's Heroes 21, 37, 97, 100–102, 105, 111, 120, 143, 159, 163, 197
Hollywood Citizen-News 135
Hollywood Palace 21, 26, 116, 147, 148
The Hollywood Reporter 55, 109, 166
Home from the Hill (1960) 123
Hondo (1953) 117
The Honeymooners 120, 190
Hooterville Television Universe 158–159
Hoover, J. Edgar 59, 60
Hope, Bob 132, 162, 193
Les Hou-Lops 17
Houston Chronicle 29, 72, 85, 129, 179
Houston Post 188
Hovis, Larry 100
How the West Was Won (1962) 199
Howard, Ron (Ronny) 159, 160
Huggins, Roy 54, 57, 58
Hughes, Alun 139
Hullabaloo 17, 203
Hunt, Gareth 141
Hunter, Jeffrey 70
Hutchins, Will 188
Hutton, Gunilla 156

I Dream of Jeannie 7, 37, 44, 90, 116, 117, 184–186, 205

"I Fought the Law" (*The Bobby Fuller Four* song) 17
I Love Lucy 64, 195, 197, 199
I Love to Eat 4
I Spy 94, 149–151, 197
I Was a Teenage Frankenstein (1957) 93
I Was a Teenage Werewolf (1957) 93
"I Wonder What She's Doing Tonight?" (Boyce & Hart song) 172
"(I'm Not Your) Steppin' Stone" (song by Paul Revere and the Raiders/The Monkees: written by Boyce & Hart) 167
Impasse (1969) 63
The Incredible Mr. Limpet (1964) 160
The Invaders 35, 37, 52, 94–96, 124, 203
Iron Horse 37, 115–116, 136, 167, 186, 203
Ironside 183
It Came from Outer Space (1953) 36
It's About Time 37, 84–86, 145
It's Alive (1974) 86
Ivanhoe 46
I've Got a Secret 51, 57

The Jack Benny Show 99, 161
The Jack Paar Program 99
The Jackie Gleason Show 49, 120, 162, 163, 190
James Bond 19, 27, 46, 59, 68, 110, 134, 138, 140, 141, 144, 145, 150
Jan & Dean 16
Janssen, David 54, 55, 56
Jason, Rick 97
Jason and the Argonauts (1963) 174
Jaws (1975) 93
The Jean Arthur Show 57, 122, 187–188
Jeffries, Dean 168
Jeff's Collie see *Lassie*
Jericho 97, 98–99, 206
Jerry Lewis Show 44, 96
The Jetsons 87
The Jim Nabors Hour 115
The Johnny Cash Show 163, 171, 175
Johnson, Dwayne 138
Johnson, Lady Bird (First Lady) 42, **43**
Johnson, Lyndon (United States President) 15, 154
Johnson, Russell 176
The Joker (Batman villain) 13, 14, 17, 20, 24, 30, 31, **34**
The Joker Is Wild (1957) 147
Jones, Anissa 197, 198, 199
Jones, Davy 166, 173
Jones, Tommy Lee 56
Junior Walker and the All-Stars 16

Karloff, Boris 111
Karvelas, Robert 135, 137, 138
Kato 21, 26, 27, 28, 29, 30, **32**, 33, 34, 35
Kay and Johnny 165
Keaton, Michael 25
Keith, Brian 197
Kelly, Brian 48
Kelly, DeForest 72, 79, 84, 127, 129
Kennedy, George 128, 129
Kennedy, John F. (United States President) 5, 20, 64
Kidman, Nichole 184
Kill Bill: Volume I (2003) 120
Kill Bill: Volume II (2004) 120
Killer Moth (Batman villain) 22
Kilmer, Val 47
King Tut (Batman villain) 14, 24
Kiss Kiss... Bang Bang (1966) 134
Kiss Kiss...Kill Kill (1966) 134
Kitt, Eartha 13
Klemperer, Werner 100, 101
Knight Rider 37
Knotts, Don 159, 160, 161
Koenig, Walter 75, 77, 79, 80, 83, 84
Kommissar X 134
Kopell, Bernie 135, 138, 174
Korman, Harvey 205
Kraft Suspense Theater 57, 58
Kristen, Marta 86, 90, 91, 92
Krokodil Today 19
Kulky, Henry 87
Kulp, Nancy 153, 155
Kung Fu 120
Kuryakin, Illya 141, 144, 191

LA Dragnet 68
Ladd, Alan 119
Lancaster, Burt 63
Land of the Giants 89
Landau, Martin 147, 148, 177
Landon, Michael **107**
Lane, Charles 196
Lane, Sara 128
Lansing, Robert 99, 127, 151
Laramie 97
Laredo 37, 100, 112, 127, 129–130, 140, 201, 203
Lassie 41–**43**, 44, 88, 89, 101, 117, 157, 163
Lassiter 63
Last Man to Kill (1966) 134
Laverne & Shirley 189
Lawler, Jerry "The King" 24
Lawrence, David 183
Lawrence, Greg 183
The Lawrence Welk Show 28, 51, 85, 109, 113, 128, 136, 147, 162, 175, 176
Leachman, Cloris 41, 128
Lear, Norman 197, 202
Leave It to Beaver 181
Lee, Bruce 21, 26, 27, 28, 29, **32**, 35, 132
Lee, Peggy 17
Lee Merril and the Golden Horns 31

Legends of the Superheroes (1976) 24
Lester, Tom 157
Let's Make a Deal 175
Let's Rhumba 4
LeVang, Neil 28
Lewis, Jerry 21, 140
Lewis, Jerry Lee 171
Leyton, John 98
Liberace 21
Licensing Corporation of America (LCA) 33
Lichtenstein, Roy 16
LIFE 15
Life on Mars 53
Lili (1952) 60
Lindsay, George 62
Linkletter, Art 196
Little, Rich ("The Man of a Thousand Voices") 203
Little Big Horn 176
Little Richard 171
Liverpool, U.S.A 166
Livingston, Barry 200
Livingston, Jay 108
Livingston, Stanley 199
The Lloyd Bridges Show 97
Locate, Pursue and Destroy 27, 97, 102
Locke, Tammy 124
Lockhart, June 41, 89, 90, 92, 157
Loggia, Robert 53, 54
Lola Lasagna (Batman villain) 23
Lone Ranger 11, 33
Long, Richard 120, 121
Long Hot Summer 95
The Long Hunt for April Savage 151
Lord, Jack 128
Lorne, Marion 181
Los Angeles Herald Examiner 116, 120, 147, 167, 205
Los Angeles Times 9, 25, 29, 50, 61, 62, 64, 67, 78, 85, 99, 101, 116, 120, 124, 127, 135, 145, 147, 152, 155, 176, 178, 179, 182, 187, 188, 191, 194, 198, 204, 205
Los Batmen (band) 17
Lost in Space 2, 7, 22, 51, 57, 86, 89–92, 94, 125, 126, 127, 128, 157, 184, 205
Lost in Space (1998 movie) 92
Lost in Space (2018 TV series) 92
The Lost World (1960) 86
Louie the Lilac (Batman villain) 23
Louise, Tina 176, 177
Love a Little, Live a Little (1968) 182
Love, American Style 189
"Love Is All Around" (*The Mary Tyler Moore Show* theme) 17
Love on a Rooftop 156, 175, 182, 203–204
Lowry, Cynthia 39, 112, 150, 180, 183, 187, 192, 194
The Lucy-Desi Comedy Hour 195

The Lucy Show 37, 84, 101, 103, 104, 147, 162, 187, 191, 195–197
Lugosi, Bela 4
Lumley, Joanna 141
Lupus, Peter 147
Lyn, Dawn 201
Lynd, Paul 181, 183, 194, 206

MacMurray, Fred 199, 200, 201
Macnee, Patrick 127, 138, 140, 141
MacRae, Heather 49
MacRae, Meredith 156, 200
MAD Magazine 16, 102
Majors, Lee 120, 128
Make Room for Granddaddy 175
Malone, Dorothy 40
A Man Called Shenandoah 103
The Man Called X 130
The Man from U.N.C.L.E 2, 38, 45, 54, 101, 104, 132, 133, 141, 142, **143**, **144**, 145, 150, 151, 178, 185, 191, 204
"The Man of a Thousand Voices" *See* Little, Rich
The Man They Could Not Hang (1939) 113
The Man Who Never Was 100, 151–152, 158
The Man Who Never Was (1956 movie) 151
Manny the Mesopotamian (Batman villain) 23
Manson, Charles 166
The Marketts 17
Marmaduke Ffogg (Batman villain) 23
Married with Children 68
Marshall, Garry 188
Martin, Dean 196
Martin, Quinn 54, 55, 56, 60, 61, 95, 99, 124, 207
Martin, Ross 110
Marx Brothers 170, 172
Mary Kay and Johnny 165
The Mary Tyler Moore Show 17, 119, 164
Masé, Marino 98
*M*A*S*H* 64
Maude 110
Maverick 116
May, Bob 90
Maya 191
Mayama, Miko 188
Mayberry (town in *The Andy Griffith Show*) 159, 161
Mayberry R.F.D 161, 163, 207
McBain, Diane 110, 201
McCallum, David 141, 142, **143**, **144**, 178, 191
McCarthy, Kevin 95
McCloud 129
McClure, Doug 127
McDevitt, Ruth 112
McDowall, Roddy 16, 95
McHale's Navy 95, 101, 132, 165, 205
McKay, Scotty 17
McKechnie, Donna 203

McKeever and the Colonel 97
McLiam, John 128
McLintock! (1963) 145
McMahon, Ed 4, 24, 114
McMillan & Wife 129
McNear, Howard 159
Men Against Evil 68
The Men from Shiloh 128
Meredith, Burgess 13, 18, 20, 111, 129
Meriwether, Lee 13, 20, 84, 93, 205
Merman, Ethel 23
Merrill, Buddy 28
The Merv Griffin Show 22, 188
Metalious, Grace 39
The Mexicali–Brass 31
MGM 41, 44, 45, 60, 93, 178, 189, 191
Miami Herald 61, 81, 116, 129, 132, 135, 187, 191, 198
A Midsummer Night's Dream 141
Miller, Cheryl 44
Miller, Mark 190
The Milton Berle Show 27, 54, 132, 133, 143
Minerva (Batman villain) 23
Minner, Kathryn 188
Mission: Impossible 98, 113, 117, 146–**149**, 150, 177, 197
Mission: Impossible (film franchise) 178
Mr. Deeds Goes to Town (1936) 187
Mr. Ed 36
Mr. Freeze (Batman villain) 13, 24
Mr. Smith Goes to Washington (1939) 187
Mr. Terrific 1, 35–38, 96, 116, 130, 177, 186, 192
Mobley, Mary Ann 144
Monday Night at the Movies 197
The Monkee Business Fanzine 173
Monkee Spectacular 170
The Monkees 2, 28, 32, 116, 117, 136, 165–**168**, **169**–173, 185, 186, 192
Monroe, Del 87
The Monroes 91, 117, 124–129
Monster on the Campus (1958) 37
The Monster Times 78, 82
Montenegro, Hugo **143**, 186
Montgomery, Elizabeth 178, 180, 184
Montgomery, Robert 180
Moody, King 135, 138
Moore, Alvy 157
Moore, Candy 195
Moore, Garry 98
Moore, Terry 21
Moorehead, Agnes 181
The More the Merrier (1943) 187
Mork & Mindy 189
Mornin' Beverly Hillbillies 154
Morricone, Ennio 128
Morris, Greg 147
Morrow, "Cousin" Brucie 16

Morrow, Vic 97
Morse, Barry 54
Mortimer, Barbara "Babe" Cushing 163
Move Over Darling (1963) 109
MTV 172, 173
Mullaney, Jack 84, 85
Mulligan, Richard 194, 195
Mumy, Billy 90, 92
The Munsters 114, 165, 176
Murder by Television (1935) 4
Murphy, Erin 181
Murray, Arthur 16
Murray, Jay 27
Museum of Broadcast Television 163
The Music Man (1962) 63, 71, 174
My Favorite Martian 101, 165
My Mother the Car 145
My Three Sons 71, 73, 179, 182, 199–202

Nabors, Jim 159, 160, 161, 162, 196
Naked City 62
Napier, Alan 13
NASA 82, 83, 184, 186
Nash, Brian 190
The National Association for Better Broadcasting 16, 29, 44, 60, 69, 88, 91, 106, 108, 111, 116, 122, 125, 142, 145, 195
"The National Association of Radio and Television Broadcasters Television Code of 1952" 185
National Football League (NFL) 197
National Lampoon's Vacation (1983) 184
National Periodical Publications **15**, 33
National Television System Committee (NTSC) 6, 7, 139, 174
Navajo Joe (1966) 61
NBC 1, 4, 6, 7, 8, 17, 22, 23, 30, 32, 35, 37, 41, 42, 46, 47, 48. 49, 51, 53, 54, 55, 57, 58, 60, 63, 64, 67, 69, 70, 71, 75, 76, 77, 80, 81, 85, 88, 91, 94, 96, 99, 100, 101, 103, 104, 106, 107, 108, 109, 110, 111, 113, 116, 118, 121, 122, 123, 134, 125, 126, 127, 129, 130, 131, 132, 133, 135, 136, 140, 143, 144, 145, 146, 147, 148, 149, 150, 152, 156, 158, 160, 161, 162, 165, 166, 167, 171, 174, 175, 177, 179, 181, 182, 183, 184, 185, 186, 187, 188, 189, 190, 191, 192, 193, 194, 195, 196, 197, 198, 199, 200, 201, 202, 203, 204, 206
The NBC Mystery Movie 129
NBC News/Bell Telephone Hour 42, 88
NBC Saturday Night at the Movies 116, 118, 147
NBC Tuesday Night at the Movies 55, 110, 123, 156, 204

Index

Nelson, Ed 40
Nelson, Ricky 167
Nelson, Sandy 17
Nesmith, Mike 166, 170, 171, 172, 173
Netflix 51, 92
New York Daily News 96, 116, 123, 131, 174, 187, 193
The New York Times 7, 14, 15, 16, 23, 27, 29, 32, 36, 37, 45, 50, 51, 52, 53, 57, 60, 62, 66, 72, 79, 83, 85, 86, 93, 95, 98, 103, 107, 109, 118, 119, 138, 139, 114, 147, 150, 159, 161, 167, 171, 172, 178, 179, 190, 191, 202
New York World Journal Tribune 85, 93, 96, 145, 167, 189, 198, 202
New York World Telegram and Sun 190
Newlan, Paul 99
The Newlywed Game 120, 175
Newmar, Julie 13, 25, 26, 205
Nichols, Nichelle 72, 77, 79, 81, 84
Nicholson, Jack 171
Nielsen Ratings 14, 23, 37, 40, 42, 55, 56, 58, 64, 73, 76, 77, 81, 83, 99, 101, 102, 103, 108, 109, 111, 125, 126, 132, 142, 146, 155, 156, 157, 162, 163, 182, 187, 195, 196, 203
The Night of the Hunter (1955) 198
Nimoy, Leonard 35, 71, 72, **74**, 77, 79, 80, 81, 83, 84, 127, 148
No Time for Sergeants (1958) 159, 161
Nolan, Jeanette 128
Norden, Tommy 48
North, Jay 47, 191
The Nude Bomb (1980) 137

O'Barry, Ric 48
Of Mice and Men (1939) 13
Off to See the Wizard 96
O'Hara, United States Treasury 67
Oliver! 166
On Her Majesty's Secret Service (1969) 140, 141
Once Upon a Time in Hollywood (2019) 61
Once Upon a Time in the West (1968) 128
O'Neal, Ed 68
O'Neal, Ryan 40
Operation Petticoat (1959) 182
Operation 67 (1966) 134
"Orange Colored Sky" (Nat King Cole song) 18, 21
Orchester Friedel Berlipp 17
The Original Amateur Hour 163
Our Man Flint (1966) 134
The Outer Limits 70, 91
Owen Marshall: Counselor at Law 128
The Ox-Bow Incident 117

Paley, William 119, 163
Paramount 73, 77, 81, 82, 83, 148, 197

Paramount Theaters 20, 21
The Parent Trap (1961) 198
Parkins, Barbara 40
The Passionate Witch (Thorne Smith novel) 180
Password 181
Patterson, Melody 205
The Patty Duke Show 165
Paul Revere and the Raiders 99, 132, 167
The Pearl Bailey Show 175
The Penguin (Batman villain) 13, 14, 18, 20, 21, 23, 24, 31
The People (British tabloid) 140
Perry Como's Kraft Music Hall see *Kraft Music Hall*
Perry Mason 107, 114
Peter and Gordon 132
Petticoat Junction
Peyton Place 7, 21, 39–41, 68, 121, 132, 156, 162, 198
Peyton Place (1957 movie) 39
Phase Alternating Line (PAL) 6, 20, 47, 139
The Phil Silvers Show see *Sergeant Bilko*
Philadelphia Bulletin 152
Philadelphia Enquirer 123, 135
Philadelphia Evening Bulletin 124, 129
A Piece of the Action (zine) 30, 80, 82
Pittsburgh Post-Gazette 52, 193, 204
Pittsburgh Press 13, 62
Pizza Hut 173
Plak-Tow 76, 78
Platt, Edward 135, 138
Please Don't Eat the Daisies 37, 45, 145, 189–191, 199, 203
Please Don't Eat the Daisies (1960 movie) 189
Pleshette, Suzanne 110
Popular Mechanics 3
The Poseidon Adventure (1972) 89
Pravda 19, 28, 76
Preminger, Otto 13
Presley, Elvis 204
Presnell, Harve 178
Price, Vincent 14, 21, 46, 206
The Prince and the Pauper (1962) 90
Prine, Andrew 95, 128, 130, 131
Provost, Jon 41
The Pruitts of Southampton 192–194
Punch and Judy 4
Pussycat (Batman villain) 21

Q: The Winged Serpent (1982) 96
Quantum Leap 94
Quibi 56
Quine, Don 128

Raiders of the Lost Ark (1981) 93
Raisch, Bill 54
Random, Bob 115
Rango 132–133

Rankin-Bass Productions 175
Rat Patrol 37, 63, 69, 94, 96, 97, 102–105, 145, 156, 196, 203
Rawhide 37, 44, 190
The Ray Anthony Orchestra 64
Raymond, Gary 103, 104
RCA 5, 6, 7, **8**, 31, 73, 106, 107, 108
The Red Skelton Show 7, 96, 122, 123, 160, 162, 163, 193, 203, 206
Reilly, Hugh 41
Repp, Stafford 13
Residence for Spies (1966) 134
Rettig, Tommy 41
Return of the Saint (1978) 47
Return to Peyton Place (1961) 41
Return to the Batcave: The Misadventures of Adam and Burt (2003) 25
Revenge of the Creature (1955) 48
Reynolds, Burt 61, 62, 63, 118
Reynolds, Debbie 178
Rhino Records 172
Richard Diamond: Private Detective 54
Rickles, Don 205
The Riddler (Batman villain) 13, 14, **15**, 16, 18, 20, 24
Ride the High Country (1962) 126
Rigg, Diana 139, 140, 141
Ringling Brothers Circus 4
Ritchie, Guy 144
RKO Studios 86, 166
The Road West 37, 130–132, 160, 198, 203
Roberts, Pernell **107**
Roberts, Roy 181
Robertson, Dale 115, 116
Robinson Crusoe on Mars (1964) 147
"The Rock" see Johnson, Dwayne
Roddenberry, Gene 70–83
Rodgers, Pamela 188, 189
The Roger Miller Show 37, 103, 196
Rogers, Roy 21
Romero, Cesar 13, 20, 21, 31, **34**
Rooney, Mickey 187, 196
Rounders 120, 122–124, 203
Route 66 145, 178
Rudolph the Red-Nose Reindeer (1964) 175
Rugolo, Pete 57, 58
Run Buddy Run 32, 36, 116, 177, 186, 191–203
Run for Your Life 57–58, 113, 122, 129, 187, 191, 192
Run Silent Run Deep (1958) 63
Rural Purge 42, 102, 119, 163–164, 197
Russell, Kurt 129
Ryan, Barry 123
Ryan, Irene 153
Ryan, Paul 123

The Saint 46–47, 52, 195
St. Elsewhere 37
St. Louis Globe-Democrat 123
Sam 67

Sam the Sham and the Pharaohs 132
Sam Whiskey (1969) 63
San Francisco Examiner 29, 61, 69, 93, 95, 101, 123, 141, 187, 190, 198, 207
Sanders, George 13
Santo, El (Mexican Professional Wrestler) 134
Sargent, Dick 179, 180, 182, 183
The Savage (1952) 206
Schafer, Natalie 176
Schultz, Keith 124
Schumann, Walter 64, 113
Schwartz, Sherwood 84, 86, 176, 177
Sci-Fi Channel 96
Scott, Brenda 130, 131
Scott, George C. 131
Scruggs, Earl 154
The Second Hundred Years 96
Secret of the Incas (1957) 206
Seegar, Sara 202
The Sensational Guitars Of Dan & Dale 16, *18*
Séquentiel couleur à mémoire/ Sequential colour with memory (SECAM) 6, 45
Sergeant Bilko 84
Sergeant Preston of the Yukon 6, 33, 106
7 Nights to Remember 21, 28, 32, 61, 102, 132, 147, 189
Seven Year Itch (1955) 178
77 Sunset Strip 59, 207
Shades of Blue 16
The Shaggy Dog (1959) 199
Shatner, William 70, 71, 74, 77, 80, 81, 84, 127
Shea Stadium 16
Sheena, Queen of the Jungle 11
Sheldon, Jack 191
Sheldon, Sidney 184, 185, 186
Shepard, Jan 132
Sheridan, Ann 112, 113
Shindig! 13, 114, 166
Shock Corridor (1963) 198
Shore, Roberta 127
Shull, Richard K. 41
Sierra (1950) 117
Sierra (1974) 67
Silvers, Phil 196
Simon, Robert F. 181
Sinatra, Frank 40, 167
Sinatra, Nancy 123, 167
Siren (Batman villain) 23
The Six Million Dollar Man 120, 128
Skullduggery (1970) 63
Slattery's People 99
Sliders 94
Smith, Hal 159
Smith, Will (actor/rapper) 112
Smith, William 129
The Smothers Brothers Comedy Hour 104, 109
Soap 194
Soble, Ron 124, 126

Sonny and Cher 167
Soul, David 49
South Pacific (1958) 84
Spector, Phil 167
Spin and Marty 199
Spockanalia (zine) 77
Squire, Katherine 130
Stack, Robert 59
Stagecoach (1966) 145
Stanwyck, Barbara 120, 121
Star Trek (2009) 84
Star Trek (The Original Series) 2, 70–84, 90, 93, 96, 146, 147, 148, 175, 179, 182, 185, 197, 201, 203
Star Trek II: The Wrath of Khan (1982) 83
Star Trek III: The Search for Spock (1984) 83
Star Trek IV: The Voyage Home (1986) 83
Star Trek V: The Final Frontier (1989) 83
Star Trek VI: The Undiscovered Country (1991) 83, 84
Star Trek Conventions 77–81
Star Trek: Into Darkness (2013) 84
Star Trek: The Animated Series 81, 84
Star Trek: The Motion Picture (1979) 83, 84
Star Trek: The Next Generation 84
Star Wars (1977) 24, 83, 93
Steel, Charles 130
Steele, Bob 205
Steele, Karen 49
Steve Allen Comedy Hour 52, 132
Stone, Leonard 187
Stone, Milburn 117, 199
Storch, Larry 136, 205, 206, 207
Strange, Glenn 118
The Stuff (1985) 52, 96
Sullivan, Barry 130, 131
Summers, Hope 159
Sun Ra and His Arkestra 18
Super Agent Super Dragon (1966) 134
Swiss Family Robinson 89

Takei, George 72, 75, 77, 79, 80, 81, 83, 84
Talbot, Lyle 129
Tammy 111, 112, 129
The Tammy Grimes Show 63, 71, 178–180
The Tampa Tribune 171
Tarantula (1955) 36
Tarr, Justin 103
Tarzan 2, 30, 32, 49–51, 111, 192, 203
Taylor-Young, Leigh 40
Teen Life 16
"A Teenager in Love" (Dion and the Belmonts song: written by Boyce & Hart) 172
Television Magazine 68
Temperatures Rising 110, 183
The Temptations 16

Texaco Star Theater 7
That Girl 173–175, 194, 197
That Girl in Wonderland (1973) 175
T.H.E. Cat 32, 37, 53–54, 117, 132, 192, 194
The Thing from Another World (1951) 117
Thinnes, Roy 95, 96
Thomas, Danny 132, 174, 175, 196
Thomas, Marlo 173–175
Thompson, Marshal 44
Three Dog Night 166
The Three Stooges 4, 64, 113
Time Magazine 7
The Time Tunnel 2, 50, 62, 86, 92–94, 101, 102, 111, 143
Timmy & Lassie *see* Lassie
To Tell the Truth 51, 98, 188
Tobacco Road 4
Tobor the Great (1954) 90
Toho 20
The Tonight Show Starring Johnny Carson 4, 56, 114, 185
Tony Award 178, 179
Tork, Peter 166, 170, 171, 172, 173
Tormé, Mel 134
Torrey, Roger 115
Touch of Mink (1962) 182
The Towering Inferno (1974) 89
Trendex 21, 29, 71, 146, 179, 190
Trendle, George 32, 33, 34, 35
The Trials of O'Brien in the Spring 51
Trimble, Betty Jo "Bjo" 73, 76, 77, 78
Trimble, John 73, 77
Tucker, Forest 127, 205, 206, 207
Tuesday Night at the Movies 55, 96, 123, 156, 193, 204, 206
Turner, Ted 177, 178
The Turtles 170
TV dinners 5
TV Guide 8, 15, 28, 32, 40, 50, 52, 72, 76, 84, 99, 102, 112, 140, 145, 146, 154, 167, 172, 175, 178, 180, 186, 190, 203
TWA 111
12 O'Clock High (1949 film) 99
12 O'Clock High (TV show) 97, 99–100
20th Century-Fox 11, 26, 40, 86, 93, 113, 114, 151, 180
20th Century Television 35
The Twilight Zone 70, 84
Twin Peaks 53
The 2000 Year Old Man (1960) 135
Tyler, Kim 190

Ugliest Girl in Town 23, 115
ultra-high frequency (UHF) 5
United Press International *(UPI)* 13, 14, 40, 57, 95, 135
The Unsinkable Molly Brown 178, *179*
The Untouchables 59
U.S. Marshals (1998) 56

Index

Vallee, Ruddy 23
Vance, Vivian 195, 196
Van Dyke, Dick 165, 204
Van Dyke, Jerry 54
Variety 166
Vaughn, Robert 141, 142, *143*, *144*, 145, 191
The Ventures 31, 134
Venus Flytrap (Batman villain) 21
Very High Frequency (VHF) 5
Vinson, Gary 112
The Virginian 91, 125, 126–129, 130, 148, 162, 178
Voland, Herb 203
Von Ryan's Express (1965) 98
Voyage to the Bottom of the Sea 2, 42, 85, 86–**88**, 94, 96
Voyage to the Bottom of the Sea (1961 movie) 86

Wagon Master (1950) 117
Wagon Train 55, 70, 103, 108, 126, 129
Wallach, Eli 13
Walson, John 5, 6
Walt Disney's Wonderful World of Color 60, 61, 86, 88, 162
Ward, Burt 13, 18, 20, **22**, 23, 24, 26
Warhol, Andy 16, 68
Warner Brothers 64, 86, 112, 205, 206, 207
Washington Evening Star 38, 61, 85, 123, 129, 152, 192, 205
Washington Post 29, 52, 69, 72, 103, 116, 120, 124, 125, 145, 152, 174, 189, 192, 193, 203, 204
Wayne, John 75, 120, 122, 196
Wayne and Shuster Take an Affectionate Look At... 51
Weatherwax Family 44
Weaver, Dennis 117
Weaver, Doodles 129
Webb, Jack 63, 64, 67, 129, 195
Welk, Lawrence 28, 32, 51, 109, 113, 136, 147, 148, 162, 164, 175, 176, 207
Wells, Carole 112
Wells, Dawn 95, 110, 176, 177
Wells, Orson 177
West, Adam 1, *12*, 13, 15, *17*, 18, 21, 23, 24, *25*, 27, 28, 29, 35, 36, 132
Western, Jonny 108
The Westerner 197
"What Are We Going to Do?" (Davy Jones song) 166
Whitaker, Johnny 197
White, David 181
The Who 17
The Wild Wild West 1, 7, 30, 50, 51, 110–112
Wild Wild West (1999 movie) 112
"Wild, Wild West" (Will Smith song) 112
Will Success Spoil Rock Hunter? (1955) 178
Williams, Guy 90
Williams, John 93
Williams, Van 21, 27, 28, 29, 30, **31**, 34, 35, 102, 132
Wills, Chill 122, 123
Witbeck, Charles 14, 48, 57, 59, 60, 68, 69, 87, 91, 102, 122, 130, 161, 162, 201, 205
The Wizard of Oz (1939) 175
Wonder Woman 22, 25
Woodell, Pat 156
World's Fair 1, 20
The Wrecking Crew (studio musicians) 166, 167
Wuthering Heights (Emily Brontë novel) 175
Wynter, Dana 151

The Yardbirds 132
York, Dick 180, 181, 182
You Are an Artist 4
You Can't Take It with You (1938) 187
You'll Never Get Rich see Sergeant Bilko
You'll Never Get Rich (1941 movie) 198
Young, Alan 36
The Young Lawyers 175
The Young Ones 172
The Young Rascals 16
Youngman, Henny 23
Your Show of Shows 84, 135

Zappa, Frank 18
Zaremba, John 93
Zimbalist, Efrem, Jr. 59
Zorro 11, 90

www.ingramcontent.com/pod-product-compliance
Lightning Source LLC
Chambersburg PA
CBHW060341010526
44117CB00017B/2916